Andrew Motion is a poet and biographer. His poetry publications include *Dangerous Play* (1984), *Love in a Life* (1991) and *The Price of Everything* (1994). His biography, *The Lamberts: George, Constant and Kit*, was published in 1986, and *Philip Larkin: A Writer's Life*, which won the Whitbread Prize for biography, in 1993.

Candice Rodd reviews fiction for the *Independent on Sunday* and the *Times Literary Supplement*.

D0293703

New
Writing 3

edited by

ANDREW MOTION
and
CANDICE RODD

Minerva in association with the
British Council

A Minerva Paperback

NEW WRITING 3

First published in Great Britain 1994
as a Minerva Original in association with the British Council
by Mandarin Paperbacks
an imprint of Reed Consumer Books Ltd
Michelin House, 81 Fulham Road, London SW3 6RB
and Auckland, Melbourne, Singapore and Toronto

A CIP catalogue record for this book is available from the British Library

ISBN 0 7493 9748 9
Phototypeset by Intype, London
Printed and bound in Great Britain by Cox & Wyman Ltd, Reading, Berks

New Writing 3 is the third volume of an annual anthology founded in 1992 to provide a much-needed outlet for new short stories, work in progress, poetry and essays by established and new writers working in Britain or in the English language. Although *New Writing* is designed primarily as a forum for British writers, the object is to present a multi-faceted picture of modern Britain, and contributions from English-language writers of non-British nationality will occasionally be accepted if they contribute to this aim. It was initiated by the British Council's Literature Department, who hoped through it to respond to the strong interest in the newest British writing not only within Britain but overseas, where access to fresh developments is often difficult. Thus *New Writing* is not only a literary annual of important new work, but also an international shop window. Like all shop windows, it can only display a selection of the wealth of goods available within, a sampling of the literature which is being produced in Britain today. The aim is that, over the years, and through changing editorships, it will provide a stimulating, variegated, useful and reasonably reliable guide to the cultural and especially the literary scene in Britain during the 1990s: a period when, to quote Malcolm Bradbury in the first issue, walls are crumbling, connections fracturing, bridges are being precariously crossed.

The first volume, which appeared in 1992, was edited by Malcolm Bradbury and Judy Cooke, and the second, *New Writing 2*, by Malcolm Bradbury and Andrew Motion. *New Writing 4*, edited by A S Byatt and Alan Hollinghurst, will appear in January 1995, and *New Writing 5*, edited by Christopher Hope and Peter Porter, in January 1996. Though work is commissioned, submissions of unpublished material for consideration (stories, poetry, essays, literary interviews and sections from forthcoming works of fiction) are welcome. All submissions should be double-spaced, with page numbers, and accompanied by a stamped addressed envelope for the return of the material, if it cannot be used. They should be sent to *New Writing*, Literature Department, The British Council, 10 Spring Gardens, London SW1A 2BN. The annual deadline is 1 April.

CONTENTS

Introduction

When the Book Marketing Council staged a promotion of Twenty Best Young British Novelists in 1983 it seemed to mark a bright new day in British and Commonwealth writing. When *Granta* magazine repeated the exercise in 1993 media response ranged from yawn to vociferous scorn. Salman Rushdie, who had featured on the original list and helped to compile the second, wrote a spirited defence of the new generation in which he spoke feelingly about an endemic British 'culture of denigration'. If the critics felt chastened by this counterblast, they showed no sign of it. There was much discussion of the perceived limitations of the young writers of the Nineties and of the social conditions that favoured, or militated against, significant new work. Less was said about the possibility that the widespread cynicism might simply be the predictable aftermath of those bracing literary days of the preceding decade.

The Seventies had been tranquil times for British fiction; most of the talent, it was often said, went into the theatre or television or even advertising. The emergence in the early Eighties of not just one or two but seven or eight confident, stylistically innovative and fiercely anti-parochial new voices had a galvanising effect. Publishers, booksellers, critics and, of course, other writers began to look unwontedly lively. Despite much talk of a literary 'mafia' (that British gift for disparagement again?) the new writers were in fact a disparate bunch. What they did have in common was the atmosphere of indifference and low expectation in which their literary ambitions had been conceived. In 1980 a young writer, no matter how gifted, would have been thought mad to give up his or her day job. The impact of McEwan, Amis, Rushdie *et al* meant that by the mid-

Eighties the writing life, complete with decent income and high public profile, began to look like a tempting career option.

There were snags. As Georgina Hammick argues cogently in this volume, the short story, still the form through which – despite its difficulty – most would-be fiction writers first flex their talent, is now under-published and under-regarded. The pressure to cut the preliminaries and launch your career with a novel, preferably a loud one, is enormous. The 400-page debut, accompanied by an over-excited press release but showing little evidence of the editorial influence that could have made it a lot shorter but a lot better, has become an occupational hazard for the fiction reviewer.

Reviewers have not been slow to bite back. If the book pages of newspapers and magazines are now more animated than for years it is thanks in part to a new breed of critic, trenchant, clever and stylistically almost as inventive as the Amis generation itself. In the Eighties you could suddenly become famous by writing novels; in the Nineties you can achieve a sort of fame by writing *about* them. Since major new novels do not appear every week while review columns do, it was perhaps only to be expected that our most vigorous young opinion-formers should grow impatient and their criticism take on a distinctly irascible and prescriptive tinge. The opprobrium that greeted 1993's 'Twenty Best' young fiction writers may or may not have been justified; its tone of sweeping dismissal was certainly characteristic of the times. The fiercely opinionated new criticism enlivens Sunday mornings – and established writers can be expected to take the rough with the smooth; whether it does much to foster nascent talent is another matter. It has always taken courage to submit that first, fragile manuscript to a publisher. It takes more now that, *if* you get into print and *if* you are reviewed, you risk being held up as evidence of terminal disease in the body of British writing. No one should mourn the days when literary 'success' meant tiny advances, tiny sales and tiny celebrity, but the alternative, in a country famously suspicious of fame and achievement, comes at a price.

A privilege enjoyed by the compiler of this kind of anthology is the opportunity to read a great deal of new poetry and prose unvarnished by publishers' hype and unfiltered through the mesh of critical consensus. Having little reason to suppose that Andrew Motion and I would necessarily share the same tastes, I anticipated what is politely known as lively debate. I was almost disappointed at how rarely we disagreed. This was not, I think, because we were pre-programmed to like the same things, but because real writing has an exhilarating way of slicing through preconceptions. We were pleased, and in the present climate relieved, to find ourselves often engaged, often convinced and often moved. We were struck too by the range of the work we selected. It would be hard, for instance, to find much in common between Rose Tremain's stunning and plangent evocation of a past world and Philip MacCann's spiky, funny and infinitely sad rendering of a present one, except for a complete integrity of voice and a formidable assurance of technique. We found comparable poise and conviction in the work of Jane Rogers, Jim Crace, A. S. Byatt, Michèle Roberts and other well-known writers (where you might expect it) and in the poetry and fiction of a cheering number of newcomers. The energy and grace of Jane Harris, Kate Sekules, Daniel Richardson, Jo Shapcott and Robert Saxton, among others, suggest that reports of the death of British writing, though they make terrific copy, are definitely exaggerated.

The Signals of Distress

Extract from a novel to be published by Viking in 1994

Both men were *en voyage* and sleeping in their berths. Hard winds swept in and put their ships ashore.

The coastal steampacket, *Ha'porth of Tar*, on which Aymer Smith had his cabin, had lifted before the wind that night as if it meant to leave the water and find a firmer passage in the clouds. It arrived at dawn off Wherrytown, hastened by the storm. Ten in the morning was its scheduled time. Dawn was too early for the harbour lightermen to be at work. No one with any sense was up and out in such a wind. The night was wild and famishing cold. A few miles down the coast from Wherrytown, the Cradle Rock, which normally would take the efforts of two strong men before it would begin to seesaw on its pivot stone, teetered, fluctuated, rocked from just the muscle of the gale.

The *Tar* shipped heavy seas as it came into harbour. There was no choice but for the five-man crew to still its paddles and shut its fires. Its passage in the wind was more temperamental – and less pontificating – than its progress under steam. The *Tar* was thrown against the harbour boom, and then against the channel buoys which marked the vessel's road. The wind pushed north. The tide tugged south. The *Tar* was only fifty yards from shore. Two sailors had to land a line by rowboat and thus secure the ship to capstans on the quay. And then they had to coax the *Tar* to dock. Aymer lay awake. He was no use on deck. His shoulder hurt from where he'd fallen from his bunk. The muscles in his throat and stomach ached from vomiting. His breath was foul. His temper, too. He should have travelled overland with the company carts, he decided. He should have stayed at home instead of meddling abroad. Yet now his ship had found a haven, he sought a haven, too, in sleep, roped to the granite of the quay. His dream was kelp and some young country wife, ensnared and going down, with Aymer drowning in the girl, the girl sucked under by the weed, the weed pitchforked like hay on tines of sea and wind.

Otto, too, was not much use on deck. His berth, at orlop level on the *Belle of Galveston* ten miles downcoast from Wherrytown, was not secured. But Otto was. He was the ship's goat by night, its donkey during the day. His ankle was held by a light chain, six feet in length and fastened to a timber rib. Shipmaster Comstock considered it a safety chain. Men far from home are emboldened by the dark, he said. His African might settle scores at night, if he were left untethered. He might do damage to himself or to the *Belle* or to the crew or to the galley rations and the grog. He might cause mischief amongst the cargo of four hundred cattle which Shipmaster Comstock had taken aboard in Montreal and whose quarters he meant to fill on the return with emigrants to Canada, if he survived the storm.

Without a porthole and with no light, Otto experienced a partial storm. It was not wet for him. He could not see the waves slap up against the timber. Or feel the wind. His cabin was a tombola. What was not fixed – the stool, the water jug, the palliasse, the black man's boots, the bed – fell across the cabin. Otto fell as well. The chain cut into his ankle. But then he caught hold of the chain and pulled himself tight up against the timbers of the *Belle* so that, indeed, the chain became a safety chain. He made a buffer from the palliasse so that the cabin's sliding furniture, the unsecured wooden pallet where he slept, would not cause too much bruising to his legs. The cattle – on the orlop level, too – were not so fortunate. They tumbled without benefit of chains. Some were concussed. Some broke their legs. They were too blind and winded to make much noise, except a tuneless carpentry as hoof and horn hit wood.

Three cows at least had heart attacks. Another choked on its swallowed tongue. The bulkhead separating Otto from twenty of the cows splintered, then fell apart. Two animals broke through the planking into Otto's berth. They had no time to find their feet. The *Belle* made reckless angles in the gale. One cow slid up against the palliasse and kicked to right itself. A hoof struck Otto on the ear. His head bounced off the wood. He fell six feet and swung like a carcass on a butcher's chain. His swollen face and ear took splinters from the deck. The anklet etched new wounds. Thank God he was unconscious. He did not feel the pain.

The Captain did his best, according to the book. The foresail on the *Belle* was lowered, the main-sail double reefed. But still the wind at its stern hurried the boat bitingly forward towards the darkness of the shore. The main and mizzen topmasts fell away into the sea, with spars and rigging too. Part of the bulwarks went. And then the foresail, taking off into the night like some great canvas albatross. Everything was swept off deck by long black hills of water, thirty, forty feet in height. The hands on board – at least those six of seventeen who were not sick, and who had managed to hold on by their eyelids to the masts and rigging of the *Belle* – now waited for the lull following every set of seven waves and sent the anchors down. But the anchors slipped. The *Belle* heeled landwards. It went in two hundred yards, found some upright purchase on a sandy bar, and stuck. The crew – excepting Otto – took to what rigging had survived. They flew their signals of distress, though it would not take a flag when it was light to signify to those on land that the *Belle* was almost lost. Comstock fired the ship's double-barrelled gun. He prayed the wind would take the sound into the bedrooms on the coast and that the people thereabouts had sympathy – and rescue boats – for sailors in distress.

Nobody came that night. But it was not long before the waves and wind abated, and a teasing, ruddy dawn thinned and thickened through the mist. The *Belle* was eighty yards offshore. The sea was still ill-tempered. Between the sand bar and the

beach, however, the water was more calm. They checked the
Belle's four long boats. Two were lost and two were smashed.
Would someone swim ashore? There were no volunteers. They
were too tired, potato cold, and fearful. The tide had turned
and out-haul waves were rocking the Belle from the landward
side. No human swimmer could achieve the shore in seas like
that. But Captain Comstock put the ship's bitch, Whip, in the
water with an ensign tied onto her collar, the red-on-white of
'I Need Help'. They would not let her climb back on board. At
last, with the good sense and resignation of a dog, Whip headed
for the beach. The cattle that had survived the night were not
far behind. Comstock opened up the orlop hatches and drove
them into the sea. He feared their frenzied restlessness would
further destabilise the *Belle*. Many did not make the shore. The
ones with broken limbs or in too deep a shock did not survive
the swim. Others had no compass sense and headed off for
Montreal. But three hundred cattle – maybe more – got to land
that day and set to work on sampling the salty foliage of the
backshore as if there'd never been a storm.

It was seven o'clock on a Saturday, November 1836, on that
far angle of the coast. Only strangers were awake. The Americans clung to rigging out at sea, impatient for a sign of life.
Aymer Smith, ready to encounter Wherrytown, packed his
careful travelstores by candlelight belowdecks on the *Tar*: his
tarpaulin coat and leggings, his books, some anchovy paste, a
Bologna sausage, some chocolate, a great bar of black bread, a
jack-knife and a leather flask. He wrapped them in a carriage
rug which doubled as a bag. Otto bled into his palliasse. The
cattle from Quebec moved on from backshore weeds and tested
the corky grass of dunes. The light of morning thinned the
wind. The final strings and shreds of cloud stretched and disappeared. The water was as clear as gin. Whip ran along the shore,
barking at the waves and cows. Finding both indifferent to her
she went in search of other dogs. She'd heard them barking,
and soon had found the wooden cottage where two large
mongrels were secured by ropes to the porch. Whip found

discarded bones which she could gnaw, and turnips. At first the
mongrels went for her, but could not reach. They were too
bored to persevere. Whip found a corner of a shed where she
could sleep, her chin between her feet. The red-on-white of 'I
Need Help' had loosened at her collar. And help was not at
hand.

It had gone nine before the mongrels were released. They ran
at once towards the hut where Whip was sleeping. Rosie Bowe
took a heavy piece of firewood as a cudgel and followed them.
At best she'd find a hedgehog for the pot. At worst? Some thief
who'd stolen lodging for the night would still be sleeping there.
There were no men about to deal with whatever made her dogs
uneasy. She had to handle trouble on her own. She was per-
plexed when she found Whip, her back bowed and her tail
between her legs, sheltering in the hut. Rosie knew the dogs
for miles around, and this one was not familiar. She pulled the
ensign from the collar and put it in her apron front. It was a
tough and decent bit of cloth. And then she let her mongrels
in. Let dog police dog, she thought. It was too cold to kick the
bitch herself. The three dogs were in a playful mood at once,
happy to chase tails. Rosie left them to it. She had work to do.
There'd be storm kelp on the beach, easy to collect after such a
tide and such a wind. Her cart would soon be full. With her
daughter Margaret's help they'd have a dozen loads before the
tide was in and (with the agent Howells paying thirty shillings
a ton for prepared kelp ash) would earn a welcome seven shillings for their efforts.

'Miggy! Miggy Bowe,' she shouted at the window of their
cottage. 'Get yourself up and out of there. This in't the Sabbath
yet.' She put her head round the door and spoke more gently.
'Come on, we'll get ourselves a good penny if we're keen.'

'No, Ma, it's hurtin' damp out there.'

'Warm yourself with work. Let's not be idle. I'll let the dogs
inside to get you up. We've three dogs now. Our two have
found a bitch to chase around.'

'Whose bitch is that?'

'She's ours, to keep or sell. She's sleeping in our hut, and that's the law. Or ought to be. Get out of there Miggy! I'm warning you. It won't be dogs'll get you up, but me.' Rosie stepped inside and showed her daughter the firewood cudgel. 'I can give a decent bruise to idle girls.'

'Oh, Ma! You gonna lay a fire, or what?'

'No fire on Saturdays. Not till it's dark at least. This in't the inn. We'll have a fire down on the beach if you move fast. I'll bet there'll be the wood washed up. Did you sleep through that wind? Well, that's like asking Does mutton dance quadrilles?'

'No, it in't. I'd like a bit of mutton though.'

'You'd better press your finery then and find yourself a farmer's son. There'll be no mutton till you do. Here, make yourself a gown from that!' She threw the red-and-white cloth onto her daughter's blanket. 'That should turn some farm boy's head. He'd turn away if he had sense.'

Margaret Bowe didn't mind. She knew enough to know she was good-looking. 'It's off a ship,' she said. 'A signal flag.'

'The little dog was wearing it for a kerchief,' her mother said. 'What kind of dog is she?'

'A hairy little sharp-toothed bitch. Much like you. Only she's up and dressed for work and running in the yard, while you're still on your back. Come on now, Miggy girl. There's been enough of this. I'll get the cart and you can earn your supper.'

Miggy Bowe tied her hair back in a knot, put on men's working breeches and her thickest smock, and wrapped the *Belle*'s cloth call for help round her throat as a scarf. It gave a reckless dash of colour to a face that had no warmth. Rosie Bowe was the cheerful kind. She'd sing in rain and mud. But Miggy was young enough at seventeen to be a pessimist. Where would she be at thirty-four, her mother's age? Still carting kelp. At fifty-one? Cold as stone, with any luck, and nothing to her name except a wooden cross. She petted her two dogs and then inspected Whip, her teeth, her paws, her collar. With luck they'd get some puppies out of her in spring.

'Come on, you little lady,' she said. 'Let's have a look down on the shore.' Miggy and the dogs ran to catch up with Rosie who was wheeling the handcart towards the dunes.

They saw the cows from Montreal before they saw the sea. They'd never seen so many cows at once.

'You called for mutton, Miggy. The Good Lord sends us beef.'

'Whose cows are they, Ma?'

'That little dog has come with them, that's all I'm certain of.'

'What's stopping us from salting one?'

Her mother did not answer. She half-guessed that there would be some wreckage and some carnage on the shore – and, if there was, then who could stop them slaughtering one cow before the excise men got wind of it? There'd be better pickings than the kelp. Bullion, jewels and plate had been beached the other side of Wherrytown a dozen years before. Tobacco, tea and lace would suit them well. There would be sailcloth and timber for the house, at least. Winter beef. Wrecks were a Godsend. Rosie almost ran.

So strong and buoyant Rosie Bowe was the first woman that the sailors had seen since they had left Montreal. They watched her pick her way between the cows and descend with her handcart down the backshore to the beach. They saw another figure, too – a smallish boy in breeches and a smock with three dogs. They'd spent six hours in the rigging but had been warmed and dried a little by the breeze and sun, so managed quite a spirited cheer when the seaman, Parkiss, who had the ship's glass, reported that the smallest dog was their own Whip. The dog, perhaps, had saved their lives.

They'd have to wait another hour yet. A kelper's handcart could not bring them ashore. Rosie sent her daughter running down the coast. The nearest fishermen were beached below the Cradle Rock, a half a mile away. They'd come out in their boats. She waved back at the sailors but did not know how she could signify across so wide and watery a gap that help was on its way. She pushed her cart along the tide line and put the morning to good use. As she had expected, the storm had deposited a lot of kelp on the beach. She chose the knobweeds and the bladder wracks because their yields of soda were the best. She kicked aside the sugar wrack. A cart-load of that would only give a quarter-bucketful of soda ash. She lifted the weed with her right hand and kept her left hand free to seize the crabs that often sheltered underneath the kelp or the lance eels which could be twitched out of the sand if she were quick enough. When she found timbers from the *Belle* and snapped lengths of rigging, she wrapped them up in kelp and hid them on the cart. She watched the water as she worked for bobbing bottles of brandies and liqueurs, but all she spotted was the ready-salted carcass of a cow, floating on its side, and masts and planking from the ship tangled in the offshore weed. Quite soon her cart was full. She pulled it back into the dunes where she had built a stone pit for burning kelp. She buried what she'd salvaged from the *Belle* in a soft dune, and spread the load of kelp to dry over the disturbed sand. She'd gathered three more loads of weed before the seine boats of the fishermen appeared beyond the bar and breathless Miggy, her breeches caked in mud, her pulse quickened by the run and what was promised by the *Belle*, reappeared amongst the kelp, the wreckage and the cattle on the beach.

One man – Nathaniel Rankin, a seaman from Boston – was dead, concussed by falling timber in the night and drowned. But sixteen had survived. They had been fortunate to end up on the bar. The three seine boats that came to rescue them were secured to the *Belle*'s hull in water scarcely deep enough. The dozen oarsmen helped the Americans to climb into the boats and find a place. They wrapped the men in blankets and gave them corn-brandy in water from their flasks. Comstock brought his charts and letters of command. He dignified himself and called down from the damaged deck, 'I trust you gentlemen will help us salvage what we can when we are warm and dry.'

There were a dozen cries of 'Yes!' They all were keen to get back on the *Belle* again. Next time they'd charge a fee.

'There's one more man.' Comstock added. 'I ought to be the

last to leave. We've got one injured party, on the orlop. Three men can shift him out.'

He took command and pointed at the nearest three – a boatman called Harry Dolly, his wildly weathered, dark-haired son, Palmer, and one of their casual hands, an old and silent bachelor known locally as Skimmer. They followed Shipmaster Comstock below decks to Otto's berth. When the cattle had been driven into the sea, a crewman had released him from his chain and wrapped him in his palliasse to keep him warm. The cloth, to some extent, had stemmed the blood. The wound and swelling on his forehead were mauve. His ankle was stiff and raw with pus. He was conscious but inert. Only one eye opened. Only one eye could.

'Are you sleeping, Otto?' Comstock said. He was discomforted by the silence and the stares of the three men. Perhaps they blamed him for the wounds. But they were speechless from surprise. They'd never seen an African before. The darkest they encountered was a youth like Palmer, a ripened russet face with sable hair. They were not used to this topography. They could not tell his age or temperament or judge his character. His hair was like black chimney moss. He seemed to have a woman's lips. He hardly had a nose. They were reluctant to hold him by his arms and legs. They could not bring themselves to touch his skin. Instead they lifted Otto in his palliasse as if it were a hammock. He was a very heavy man, and it took twenty minutes negotiating the carcasses of cows, the timber debris and the companion-ladders, before they reached the deck. They put him in the Dolly boat and pushed off for the beach. Already there were forty people and a dozen carts waiting with Rosie and Miggy Bowe. Two harnessed horses pulling carts and one unharnessed horse ridden by the agent, Walter Howells, stood backs against the sea, on the shingle. It was too cold to wade in to help the Americans ashore. They had to manage it themselves – except that when one older sailor fell into the water, Walter Howells, to some derision mixed with cheers, rode his horse into the breakers and hauled the sailor out by the collar of his cork safety-jacket.

Otto was not touched. Comstock threw sea-water in his face to rouse him. He found the energy to swing his damaged legs across the bows of the rescue boat and try to find his footing in the shallows. He sank into the water. Its iciness awakened him. The salt was painful on the wounds, but cleansing, too, and healing. He was the last to make his way to shore. They found a bed for him, in seaweed on a half-loaded horse-drawn cart. They gathered round to point and shake their heads and giggle nervously. Miggy was the first to stretch her arm and touch him on the toe, where dry, dark blood had been made pasty by his short walk in the sea. Then everybody touched the toe, in turn. They ran their fingers across the nail and felt the skin, the pink below the toe, the brown above, the blood, and cold.

The beach was never busier, except at pilchard time. The sailors and the locals hugged and shook hands. Three dogs ran wild, experimenting with the sea and crowds. The cattle moved inland. Miggy looked for Palmer Dolly. Perhaps he'd shake her hand. Or they might hug. But he had gone off in his father's boat. Instead she made do with the attentions of the younger Americans, who now could see, despite her breeches, that she was a girl, a pretty one. She wore their ensign round her throat.

'This Miss is calling out for help,' they joked. 'All hands stand by.'

One sailor – blond and teasing – attempted first to take away her ensign scarf. And then, affecting innocence, touched her at her waist. The whole of Miggy flushed. She'd gladly press her lips on any young man there. A fire was lit – in her, and on the beach. They warmed and dried themselves as timbers from the *Belle* smoked grey. The three seine boats pulled now beyond the bar and soon were out at sea. The *Belle of Galveston* settled into the wet sand of the bar. The Americans – with Otto sleeping in the cart, and Whip in tow – embarked upon the eight-mile walk to Wherrytown where there was food and lodging and where, by now, Aymer Smith, that other dreaming voyager by sea, had found the only tolerable inn. The air – scrubbed and quietened by the storm – was now so still that Miggy and her mother could take a lighted piece of wood and carry it the half-mile to start a celebration fire in their own home. And what was there to celebrate, besides the passage of a storm? Much. Much. Much.

Samhadrarow and the Partial Exchange

Yellamanchili, Andhra Pradesh, 26 December 1992

i

Marcus stands still in the road, alien. He has lost weight; fat shat away with chillies and dhal. His bones are long and clumsy, his flesh slack and white. He wears Bermuda shorts and a tie-dyed shirt from Puri. His hair is blond and straggly. He is sweating.

The Indian, the boy, convulses below him, his arms and legs flapping and slapping against the road, raising plumes of red dust. The boy's lungi and hair and tight brown skin are caked in it.

'*Baksheesh! Baksheesh!*'

All the world swoops around the boy's fit. The vultures and the coconut palms and the ten o'clock sun and the thick air and the cucumber fields and the haze. Marcus is vague, confused, dizzy.

ii

Marcus has spent ten months in India. He has consumed it like a box of Quality Street, rummaging through the confectionery glitter, selecting always the richest, the most fondant. Saffron cloth, Golden Temple, Snooty Ooty, silk. Taj Mahal, Bengali burfi, Elephanta, ghee. He has ridden an elephant. He has learnt a mantra. He has travelled First Class on the Rajdhani Express.

He has gorged and sickened, then discarded the fancy packaging, still full of sweets, unable to bear its rustle and glare. So he has found Good Work. Only three weeks left in India, but time for Good Work. Time to help. They need help.

iii

Yesterday, Marcus spent five hours at the tree nursery, doing his Good Work. The Indians were all around as usual, packing the red soil into polythene seedling bags; crusty brown fingers nimble. They were toddlers, sons, widows, daughters, newlyweds, twins, teenagers, mothers, grandparents . . . but Marcus did not see them. He might have been told a name, he might have remembered it for an hour. He might have mistaken a fourteen-year-old girl for her thirty-year-old mother.

Eyes hidden behind duty-free Ray-Bans, he yearned for England the whole day. Scenes from films. Song lyrics. Rugby. Friends. Roast beef. Christmas.

iv

And then, as the sun faded into the dusty horizon, Marcus came to loathe the sugar in chai. It seemed that someone had brought him a sticky cup of the stuff every hour. He had not tasted the sustenance, the vital energy of carbohydrate, where protein and fat are scarce; he had tasted only the sweetness. He wanted water, but had run out of tablets. He could have afforded cold Limca or Kampa Kola from the stand along the road, but he loathed them too; they too were full of sugar.

v

Now Marcus tries to steady himself in the road, his vision blurred, the boy still fitting beneath him.

'*Baksheesh! Baksheesh!*'

The world swoops faster round the boy. Marcus sways on his feet and closes his eyes. His mind arcs away with a vulture and he is transported back five minutes to recognise his body, his own ridiculous body, trudging along the road from the headquarters, on its way to the nursery:

> The sandalled white feet, kicking up dust. The massive white toes jutting from leather. The hairless, lumbering white legs, wrinkled at the knee, trunking up to Authentic

Indian psychedelic shorts. The thick white neck rising from broad white back and shoulders. Like a sweaty ox. It should be pulling a cart.

And the Indian, the boy, in the distance, perched on the broken-down fence, at the side of the road, swinging his legs. Laughing.

'What is your name? My name is Samhadrarow. What is your age? My age is ten years. What is your country? My country is India. What is your father? What is your mother? What is your breakfast?'

And his approach to the boy, through the thick heat, not bothering to acknowledge him – to namaste or smile – until the boy jumps from the fence and is running into the road and standing, feet apart, in the middle, laughing.

'*Baksheesh! Baksheesh! Baksheesh! Baksheesh!*'

And the boy flopping to the ground.

Marcus opens his eyes. It is a laughing fit. The Indian is having a laughing fit. The world is steady now. The fields and palms and vultures and sun are back in place. Marcus stares at the boy on the road. The emaciated legs, arms, chest. The ribcage pushing against taut, brown skin. The brilliant white teeth, scrubbed with neem. Marcus will not look at the eyes. The boy is a beggar. He has been saved from the street to work at the nursery. But he is still a beggar, and he has the gall to laugh at an English man. That is how they are here.

Marcus steps back and pulls out his camera. He laughs in return, with a sickly grimace, and takes a photo

★

which is whisked from his hand, as he stands outside the colour developer's in Delhi, up into the hot air, through the storming dust and cries from the bazaar, through the rainless clouds and thunderclaps, and struck by lightning, smashed to atoms, drawn up through the exosphere and out to the vacuum and junk and satellites and radiation and radio waves and telephone waves and television waves, and gathered by and mingled with these criss-cross ribbons, round the spinning earth:

East to West, West to East, North to South, South to North; the urgent news; floods and droughts and famines and fires and wars and crashes and coups and murders and stocks and shares and urgent news; the lust and tragedy and hate and scandal and envy and action and pity and romance and shame and urgent news

and released again as atoms, from the tangled ribbons, to be pulled down through the exosphere, channelled through snowclouds and snowflakes, frozen into black and white and sucked through the cold wet air and slushy roar of taxis and double-deckers into the portfolio of a man on his way to a job at a photo library in London.

*

Radlett, Hertfordshire, Christmas night 1994

i

Samhadrarow stumbles from the photo, three inches tall and still laughing, into darkness. His big toe strikes metal and he freezes. He stretches his eyelids wide and waits. A stench of mouldering bread and meat and cheese fogs his nostrils. Goose-pimples rise on his flesh.

His eyes grow accustomed. A wall of metal and plastic towers in front of him; arteries of electrical cable snaking through and around a grid of aluminium pipes. The ground is strewn with boulders of rotting food and ropes like hair, all piled with dust.

Samhadrarow turns to the huge square of paper from which he fell. It is propped up in the dust and the food, confined in this dark alley. Peering up on tiptoe, he deciphers letters the size of his head:

SAVE THE CHIL

The earth quakes and

ii

Samhadrarow runs from behind the juddering fridge, abandoning the already abandoned charity envelope. He skirts the side of a dishwasher, in the shade of a worktop, and emerges into the bright light of a fitted kitchen. His feet slap against multi-hued, tile-effect linoleum. He stops in the middle and notes that his skin has faded to monochrome, then looks up past the front of the fridge and the dishwasher, to the worktop.

Curling over the edge, beckoning, are the remains: a turkey carcass – pink scraps clinging to blood-spotted bone; sprouts and potatoes – soft and wasting, skins blotching dry; half-eaten pudding and pie and cake – fruit, sponge and pastry mashed into crusting custard.

Samahadrarow's stomach rumbles with nausea and desire. The worktop is too high. He waits. Morsels of the stuff detach and rain down on him. He gorges.

iii

It is five a.m. A clock chimes. Samhadrarow runs out of the kitchen, through deep shag pile, into a dim lounge. He stops in the middle of an Afghan rug. The air buckles with booms and rumbles, and trembles with shrill, tinny music. Samhadrarow's bones tickle with it. He raises his head to meditate on the huge tree in front of him. Red, blue, green and amber lights, winking on and off, glimmering on baubles and tinsel, something like Diwali. He finds some peace, but it is soon curdled by the acrid waves of pine, flooding down. He feels dizzy and sick and turns away, to a giant in an armchair.

A man, a fat English man, snores thunder, mouth agape, flesh ghost-blue in the light of the television. Samhadrarow crosses the rug, approaches the man's legs and grasps up at a red silk dressing gown. He grips the material hard, scrunching it between his fists, pulls himself up, and clambers onto the man's lap. The man's stomach balloons and deflates in folds beneath a string vest, pushing through the front of the dressing gown. Samhadrarow finds footholds and ascends to the man's shoulder. He edges round to the tunnel between the blubbery, stubbly neck and the armchair's upholstery, gripping at spiky hairs for balance. Bending to a label sticking from the dressing gown's collar, he deciphers letters the size of his head:

MADE IN IND

The earth quakes and

iv

Samhadrarow tumbles backwards into the coughing man's lap. A hurricane of breath, rich and foetid with whisky and half-digested food, roars against him, blows his lungi up against his chest, and throws him head-over-heels back onto the Afghan rug. Samhadrarow lies still, till the hurricane calms and the snoring resumes. He sits up and gazes at the television screen, which stretches vast above him. A Hindi love story rides the night-time schedule, the sound turned down low.

Samhadrarow is entranced and transported. His mind is lost in a hazy blue cloud and he drifts back to all those evenings in the gallery of the cinema in Yellamanchili

> where the bench splinters into his thighs and his friend, Ram Babu, has drifted to sleep on his shoulder. Where, in the dark, the chatter and restless rustlings flutter up from the stalls. Where Samhadrarow is peaceful. Where the screen flickers. Where the soundtrack bounces a clean echo off the walls, and Samhadrarow remembers that

>> the heroine, her love unrequited, has followed the hero across the sea in a jumbo jet plane and now, mid-

bhangra, luminescent goddess and god in sari and suit, they whirl and trill through a dream of England: a luxury mansion; a fitted kitchen (all mod cons); a Porsche; a Jacuzzi; a glass of champagne and here, in England, suddenly at Alton Towers, riding the roller-coaster, they finally embrace and

the crowd cat-calls and tosses fried dhal at the screen, and Ram Babu stirs and opens a sleepy eye, and the adverts cut in and

Samahdrarow jolts back to the lounge. Confused, then amused, he sees that, cross-legged on the rug, he has grown to fill half the room. His head is close to the ceiling; the tree and the television and the still-snoring man are tiny below.

Samahdrarow laughs and a myth is uninvented; a pack of lies collapses; a ten-year-old boy, face frozen to listless grimace, black and white in the dust, moves free and tall.

This England is small. This whole world is small. And Samhadrarow laughs because he knows it.

His flesh has regained its colour.

v

Samhadrarow hears a tap of heavy fingers on glass, and stoops through the lounge, into the hall, to answer the front door.

There, in the cold, he faces himself. His tall, glowing self, standing on the doorstep, shivering and laughing, fresh and multi-hued with knowledge. He passes out of the house, hugs himself, sees more of himself, all along the street, outside all of the houses, laughing in the snow. Samhadrarow. A legion of Samhadrarow, stretching past semis and lamp-posts and tarmac, to the horizon.

They have all stumbled tiny and grey from a photo on an envelope, onto a carpet or a rug or a coffee table, or into a swing-top bin . . .

They have all discovered and explored what is England inside the houses, and they have all dreamed of Yellamanchili.

They have all grown tall, and stepped out into the street to see themselves.

And, in the distance, one of them, Samhadrarow, is holding an envelope. In the distance he is staring at the silhouette on the front, from which he stumbled. In the distance he is lighting a match and burning an image . . . and the street is on fire.

Marble worktops squeal and crack, hurtling fiery splinters into old teak chests. Silver bangles melt to puddles, sending cotton blouses up in smoke. Windows bulge and shatter. Beams groan and crash to earth. The houses tumble.

Samhadrarow dances and laughs in the snow, warmed by the flames. He watches England flake to ashes, and is ready to go home.

Those Nails

She sat through the late afternoon, smoking, lighting one cigarette from another. She sipped golden liquid from a glass until the evening breeze began to twitch at the curtain. The park bench, the last night, those fingernails. It was what she and Harry had wanted. No need for shame. They could say what they liked.

In the half-light, she spread her fingers out on the cracked leather arm of the seat, examined the veins, the liver-spots. The nails of course were all wrong. There were far too long, uneven. Like claws. She reached into her sewing basket and picked out the scissors, the medium-sized scissors, the ones with the keenest blades. They had a pleasing, symmetrical shape, and 'Empire' stamped on the handles. The cutting edge would make the left hand easy. Just a slice here, a trim there. The right would be difficult. Had been for as long as she could remember. Even before the arthritis. She stubbed out her cigarette, touched the rope of false pearls at her throat, remembering. Ten years ago, she hadn't needed to trim her nails. They'd been just the right length, and she'd only had to neaten them up with an emery board.

She threaded her finger and thumb through the scissor handles, the metal cool against her skin. Moved the blades towards her thumb nail. With the right hand, it was a question of hacking, half ripping, an unsatisfactory process, that left the nails uneven, battered looking. A reminder that she was on her own. She'd have to file them after her bath. But that was fine. That would keep things in the right order.

Snip-snip.

She listened to the scissors in the silence of the room. If Harry had been there he could have helped her. Perhaps cut them for her. Sat her on his knee and held her hand in his great fist, trimmed each nail, taking off just enough until they were perfect. Finishing with her little finger. She glanced up at a silver-framed photograph on the mantelpiece. Harry in his suit, outside the furniture shop. No tie, so perhaps the picture was taken on the morning of the staff outing. He stares past the photographer, as if something has just caught his eye. The arrival of the charabanc? A big, passionate man, his hair flopping into his eyes.

Snip-snip.

And once he'd finished cutting her nails, he'd surely have pressed kisses to her mouth, maybe patted her backside as she stood up. Slid his hand up her skirt.

Snip.

She ought to be past all that. She'd read about it. The withering. The fluids ebbing. And Harry, well, he'd have been over seventy. The very thought. All creaking bones and coughing, it was meant to be at their age. And what romance was there anyway in how she was supposed to live now? Pension-books and hot water bottles, a bit of fish once a week and tinned soup for lunch. Shopping with a string bag (she refused to use the tartan trolley Richard had bought her, as if he wanted a stepmother who was ancient before her time). There was the gym, of course. Her sedate circuits. Pump up the gym, pump it up. Work that body. Body. Work that body. That infuriating computer bicycle. The film-club. Avant-garde, my word. And every few months a flutter on the horses. For a thrill. Making ends meet. Passion-killing, that's what it was. That's what Harry would have thought too.

She built a little pile of nail cuttings on the arm of the chair, like a cluster of tiny new moons. Nails probably weren't that important to most people. They were just things on the ends of their fingers, handy for pulling out thorns and soothing irritated skin. 'I'll scratch your eyes out,' people say, though they seldom do, preferring to use their nails for more or less sociable pursuits, like tickling the wrinkled soles of baby's feet and drumming the Post Office counter to show they'd been kept waiting too long.

She glanced at the mantelpiece again, checking the time. Richard and his wife Mona would pick her up in the morning, in their matching quilted jackets and sports shoes, and she'd sit in the back, beside the baby, on the way to the cemetery, listening to them bicker about his driving or the child's feed. And, when they'd stood a while around Harry's grave, shivering and shuffling their feet as they'd done one Sunday a year since his death, they'd go somewhere for tea and Mona would fill the silences with chatter, smiling, yet somehow managing to look right through her. As if it was her fault. And all day, Richard, remembering Harry's wishes from his childhood, would call her 'mother', the word sounding, at best, like something which made her disappear, and at worst, like the twist of a knife.

She gathered up the nail slivers and trickled them through her fingers, listening to them tap against the metal bin. Once upon a time she never cut her nails at all. Oh dear me no. That would have been disastrous. Emery boards only it was then and hand cream and rubber gloves for the washing-up on Lily's day off. A pretty penny, that's what they'd earned her, those nails. The hands.

Difficult to believe, looking at them now. She pinched the flesh and the skin puckered, crept back into place slowly. Looked at the nails, ridged and misshapen. The knuckles thickening, bones beginning to twist. The amber stains from smoking. 'Another nail in the coffin, Peggy,' Harry used to say, every time she lit up at one of their poker nights, and round the house he'd go, sniffing, as if there were something dead in the ashtray, instead of just a Du Maurier. Irritating. She would tap the waxy backs of the playing cards, spread out in front of her on the baize, and roll her eyes at Billy or Sinclair. It was the only thing they ever quarrelled about. The smoking. He didn't complain about the pounds, shillings and pence, did he? Or the fact that he was married to a celebrity.

The bath was next. It was important that tonight, everything was the same. Ten years ago to the day, she'd been so tired, so very tired, that the bath was a pick-me-up, as much as anything. Though she had wanted to make herself beautiful too. She went up to the bathroom and fumbled with the plug. Nothing seemed to be made right for her these days, even turning on the tap was becoming an effort. But she still had her pamper-session one night a week, just like always. Still rubbed cream into her skin. Looking after her assets.

'See those hands,' Harry said once, when Sinclair or was it Johnny Tenby and a few of the others were round and someone, happening to flick through a magazine, had come across an advertisement for whatever it was, for 'Passing Cloud' or 'Mansion Polish' or 'Lifebuoy'. 'Peggy's hands. Those are our Peg's. Got a packet for that one didn't we, pet?' And because he'd crunched his way through the ice in a few too many Martinis, he pulled her onto his knee, bending his head to kiss her fingers and she smelt the Bay Rum he'd sleeked into his hair. 'Midas Fingers,' he called her, because every time her hands were used in a magazine she'd nip up to London on the train to collect a slim packet of notes from Adam at the agency. Then Harry would meet her at the station, and off they'd go through the park, to the pictures, or the golf club, or the steak house, to celebrate.

She had a dim recollection of perfuming the water that last night, so she tipped a scented bath oil under the hot tap and watched the foam gather. Lilacs. Lovely. Pricey. Of course, when she was modelling, they got all sorts of stuff free. Toiletries, cigarettes, even clothes, all sorts, until she got too old and they dropped her. Past it at thirty-five. 'The freckles darling,' they said at the agency. Even that dear old handbag, Adam. 'Well dear,' he said, 'We're getting a teensey bit crepey around the old knuckles.' And by that stage, well, she was too old to go back to house-modelling. So she'd taken her little hostess job in the VIP lounge and Harry's shop had ticked over and things went on much as normal. But they'd never thought to put anything aside, never dreamed how much of a struggle it might be. Being old. And alone. 'Two can live cheaper than one, Peg,' Harry had said. Some dance hall, on the Isle of Man. And then he proposed they get married. Quite matter of fact. He was. Though he'd had go to the men's room for five minutes first. Prepare himself. 'What would you say Peg, if I asked you to marry me?' Well. When he said it, the room started to spin, just like that scene, that scene late on in *Last Tango In Paris*. The ballroom scene. All those years later, all the fuss about the film, and when they went to see it, she kept thinking, that was just like, just like. . . . But when he proposed, that was 1950. When nothing seemed to matter, when their lives were filled with potential and tenderness and hopes about the shape of the future.

She turned on the cold and perched on the toilet seat. She listened to the jets of water thunder as they fell, watching the steam rise up to swirl beneath the ceiling, thinking about the great Isle of Man adventure.

One of the girls had got friendly with a chap with a car on the way over, and that night, they'd all driven down to the front. And in the excitement of a first holiday away with her girlfriends, of all the handsome young men on the promenade, of just being there, she'd closed the car door on her finger. A strange sensation that was. Numbness at first, and then, when she realised what she'd done, an intense, throbbing pain. She cried out, pulled her hand up to her face in horror, to see the damage, but her eyes were clouded with tears and before she could blink them away, she felt a light touch on her arm. Turning, astonished, she watched a complete stranger guiding her fingers straight into his mouth. Harry. Passing with his friends, he'd seen what had happened. And there he stood in his baggy suit, like he'd been planted in the pavement, sucking her hand. He stroked her face, the back of her neck, all the time staring straight into her eyes, as if to say, 'It's all right, pet. It's all right.' The others gathered round, giggling, until Harry sent them for First Aid. What with the shock, the embarrassment,

she almost forgot the pain, the tears coursing down her cheeks
and oh my Lord, her new mascara. What a mess. But Harry
didn't mind.

Such a holiday that was then, her with a great black finger,
running about the island in cars, falling in love. For a while they
thought she might lose the nail. But miraculously, it healed, and
on the day Harry slipped the engagement ring onto her finger,
the skin was only tinged a faint yellow with the last of the
bruising.

She tested the water. Beneath the cool froth of bubbles, it
was scalding. She turned off the hot tap, left the cold running.
Ten years ago there'd been an urgency about the bath and she
remembered filling it only half-full. Tonight, though, there was
more time. What pleasure was left, if she couldn't enjoy a good,
long soak? It was the order of things that was important.

And, well, if Harry hadn't been entirely honest with her at
first, did it really matter? He'd said if she knew from the start,
she might have avoided him, he'd have lost her for good. And
perhaps there was some truth in that. After a couple of weeks,
when he did tell her, there was no question in her mind. She
loved him and if he'd been married before and had a son and
was a divorcé, then she'd jolly well just have to lump it. And
when Richard's mother died, hadn't she tried her best, accepted
him into their house? Sullen little lad that he was. That time in
the park, early on, when she was so unsure how to be with
him. A child. What to say. And they'd studied the leaves of a
tree. A chestnut tree it was. No doubt about it. And Richard,
age nine, kept insisting it was a maple. When it was obviously
a chestnut. And what were you supposed to do? Argue with
them? Or let them win points, just for the sake of it. It was
beyond her. The huffs. Pining for his own dead mother. And
all when she'd found she couldn't even have one of her own.

She wiped steam off the bathroom cabinet mirror and
inspected her hair. Thinner now than years ago, and shorter,
but the hairdresser had done a good job. Blonde and wavy, just
the way they both liked. On their honeymoon, she'd found it

embarrassing at first, the way Harry let his eyes travel across her hair, her hands, her body. Like she was a precious jewel with multi-facets that he wanted to commit to memory. He'd watch her hair fall through his fingers onto the pillow, or press a handful to his cheeks with his eyes shut, breathing in her scent. Then he'd stroke her fingers, slip them into his mouth. And later, when her own love-making became more adventurous, she'd wrap his penis in hanks of hair, rubbing it across his skin so it felt like she was holding a bulging, silky purse. Mind you, that was when she hadn't her rollers in. Passion-killers, that's what they were, Harry said.

She tested the water, turned off the cold. Started to undress, caught sight of herself in the mirror. Remembered Richard, breezing into the bathroom once when she'd forgotten to draw the bolt. Her, naked at the sink, Harry getting out of the bath. 'God, sorry,' Richard said. Flustered. Bless him. His cheeks all pink. Backed out, 'Sorry, Mother.' Yes. Mother. He must have been nineteen by then. Easily embarrassed. Or was it something else? There were all those years before, when he was there in the house, having to be careful about love-making. Circumspect. Quiet. Once or twice, when he was younger, they must have got a bit carried away, until they heard him stomping around his room next door, banging things. The following day he'd be all glares and silences and disapproving looks. As if she was disgusting. Never Harry, just her. As if ladies aren't supposed to do it after the age of thirty. And at one point, in his teens, his awkwardness, a notion had come to her. God forbid, the boy fancies me. But she'd dismissed the thought, quick as a blink.

She slipped out of her knickers. She'd long given up on roll-ons. Torture, that's what they were. But she'd needed a perfect figure for house-modelling. Thinking about it now, she'd never really been the type. Not brash enough. Pretty, that's about all you could have said. Fine knees, a good mouth. A bit on the short side. The only part that could ever have been described as beautiful were her hands. Ten perfect oval nails tapering to a point, the fingers long and slender, the skin tan. Smooth.

She gazed into the mirror, trying to remember how she'd looked that night. Tired. The bags under her eyes seemed worse then than they did now, though perhaps that was her imagination. Tonight, the skin was looser in places, more mottled in others. She shrugged her shoulders, watched her flesh jiggle and sag. Not that ageing ever mattered to Harry, she thought, stepping carefully into the bath, the bubbles tickling her calves. He'd always loved every bit of her. Every rounded inch, he said. He must have kissed every inch too. She lowered herself into the water. It was just a little warmer than her skin, hot enough to relax her without turning her lobster-pink. She'd been careful about that on the last night, too. She rested her head, keeping her hair out of the wet and reached for the soap, noticing the usual inexplicable bruises on her legs.

There was a boy once. In a picture at the film club, a few years back. A Scottish boy. 'See me,' he said to the girl, 'I bruise like a peach.' And she'd missed most of the rest of the film, thinking about Harry.

The marks they made on each other. Sometimes, when they made love it felt bestial. Like they were animals. That was the only way to describe it. Not violent. But not human. They held each other very tight, but it was passionate, not vicious. Never intentionally vicious. She'd roll over, and he'd press his teeth against her neck and shoulders, like the lions in nature films. The same places she was soaping now, he'd bite into, sending shivers down her spine. And sometimes he'd leave faint imprints in intimate places, nothing that showed when she put her clothes on, maybe just a little something, there beside the stretch-marks on the inside of her thigh. Matching fingerprints on the backs of her legs. But then, they both did mark easily.

She scrubbed her back with a rough cloth, watching milky particles of dead skin float away from her towards the taps. Ten years ago, she'd washed in a hurry, but tonight there was more time. Somehow, she wanted to savour these moments. She pressed her fingers across her calf, picking up tiny rolls of damp grey stuff, and let them fall to drift, suspended in the clouded water.

Harry loved it when she dug her fingers in, dragged her nails across his back, his stomach, his thighs. She left fine red weals on his skin that would be there hours later, parallel lines, faded to purples and pinks. 'Am I hurting you?' she asked the first time it happened, but he looked surprised, then laughed and said no. 'God no,' he said. And 'More'. Even if they'd lived in a cave in pre-history, or been servants in a hayloft in the middle ages, she was sure they'd have done it just the same way. It felt ancient, like they could have been born in any form, at any time, anywhere and it would have been the same. Animalistic. But that couldn't matter, could it, if they both enjoyed what they did?

Outside, the wind picked up, moaning through the chimney-pots. She lay back to soak. Harry used to come in sometimes when she was having her bath, and sit on the toilet. They'd chat about this and that. Twice, after the unit was installed, they'd tried taking a shower together, making love beneath the running water, but both times, they dissolved into giggles, because Harry kept slipping and the soap got in her eyes and they could hear Richard stamping about on the landing. 'Not like the pictures at all, is it?' Harry said. So that must have been late on, because they didn't make films with shower scenes when they were younger. Not at all. No siree. Doris Day never took showers. And if she ever did, she took them alone.

One night, not long after Richard and Mona's engagement, she and Harry were on the way home, and stopped on a bench in the park. The avenue was dimly lit, the only sounds were the rustling of the trees and traffic on the ring road. They sat for a long time, holding hands, looking up at the stars. Then she'd remembered that she had on her best underwear, a one-piece that fastened between the legs, 'Sailor's Delight', Harry called it. And she was wearing a dress. She slipped onto his knee and kissed him. And after a bit of fumbling with press-studs and zips, she'd pulled him inside her, thrown her head back to look at the sky. They stayed like that for some time, holding each other, moving softly in the dark. And it would all have been a bit of a giggle really, if Richard hadn't happened along the avenue with his new fiancée.

She felt the skin on her feet and fingers begin to wrinkle up like walnut shells and pulled herself out of the bath. Patted herself with a towel. It didn't seem right, to be dwelling on Richard and Mona. Their disapproval. She and Harry had done nothing wrong. She should concentrate on him, remember their last days together. The order of things on their last night. Of course, they hadn't known then that it would be the last night.

She remembered that she'd moisturised her skin, so she poured a little pile of lotion onto her hand and sleeked it down her thighs and up over her breasts.

Looking after her assets.

There'd been a huge fuss about whether he should come home or not, towards the end. Richard and Mona were dead against it, thought he should be kept at the hospice, with all its medication and nurses. But it was so painful to see him on the ward, lying for weeks against those relentlessly white sheets, wrapped in blankets, with tubes spearing his body, draining fluids into jars around the bed. Doped to the eyeballs. He seemed half his normal size, propped against the pillows with his mouth tugged down at one side, like a man who was already dead. 'The Big C', Richard kept calling it, in some failed attempt at diplomacy, his eyes shining, like a desperate dog's. The Big C. But it still meant the same thing. The doctor was very unambiguous and honest about what they could expect, she'd to give him that. He said the decision should be left to Harry. And thank God, when they asked him, he'd whispered, 'Take me home, Peg.' He squeezed her fingers beneath the blankets, like he always used to do at the pictures, and she'd to dig the nails of her other hand into her palm to stop herself from crying. They collected him in Richard's car and drove him home, Richard with his jaw set, staring straight ahead into the rain, and poor Harry, swamped in coats and scarves and blankets, though it wasn't cold.

She finished moisturising her body, and taking an extra dollop from the bottle, rubbed her hands together in a washing motion until all the cream was absorbed. Then she slipped into her robe, the same robe as before, kept in a drawer all those years, and went down to the living room to put on her make-up.

A week was all they'd had. As it turned out. One week together, holding each other, not really talking much. Richard arriving at tea-time, making stiff jokes and sniffing the air in the bedroom, his lip curling at the fact that sometimes she wasn't dressed. And after he left on the last day, she and Harry had talked about it, and agreed that it would be a lovely, lovely idea. To at least try. And before she went for her bath, they drank a cocktail together on the bed, hers a Marguerita, his the Morphine mix the hospital had provided. Harry insisting she give him less than the usual dose. 'I want to know where I am,' he said.

She'd kept the eyeshadow and lipstick in her drawer for ten years. Not that she'd planned this. The idea had come only last year, and right up until that afternoon, she wasn't sure whether to go through with it. But after a couple of sherries, it had all seemed inevitable. She applied foundation cream from a bottle, checking in the mirror for streaks, and pressed powder onto her nose. Then she stroked an applicator across the chip of shadow and drew it across her eyelids. The lipstick had hardened in its case. She tried softening it with a brush and some face cream, but it crumbled away and her fingers had begun to shake, so she resorted to the newer stick in her purse. Then she blinked mascara onto her lashes from a wand. It had been a cake mascara and a brush before, but she couldn't expect to get everything exactly the same. So long as it felt right. In the right order.

When they were younger, Harry used to like watching her prepare to go out. He'd lie on the bed with his hands behind his head, his eyes following her around the room as she dressed, put on her face. She'd catch sight of him in the mirror, smiling at her, with a glint in his eye. 'Bend over like that again?' he'd say.

She finished with a brush of rouge across her cheekbones then took the emery board from the mantelpiece and drew it across a nail, watching the little particles of protein build up like fine white sand on the end of her finger. The bath had made her nails translucent, like a child's. Last time Richard and Mona had come round they'd brought their baby and she'd asked to hold her. She tried not to notice the slight hesitation, the exchanged look, before Richard ducked his head in a nod and plumped his daughter in her lap. As if she was a bag lady. Or the Wicked Witch of the East. She turned the baby round on her knee, cuddling her close for a moment, sniffing the warmth of her downy head. The child grabbed her hand, and she noticed that her little fingers were like pale slugs, her tiny nails like half-formed pearly shells. And then Mona snatched her away, saying it was time they were off.

The varnish she'd worn on the last night had long since hardened, but she'd found what she thought was a similar shade in the rack at the chemist's. She shook the bottle, listening to the little silver balls rattle against the glass. Comforting. How many times had she heard that sound over the years? She unscrewed the top and stroked colour across her index finger-nail. Faded Rose. It would need a couple of coats, but there was time. Ten years before, she'd made do with just the one.

When they made love in the early days, she used to look at her hands against Harry's naked skin, at the beautiful shapes they made, the bright red patterns of her varnish as she caressed his back and chest. Before they got to know each other properly, before Harry found out what pleased her, she used to feel a tingling sensation in her hands and feet, a breathless, heady feeling. For weeks, she convinced herself that this tingling was a female orgasm. Of course, later, when she actually did have one, there was no mistaking it and she realised that the dizziness she'd felt before was only hyper-ventilation. It still amazed her how things had got better, through the years. How she'd become more comfortable, less inhibited. And how important it was for Harry, even when he grew older, to perform, not to let her down. Though of course, as they grew older, everything took longer.

After the second coat, she screwed the cap back into the bottle and waggled her hands around, blowing at her fingertips. This was the last stage. On the night of Harry's death, she'd despaired of even the one coat ever drying and had gone up to him, before it was quite done. She spread her nails across the seat, examining the new varnish. It was too red, the colour of blood. Have to do though.

She took the stairs one at a time, feeling slightly nervous. It was eight o'clock. As she pushed open the bedroom door and slipped out of her robe, she had a vision of Harry lying on the bed, waiting. He'd winked at her and tried to sit up. But he was so frail, from the illness, from the drugs, from dying, that she had to help him. He lay, naked, against the pillows and they kissed for a long time before she dragged her hair down across his stomach. He was smiling, and then suddenly, as she pulled her nails down his side, he grabbed her other hand, linking his fingers with hers, and stretched his arm out behind his head in the most healthy gesture she'd seen him make in weeks.

She stared at the empty pillows, side by side, then slipped between the sheets. Of course, they hadn't managed the whole thing, as they might have done when Harry was well. But it was enough. Enough for them both. And, yes, quite beautiful.

When Richard and Mona had arrived, it was gone eleven. They'd driven over as soon as they got her call. She'd rung the doctor then made herself a cup of tea and was drinking it, and smoking, when they came in. 'Mother . . . ,' said Richard, and stepped forward, awkwardly, to embrace her, but she shook her head and moved into the kitchen. When the doctor arrived they all trooped upstairs, in a sort of procession and stood around the bed. Harry's eyes were closed. The doctor turned on the overhead light and drew back the sheet to examine him. And it was then that Mona gasped and Richard stepped forward, frowning, staring at his father's naked body. The doctor reached out and touched one of the weals on Harry's chest, drew a hand down over the scratches on his side. Then he glanced across at her, his eyebrows raised.

They could think what they liked.

She arranged her hair across the pillow and stretched out to caress the place where Harry's head would have been. The linen felt cool beneath her touch and she spread her fingers out against its surface. 'You have the most beautiful hands I've ever seen,' he'd said, holding them against his cheek. His voice was weak, his breathing, which had been fine for so long, even though the doctor had said it would soon go, was finally laboured. She kissed his eyelids, stroked his pale, damp forehead. 'Even now?' she asked, eventually. But he seemed to have fallen asleep.

Richard had glared at her, the muscles in his jaw twitching and for a moment she'd had the irrational fear that his face might fly apart, that he might leap across the carpet and attack her. She sensed Mona flouncing from the room. Richard turned to the doctor. 'I'm sorry about this,' he said. Then he shook his head and walked out, without looking at her again. She could hear them hurrying into their coats in the hall. They could say what they liked. The doctor cleared his throat. He shrugged, and she thought she saw a twinkle in his eye as he pulled the sheet up and draped it over her husband's head.

The wind had died down and it had begun to rain. Heavy drops bounced off the slates, spattered the bedroom window. She stroked the sheet, watching the shapes her flesh made as it moved, the indentations on the pillow's surface as she kneaded it. Waiting. Towards ten o'clock, she uncurled her fingers and slipped them, one at a time, into her own mouth. 'It's all right, pet,' she thought, 'It's all right.' She lay awake for a long time, sucking at her fingertips, listening to the soft tick-ticking of the clock, to the raindrops, and the sound of blood moving through her veins.

Ways of Behaving

At Charm School they teach Angelica Stralka and me how to cross our legs properly. We sit on the spindly ballroom chairs set in a circle on the top floor of the downtown Higbee's department store and practise crossing our legs properly. One leg is wrapped like a snake around the calf until the toes of the top leg touch the inside ankle of the other. While we wait for the tea and cookies to be passed around I gaze across at the building opposite Higbee's. The Ohio Ballet practises there, and I can see the dim shapes of the ballerinas dipping and turning behind the soot-stained, greenish-tinted windows. Mrs Stralka, Angelica's mother, teaches ballet to little girls in her basement. A cramp begins at my calf and works its way up to my thigh. The smokestacks beyond Euclid Avenue give the taste of sulphur to my tea.

The bachelor lives in an apartment above the garage of the Stralkas' house. He moved in a few months ago. He is tall and thin and uses Brylcreem to keep his hair off his forehead. He plants crocuses for Mrs Stralka around the house. When he stands up from where he is planting, there are stripes of dirt on his khaki trousers. Despite his slenderness, his legs are thick and the stripes of dirt look like the wrinkles at elephants' knees. Whenever we drive down South on vacation, I see lots of billboards advertising Brylcreem. The men on them have teeth the size of Volkswagens.

My parents are away for most of the summer. Leonora, our cleaning lady, is staying with me. The kids in the neighbourhood are afraid of Leonora. She drives an old green Continental she calls her green hornet and keeps an axe in the back seat. She tells me she will use it on any of her dozen boyfriends who get fresh before she is ready. Any of the kids in the neighbourhood who don't believe the part about the dozen boyfriends are shown the pictures in Leonora's wallet. My favourite is one of Leonora wearing a blonde wig and a long green dress that barely makes it over her hips. In it, Leonora stands next to Shane, one of her boyfriends, smiling so wide that the fake pink gums of her dentures show. Leonora tells me that her Daddy pulled out all her teeth himself when she was twenty. 'That's what kissing too many sweet talkers gets you!' she says and laughs so long and hard that I have to hit her on the back.

The Stralkas live across the street from me. Mrs Stralka drives Angelica and me to Charm School on Saturdays. Mrs Stralka is French. Her first name is Monique. Sometimes her daughter calls her Monique. Mrs Stralka becomes angry when her daughter calls her Monique, but for an instant she is much younger. She gives Angelica a look in the rearview mirror and her hands tighten on the white leather steering wheel and she says, 'Don't call me that.' She smells of lilac and sometimes when she drives she holds her fingers splayed outwards, just the heels of her hands touching the wheel and gazes at her fingernails. They are perfect pink ovals and the tips are very white. Sometimes I am afraid she will run a red light.

Ms Murphy and Ms Phillips are our instructors at Charm School. They seem to have walked off one of the alphabetic ribbons that run across the top of most elementary school blackboards. Ms Murphy is a capital 'T' and Ms Phillips is a small 't'. Ms Phillips always plays the male counterpart when they act out etiquette. They seem like those Hollywood couples – a short Italian director and his tall glamorous wife. Today we are staring at each other. Ms Phillips is talking. 'Every once in a while you meet someone who stares at you, whether he or she is speaking to you or not. It is not good etiquette. Do break such a habit if it is one in which you indulge.' We are supposed to be learning by example that being stared at is uncomfortable. We cross our eyes at each other until one of us laughs.

Leonora spends most of her time with her dozen boyfriends. She has to change her rings each time she goes out with a different beau, according to which rings that particular beau has given her. But she always leaves her wedding ring on so Harry her dead husband won't start chasing one of them wicked angels. 'Bye Sugar – be good!' she yells as she rushes out the door. Her green Continental backfires as she leaves the driveway. I have a lot of time to myself.

Absinthe is a green liquor made from wormwood, now illegal, which can cause brain damage. Acteon was a mythical god who was attacked and eaten by wild dogs because he saw a naked woman bathing. I rediscovered the *Encyclopaedia Brittanica* in my father's study. I plan to work my way through to Z. I like accumulating facts. Each fact has its own texture, taste. You can roll them around in your mouth like hard lozenges and two together make a new flavour.

Like my parents, Mr Stralka has been away. I do not know when he will return. He owns a large company and has to be in the Orient a lot. He is a very big person. Not just in size. He enters a room with the air of a performer entering a sold-out hall. I always picture him just having arrived off an airplane, its engines still throttling in a darkened field.

'You look like a couple of harlots,' Mrs Stralka says to Angelica and me when we meet her at the Higbee's cosmetic counter after Charm class. She hands us Kleenex from her purse to wipe the lipstick off our mouths that we just learned to put on properly. The Kleenex smells of lilac, Chanel, cigarettes. Women's purses make me think of hidden doors, secret staircases, the moving eyes in paintings in old houses. I picture Mrs Stralka's mind full of secret staircases, moving walls, hidden rooms, her other language slumbering behind the doors like a mythical creature. We move along the glass cases to the jewellery. Mrs Stralka buys four gold chains. 'No box,' she says and fastens each one around her neck.

Alchemy is a medieval form of chemistry, seeking to turn other metals into gold. There is a line drawing of a medieval alchemist – a crazed-looking man surrounded by steaming vials. To the alchemist gold represented the eternal spark in the human body. Gold was the embodiment of incorruptibility in the physical world. In trying to transmute base metal into gold, the alchemists were seeking to extract the quality of permanence from the everyday.

Leonora tells me that mirrors have the most memories.

Mrs Stralka is having people over for tea today. Her cleaning lady called in sick and Mrs Stralka is in the kitchen. Her high heels sound angry. She calls Angelica and me. She wants us to get the tea cups and saucers, spoons and sugar together. The bachelor is outside the kitchen window, planting something around the border of the fountain in the courtyard. 'I like the smell of dirt,' I heard him tell Mrs Stralka when she protested about all the work he did for her. He comes to the open window, asks for a glass of water. My hand shakes as I hand it to him. Mrs Stralka opens up a box of orange sponge cake. '*Merde*!' she shrieks. The sponge cake is covered with large black ants. The bachelor puts his glass of water on the sill and reaches for the box. Mrs Stralka hands it to him. He tips the box upside down, holding the cake with the tips of his fingers. He gives the box a shake. Ants rain down upon the stones. He hands the box back to Mrs Stralka. They stare at each other for a moment. Then Mrs Stralka laughs and puts the cake on a tray.

Mrs Stralka reminds me of a zebra, or one of those creatures that look like small deer and have stripes and seem to be wearing high heels. Mrs Stralka wears high heels. She walks across the highly polished wood floors of her house and her heels make the sound of Martinis being stirred in a high pitcher. The Stralkas' house used to be a hunting lodge.

Angelica and I are in Mrs Stralka's bathroom. On her dressing table are rows and rows of bottles of perfume. She buys a new bottle every Saturday at Higbee's. She has the saleslady wrap them up like presents. The wrapping paper is blue and gold. But she keeps them. I see the wrappings from her last purchases peeping out of the wastebasket. Angelica and I try on Guerlain's *Sous le Vent*, Prince Matchabelli's *Evening in Rome*, Bonwit Teller's *721*. I start to get a headache. An aphrodisiac is a substance which arouses sexual desire. The encyclopedia gives examples of natural aphrodisiacs. Certain moths release aphrodisiac perfumes from the ends of hollow hairs on their abdomen and then wave the potion over the female by fluttering their wings. On the same page is apoplexy. It is the sudden inability to feel or move.

'If you are walking up stairs into an attic, even if you are wearing trousers, the polite male will proceed first, saying "follow me" rather than "after you". He will always come down last.' Now Ms Murphy is demonstrating how to take a seat at a restaurant. I am wondering how many opportunities there are for the young lady and her polite male to go up and down attic stairs. Ms Murphy's peach blossom lipstick is bleeding around the corners. She leans engagingly towards Ms Phillips, her polite male companion at the dinner table. I picture her on dark attic stairs. A man who has shiny hair like Dean Martin is on a stair below her. The air smells of peach blossom lipstick and the garlic of a spaghetti dinner. 'Follow me,' Ms Murphy whispers.

There is a ravine behind the Stralkas' house. Huge old trees stand in rows like frozen tribes. I see the bachelor there. From far away I thought he was Pan. I move from tree to tree, remembering the Indian steps I used when I was younger. When I am opposite him, a few yards away, I stop. His head is bowed. The tree above him sways its branches erratically like a neighing unwieldy horse. The sun straining through the branches creates shadows, minnows swimming upstream over his head. I realise he is praying.

Some African tribe believes that the hands have a separate soul from the body. I think of Mrs Stralka's hands on her white leather steering wheel. When Leonora speaks, her hands move with what she is saying – they make elaborate pictures in the air. Angelica sometimes puts her hand up over her top lip when she is talking. It makes you think she is telling you a secret. I think of the bachelor's hands – how they were clasped together when he was praying – quiet obedient twins.

Praying seems like something strange and illegal. Like absinthe.

Mrs Stralka is teaching ballet to a group of seven-year-olds. Angelica and I sit on the basement steps listening to Chopin and Mrs Stralka giving orders. '*Un, deux, trois, plié.*' We hear the moving feet of the little girls. They sound like dead birds dropping out of the sky. I think of the beautifully polished blond wood floors and bars Mrs Stralka had installed. When she limbers up for her classes, she bends into positions that seem impossible. The little girls climb up the stair past us for a break and some iced tea. Their black leotards bag at their bottoms, their pink tights sag at their knees.

The bachelor teaches high school biology. Nothing seems to fit together. He is slender yet his legs are thick, his feet are small and his hands are large, his mouth is large and his nose is small and his hair springs up when it is not held down by Brylcreem. Yet my hand shook when I handed him a glass of water.

'In the church of my heart the choir is on fire!' Leonora wakes me up in the middle of the night to tell me this after one of her dates.

No one has ever seen the atom. Niels Bohr stands next to a gigantic electron microscope. Belief is faith in the invisible over the visible.

Angelica and I decide that the bachelor is a romantic soul. We imagine him saying words like 'swoon' and 'unguent' with conviction. We leave a copy of Keats' 'Ode to a Nightingale' in front of his door. We sprinkle some Prince Matchabelli's *Evening in Rome* on it. Our teacher Mrs Percival cried over this poem last year. It embarrassed everyone.

'When two elephants meet on a desert savannah after an absence of several months, they charge at each other in happy recognition, urinating and defecating with the joy of seeing one another. Ladies, it is etiquette that sets us humans apart from the animal world.'

Mrs Stralka receives lots of letters from France. They are airmail letters, light and blue and the handwriting is strange. Mrs Stralka leaves a trail of these opened letters around the house, a personal map of memories – on the entrance table, in kitchen cabinets, in between sofa cushions, between stacks of records – once Angelica and I found one tucked under the breast of a stone swan in the garden. Sometimes they remind me of Easter eggs, hidden surprises to find. But most of the time I find it embarrassing, like dirty underwear left out in the open and underfoot.

Animism is one of the oldest religions and suggests that all objects have two aspects. One that is external, objective and real in the sense that it can be perceived by the usual senses; the other imperceptible to but a few, the animus.

I am awakened by Leonora's voice. 'For Lawd's sake stop trampling my petunias!' she yells, accentuating petunias, delicious and dark. I stand up on my bed and look out of the window. I think I see the bachelor crossing the street, or is it just my imagination? The next day Leonora practises shots in the front yard with her axe, mumbling about robbers, until one of the neighbours asks her to stop.

'Never kiss and tell for that is the road to hell.' It is humid in the Charm School classroom today. Ms Phillips has opened the windows and I can see more clearly into the dance studios across the street. One dancer lifts another high into the air and spins around. Ms Murphy is wearing fawn-coloured stockings and tan suede shoes today. One leg is wound perfectly around the other. I read about Amazon pythons this morning. This is how one attacks you. It wraps its coils around you, pins your arms to your side. It doesn't squeeze hard but tightens its grip each time you exhale, making it increasingly hard to draw the next breath. It doesn't bite, but holds its face close to yours, watching, while its forked tongue flickers around your nose. 'They watch you very closely,' said Sir Wilbur Phillipus Von Hohenheim, a nineteenth-century survivor. Ms Phillips pulls back on my shoulders. 'Don't slouch!' she hisses. 'While the man is allowed to originate the embraces,' Ms Murphy is saying, 'the young lady has the privilege, which must be assumed sacred, to say, "Stop. No further." '

The bachelor owns two grey Persian cats. When they are running around in the dark, you can't distinguish their bodies from their shadows. Sometimes I wonder if they are not living or dead but somewhere in between. Their eyes look red at night, like rubies set in the sockets of mummy shrouds. I decide that they are the bachelor's familiars. That he is a warlock.

August Strindberg searched for the animus with a bottle of liquid lead acetate in the cemeteries of Montparnasse.

Angelica and I are lying among the weeds on the Stralkas' delapidated tennis court, trying to get a tan. The Persians are lying between us, licking their fur. Angelica and I rub suntan oil into our skin and admire our newly painted toenails. I am reading *Peyton Place*. I found it in the drawer of my mother's bedside table. We can hear the bachelor laughing. I've never heard him laugh before. He is standing by Mrs Stralka's car. She is sitting in the driver's seat. I wonder if her fingernails are splayed outwards on the driving wheel. The bachelor has a deep laugh. It is like dark wood and you can feel it drumming inside you. Mrs Stralka's laugh sounds like a tray of delicate tea cups falling. 'Are humans the only creatures that laugh?' I ask Angelica. 'Probably,' she shrugs. I spend the rest of the afternoon trying to make the Persian cats laugh.

Mrs Stralka is having a party. She moves among her guests, introducing people. The bachelor stands at the edge of the lapping tides of a large Oriental rug. A piece of his hair has slipped free from its Brylcreem embrace and stands up straight. 'If you are present at a gathering and notice somebody looking bashful, do not hesitate to approach them and comment, "Isn't this a nice do?" or something suitable. A more subtle way is to get a tray of nuts or sweets and offer them, thus making a suitable excuse for conversation.' I go and get a bowl of salted peanuts, but when I turn back I see the bachelor is gone. I wander around looking for him. Later, through the kitchen window, I see him in the courtyard, dipping his fingers in and out of the fountain.

Pine trees are more stern than maples. People are their faces, bodies, belongings. I try to picture Mrs Stralka with different colour hair, wider hips, orange shag carpeting and she dissolves like sugar.

'Indian summer is like a woman. Ripe, hotly passionate, but fickle . . .' I am underlining all the good parts in *Peyton Place* for Angelica. This line runs through my mind, over and over, like a radio jingle.

It has been raining all week. There are worms all over the sidewalk. I used to step on them when I was little. Then in biology we dissected them and I saw how much was inside them. The frogs are out too. They sound like thousands of jump-ropes slapping on sidewalks. It is dark and Angelica and I are hunting for frogs. I don't know what we will do when we catch them. I run around the side of the Stralkas' house in hot pursuit of one. It jumps into one of the basement window gutters. Angelica and I see it at the same time and slide on our bellies in the wet grass to reach for it. The lights are on in the basement. I am about to grab the frog when some movement inside catches my attention. Mrs Stralka and the bachelor are leaning against one of the bars, entwined in an embrace. Their image is repeated on the three walls of mirrors. For an instant I think Mrs Stralka is giving the bachelor a ballet lesson. 'Baby where are you?' Leonora's voice echoes through the neighbourhood in orange swells and waves. I leave Angelica lying in the grass, looking in the window. Ms Murphy's voice chases me home – 'Never kiss and tell for that is the road to hell . . .'

The next day I go to the Stralkas'. It is Saturday. Charm School day. But no one is home. It is so quiet. Like a ghost town. I feel as if I could push on the house and it would fall over, a two-dimensional set piece. I look in the windows. There is a pile of blue airmail letters in the centre of the floor. They remind me of a pile of autumn leaves, ready to be burned. The garage door is open. I go inside and then up the stairs to the bachelor's apartment. 'Follow me.' I knock at his door. No one answers. I sit on the top stair. In the gloom behind me I see the Persians sitting on a spare tyre. They look inanimate, like the paperbacks one leaves behind at a seaside cottage. Their eyes are azure. Azure is the last word in book 'A' of the *Encyclopaedia Brittanica*.

The Nature of the Trade

After the big build-up they'd given him, you can imagine how I felt when I saw him in the wine bar, drooping over the table like a half-cooked ribbon noodle. I don't want to be unkind, but he was one of the least attractive men I'd ever seen. I suppose he had youth on his side – he was twenty-seven or eight – but his feathery-looking hair already had a dirty grey in it. He was five foot six when he stood up to say hello: small eyes, bad skin, soft voice.

I have to admit that he worked hard at being charming. He did it in the way you're told you should; he got you to talk about yourself. Slow down, Michael Parkinson, Cheryl said, after the first ten minutes; he was quizzing me incisively about my prospects, hopes, wishes, dreams. He was a salesman, from a family of salesmen, and what he was doing was selling me myself.

Almost all the people I knew at that time in my life were in sales. I used to sell dresses. It was a point of pride with me that I never let a customer out of the shop with an item that made her look more of a fool than she needed to. For this reason, people used to remember me; they'd come in and ask for me by name. We in turn used to keep lists of our clients' names and addresses. In theory this was so we could send them cata-logues and lists of special offers, but in practice it was in case we got a bad cheque. Over a six-month period, I had a Mrs Haddock and a Mrs Herring, and I used to keep praying they'd come in together and I could introduce them. I had a Mrs Pott, and a Mrs Kettle (you must trust me in this matter) and in due time there came along a Mrs Black.

Our shop was in Manchester, at the back of Piccadilly Station. It was an old district of dying enterprises; small dusty windows, adequate for Victorian eyes, looked out onto dusty back courts. Damp and fog hung in the air; war damage was still evident. The buildings grew haphazardly, some turning their sides to the streets. High on our fourth floor, written in letters two feet high, were the words MANTLES, GOWNS. They were painted in the 1880s, I used to think, by some immigrant hand, by some Jew from Hamburg or Lodz. Every day, as I bowled down the street at twenty-five to nine, I would look up at the fading legend, and the cream-wash greyed by many winters. Then I would let myself in with my key, push through the tacky old swing door, snap on the lights, pull off the dust covers, and take out my notebook to count the mantles and the gowns. Sometimes, it seemed, they travelled in the night; teleported themselves to distant stockrooms up or down uncarpeted stairs. Our showroom occupied the two lower floors; the others contained stranded rails with wheels off, and rattling bundles of wire coathangers, and boxes of unsaleable trash that was old when the New Look was new.

We called ourselves a wholesaler but we did a lot of retail, albeit in improvised circumstances. Our curtained fitting rooms were rather *ad hoc* and shrunk in size when we had a lot of new stock in. Sometimes there would be a ball of twine in one corner, or a stack of flat-packed cardboard boxes, or a mannequin with a bald head and one arm. We were always pushing about those big mirrors on castors, so that our ladies could have a front and a back view. You will wonder who came to us; but we had our regulars, as I've said. We were patient and tactful saleswomen, who never jibbed at the most unpromising figure. Though I could not sew, I knew what our alteration hand could do, and I was able to nip and lift and pin the garments to accommodate them to our customers' strange elderly shapes. I seemed to specialise, somehow, in dowager's humps. I often thought of quitting and opening up for myself: Quasimodo Modes.

Mr Wagner, the owner, knew all our customers by name or by reputation. He had different prices for different ladies: without the need to enquire, he knew what each customer thought she could afford. When I went to work for Mr Wagner at first, I thought that this was because so many of our customers were Jewish, and he knew them socially, knew their families. Later, though, when I saw him price up obviously Gentile strangers, lost souls who'd strayed in from the big stores, I began to think it was some sad telepathy that he possessed. Incidentally, it was 'Wagner' as in what a dog's tail does, not as per the composer. He was bald, harassed, mean in small ways, unpredictable too; but we did not have much to complain of.

My friend Cheryl had worked at Wagner's briefly, then skipped on to better things. One June she'd come back from Eilat deep brown and feeling brash, evaluated her prospects and said she couldn't take another autumn, she'd like to be selling some less stolid commodity. Maybe something financial? She didn't mind a low basic and a high commission; it made her feel she was teetering on the brink of a more exciting world. If this had happened in the eighties she'd no doubt have left for London and gone into some form of noisy brokerage and become a quarter-millionaire. But at the time these opportunities weren't open to her, and anyhow she was being pulled two ways. She was twenty-four and her grandmother had been telling her she was on the shelf.

She left Wagner's after the tape measure incident, which everybody agreed was the final straw. Mr Wagner was out on the floor himself that day: 'Cheryl,' he said, 'put a tape measure round Mrs Cantor.' So she did; she stepped up to the huge, bluff, beaming lady, and pressed the end of the tape to her vast stomach, and said 'Would you hold that, Madam, please?' Mrs Cantor looked bemused, and she dropped her beefy finger on the end of the tape; then Cheryl held the tape taut, and stood off, and began to walk around Mrs Cantor in a circle, as if Mrs Cantor were Stonehenge and she were marking off a track for the tourists. It took her a long time to get around, moving as she did at a stately pace. Mr Wagner, looking on, grew mottled in the face. 'Step forward, Miss – ' he said, forgetting my name in the agony of the moment, though I had worked for him for three years. 'Mrs Cantor, this young lady will attend to you.' And to Cheryl, with a snarl, 'Be so good as to count the sheepskins.' Mr Wagner managed a smile for his customer, then scuttled off to his tiny office, and fulminated behind the smeary glass panes.

To appreciate the story you'd have to know Cheryl. But as you don't, please try to imagine her pert bust (for there is no other term, in the trade): her twenty-two inch waist and her curvy legs, long in the calf. Imagine you see her as she sets down her dainty red shoes on the dusty carpet. (She had size 3 feet, always had marvellous shoes because she bought them in the sales.) Now: see the way she tossed her head. She shook it at Mr Wagner: she shook her curls, smiled a sack-me-then smile.

Counting the sheepskins was something of a penance. It was August when the tape measure incident occurred, and the coats were stowed away until autumn. It was dust-choked in the little hole where we kept them, it was stifling, close; there was a tiny window high up in the wall where hopeless flies knocked themselves hour after hour with dull buzzing thuds. The coats stank of beast; they were heavy to move, as if there were bodies inside them. Mr Wagner was always wanting them counted: as if they might resume their animal nature and flock off somewhere. In September they would be transferred to a shinier rail and pushed out onto the floor. Mr Wagner would pass a chain through them, down the necks and through one sleeve, roping them together, so valuable were they; in case Pott, Kettle or Black, in some menopausal fit, should decide to rustle one. Theft was a major preoccupation with us. Up and down Market Street, from showroom to store, we'd exchange intelligence of shop-lifting gangs.

After Cheryl left Wagner's she had three jobs within the year. She was restless, and her mother had begun to add her hints to Grandma's. It was expected in their community that girls marry with the bloom on them. At twenty-four, her mother had

Howard at nursery school, Cheryl in the pushchair, Lindsey in the womb. She had known very precisely what she had to look forward to. There were no areas of mystery in her life.

Sometime in the post-Wagner year, Cheryl started to call herself Cheri, pronounced Sherry. Her grandmother Ruthie, a cake-eating lady, came in to see me one day, and said what did I think of that? Ruthie twitched our stock about for appearance's sake, while she chatted, but really she hadn't come either for a gown or my opinion, she'd come to air her grievances. I said I supposed it was symptomatic, of something or other. Mr Wagner, seeing I was being kept from my customers, came over to Ruthie with a hearty handclasp and said 'So! How's Ruthie these days? How's my old pal Sydney keeping?' It was like that; caricature stuff, I'm afraid. I'm sorry if I make it sound like a caricature. But it was quite true: everybody knew everybody else.

This is where I came in. I was an outsider, and so I had some value for confiding in, for using as a sounding board. You see, I was not really Cheryl's friend – more her mother's. Though Cheryl and I were quite near in age, there was a line drawn between the married and the unmarried state; fun on one side, eye-rolling self-sacrifice on the other. I was on her mother's side of the line. I might be separated, I might be childless, but there was an unspoken belief that I was an initiate in that world, where in kitchen or bedroom you catered to a man's whims till your cheeks burned and your feet or pelvis ached. You know what it's called: giving till it hurts.

Her mother, Rachel, was always called Ray. I once heard Mr Wagner describe her as 'a flighty little woman', but she was flighty, if at all, within narrowly respectable limits. To look at, she was small and neat, like her daughter – Howard, Cheryl and Lindsey having made no impact on her figure. She never seemed to eat anything; would lunch on a cup of coffee and dine on a starch-free roll. She had short fluffy hair, streaked blond. She shopped a lot.

I liked Ray very much. She was funny and sharp, and I

sometimes felt in her company that fizz of excitement you get as a child when you're on the loose with your best friend and the weather's fine. She liked me too, trusted me on sight. 'I tell you things,' she'd say, 'that I've never told anyone.' Sad to think that after a certain age, or a certain span of enduring marriage, confession is the greatest excitement a woman has left.

We saw each other every time our lunch-breaks coincided: Mondays always, Wednesdays if we could fix it. Sometimes we'd have a cup of coffee and I'd have a sandwich; sometimes we'd just go round the shops, laughing at the stock or saying hello to our friends. On these days we'd buy a paper bag of fudge from Woolworth and eat it between us. It used to be quite sustaining, not sticky or bland. Of course they've changed the recipe now.

Ray worked three days a week, just round the corner on Ducie Street, at a similar place to Wagner's that belonged to a cousin of hers. Her husband Allen had a shirt factory; it did quite nicely. She didn't – as people said in those days – *need* to work. But she liked to have money of her own to spend on clothes, and she was always slipping the odd cheque to Howard, Cheryl and Lindsey. Besides, at home she had standards of comfort to keep up.

I visited her sometimes, though less frequently than you would think. Their house was modest; a three-bed detached in Whitefield, built cheaply between the wars on a narrow plot of land. Inside there was no skimping. There were thick fitted carpets, and the heating was kept at 80° F. There were cupboards full of crystal glasses and fine china, each piece dusted and tabulated, the date of its purchase and its price filed away in Ray's brain and available on request. There was a linen cupboard where everything matched; she was the kind of woman who has to have the curtains matching the quilt cover, and one of those poly-cotton frills around the bed. She employed a woman to come in Mondays and Thursdays to mop and polish and iron these frills, and this woman used to borrow money from her, so by the end of the week her purse would be pretty light; this wouldn't stop her dropping in at Wagner's on a Friday morning with a bag of Danish pastries for us, or from treating me to lunch if I looked a bit down.

Then, in the course of a long hot summer – but in our trade, hemmed in from July by the winter stock, all summers were long and hot – Cheri met Jonathan. By September, her family's cautious hopes had become conviction; at last she'd found somebody she was serious about. He's a lovely boy, Ray told me, not what you'd call good-looking, but if she doesn't mind, should we? The family are in business, from what I hear they're well set-up, they've asked us over, I'm telling Allen he should order a new suit. What's the point of a smart shirt if the rest of you doesn't live up to it?

Ah, the relief! The relief that was transmitted, from Ray to me, from Grandma to Wagner: even our rarer customers would come in, beaming about it. I asked myself later, why weren't we forewarned?

Let me stop the story here. Let me say at once that it wasn't that Cheri attached herself to a pervert, or to some pig with four concealed bastards on a council estate. No mistake of that sort could have been made. But I had supposed, and for a few months continued to suppose, that nothing was hidden from the eyes of my friends: that they had Mr Wagner's talents, and read each other like an open ledger. In this I was mistaken. And there – I've tipped you off now. Well, I'm not the sort of writer who springs surprises.

If I can offer an excuse, it was that the whole thing happened so quickly. One week there was Cheri, a blighted spinster in her Grandma's eyes; the next week, Grandma was talking about the joy of seeing her great-grandchildren before she died.

Cheri and Jonathan were introduced through friends, which Ray considered the nice way of saying they met at a party. They went to a couple of films, and quite possibly afterwards for a pizza: strolling through Manchester's silted midnight heart, pretending to be Woody Allen and his date. They went – they were trying to impress each other – to a harpsichord recital given by George Malcolm, in a near-empty civic chamber. Ray came into Wagner's. 'I don't want to build on it,' she said. 'But.' I wanted to kick her. Run up and kick her on her delicate shin. Already she was thinking about who they'd engage to do the video; and in those days, it was only the rich or the distrustful who put their weddings on tape. I'd have liked to say, why is marriage an end in itself? Why do you think it is?

But of course, for Ray it *had* to be an end in itself. The man she wanted had married someone else: Allen was her second choice. She'd been happiest on her wedding day; after that, life had been difficult. And disillusioning? No, not that. It was a point of honour – no, a point of necessity – not to let disillusionment enter her life. Unhappiness on a personal level, yes – she could admit this to me, and did. But not on a philosophical level. If your soufflés fall, you can still eat other people's; you don't say life's a bitch just because she's nipped your ankles. From time to time little whiffs of misery came from Ray. I said that to her once. 'No,' she said, 'it's *L'Air du Temps*. I've always worn it. Have another cup of coffee.'

On the Sunday appointed, Ray and Allen went out to meet Jonathan's parents. It was 11.30 when they turned out of their drive, and it was one of those summer days that, in the suburbs, turn out hotter than you think. The sun's trapped by mellow red brick and polished plate glass; by three in the afternoon, there's not a breath of wind. Ray, the great anticipator, dropped into her bag a roll-on deodorant: the unperfumed sort.

They drove down Bury New Road with the windows open. They made small talk, each sealed in their apprehension; they wanted to do well, not say the wrong thing, come home to Cheryl and report that they'd made an impression. They drove past the old dog track and crossed the Irwell, avoiding the city centre: down Stretford Road, past Old Trafford. Onwards, through the leafier suburbs: into the drone of lawnmowers and

the hiss of potatoes, par-boiled, scooped into a thousand roast-
ing pans.

Halebarns.

Of course, you don't know the area. So imagine the first line
of a prayer: Hale barns, full of grace, hallowed be thy name . . .
It was the kind of place where First Division footballers set up
house: the kind of place where private doctors live, the sort
referred to as 'the best Chest Man in the North-West'. Acres of
green. Drinks trays. Sunday morning sloth. The *Observer*
draped apart across sofa cushions; wives, their bare ankles
crossed, skimming reviews of *La Traviata*.

'This must be it.' The drive was a semi-circle, a sweep. They
relished the spit of gravel. As Allen pulled up the Austin Maxi
next to the BMW, it seemed to catch good manners. It positively purred to a halt. But then there was the panelled front
door to face: gleaming, lacquered, fronted with a lion's head.
Next, the delay – which they should have anticipated – before
the couple frolicking in the garden were made aware of their
presence. During this delay they exchanged a glance: not nervous exactly, just a glance.

Jonathan's father Leo opened the door. He looked cool and
casual in his light grey flannels and his short-sleeved, bright-
striped shirt open at the neck.

Allen, of course, wore his new suit. He half-shed his jacket,
while at the same time he shook hands. As they were ushered
through the dim mansion to the dazzling lawns, he tried to
jettison his jacket somewhere. If there had been a burning fiery
furnace, he would have consigned it to the flames. As it was,
he found himself thrust into the sun again, blinking at the
expanse of shaven green, with the jacket hanging before him,
over his clasped hands: it was big and hot and grey, like a
marsupial baby that won't leave home.

They had not expected a trial by patio. They had expected
an indoors Sunday lunch, with hot earthenware, vivid with
fashionable veg, passed by cheery oven-gloves from hand to
hand. Afterwards Leo and Allen would do a cigar and Ray and

Rosalyn would tiptoe through the mansion, glass-case to glass-case, speaking with reverence of Royal Doulton.

Rosalyn clattered a little as she came out to greet them. But Ray would always say, if you've got nice things, if you've got jewellery, why not have the pleasure of it? Once outside, there was a good deal of business with little striped cushions: patting them, placing them in the small of Ray's back. The garden chair, white wrought-iron, martyred her buttocks. But that is the rule about cushions; people never put them where you want them. They intimate, as they place them, that they are superfluities, and that you are indulged. They like to make the gesture; your subsequent discomfort is no fault of theirs.

I hear in my mind the clink of ice; small gins are dispensed. Rosalyn said 'What we do, Leo and me, we like to relax on a Sunday.' She turned up her face to be baked; and the sun here in Halebarns was hot and strong, no city sun, nothing weak or filtered or conditional. 'I should have worn a sun-block,' Ray said.

Rosalyn answered, lazily, 'We can go up to my bathroom, honey. Or you'd like to move in the shade?'

Seemed ungrateful, to move in the shade. Over a bowl of olives, they felt their way into conversation. Common friends, common problems. Kids! Rosalyn said. Jonathan had just one baby sister, seventeen, and if Ros says it herself, fantastic looks – offers from *Vogue*, also the continental magazines. But no fool either, she knows looks don't last forever – not at the international model level. So, she's at Berkeley. It's in California. Gives her a degree to fall back on, meanwhile it puts her in the part of the world where she can be noticed. Tastefully, she ejected an olive pip from the side of her mouth.

Allen was torn: resentful, yet fascinated. On the one hand, he could see that there were to be these small gin and tonics, replenished long after your ice had melted; and that there would be no food. You eat air, he supposed; somewhere between Whitefield and here, you are mysteriously nourished. Yet he could not pluck his eyes from Rosalyn, who now lolled, like a

Southern belle, on a sofa beneath a canopy, the whole decorated with fringes, with bursting flowers of white and tangerine. As Rosalyn lolled, she flexed her tanned calf, to admire her painted nails; her instep had a curve to please a fetishist. Sunday light glanced from her shin-bone: cream-gold. Opulent Rosalyn! She put out a fingernail and scratched up another olive. Her eyelashes wafted: they caught the light, shimmering teal-blue. Usually a mistake, blue mascara. She must be forty-five, Ray thought.

Keep in mind this moment, this summer afternoon: somewhere far-off, a radio playing Gershwin, the sound leaking from lawn to lawn. Between the fronds of shrubs, shrubs of deep green, the glint of the swimming pool. Its chlorine whiff carries to them, vying with cut grass scents, and from other gardens the aroma of crushed garlic and tomatoes, borne to Allen on the breeze.

Look: I have no wish to represent to you that I was there on this Sunday afternoon in Halebarns. At this time I lived in my own small flat – left in it, after a marriage that hadn't worked out. The break-up was not dramatic; you might see it as a cooling of what was already tepid. During the two, three years this story occupies, I was a spectator: I felt I looked in at other people's lives. Despite what people think, this is not a bad sensation to have. You learn a good deal: the lessons may not be palatable at first, they may not be digestible, but they are worth chewing over. You will learn general principles, which help you in your own life: also, specific tricks. Before too long, someone will say to you: you are so *wise*. You should enjoy this moment; it is hard-won. No, my dear, you will say: I am simply experienced.

Three weeks after the families had met, Jonathan proposed to Cheryl in the most romantic manner possible.

He took her to a little Italian place on Princess Street. I knew it from my own days of dining *à deux*. It was pretty and intimate, with green-shaded lamps, and green candles flaring in bold, brass-bronze arches. The food was routine, but no one minded that.

Cheri wore white. Her reddish-fair curls spilled onto her shoulders. Her short, clear-varnished nails fiddled with the book of matches on the table, and with the thin gold chain around her neck. Jonathan reached out and placed his hand over hers, very briefly. His calloused fingertips brushed her throat, touched the pulse-point. He guided her nervous hand to the table, laid it palm-down. He patted it: one, two, three times.

They commanded antipasto: both easy, for the moment, with their faith and its prohibitions. Then – unwilling to evince too great an appetite for flesh – they both chose the Dover Sole. The waiter performed the usual phallic flourish with the pepper-mill; Cheryl, smiling, waved him away. All evening – though she was enjoying herself – she had the feeling that people were watching her. She voiced this to Jonathan. He said, 'They're not watching you, they're admiring you.'

After the fishbones were taken away there was a hiatus. Cheryl expected the dessert-trolley to be pushed in their direction. She had a sweet tooth, like her grandmother, and even while her knife eased away flakes of sole from the bone she had been eyeing the mousses and cheesecakes and flans. Jonathan sat looking at her, smiling. The head waiter approached.

She looked up expectantly. He set before her a white china plate: upon it, a single peach.

The other diners seemed to shift in their chairs; they did not look over their shoulders exactly, but there was a ripple of attention, table to table. Lifted forks were replaced on plates. The head waiter's nicotined fingers brushed – 'excuse, Signorina,' the peach's fuzzy skin. He parted the delicate cheeks – sliced already with a silver knife – and there, in place of the rufus, crinkled stone, was Cheryl's engagement ring.

She leaned forward; reached out, and plucked the symbol from the scented heart of the fruit. A tiny exhalation from the room. Men smiled warmly. Women smiled too, in a fashion more embarrassed.

Jonathan inched towards her, shuffling on his rush-seated chair.

'Just a little ring,' he said.

She held it up to the candlelight. It was late Victorian and very charming, made of thin, cheap, coppery gold. There were two tiny stones: one grey white, one a stormy-weather blue. 'A sapphire and a diamond?' she asked.

'A sapphire and a sapphire,' he said.

She said 'Not all sapphires are blue?'

'They can be yellow, or white.'

She peered at the ring. Her eyesight was not good. 'Shall I put it on?' she said.

He said 'You'd better. Or you'll spoil the evening for all the people here.'

Cheryl flashed a glance across the room. She blushed; he found this charming, and she knew he did. Her bare throat mottled: an orgasm of self-consciousness. 'Put it on,' he said. 'A little ring. The proper ring we have to choose together, don't you think?'

The waiter brought champagne.

Cheri smiled. She held up her glass to him, then dropped her eyes becomingly. Just as well, or she might have read the label. A hectic fizz hit her hard palate. After that she was not her own woman at all.

Immediately, preparations for the wedding began. Ray consulted me about dyeing satin shoes, and other arcana. I gathered that Allen was to be practically bankrupted by the cost of catering per head – for four hundred guests – but was not to realise it till after the event. 'I don't expect,' Mr Wagner said, 'that this affair will bring business our way.' He shook his jowls.

'Oh, Mr Wagner,' I said. 'This is the Halebarns set.'

'They'll buy from Kendal Milne,' he said. 'The "Designer

Room". Seen it, have you? The so-called fitting rooms in the middle of the floor, made out of curtains just?'

'Curtains just,' I said. (You will think my friends cannot possibly have talked like this, but I am afraid they did, because I encouraged them.) 'That stout woman who runs Jean Varon – '

'I know her,' Wagner said.

' – beats their junior sales with a coat hanger.'

Mr Wagner rocked with silent, mirthless laughter.

'Anything,' he said. 'If it makes the day.'

The phrase goes round in my mind, now. You've made the day, in the language we used, when you've achieved the sales target set for you, based on last year's figures. In the big shops they have (perhaps) sophisticated ways of working out what your sales target should be, but for Mr Wagner it was enough if we took the same money as last year. He had his areas of shrewdness, but they were limited indeed. He did not take account of inflation, or his own costs, or of the fact that within five years most of our customers would be in the market for a one-size-fits-all shroud.

I thought a good deal about what, on my salesgirl's wage, I could give Cheri for a wedding present. In the end I settled on a set of kitchen knives. At the back of my mind was something that – I think – Edna O'Brien says in one of her novels. That it's not enough for women to have the vote: they should be armed.

You'll say now, I'm tired of this narrator and her prescient voice; but stay with me, just for a little while. The one fact that worried Ray was this: the weeks to the wedding went by, and the big ring never appeared. We knew about diamonds, we knew about fiancés, and we knew what Cheri should expect. The cut should be Brilliant, the quality flawless or near so, the colour much much nearer silver than yellow; there were areas of compromise here, but the weight should be one carat. Half a carat would do, if the boy was struggling and saving hard, but on the first anniversary he must give again. It's what we all need; that flash of fire when we turn our hands against the light. And the valuer's certificate, kept in a chocolate box with the marriage lines.

The little ring was perfect of course – as a token. Everyone cooed over it. It was so unusual. It was *sweet*. And her acceptance of it proved Cheri's sweetness of nature; it showed she had a sense of humour.

The wedding day approached. I did not expect to be invited; this was an insider enterprise. Still, I was party to the unease: no major diamond yet. Minor jokes were made. Just tentative ones. Still, Cheryl continued to wear the little ring, the token – and to show it off, and describe it as such. Finally Ray said, sounding irate: 'Oh, what does it matter? Any boy in his position has enough to spend on. My feeling is,' she smiled, 'that he's saving up for something special on the honeymoon.'

Like what? I thought. Hiring himself another body? If Cheryl was making a mistake, at least it wasn't the kind I'd made. Trusting to my own intelligence to carry me through life, I'd married for looks; women sometimes do, you know. Cheryl was marrying for a penthouse in Didsbury, for rich in-laws, his meagre person and his prospects. I did not deal in words like 'penthouse' and suspected those who did, but I understood the idea very well; you would look out on treetops, someone else would clean your bathroom, and you would always be warm.

Do you think this is not much to want? You try getting it, then! I could put a price on what Jonathan was offering, but that does not mean I despised it. I felt it as a personal cruelty, just after the marriage, to be asked by Ray to her house; to be taken to her close-carpeted bedroom, and shown the wedding gown of heavy cream lace, with its floating scalloped cape: and the tiny, chic veiled cap that Cheri had worn. Ray perched it on the crown of my head, and turned my chin, with gentle fingers, so that I glimpsed myself in the triple mirror.

I could not help but smile. My ex-husband had liked me to wear hats – cheap straw hats you get off market stalls, hats with floppy brims, the kind of hat you finish with a scarlet ribbon and a bunch of plastic cherries.

Once we had separated I understood that he had been making a fool of me. I had given up on hats. Now I saw there was a kind I could wear. I dipped my head forward, to see the effect from three sides. Ray lifted a piece of my hair – for my hair lay in pieces, each one carefully supervised by my hairdresser – and touched her lips to the nape of my neck.

My hairdresser – if we may change the subject, as I think we should – was employed at Lewis's department store, on Market Street. He called himself Juan, and carried his personal scissors in a black leather pouch embossed with a toreador motif. He fooled a few of his elderly clients, the ones whom Mr Wagner put in a taxi for the quarter of a mile down Piccadilly. The rest of us were happy to take him as he was: a misrepresentation. People had seen him in the queue for the Oldham bus, conversing with fellow passengers in tones that were far from Seville.

I have noticed this: that there is a disposition, among some people, to take umbrage at what they term 'misrepresentation'. Once I shared this disposition – I am temperamentally inclined to it. But temperament is nothing. It can be altered, overcome. All of us can change, at any point; this is the only thing I believe.

So, now, the marriage took place. As I say, I didn't go. There was so much family to be accommodated: fewer on his side than on hers, but that was because, Ray said, they were mostly in America.

Before the wedding, Ray took the week off to shop. Several times she came into Wagner's, with Manchester's best carrier bags depending from her wrists. If I was with a customer, she looked understanding; she leaned against a glass counter and lit up a Rothmans, which I knew was anathema to our proprietor. When I clustered around her with the other girls, she would pick from her wrists the cords of green silk; inside her bags were the damask napkins, the plump Turkish towels, the Irish linen sheets with the scalloped embroidery at the hems. 'The least I can do is furnish the airing cupboard,' she said: her smile vague, secret, pleasured. 'His family have given them the air-tickets, on the honeymoon they'll be visiting his relations. It will be good for business if they see the bride, there's all sorts of transatlantic – ' she broke off. 'Feel that,' she said. My fingers massaged folds of fabric, soft as sunlit flesh. 'Transatlantic connections,' she said. 'And plans. You should hear the plans the family have for him.'

'Ray, you know I'm pleased for you,' I said. 'I'm thrilled.'

She whispered to me, as if it were confidential: 'They're very nicely situated, his family, very nicely situated indeed.'

You may think this turn of phrase ridiculous. But – one thing I do – I write down faithfully what I have heard. Did I ever laugh at Ray? No. Her family came out of Russia, with their possessions on a handcart. Suppose they'd not tramped quite so far? Suppose some town had detained them: violins in the square, lemon pastries light as lies. Then Ray would never have been born; Grandma would have been ashes on the plains of Europe, vapour in the wind. It bears thinking about, and with such thoughts in your head you don't despise security, even if the rest of the world fails to see the point. Laugh? I dare you.

After the honeymoon, Cheri and Jonathan moved into the pent-house. This, it turned out, was not so much in Didsbury as in Withington, an area of lesser standing. After three months, when all the friends of their own age had been entertained, and wedding gifts from the older generation had been repaid in hospitality, they asked me over for the evening. Cheri still had the shadow of her honeymoon tan, though she admitted she was boosting it with a sun lamp. She whirled me round the flat and told me her plans; so far, she said, she'd simply been too busy to implement them. 'The lounge,' she said, 'we're doing out thirties-style. We won't have our books in it, it will be just for – '

'Lounging,' I suggested. She gave my arm a squeeze. 'This

is going to be our den, our cosy, comfy den, with a squishy sofa that we can sink into. Subtle, brown-beige-cream walls, I thought. The kitchen farmhouse-style . . .' Remember in charity, reader, that all this took place some years ago.

It occurred to me, as she waltzed me from room to room, that it was very much a bachelor apartment still, sparsely furnished and chilly. This surprised me; surely a diligent, clever girl can spend money faster than the speed of light? When family and friends had asked what they wanted for presents, they'd mostly said 'cheques, please', smiling so bashfully that no donor could feel her taste was being impugned. 'Jonathan thinks it's best,' Cheri had explained. 'A nest egg.' Now the only signs of luxury were the linen on the table and the thick cream towels on the rail; and those had been disgorged from Ray's paper bags in that last mad week of shopping.

When the front door closed on me that night I stood at the top of the stairs, quite breathless from the warmth of the welcome I'd received. Like Ray, Cheri had a way of seeming to take you into her confidence. 'This squishy sofa,' she'd said, 'keep a look out for us, will you?' These days, she wasn't in town as often as I was. When she married, she'd given up her high-paying commission-only job, because it meant odd hours, evenings and weekends. She said she wanted to go part-time, so that she could entertain and do out the flat; she had looked around for what was available, and ended up at Kendal Milne, working just yards from the violent manageress of Jean Varon. Part-time is the death of ambition; you will never climb to be a Deputy Manageress. Her take-home pay must have been pitiful, compared to what she'd been used to; but she shook her head, smiled, said 'It's just for the moment, it gives me some pin money, and of course I see all my friends.'

So, commissioning a sofa, she'd squeezed my arm again: 'I'd trust your taste anywhere,' she said.

'Right.' In the face of such bubbling happiness, I was glad to know there was a tiny practical thing I could do. 'I see the colour you want, terracotta, brick, Bill and Ben the Flowerpot Men.'

'In a natural fabric, fairly open weave, linen-look.'

'But which will wear well, even if you should buy a cat?'

Cheri smiled. 'We won't buy a cat.'

'No claws to snag? You need to think. Sofas at the price they are.'

'He's allergic,' she said.

I might have imagined; little sneeze-bag, pale eyes sore. I said, 'If we agree on the basic shape and cushion filling I can track down the fabric and take it from there. Give me a price guide,' I said. 'To the nearest two hundred.'

She hesitated. I saw at once that her request had been fake, a means of ingratiation. 'We don't want to lay out too much,' she said. 'Because of course, saving is the priority. For a house and a baby.'

'Does Jonathan say so?' I asked.

She nodded.

'So in the short-term – are you re-decorating or not?'

Cheri folded her arms, hugged herself, smiled ruefully.

'Cash-flow problems, you know? We have to economise, just for a month or two. But look – don't go worrying about us. You've got yourself to sort out.'

One day, just a fortnight after this, Cheri was putting away her husband's clean underwear, as a young wife should. Her fingers found something, beneath the lining paper of the drawer: she felt the flat rectangular outline of an envelope. She paused for a moment, thinking of the implications; she was not unsophisticated. She slid her fingers beneath the paper and found more envelopes, laid one by one across the drawer, like paving stones.

They were not love-letters, that was obvious at once. They were official letters, in long stiff envelopes. She thought for a moment, then eased out other drawers. In the drawer where Jonathan kept handkerchiefs and cufflinks, small change and old cheque-stubs, she found another graveyard of envelopes, seemingly from a different credit card company; her husband's name inscribed upon each.

She studied the postmarks and waited for Jonathan to come home.

When he saw the envelopes neatly stacked, on the scarred teak table they had not yet replaced, he asked her to pour him a whisky and to pour one for herself.

She said 'I don't like whisky. And there isn't any. You said you'd be in charge of drinks. The thing is, if I'm to do the shopping, I need some money.'

You would hardly believe an intelligent girl could be taken in by the stories Jonathan had told, but we did have to believe it, Ray and myself and the ladies about town. There had been all sorts of reasons, to do with his father's business, why they couldn't have a joint account at his bank; he was a director – junior, of course – and could sign company cheques, but really it was tidier if for their private spending she paid out of her account, which he would top up monthly . . . do I need to go on? It's such a commonplace story. He hadn't paid his mortgage for eight months. He'd run up several thousand on the elastic plastic, and he had – this I know, for in the wine bar I'd had a quick flash of the inside of his wallet – just about every credit card known to man. As he told her about the scale of his debts – which I suppose were pitiful enough in all truth – he shivered, and his pale eyes wandered over the white-painted walls. He had known what the envelopes contained – threats – and he had not been able to bring himself to open them.

'The flat will be repossessed,' she said.

'Yes.' His tatty head drooped.

'You couldn't have trusted me with this?'

'I dropped hints.'

'Hints? You said cash-flow, you said savings plan – you didn't say the bailiffs would be in.'

He looked away.

'I can earn,' she said. 'We can put off children. We can work this out. We can beat it.'

Certain lines, half-remembered from films and songs, came tumbling from her mouth. She had heard of a world in which you fought for your marriage and your man. She was a brave girl.

'I forgive you,' she said.

He didn't answer.

'Why didn't you tell me?' she said.

'I couldn't.'

'Your family,' she said. 'They'll help us.'

'Oh no,' he said. 'We may have to help them.'

God knows what was in his father's underwear drawer. I gather it was something similar, but much much worse.

After this, the collapse was rapid. It proved there was a thumping mortgage on the house at Halebarns. The family business – the exact nature of which was never revealed to me – was tottering into the hands of the receivers. The creditors were likely to get nothing in the pound, and it seemed there was some question of Leo and Rosalyn going to prison.

A commonplace story, as I say – certainly common enough these days – but it was a cruel blow to Ray and Allen. It was the deception that hurt, Ray said. Not the *debts*; it was the *lies* that turned the knife in the wound. And the fact that one could not trust one's own perceptions, any more. What was the point of anything, if you could be deceived like this? 'Perhaps,' Ray said, 'other people knew. Perhaps they wanted to tell us. Do you think they did? Just didn't know how? Could that be it?' I thought of when she came into Wagner's, her cheque account emptied; now, as then, her cigarette smoke spiralled into the air. I sat opposite her. Her elbow rested on her kitchen table. I loved the way she held her cigarette, her hand flicked back at almost ninety degrees to her forearm. It was too elegant for our age.

What surprised Ray, as much as anything, was how little Jonathan's parents seemed to care. Once the threat of gaol was lifted, they cheered up remarkably: they still had to face the loss of the swimming pool, but the marriage was an incidental casualty. They waved it away, bantering, smiling. Little marriage. Little ring. Little people. Other business opportunities would open for them. Lenders would be found. Confidence created. Though not in us, of course.

Cheryl stayed with her husband for another three months, getting him through the worst of it. Then they were officially separated, with a view to no-fault divorce after two years. She didn't leave him because he had no money; she left him because he'd lied, and she knew that when the need arose, year after year, he would lie again. He must have loved her, you'll say; but must he? He'd simply seen her and wanted her, and bought her with a cheque that bounced. As she said, how would you know what he was doing, behind your back? Setting up a mistress? Putting a deposit on a country house? It would always have been the same; the pale desire, the shallow charm, the optimism, the evasions, the day of reckoning. I was glad to think that she wasn't going to waste her life.

She moved back in with her parents. Her savings had been spent, and jobs were tight at the time. Prospective employers considered her unserious; only six months before she'd given up a job for a transient man, so who knows what she might do next, turn out to be pregnant or something? In those days employers thought like that and were entitled to tell you so. She ended up on Ducie Street, working for Ray's cousin; what happened in fact was that Ray gave up her own job, so that her daughter could take it. Cheryl picked up with her old crowd, after a fashion. People were inclined to say she must have known, or what was she, brain-dead? A cloud hovered about her, moving as she moved.

Over that difficult season, when Ray was disinclined, for reasons of suspicion or shame, to spend time with her own friends, we became closer than we'd been before. I knew this state of affairs would not last, but I enjoyed sitting in her kitchen, strong coffee in a china pot between us, and hearing her thoughts and her reflections on the course of her life. Mainly she moved about the same sad axis: disappointment, loss. But one day, brooding on these themes, she told me a singular story, which may – and you will be the judge of it – have changed my life. Here it is.

A family known to her, wealthy (and their wealth attested) had adopted a child. Not, I think, from an official orphanage; there was some disaster to be covered up in the neighbourhood, some instance of miscegenation among the children of friends, drink possibly involved on the night the deed was done. The child was a girl, a sweet little thing: she used to look as cute as anything with her hair-ribbons braiding her kinky hair and the white frills of her dresses setting off her coffee-coloured skin.

Do you know, Ray said, it was remarkable how everyone just simply accepted it? They took her at six weeks old, and made no difference between her and their real children. All the cousins, even the older people, they were wonderful about it. The black baby, she had just what their own two had – the clothes, the private day-school, the ballet and music classes.

'But goodness,' I said, 'what was she to think? When she was older?'

For she was an outsider, after all. And sooner or later, she would see this.

'The grandparents,' Ray said, 'who were in a very nice way, I can tell you, had said that she would inherit from them, equally with the real children. And the hope was, of course – and this was what all the family wanted – that she would go to Israel, build a lovely life there as a black Jewess.' For in Israel, Ray said, there would be no discrimination against a dark-skinned person, simply no feeling of that kind at all.

But Ray put down her coffee cup. I could tell where this was leading: children never turn out as you hope, she was going to say. 'Until she was thirteen, fourteen, no family could have had a more perfect daughter. She grew up, if anything, more attentive to them than their own two; they blessed the day they'd decided to take her into their home. But then, a change set in. She *would* leave school.' Ray shook her head. 'Failed her 'O'

Levels and then played truant, till in the end they removed her
– they had to face it, they were paying the fees for nothing.'

The black girl hung about at home, sulking.

A bit like Cheri, I thought, in recent months. Suddenly I saw
the girl with her braided hair and her black cloud, her piano
music shredded, her ballet shoes stained, ragged, chucked at the
back of the wardrobe. I put my forehead in my hand. I had an
urge to reach for pencil and paper, begin to write down what I
saw.

'And do you know what she did then?' Ray lifted her eyes to
mine. 'After all the advantages she'd had – just to get back at
the family, just to spite them – she went to work in a factory.'

'What kind of a factory?'

'The soap works,' she said. 'You know, Kersal Vale? But it
didn't last. She used to take samples off the line, and go off into
the Ladies and start persistently washing and scrubbing herself.
They put up with it for a bit, they were glad to have a nice
clean girl – but after all, they were supposed to be making it,
not using it.'

I imagine my jaw dropped; but not indecorously, I hope.
'How long did this go on?'

'A few weeks,' Ray said. 'She went schizophrenic, I think.
One day she started throwing the soap around – well, imagine,
it's like bullets, thuds into you. The supervisor almost lost an
eye – but luckily, the tablet glanced off her temple.'

'And the black girl?' I said casually.

'They took her away.'

'She had a private bed?' I asked.

Ray said, 'Of course she had a private bed.'

After this conversation I felt sure: I must take a chance on
my new trade. The last few months had taught me something
about the nature of life. I had learned that representations count
as money in the bank. That most of life – perhaps all of it – is
fake. That seeming can be just like being, for a while; and they
don't gaol you for it. There and then, as I sat in Ray's kitchen

with my coffee cooling, I decided to add my representations to the rest. If life is fake, why should only I be true?

I asked Mr Wagner about going part-time, three days including Saturdays. He was reluctant. I was a first-class sales, he said, he valued me. Would another five pounds in my wage-packet persuade me I had a future with him? I explained that I was serious, that I'd decided to try my luck as a writer – I mean, not mess about as everybody knew I did, scribbling between customers, jotting conversations down, but really put the hours in, give it a go. Mr Wagner shook his head. He said, 'I'll keep the job open for you for four weeks. You're honest,' he said, 'that's your sterling asset, Miss – ' In times of stress, he always forgot my name. He ducked beyond his partition. If his eyes were misty, I never knew about it.

As Mr Wagner could not accommodate me, I went to Lewis's, secured a per-diem pay rise, and worked in Coats, Monday, Wednesday, Saturday. I had some success in my other new career. Well, I must have had, of course, or you wouldn't be reading this now.

Since then a number of years have passed. When these events took place I was twenty-six years old, but now I am what Mr Wagner would call the Mature Woman with a Fuller Figure. Like every writer I survey my life to see what use I can make of it, and in some respects my notions have been overturned. Then, I had to give myself permission to take wings to the realms of metaphor, image, untruth; for the first few years you must drive your imagination so it becomes supple and strong. But my standards are high, and I would never dare invent a black girl in a soap factory, or dream up a storyline so bald and mundane as this. Increasingly I think, why invent? Truth is free.

What a debt we owe to the past! God forbid it should ever be called in. And Ray, and her daughter, and the ribbon noodle? I'm afraid I don't know what happened to them. We lost touch. We had to. I cut myself off from them. That's the nature of the trade.

Finding Shelter

Jay was pretty and smart. His wife, Louise, looked as if she were hearing bad news, and she wore tights with ladders and drab skirts with ratty hems, but it has been rumoured that when she shucked her clothes she was gorgeous, like an angel from paradise.

Jay had been prosecuted and convicted of fraud in connection with benefits: of working while on the dole, and of trying to appear to be at least two different people at once, or of conspiring with others to create this impression, in order to make extra claims. He wasn't guilty as charged, he would have said, but he was guilty of something and it became too difficult to explain the truth. It was a fact that he had been caught with a paintbrush, and wearing dirty overalls. He had a funny look on his face. He had also been caught trading in wind-up ducks, or at least standing near some ducks on a card table in an open market. There was a lot of evidence of related offences.

The prison he went to wasn't the sort of place with watchtowers, but more like a severe and compulsory hotel, to teach a lesson to scroungers. It was semi-open in the sense that sometimes a judge or MP would take one or several of the young men out for the afternoon and bugger them, or try to at least. The idea here was that a member of the underclass who got a glimpse of some of the finer things in life might tend, in future, to adopt a more socially useful posture. Fortunately, it is not true that political influence and power stimulate or simulate sexual capacity.

Jay escaped by climbing up a pile of laundry and out of a window in the back. Then he changed his name. He had changed his name before in the sense that he hadn't corrected misunderstandings which had arisen from his unclear handwriting. Over a period of time there had been a name drift, from Hair to Hart to Harris. He believed he had the right to allow his name to change.

His wife Louise and son Tony were living in Brittany then, in a hotel where she worked as a cleaner. Jay and Louise had become estranged and had separated with what seemed at the time to be bitterness. Her complaint was that he was neither practical nor honest, and his was that she did not respect him. She wanted to respect him. She almost did, she liked him. But she found it horribly dreary that he had been caught. She was frightened and depressed by the law and its procedures and institutions. Everything was out of her control, and it seemed an improvement to say goodbye and to leave the country.

Jay, under his new name, claimed a technical qualification, and got a job as a computer salesman. He wore a dark suit and stood around in a showroom with other desperate fellows under flickering fluorescent lights. All of them, even the genuinely qualified, were low-paid, knowledge being cheap.

He wrote a short love letter in blue biro to his wife, not saying directly who he was. The previous anger was no longer of central importance to either of them. She wrote back and Tony, who was five then, and wanted his parents to be together, sent a drawing and some seaweed.

Louise and Tony came to live in the provincial city again. They got a bedsitter, and Louise claimed benefits. Jay surreptitiously lived with them. It had to be kept secret that she was cohabiting with anyone, especially him, since otherwise her money would be reduced. Even if he could pass as someone else he couldn't be there. The bedsitter was expensive, uncomfortable and dirty, and guests were not allowed. Jay and Louise made love very quietly behind a curtain while Tony slept.

I'd rather have you here than not have you at all, Louise said. I'd live anywhere. But I don't like you having to sneak around.

It suits me, Jay said. I don't care, he added.

No you don't, Louise replied with surprising anger. Everything in my life, she went on, is saying to me I'm no good. Everything I have. It's supposed to be clear that I don't deserve it.

Don't worry so much, Jay said. Jay frequently expressed the idea that anything could be looked at in several different ways, and nothing was ever pure white or pure black.

She wondered if he intuitively knew something which she did not know. But she was only a little soothed by his telling her not to worry. Jay couldn't understand how shabby everything seemed to her and how much it got her down. She felt she really hadn't got any grip on anything; and rooms and streets and dirty windows really talked to her and they said what she said to Jay, that she was no good.

Besides eating and sleeping and arguing and making love in that room, they read a lot of children's books. Jay and Louise read to Tony for hours, in relays, out of respect for his imagination. He often didn't get to bed until after midnight. Tony was especially interested in the seething, inventive early stages of evolution and life in the deep sea. They read all the books about this that they could find in the children's section of the public library. Their favourite phylum was the coelenterates, translucent animals in the form of sacks, usually with tentacles around the mouth. They looked at photographs of polyps and free-floating medusae and the soft-branched corals. They pretended that shopping bags were jelly fish, and red cabbages were lurking sea anemones.

One morning after a quarrel with Louise, Jay walked over the bridge into an unfamiliar part of town. The weather was good. It was sunny and a little breeze was moving bits of cloud over the sky. Jay had some money in the pockets of his raincoat. He felt he might be any respectable citizen. He went into an estate agent's office, open although it was Sunday, and said to the woman there that he was interested in buying a small house. He admitted that he didn't have any money; but the agent, a nice woman with glasses, replied that it might be possible to arrange a one hundred per cent mortgage. Does that hundred per cent include the expense of moving? he asked. No, she said. Just the cost exactly, Jay said. Yes, she said. She gave him a stack of papers. Each one held a smudgy photograph of a house, taken from, possibly, its best angle, as with the mail order brides of the Philippines. Dining room, Jay read, 13' x 10'3", tiled fireplace, inset Rayburn Rhapsody, UVPC window and double-glazed Roman glass roof light. Although, he read, the interior is in need of updating in part, the benefit of a garage must be regarded as a tremendous asset.

Jay had always liked any sort of trading or buying and selling, and the associated figuring-out processes.

He walked up hills and down to see houses. He stood on tiptoe, craned his neck and looked in windows. He walked until his feet ached. Returning home, grinning, instead of continuing the argument they had been having, he said that they ought to buy a house. Louise was confused by him. She didn't know what he was going to do next, or what his priorities were. They went to bed, which made agreement.

Like generals, consequently, they studied maps of the city. They walked all over. One hundred per cent mortgage, Jay whispered in his sleep.

They concentrated their efforts on a neighbourhood around an attractive green mosque, where the hills were so steep the thin houses looked stacked up crooked, and the roads were full of skips and bins. There were discarded things, which might be useful, such as armchairs, or, for example, a pink bathtub, out on the pavements. Every house they imagined living in. The one they liked best had French windows onto the back, several rooms upstairs, lots of bumpy wallpaper, and a purple clematis over the door. Jay made an offer for this house and he applied for a one hundred per cent mortgage. Then they waited. We won't get it, Louise said.

The reply from the building society, when it eventually came, was disdainful. They said in their letter that the house needed to have a lot of work done on it. A new roof might be necessary, although it said that the surveyor hadn't been able to get access to it. (It was high off the ground of course, Jay thought. Tops of houses often were. Didn't he have a ladder?) It would be required to demolish the kitchen at least, the insulting letter continued. It would also be required to commission a more extensive, more expensive survey to find out what else was wrong. (The more expensive one, Jay said, is where they get up on the roof no matter how much trouble it is, even if they have to use a ladder.) Even if all this were done, they were only willing to part with seventy per cent of the price, and then only reluctantly, it seemed.

The estate agent said that she could not understand the attitude expressed in this letter. Her lipsticked mouth dropped open in surprise. A report always depended, she explained, on how the surveyor was feeling that day. He had been in a bad mood, whoever he was. She strongly suggested that Jay try another building society. She said that she knew the surveyor for the other society and would have a word with him, a quiet word, one professional to another. There was nothing crooked about it, she said, but it would be all right.

In this way, they achieved the hundred per cent mortgage on the second try. Jay had ideas about how to do everything. Louise and Tony moved in as tenants. They got housing benefit for the rent, which was paid to Jay in his role as landlord. Louise was still on the dole also, which depended on her not living with her husband. The housing office were given Jay's work as the landlord's office; and the building society was told that Jay lived in the house with his wife and child, which was true. The house was in Jay's name only so that Louise couldn't get into trouble for claiming benefit. It all worried Louise but she went along with it. Sometimes, first thing in the morning for example, it was hard for her to remember it all. Who was sending cheques to whom and for what reasons? Is everyone doing this sort of complicated business? she wondered. It's just about the truth anyway, Jay said.

Tony had a room to himself and they painted scenes from the great barrier reef on the wall. They found furniture in skips.

Louise found an old television on the pavement and lugged it home. If you slapped its side it usually worked. They didn't get a television licence since you don't need a licence for a television that doesn't work. What they had was intermediate between a television and a box. They all watched wildlife programmes. In general they were happy.

In the neighbourhood pubs, they noticed that a lot of the conversation was about houses. Grants were mentioned, and subsidence, and huge sums of money. The place was alive with schemes. About half the population seemed to be builders, and the whole neighbourhood had been designated by the council as urgently in need of repair.

A damp patch appeared over the bathroom ceiling, soaking through the new wallpaper. This was right under the lowest part of the roof, to which no one had been able to gain access. One morning when Jay was at work, a friend who was employed by a builder came, full of professional knowledge, to look at the leak. He stood on the bathroom window sill and hoisted himself up. Louise watched him, and was ready to catch his legs if he slipped. She saw his belly button and his underpants while he looked at whatever was on the top of the house. He came down looking tragic. His face was altered. If she hadn't been watching the torso the whole time, she might have thought it was a different man.

What is it? asked Louise. What is it? Let's sit down, he said. They went downstairs and Louise made him a cup of tea. It is a valley roof, he said. That means it's in the shape of a vee, with the valley at the bottom and the main beam just below the valley. In your case the valley is perished. That means the main beam will rot, if it hasn't already rotted. And that main beam is the only thing holding the house up. He looked the way surgeons do when they tell you the worst. Can't the main beam be fixed? Louise asked. Replaced? He shook his head at her simplicity. Not only do you have to take the roof off, he began, you also have to take off the whole front of the house. What would be left then? Louise asked. Well, the side walls would be there where the other houses were. And you'd still have a back door. She watched him drink his tea. Before he left, he poked at a skirting board in the corner of the room. Dry rot, he said, shaking his head. It's a fungus which can eat up a whole house in a matter of weeks, he explained. One day you close the door and the place falls to powder. If I were you I would just move out of here.

I think we were cheated, possibly, Jay said that evening when she told him. Still, it's nice while it lasts, isn't it? he said as cheerily as he could.

This is just a disaster, Louise said. And it is going to get worse.

First he accused her of always being gloomy. Then he tried to comfort her, but he also was frightened. He felt the ice of misery in his stomach. He thought at any moment the house would fall down, either from the wet rot in the main beam or the dry rot in the floor.

Or maybe they will cancel each other out somehow? Louise said.

Jay tried to laugh about it but he felt that the world was full of laws with teeth and the house was infested with dark aggressive mould.

However, they got a lodger to help pay the mortgage, a girl named Sophia who was in a grouping called Class War. They warned her that the house might fall apart, but she said she'd take the room anyway. She got housing benefit too.

Jay got a book from the library which told him how to deal with dry rot. He went to a do-it-yourself place, and there he bought a tape measure and a hammer and a saw and a paint brush, and a tin of fungus killer. He took up the floorboards by the television where the dry rot was. A breath of decay wafted up from the darkness. Seek the source of the dry rot, he read in his book, which he had propped open with his hammer by the hole. He fished around with the tongs under the floor and found a piece of board that was covered with white fungus, like a white beard. He took this out and burned it. He replaced the rotten wood and painted everything in the area with evil-smelling fungus killer. It seemed as if the house had had a decayed tooth and he had painlessly removed it.

After some hesitation he applied to the council for a grant to get the roof fixed. Grants were available for owner-occupier families only. Now, he said to Louise and Sophia, when the council surveyor comes, I live here, right? I'm not the landlord. Sophia is not a tenant. She is just visiting. And who am I? asked Louise, momentarily confused. You are my wife, said Jay. He gave her his fishy look, blue-green eyes softly glowing.

They made sure that when the surveyor came there were no housing benefit cheques in sight. Louise and Jay had an odd feeling pretending to be just themselves. Both of them checked in their thoughts before speaking on any subject, like double agents. The surveyor was a big friendly man with a briefcase, and he was helpful and encouraging, and didn't seem to notice anything wrong. He sat down in their old sofa with a sigh, like a hippo submerging. He said that the council might give up to seventy-five per cent of the cost of repair for the roof. So Jay got estimates and applied for a grant.

Tony's room was spacious but he filled it with his toys and his collections and his books. Next to his bed, Jay made for him a house out of big cardboard boxes and masking tape. This house had a front door and a back door, big enough for a child to crawl through. It also had an upstairs and a downstairs and flap windows which opened and closed, and a pitched roof painted watercolour red, which opened and closed from the top. The house jiggled when Tony played in it, and sometimes part of it would collapse or rip but then Jay would patch it together with more masking tape and cardboard. Tony and Louise and Jay drew pictures on the walls of Tony's room. There were pictures of sea creatures such as portitia, and the sea gooseberry, and the moon jelly; and there was a Portuguese man of war, whose purple tentacles came out of the room and extended down the bathroom corridor.

The house hummed, performing its function for the humans.

There was no sign of imminent collapse. Class War had regular meetings in the front room. Louise made twenty gallons of strong rice wine. Jay took Tony to school in the morning over the park, holding hands. Louise got a job, which was paid in cash under the table, for a slovenly vicar and his family, who were boring and disgusting, and took the solidity of life for granted.

On the television they saw financiers being criticised, or even having to appear in court, for insider trading. Lock 'em all up, Jay called from the drooping sofa.

Also in the news, the Easter issue of Class War newspaper featured a photograph of a crowd beating up a policeman, under the insensitive banner: *There ain't nothing like a good game of piggy in the middle.* Sophia and her friends were arrested one afternoon while trying to sell these newspapers in town. The police put them in cells, clanging the doors shut. They took everyone's keys, and then they went out and searched every residence.

Tony was in school and Jay was at work. Louise was just about to have a bath after coming in from her cleaning job, when three policemen came rushing and bungling up the stairs, like cows in heat. Do you have a warrant? Louise inquired meekly. They said they didn't need one under the new law. What is it about? cried Louise, afraid she might lose her house or her husband, or her child might be taken away into so-called care. Never mind, said the leader of the policemen, just stay out of our way. Law-abiding people have nothing to fear from the police, he stated dogmatically. He questioned Louise about who lived in the house and what lives they had, including who slept with whom, since any information may come in handy when dealing with potential terrorists. She wept and uncontrollably told the truth, saying she lived with her husband and her son, and the lodger Sophia who was just a friend. Meanwhile two of the police hunted and rooted in every drawer and box. They found only some back copies of the newspaper, which they took away, when they departed.

Jay was shocked. They should have a warrant before they

search a house, he said. They can do what they like, said Sophia.
What they like is to lock people up. Their problem is they don't
have enough cells. But Jay, in spite of his experiences, believed
that the police were OK really, deep down, as long as they
followed rules, which were stated in advance. If they didn't
follow the rules he thought they should be severely repri-
manded. He wanted to complain, to write to newspapers and
to Parliament, but Louise was frightened, and asked him to
keep his head down. The police had really wanted to find
something wrong, she knew, and they had scented illegality,
but had been in too much of a mad hurry to locate it.

They received a letter in August to say that the council had
approved the grant for their roof. Whatever you do, the surveyor had said, don't give anyone any money in advance. The
cheaper of the two estimates was £4682, given by a man named
Harry who lived around the corner with his girlfriend. He told
Jay that he could start in November. Jay asked him whether he
might do some of the work himself, and Harry might unof-
ficially pay him for it, as if he were subcontracting to another
person. Harry said that was possible. A man should be able to
work on his own house for goodness sake! he said. He mentioned he was having cash-flow problems. Jay said that he could
perhaps give him five hundred pounds in advance, but then all
the rest of the money would come either from the council or
Jay's work. Harry said that might be all right, if the work were
good enough. He said he would let Jay know about the starting
date.

November passed without work beginning. Water was
coming in the bathroom ceiling most of the time, and also
into Sophia's room. It was collected in pots and pans. Sophia's
boyfriend, a karate expert and, by the sound of it, fantastic
lover, frequently tripped over them in the dark. The word
'landlord' was mentioned.

Harry explained that he didn't want to take the tiles off in
the winter. He might start in March, he said. March was ideal
for roofing.

Jay called Harry in February. Harry said that he had just started on a new job and he didn't know when he would finish. He also explained that he would really like to have at least two thousand pounds in advance. Jay replied that he would try to borrow it.

Jay borrowed one thousand two hundred pounds from the bank. There didn't seem to be any obstacle to borrowing any amount. He called Harry at the end of February. Harry said that he wasn't sure when he could start even if he had the twelve hundred in advance. Jay said firmly that he intended the work to start in March.

In the first week in March, Harry wrote to say that he was having cash-flow problems, since a solicitor he was working for had refused to pay the last one thousand pounds which he owed, for no reason. Harry said that unfortunately he would not be able to do the job. But he suggested a friend of his, Steve, who also lived around the corner and was conscientious and a tidy worker.

Although Steve was already working full-time, he was due some holiday and he thought he might be able to take a week off to help if Jay wanted to do a lot of the work himself. I have never done a valley roof before, Steve said. By the way, I don't want my name on any documents. What about the council? Jay asked. Steve understood this because he had worked for Harry before on grant jobs. They pay you, not me, Steve said. You can always make up a builder, can't you? Then Jay gave Steve three hundred pounds in cash for lead, felt, battens, sand, cement, and paving slabs.

Jay went back to the do-it-yourself place, where he had gone before. It was in a big multicoloured shed. He felt hypnotised. There were crowds of men in the place like himself, wandering in the aisles like zombies, or standing, fingering the screws and fixtures. You couldn't help but feel sorry for them. The whole emotional atmosphere was so strong it was almost painful. It must be similar to what beavers feel about their dams, Jay thought, an uncomfortable eagerness. Not wanting to fight instinct, he bought himself a pair of white cotton gloves and a brick bolster.

At home he thought about the roof. Maybe the first thing would be to take all the tiles off. He thought of standing on the roof one morning holding the bolster, about to chip away the cement above the first tile at the top.

He studied the manner in which roofs were put together, each strip of felt lapping over the top of the one below it, and the felt sagging in between the timbers so that, when it rained, if any water got in it would run away from the holes where the nails went through; and the battens over the felt, soaked in arsenic so that they wouldn't decay; and the tiles hanging by their own weights on little nubs from the battens, each tile overlapping the one below it and the one to the right, and overlapped by the one above it and the one to the left. He anticipated the tensions and balance of the roof in his muscles.

On a grey Saturday morning in the last week of March, the two of them began work, or at least Steve did. Steve brought rusty pipes and other scaffolding pieces through the house. He put up the first level and then swung himself up like a monkey and put up the second level. A ladder went up to the edge to the lowest part of the roof at the bottom of the valley. Jay passed some boards to Steve who placed them over the top level of the scaffolding. You're not going up there, are you? Louise asked Jay, craning her neck way back to look up to the top. Yes, Jay said. He climbed up.

To picture this: if you cup your hands in front of you, as if you were begging, to represent the roof, your fingernails would be looking out over the street, your palms would be the tiles and the scaffolding would come up between your wrists. Jay felt OK when he was sat down on the zinc, in between the roof slopes.

Steve said that there was nothing much wrong with the valley as far as he could see, except that it was zinc and the council required lead. They peeled back the zinc valley, exposing the main beam, which was as big as a ship's timber. Sound as a bell, pronounced Steve. What's all those holes? Jay asked. A little woodworm, but that doesn't matter. He poured timber preservative on the beam. Then he began measuring and cutting wood to make a sort of cradle over the main beam to hold the new valley.

Jay chipped away and hacked and beat at the rendering on the chimneys and the parapet wall at the side of the roof. The rendering was quite hard, but the bricks underneath seemed to be just stacked up on top of each other with something like damp ashes in between them. That's how they used to build houses in the old days, Steve said. They just put them up any old way. There was not much holding anything up, Jay realised. All these houses were condemned in the Second World War, Steve remarked, but they never got around to pulling them down.

At the end of the day, Steve unrolled the old zinc valley and tucked it roughly back under the skirt of the tiles. There's nothing to construction, Steve said. It's just humping stuff around really.

Steve had bought from friends several strips of lead about two feet wide, which were rolled up like stair carpets. On Sunday morning, they put a rope through one of the rolls and pulled it up to the roof, Steve taking almost all of the weight, bracing his feet against the boards on the top level of the scaffolding. Jay was not really committed to the rope. He was tentative and watchful, since he thought the weight of it could drag him over, which was true. When the roll was halfway up, Steve's foot slipped, he staggered, jerked forward, changed colour. Jay wasn't holding very determinedly, but Steve recovered himself at the edge. Steve didn't say anything. Maybe he decided then that he didn't want to kill himself for Jay. He gave Jay a sharp look which Jay understood to mean: Are you doing this or what?

They lifted off the zinc and unrolled the lead out over part of the cradle. This first piece went from the bottom, at the back of the house, where the valley emptied into an ancient cast iron drainpipe, up to just below the first of the steps in the cradle. They hauled up the other roll and put it down from the bottom of the first step up over the second step to the top of the valley where it met with the wall at the front of the house.

The lead was soft and clean and curvy and had a dull glow to it, as if a cloud had been polished. That will last about five hundred years, Steve said. He tapped the lead gently down over the steps. Each of the steps was now about one inch high, and the valley was gently sloping. Louise made tea. She leaned out the bathroom window and yelled up to them that it was ready. They went down and drank the tea. Louise came up the ladder far enough to see the new valley. It was still just the afternoon. They experimented by pouring a bucket of water onto the top of the valley. The liquid rushed nicely down and into the drainpipe. The valley was more like a metal violin or a metal Marilyn Monroe rather than only part of a roof.

Steve studied the sky with dubious eye. It was true that there were dark clouds in the south. Who dares wins, said Steve eventually. Let's go for it. They began taking the tiles off. Steve struggled and bashed at the ones on the top. Then he began quickly stripping them off and handing them to Jay who tried to stack them up neatly on the scaffolding platform. On the ribs of the roof Steve clambered like a long-legged spider. Jay uncertainly mimicked him. He had to think about where he was stepping. If he put his foot in the wrong place he would probably go straight down. In his mind was a picture of himself going through the ceiling.

Above, the sky darkened. They pried off the battens, and pulled away the old roofing felt. The void was exposed to the light. Clouds of ancient filth flew into the air. Underneath the felt the timbers were decayed at the top, where there had been leaks for many years. They are OK, said Steve. The two of them were covered with black greasy dirt. It got into their clothes and hair and eyes and into their ears and noses. When Steve hit a nail down into one of the timbers, it snapped off at the top. He got a piece of wood and propped it up from underneath. It's something and nothing, he said, to calm Jay's fussing. I want everything to be perfect, Jay said, smearing his face with his elbow. It's stronger now, Steve said, triangle of forces and all that. As far as Jay could see it was only held together swivelling on one nail. They pulled all the rubbish off the roof and dropped it over the side of the house and into the garden. After a while the garden was obliterated. It began to rain. They tacked plastic sheets over the timbers and nailed battens over them to hold them down. A deluge of rain came down. The sky was solid black.

It rained all night and all the next day. The rain streamed and gurgled into the house down the walls and dripped in through cracks which opened in the ceiling. There was a constant noise of dripping. It doesn't seem like a house any more, wailed Louise. Don't worry, Jay said. It will be all right. You always say that, she yelled at him. She tried to control herself. Tony cowered miserably in the corner of the room and tried to be polite, like a victim of violent abuse. I can't stand it! Louise cried. She threw a coffee pot at Jay. Don't start that, he snarled at her. He had a face like a ferret, she thought with horror. She went out into the rain and flapped her arms and yelled AAAAAAAA. She came back in. I should never have had anything to do with you in the first place, she said.

Jay didn't reply, since he was too anxious for speech. He turned off the electricity, because the water was running in over the meter. The water ran in all over the paintings in Tony's room and ruined them.

In the afternoon of the next day, Steve and Jay went up onto the roof and tacked down more plastic sheets. It wasn't possible to do anything else. Some of the leaks stopped or diminished. Steve hired a stone-cutter and he made a plastic tent outside the kitchen door and cut paving slabs to make coping stones to put on the walls around the roof. Jay gave Steve some more money for the stone-cutter. He didn't understand why Steve didn't just buy coping stones, instead of making them himself. He suspected that Steve wanted to use the stone-cutter for something else that he was doing in the evening. He suspected all sorts of things. The rain poured down. Inside the tent, Steve worked cutting paving slabs in a white cloud of probably life-shortening stone dust.

The rain stopped on Thursday. In the afternoon they brought up the rolls of felt and the battens. The sun appeared briefly. Jay crept around on the roof, bracing hands and feet on the timbers, and cautiously cutting battens and knocking in nails. He measured all the lengths twice. The timbers were not at an even height and the battens dipped and bent with the shape. Jay fondled the rough felt, smelling of sweet tar, to make sure there was wood underneath, before hammering each nail. Everything seemed OK. Louise and Tony came up the ladder in the evening and they ate a take-away curry in the valley and looked out over the prospect of the neighbourhood.

Later after Tony had gone to sleep, Jay talked Louise into coming up to the roof again, and they made love in the valley on a grey blanket, which Louise insisted on having underneath her. But I like it best in bed, she said, ordinary and comfortable. She slipped and slid and pulled with her arms and legs. It wasn't her rhythm only or his rhythm but an architectural combination, such as between bricks and mortar, main beam, and multiple tiles in overlapping balanced layers.

On Friday Steve and Jay put the tiles back on, and Steve did some of the flashing. Jay lifted the home-made coping stones up one by one. He had a rope over the pipe at the top of the scaffolding. He looped the rope around one stone, and warned Louise not to come out the kitchen door. Then he would go up and haul it about halfway up, and then loop the slack around a pipe and stop for a minute, to breathe, and then pull it up the rest of the way. They put a strip of plastic damp course on top of the wall and lined the stones up on it. The stones rested on the wall. The plan was to cement them the next day.

On Friday afternoon bad weather was predicted. On Friday evening a storm began. First branches were blown off trees. Then walls were blown over. On Saturday morning several derelict houses of the neighbourhood, whose main beams really were rotten, collapsed under the buffeting. Bins full of garbage scuttled down the street, propelled by the wind. People were pushed along too. Out of an upstairs window, Jay saw an old lady almost lifted off her feet as she hung on to a fence. From every direction in the neighbourhood there were breaking and cracking noises. About eleven in the morning there was an awful, intimate slipping grating noise from the roof, like the sound of your own tooth being pulled. Don't try to go up there, Louise said, it's crazy. Of course, thought Jay. But he went up anyway.

He climbed the ladder, clinging to the pipes of the scaffolding and to the side of the house. The air was full of flying grit. The wind pulled at his clothes. At the top, he looked quickly over the edge onto the roof. The wind had got under the plastic below the stones at the top of the wall. Some of them had been blown off and slid down the roof, breaking tiles on the way, into the valley. Between the remaining stones the strip of plastic was jerking and billowing like a black sail. The wind shifted in direction and intensity. There would be a run of little gusts and then a big gust. Each big gust lifted the slabs towards the edge. Jay crawled up into the valley. The slabs which had come down had mashed corner first into the soft lead. Flattened to the slope of the roof he hitched himself up towards the flapping plastic. The wind was stronger than he was. He held the plastic down so the wind couldn't catch it. He slid the stone on the end off the strip. The plastic end pulled away and sailed up in the wind. Jay reeled in the free end and rolled it up and held it down with his elbow. He inched along, belly down, pulling each stone over the top and rolling up the plastic. He slid the stones all the way down into the valley and put one of them on top of the rolled-up plastic. That was the end of what could be done. He crept down the ladder, and into the shuddering house.

The next day was calm. Steve repaired the damaged lead as well as he could by dropping melted lead on top of it. They cemented the stones up onto the wall. Jay paid Steve fifty pounds for each day he had worked.

Jay had arranged for the council to inspect and pay for the work in four stages. Steve said that they never inspected very much until the end, and he had never heard of an inspector going up a ladder onto a roof.

On Monday afternoon the council inspector came. He wasn't the same man who had come before. He looked at the house without enthusiasm. He wouldn't take off his coat, or sit down, or let go of his clipboard, or drink a cup of tea. Bottom wobbling, he clambered straight up the wobbly ladder to the roof. He said that the coping stones were not wide enough, and that they were just paving slabs anyway and would have to come off and be replaced with proper ones. He said that the steps in the valley were not big enough. They had to be two inches at least according to regulations. He shoved aside the tiles over the valley and he peeled back the top sheet of lead. This is done completely wrong, he said. The bottom piece of lead ought to come up over the top of the step, not end below the step. Think about it, he said, almost rudely.

They went down. Jay was hurt that he hadn't liked the roof. What about paying? Jay asked. The inspector said that he would not make any payment until everything was right. He wanted to know who the builder was. Jay said he had already paid the builder and he was gone. I was told he was very reliable, he said. He mumbled one of his old names. The inspector repeated that a lot more work had to be done before any payment could be made. He also required an account from the builder.

It's time to do everything straight, was Louise's reaction, when they talked about it that evening. Yup, Jay replied.

In the meantime the rain wasn't coming in. They found another builder who agreed to take over the work. Jay decided that since Steve didn't want his name on any document, he would have to invent a builder who would be said to have begun the job. He gave one of his old names, and the address of the bedsitter where he had lived with Louise, since nobody knew for sure who was living there. He made an account on the computer drafting system in his office. It looked excellent. At the top he put a house with a chimney and smoke puffing out. Getting carried away, he put a child skipping rope down the left-hand side. O'Hara and Associates Builders, he called it.

During his lunch hour, he got a fat sandwich and went to pay a call at the old bedsitter where it had never been possible to acknowledge that he lived. He knocked on the door. When a balding and responsible-looking man he didn't know answered the door, he asked for O'Hara. The man was friendly but looked puzzled. I think he might have lived there once, the man said. He claimed to be running a construction business from here; you're not a relative of his are you? Jay asked sharply. Oh no, the man said.

Jay went back to work feeling pleasantly detached, recreationally schizophrenic.

In the early evening, however, he began to worry. He and Louise and Tony went to the park. He was silent. There were two steps in the valley, he was thinking, and they had to be increased in height to two inches at least. They were one inch now. Jay made levels with his hands. So that meant that the top of the valley would be two inches higher than at present, or would it be four inches. No it was two inches higher, but even that would lift the bottoms of some of the tiles until they were almost level. When the new builder discovered this, what would he do?

In the last sunrays, Louise and Tony tried out the swings. Louise smiled at him, and swung back and forth. She was wearing her old frayed green skirt. Jay saw darkness ahead.

Maybe the builder would be led to take off the felt and build up the timbers underneath. Then he would discover that piece of wood propping it all up, and that nail. What's the matter? Louise called happily. Her face was wide open, childlike in the best sense of the word. Worry, said Jay. It's OK, said Louise, I can tell. No don't worry, said Tony.

But what if the builder found the woodworm in the main

beam? Oh Jesus, Jay thought. It was like everything, impossible, and lies were piled on lies. Where was the money going to come from?

On the other hand, suppose the builder was not so fussy, and managed to make it look all right. Then there might be a big snowstorm in the winter, and the roof could collapse, right on top of all of them. He could see it and feel it, the split timbers, the broken tiles, the felt, the dirt, the snow, right on top of them in bed. He wanted to hold it off. He held the roof up with his mind.

Go for a drink? suggested Louise.

No money, said Jay.

The three of them walked up the hill. I'm terrified, said Jay. The house will fall down or the builder will cheat me, or he'll find the woodworm in the main beam, or the building society and the housing benefit will get together and nail us, or the police. I can't move either.

We have an address now, said Louise.

They know where to find me, Jay wailed.

You are a big bundle of nerves, she said.

They walked up a steep alleyway. Everywhere Jay looked he saw broken tiles, decayed window frames, coping stones that were on wrong, and perished gutters. He had an eye for it now. He could see half a dozen dangerous chimneys and cracked walls. All these houses! Jay exclaimed in wonder. All these people!

She stroked his back and nice tight bottom and the tops of his legs. Tony held onto her skirt. She put her right arm over his shoulder and her left hand just inside the top of his trousers. She licked his ear, and they slowly progressed up the alley.

Mouth

Extract from a novel in progress

You always did look with your mouth.

The sun-warmed pebble, salty-smooth against your tongue. Oh Jesus, she's swallowed something again – your Mammy prising open your mouth like you did to Tiny, the Jack Russell. Come on, now, spit it out, spit it out. Your gums aching from clenched teeth, sand in your eyes from your tussling. What's got into you, at all? Mammy embarrassed before her friend. Do what Mammy says – her nails clawing at your jaw – spit it out, now. She won't be vexed. Its smoothness, its grainy smoothness against your flesh. Now I'm warning you – that note of dying patience in Mammy's voice. The struggle would soon be over, you would have to yield to her nails and sharpening tongue. Open up, come on, now.

The pebble dropped into the sand. You watched it fall with sad resignation. Your mouth was empty, now; void of the fullness which had moulded to the shape of your palate.

You'll choke on one, sometime, and then there'll be tears. The pebble sand-saliva-sticky in her hands. You're bein' bold. It's nasty. A dog could have done a pee-pee on it and there's you, suckin' it. Mammy's arm poised high as she threw it back into the foam. We'll put it back where it belongs, shall we?

You sulked, digging holes with the point of your shoe. Don't be so contrary. Mammy'll get you a nice ice-pop to suck on the way to the shops.

But you didn't want a nice ice-pop, the dye colouring your teeth for days. You liked the wooden stick, but that gave you splinters which Mammy had to take out with her tweezers.

You wanted the grain-pocked smoothness of stone, the delicious shiver from sour-grass, the gritty fullness of soil.

I blame it on meself, y'know. Mammy posing with a cigarette, her friend and she again sophisticated ladies from magazine covers.

I ate coal when I was carryin' her. Imagine! Coal! The crunch of it between your teeth, the thickening saliva all black and bubbling. Down on me hands and knees before the scuttle and y'man coming in, thinking I was gone doolally. Mammy's social laugh, all tinkly and false. And raw meat. Couldn't wait to get a bit of blood rare beef into me gut. Like whatsisname – y'know, that fella that drinks blood.

They laughed, home-permed heads together, you forgotten. You sat on the damp sand, feeling its coldness compressed against your bare legs. You shivered, the day growing chill, only the shallow pools within the black rocks containing any warmth. The black rocks with their yellow speckles of age, their roughness, their unwelcoming juts. Careful over there – Mammy's voice reaching out across the sand to caress you, to encircle you in her love – don't go splittin' your head open on them rocks.

The winkles stuck to the surface, the ageing seaweed buds, dirty-looking and crawling. You popped one, its soft tautness spurting jelly onto your hand, against the fingers, down to the slight web of skin between the bones. The last ray of sun on the water; something moving, alive. A sidewise scuttle, a wobble of stalked eyes. You watched each other, motionless, each willing the other to move. The heel of your palm against the pointed dome of a shell.

You wanted it, this cluttering creature, the welts and crusted parasites on its hard-case shell. You wanted it, but not to own; to trace the rhythms and undulations with your internal skin. To remember it. To best understand its surfaces, dimensions, taste. You wanted to look at it, without your eyes, like the furriness of the bee whose scalding sting shot through to your bone. Mammy holding the blue iodine bag against your lip, you bawling, nose running, eyes screwed tight.

Now that'll teach you – Mammy worried, her concern manifesting itself in cruel harshness. Whoever heard of anyone sucking a bee? Honest to God! If you want something, have some of Mammy's nice Turkish Delight. The jewelled jelly, its perfumed texture of fruit-flesh. You disliked its dusted decadence, preferring the raw rose petals to chew to a pulp and make you sick.

It moved, its impatience and fear greater than your own. The sound of horn, of bone, of shell as it scuttered across and into the water.

Mammy's voice, plaintive, finally reaching your ears. Come on, now. I'm hoarse with calling you. We're going. The wind flattening the skirt against her legs, her arms raised to shield the blowing sand from her eyes. Mammy's friend shaking and folding the blanket, their white cardigans on against the changing weather.

I'm tellin' you – Mammy's grip on your arm tight, incisor-like. You answer when I call. Her nails clawing inwards, your skin viced. I'm not having you show me up before me friends. Her voice snappy as the pincers had been, her flesh-covered bones digging into your flesh-covered bone.

And you cried as she dragged you along the Strand, your feet weighted, making tracks in the sand. You cried at the loss of your shelled friend which Mammy now resembled more than it did itself.

Hard. Encased. And crabby.

An Apprenticeship in Assimilation

'*Every migration, irrespective of its cause, nature and scale, leads to conflicts. Self-interest and xenophobia are anthropological constants: they are older than all known societies. To avoid bloodbaths and to make possible even a minimum of exchange between different clans, tribes and ethnic groups, ancient societies invented the rituals of hospitality. These provisions, however, do not abrogate the status of the stranger. Quite the reverse: they fix it. The guest is sacred, but he must not stay.*'

Hans Magnus Enzensberger

On a cloudy March day in 1937 a young woman in her late twenties, dark hair and brown eyes, boards a plane at Northolt Airport in London. The plane is going to Berlin. The woman is carrying a six-week-old baby. The baby too has brown eyes, and a tuft of black hair. I am told by my mother, because that baby was me, that before the plane reached Berlin I grew very hungry, and yelled at the top of my voice. She describes her relief at getting there, the prospect of being met by my father, of being able at last to feed me. (No middle-class German woman at that time can breast-feed her child in public, *Das tut man nicht*.) As she walks down the steps of the plane and onto the runway with me in her arms, a fellow passenger, English, a distinguished-looking middle-aged man with silver hair and elegant grey suit, turns to her and lifts his arm in a mock Nazi salute. 'Goodbye, Madam and baby', he says. And he is gone.

An understandable mistake, my mother has always said, laughing. 'He thought I was a good Nazi sympathiser, returning to the Fatherland to support my Führer.' After all, it is 1937, and who else but a Nazi sympathiser would be going into Germany at such a time with a baby?

Who knows whether she thought it funny at the time. When I am growing up, and becoming an indignant and slightly self-righteous radical, I feel outraged at this story, just another example of the insensitivity of the privileged. I am angry that my parents take it lightly. But then I'm also angry about my relatives expressing relief that, in 1938, they took refuge in a country where the burning issues in the correspondence columns of *The Times* concerned the condition of laburnum trees. In the heat of my new-found political passions, I refuse to understand such relief.

*

I seem to start my apprenticeship in assimilation in the womb. My parents are German Jews, born in Frankfurt in the first decade of this century. Neither family is Orthodox, and both are highly assimilated into German bourgeois life. My family has never denied their Jewishness. On the contrary, my parents often made a point of it, even after they became converts to Christianity. No one in my wider family supports the Zionist movement; many of them see assimilation as a positive good. It is easy to dismiss this as a craven desire to belong, but nothing as simple as that makes sense.

My father and mother, three years apart in age, grow up in the same part of Frankfurt, Westend, within shouting distance of one another, inhabiting those tall bourgeois houses, divided into flats, with large gardens. Many years later, my father takes me round the streets. He knows the names of almost everyone who lived in the neighbourhood at that time. My parents' account of their teenage years always sounds to me rather idyllic – a tight-knit, talented group of men and women, many of them future scientists, like Hans Bethe, the Nobel Prize-winning physicist. There were dancing classes and skiing trips, a lot of fun and companionship: the photograph albums confirm it. But of course I romanticise, or rather suppress things (perhaps they do too). The shadow of anti-Semitism lurks there too.

When my parents marry in 1932, they move to Berlin, where my father works as a chemical engineer in a family firm. My mother does not work. In 1933, the year that Hitler becomes Chancellor, she is pregnant. My parents, especially my father, are people who plan ahead, who don't have a high tolerance of uncertainty or disorder. I marvel at how they were able to make a life in Nazi Germany at all endurable.

A perspicacious friend of the family visits. He says Hitler's intentions towards the Jews are clear, and that my parents must prepare. He proposes that my mother go to England to have the child, giving the baby British citizenship, which will make emigration easier when the time comes. (A clear-sighted prediction in 1933, when many Jews still hope they won't have to make the painful decision to leave.) So my brother is born in Leeds in November 1933. (In 1951 this entitles him to do his national service in the Royal Navy.) When my mother is pregnant with me, she does the same, travelling this time to Oxford in 1937. And so I too become a little British citizen, ready when the time comes to return to my homeland. My parents carefully choose bilingual names for us (they couldn't know then that Ursula is almost always the villain in every English school story I read). Everything is prepared.

In July 1938, after hair-raising struggles with the Gestapo for exit visas, my parents leave Germany for good. They leave without my brother and me. We remain with our grandparents, who, like many of their generation, are reluctant to go, feeling that the 'nonsense' of political extremism must soon pass, but they will eventually also have to leave. When I question my parents about this – why did you go without us? – they always say, a bit puzzled and defensive, we wanted to settle down, to bring you over when we'd found somewhere to live. How could you have taken the risk? I say. Now I would no longer ask. I accept that it's impossible for others to make sense of the contradictions of living under Fascism; on the one hand the fear of the knock on the door in the middle of the night – the constant vigil in case you are picked out; on the other, the insistence, often only half conscious, that life is normal, and that normal decisions have to be made. I hear endless stories of such contradictions through my childhood.

In August of that year there is Munich and appeasement. My parents are alarmed and ring my grandparents. My four-year-old brother and I are taken in a train with an Aryan maid across the Dutch border, where my father is waiting to meet us. For years I hear this story and accept the way it is told – as unproblematic, routine. Two years before my father died at the age of eighty-four, I asked him whether he was frightened at the possibility that it could all go wrong, and he said, simply and vehemently, yes. The expression of a strong emotion about these events surprises me. I realise that my parents always talked about their experiences in Nazi Germany with the minimum of drama and no self-pity. During the war there are many anecdotes exchanged between them and their friends, which I listen to carefully and remember in great detail. But they are usually of narrow escapes, of bravery, rarely of death and terror. I guess this is a policy decision about not frightening us, about making the best of things. So as a child I can be proud without being scared at the thought of my mother at the 1936 Olympic Games refusing to raise her arm in the Nazi salute to Hitler, shaming the woman next to her into lowering hers.

There are also the stories of Germans who behaved well. There is the customs official, who, seeing the giant J on my parents' passports, hurries them through without looking at their suitcases, while the SS officer behind them is made to open everything for examination. There's the Gestapo officer who knocks on my grandparents' door at 5.00 a.m. on Kristallnacht, November 1938. My grandparents naturally believe this is the knock that will take them away, the knock that spells the end. He is not what they expect. A former pupil of my grandfather's, he tells them that he joined Hitler Youth in 1933 in a spirit of hope, believing that Hitler might save Germany. His disillusionment came quickly, but he cannot leave the Party. So he has made it his business to knock on people's doors at five in the morning, not to take them away, but to warn them to flee. My grandmother testifies in his favour in the de-Nazification procedures after the war.

Like all good stories, they get told often, and each time I wait for the endings as if I'd never heard them before. It's only later that my parents' own fears and dramas sometimes get put into their stories, and some I hear only when I ask questions.

★

Is it justified to feel an exile in a country to which I came at the age of eighteen months? In fact the odd thing is that I have felt so English for so many years. My parents speak with strong German accents and small English vocabularies, we eat German food, our social and family life is almost entirely German in its patterns and habits. Looking back, I see how hard I work at being a little English girl. I live a double life without being conscious of it. It isn't until I am in my twenties that I really begin to understand I am in an important way a foreigner. And it isn't until my late thirties that I begin to see that being an outsider is a sort of gift, bringing a particular sort of energy for which I am grateful. It takes me some time too to realise that politics entered my life long before I had the faintest notion of what politics was.

The English are, after all, a decent people, and they will give some people refuge from some situations, sometimes. But, like most host nations, they have problems when immigrants stand out, don't become enough like them, don't fit in. In 1989 I hear the historian Bill Williams give a talk on Jewish immigration to Britain at the turn of the century. He describes a list that was produced by the indigenous *Jewish* community for the new immigrants, telling them what to avoid – speaking their own language in public places, talking loudly in buses, wearing the wrong clothes – in other words anything that made them appear un-English. Nothing changes much.

My parents discover this very early. We, their children, will be their English representatives in their new-found land. They will not try to be English themselves – they are shrewd enough to know they'll never succeed. (One of the many immigrant jokes they tell is the one about the German refugee who lives in Scotland and decides to change his name to Mackintosh. Then he has to change it again because he is always asked, 'Mr Mackintosh, what was your name before?') Ours is a bilingual household – they speak German to us, we speak English back. We learn each other's languages, and much later I realise I don't feel quite at home in English, that I speak in translation more than I thought.

I turn out to be a brilliant assimilator. A conformist child, I take to it like a duck to water. I am duly embarrassed on buses with my relatives, who do talk loudly, sometimes in German. My parents' conversion to Christianity soon after they arrive in England must help, though I am not greatly conscious of it. My parents are confirmed at the same time as we are christened, and my mother actually teaches Sunday School in St Mary's, Oxford when we are evacuated there.

At school I am extremely shy, and very silent. An early report says 'Ursula seems to be an intelligent girl but she does not speak.' In my teens I gravitate towards the most English of friends. But I also live a sort of split life, becoming close to two girls whose parents have also come from Nazi Germany, and spending time with their families. They make me feel uneasy. The accents, the food, the aspirations – they are deeply familiar, and yet they jar. I am busy with my apprenticeship in assimilation. They are not the route to belonging.

I work hard too at trying to be a success at the local tennis club, to acquire boyfriends who are the essence of Englishness, to be a star at the youth club dance, to make jokes in the best colloquial English. Socially, my teenage life seems to me a failure. I am too shy and awkward. I don't speak a lot even now, and I apologise too often. I don't have the patter, the inflections, the speedy responses. I don't dress right, still much under the influence of my parents, who remain resolutely continental and old fashioned in their tastes, and disapprove of makeup long after English parents have succumbed.

My father is kind, charming, autocratic. He is likely to be angry if we are even a little late for meals. If he wants a fork at table, he announces it, and someone leaps up to get it for him. Talk at meals tends to be rather formal, sometimes educational. One day it is revealed that I know nothing about the Peloponnesian Wars, and don't even know where the Peloponnese is. He is shocked, instructs me to bring the atlas down from upstairs, and proceeds to show me. In his mellower years, I can tease him about how he can't catch out my daughter, who's doing Ancient History A-level. But teasing is not part of family life when we are children. There is too much at stake. Both my parents have strong feelings, strongly expressed, about how one should behave. *Das tut man nicht* is a phrase I often hear – an expression partly of their generation, partly of their Germanness. I find it difficult to do things of which they disapprove.

One summer, my mother takes my sister and me away, to Dawlish Warren in Devon. It is a time of unhappiness between my parents, and they are having separate holidays. My father takes the son, my mother the daughters. We stay in a large and smart hotel, with tennis courts, full of young people who seem to know how to live. I remember walking up the drive, my feet kicking the gravel, watching them playing tennis so confidently, so at ease. I felt a hopeless alienation, a recognition that I could do nothing to turn myself into one of these people. I envied my sister her happy five-year-old's oblivion.

That evening there is a fancy dress competition after supper. My mother, rather admirably, for she too feels out of things, and has no husband to support her, encourages me to enter. I must have wanted to, just to be part of things. All I could think of to dress up in was my pyjamas. So I got into them, and as the music played and we walked round in a circle being judged, the other children in pretty dresses or fancy trousers, in funny hats and with make-up on their faces, I slumped round and round, dragging my feet, looking as awkward as I knew how. Somehow I was given second prize. Were they sorry for me? Or did I do a rather brilliant unintentional imitation of a street urchin, which impressed the judges? I shall never know. It was a consolation to me that I was given a prize, but it did nothing to bring me closer to those golden girls and boys who messed about so happily on tennis courts and laughed with each other on the lawns.

Perhaps because it was the first time I realised the gulf between my parents was serious, that holiday imprinted otherness with particular intensity. The next day my mother went swimming across the river estuary, which turned out to have dangerous tides. A boat rescued her, though she herself did not feel in danger. As she was brought back to us in the boat, I noticed that she had forgotten to take off her pearl necklace. She seemed embarrassed about this, indeed about the whole episode. She clutched the pearl necklace and giggled a little. Her accent seemed stronger than ever. I was more than embarrassed. This absurd episode seemed to confirm our otherness for ever. It was so clear that I stopped aspiring to the condition of a Joan Hunter Dunn tennis girl, and began, at least on that holiday, to accept that things were as they were. It was a sullen and depressed acceptance, but some sort of acknowledgement of the reality of my life. I did not yet see the strange gifts of alienation – Adorno once warned his fellow refugees that if they lost their alienation they'd lose their souls – but it was a beginning.

*

I grow up feeling confusion about what language can do. My parents express nuance and humour in German. But my attempted subtleties are earnestly imitated from friends. I have no real confidence in my ability to express precisely what I am feeling. I use words experimentally, testing them out on what

I think of as my critical audience. (I was well into my thirties when an irritated friend told me that I used swear words as if I was a child, with a desire to shock but without any real conviction. I was shaken as much by her irritation as by her insight.)

When Eva Hoffman's book *Lost in Translation* comes out in 1989, I feel an extraordinary lurch of recognition:

> 'My speech, I sense, sounds monotonous, deliberate, heavy – an aural mask that doesn't become me or express me at all. This willed self control is the opposite of real mastery, which comes from a trust in your own verbal powers and allows for those bursts of spontaneity, the quickness of response, that can rise into pleasure and overflow in humour. Laughter is the lightning rod of play, the eroticism of conversation; for now, I've lost the ability to make the sparks fly . . . I become a very serious young person, missing the registers of wit and irony in my speech, though my mind sees ironies everywhere.'

Even so late on in my life, when I think I have dealt with much of all this, I am deeply comforted by reading about something so recognisable, and still surprisingly painful.

*

Influence is even more significant for us than it might be for an English family. My parents, like all parents, want certain things for their children, but perhaps more ardently and anxiously because we are the outward and visible signs of their success in coping with exile. I suspect they listen out very intently for signals. It isn't easy for them. The signs are different. For instance, none of my family ever have any problems about shouting when they are angry. For them it is not a social taboo, as it is in their adopted country. (I inherit this characteristic. There are rarely other raised voices in my street. And how rarely my daughter, friends, lovers, or anyone English I know

raise theirs – and how they struggle with their embarrassment
when I am shouting.)

The issue of class arises in my life. In these terms, I am less
of an outsider. Although working-class girls come to my school
on scholarships, it is overwhelmingly a middle-class school in
population and attitudes.

My parents buy a house in a suburban street which today is
mostly inhabited by barristers, media people, successful pro-
fessionals. Then it was different – respectable, but full of out-
siders and eccentrics: a man shell-shocked in the war living in
the house opposite, an Austrian refugee family down the road,
spinster sisters and their long-suffering servant four houses
down, two Plymouth Brethren families, one Christian Scientist.

One awful day, when I am about twelve, the elder daughter
of the Christian Scientists and I (we are at school together) dare
each other to hide under my mother's bed and watch her dress.
We are bound to be caught, and indeed we are discovered partly
because we are so overcome with horror at what we are doing
that we reveal ourselves by shifting around noisily. My parents
are angry and shocked, but the brunt of their anger is for my
friend, who they say is vulgar, and a bad influence. She is from
the wrong class. They more or less forbid me to see her, and I
capitulate. I do not like being disapproved of. Looking back, I
see that they were truly afraid. They were immigrants and so
had even less control than other parents over what was happening to me because they didn't know what to look for.

I make up for my lapse. I am diligent. I am a reasonably
clever girl in an exceptionally clever class, and I have to work
hard to stay at the top end, where I have so far always been. I
throw myself into sporting activities, eventually becoming Head
of my House, hockey captain, a member of nearly every school
team. I am devastated when I am made only Deputy Head Girl.
But I am successful enough at being a Good Girl and an achiever
to keep some of my sense of otherness at bay. It is precarious,
and I never feel really safe. Of course, aspirations to be good
are not uncommon in girls, and there are many pressures to be

so. But I am representing more than myself. I have my parents' desires to consider. They want to give us a new world and for us to create a new life, and at that time I don't know any other lights by which to act.

Culturally there are things my parents bring with them from their past which they give us with great confidence – music above all. I am taken to concerts and the opera. I quite often don't want to go, but to protest would be inconceivable. I hear the late Beethoven Quartets at the Victoria and Albert Museum when I am fourteen. My memory tells me I was bored, but since I get such pleasure from that and so much other music now, I suspect I just thought that bored was what I should be. And even when there is great unhappiness between my mother and father, we go on making music as a family at home. In my adult life, I am very grateful for this gift of music.

My parents take pride in me. I am a good pianist, and play each year at the Wigmore Hall in a concert given by my teacher's best pupils. One year, the last as it turns out, I am due to play on the same day as the final of a rounders match at school. My mother says I must miss the match, it will affect my piano-playing in the evening. I insist that I cannot. It is not simply that I can't let the team down: it is clear to me that no one will conceivably understand that a concert is more important than such a final. It would be humiliating even to propose such a thing. I defy my parents. We win the match and then, later, I make a mistake in the concert. I recover myself, but my mother is in agony. I have let her down, and she can't conceal her feelings. I am angry about that and miserable at my less than perfect playing. I feel, as I often do, that this person who my parents are so proud of is mysterious to me. Who is it they're praising anyway? What does this person really want?

Surely I exaggerate these feelings? After all, I enjoy my school life, I am popular, I have friends. And I get pleasure from some of the things I am good at. All children have to assimilate to something and I am not unique in this respect. But I am precarious in particular ways. I am not really making sense of the two worlds that I am growing up in. I am never sure why people like me or whether they will go on liking me, whether I will go on being clever or in the school teams. One skin too few, someone once said about me. I need too much to be part of things, things I don't feel are available to me. Much later, of course, I want to discard a lot, some of the very things I wanted so much to belong to then.

And even at this stage there are times when I rebel against my need to be part of a world that eludes me. In my teens I go and stay with a Jewish friend and her family in Golders Green. I love their Friday night ceremonies, and long for us to have this in our lives. It's another kind of certainty, and I try it out on myself. It never lasts much beyond the visits, but it's some recognition that there are alternative worlds which I could join.

There is more to this desire to belong. My parents seem to discard a lot of their past when they arrive here. A friend says one day that she always felt our house had no history in it, and I am reminded that I felt something like this – that the house seemed frozen, with no past or future. The rooms are tidy and somehow empty of life. If they express anything it is a kind of careful feeling of our way into a new world. My own room reflects this – in my choice of objects, pictures, curtains. No breaking out, nothing that is particularly me, apart from my collection of glass animals. My room reflects the caution with which I view myself.

Photographs are almost entirely absent in this house – a few rather drab framed photos of Riemenschneider carvings on the staircase wall, one of my grandfather on my father's desk – that is all. (Interestingly, when my parents divorce, my mother's rooms have many more pictures and objects from the past.) Later, when I acquire a house, I fill it to overflowing with photographs, obsessively, on every shelf, fading and bending, my grandparents, parents, my daughter, friends, lovers, constant reminders of who I am, where I come from, where I place myself.

There are of course some signs of their past life in Germany in that first house I grew up in – my parents managed somehow, in those extraordinary times, to bring over a grand piano, furniture, china, some books, some framed prints. Yet these things do not seem to have resonance, or connect us with the past. I am sure now that, consciously or not, they wanted us to start afresh, have a chance to be part only of one world, not to feel divided between two cultures. In retrospect I am moved by their attempts to help us on our way to being English.

But there are drawbacks to these efforts. For a long time, and always recurrently, I don't know how to judge things, don't have a sense of certainty, of a structure against which to measure things, for myself. I have no sense of the normal. I am often sure that I'm not normal, and I want to be, badly. (My father, in a row we have over politics much later, says majority opinion matters because it *is* the majority. I argue hotly against this, but I know too that my relationship to majority opinion is ambiguous.) All my life, especially when the going is hard, I try and assess myself against such normality. Do other people do such and such, feel such and such? It's a hopeless task, and not fruitful. But it's hard to give it up. And it produces a sort of obsessive frozenness about decisions. I am looking for some context into which I can fit human behaviour, my behaviour. I seem to live so much with extremes of feelings, though I find it hard to understand what they mean. I want life to seem less black and white. I would like to inhabit the middle ground more. It would mean too that I could accept myself more. It is years later that I acknowledge that there's no such thing as normality, and where there is, that it's rarely useful to me.

*

Other things conspire in my sense of being an outsider in my teens. My mother is ill a good deal, and spends time in mental hospitals. In the 1950s, mental illness is a taboo subject for conversation or even acknowledgement in a school and milieu like mine. I go to tea with a friend whose mother is divorced from her Indian Army husband. It is the most English of houses, and we have tea in the slightly gloomy drawing room, out of china cups, with polite chat and sandwiches with the crusts cut off. I think this must be one version of normality, how it is to be English. Years later, this friend tells me how much she wanted to talk to me about how isolated she felt, having divorced parents. She knew I too had a secret and thought we could talk more easily. But we never did talk. It is enough to cope with being an outsider in such circumstances, too dangerous to acknowledge it or share it.

R. D. Laing's writing comes out just in time for me to believe it possible that I will not go mad. I am close to my mother. Mental illnesses in the early fifties are considered to have specific symptoms and their own pathologies. Some are thought to be inherited. I read about them, as much as I can face, and I am frightened. *Sanity, Madness and the Family*, the book Laing wrote with Esterson, is an early exposition of the idea that mental illnesses can be the result of social interaction, can be largely social creations, that families may sometimes choose someone to be ill for them, that some illness is to do with the denial of people's experiences. At least it offers an alternative view. It is probably the first book to politicise me.

Politics has not been part of my life thus far. School does not encourage it. None of my close friends are interested – nor am I. A kind of liberal Conservatism is a given position in my family. I know nothing about Socialism, and indeed have never met a Socialist. The history of my family in Germany is Liberal or Conservative, sometimes arch Conservative, with the exception of one remarkable great-grandfather, Richard Grelling (friend of Rosa Luxemburg and the radical playwright Gerhardt Hauptmann) who wrote a notorious book, *J'Accuse*, claiming that Germany started the First World War, and was forced to go into exile for writing it. My family are proud of him, but at a safe historical distance. I know of only one girl at school whose parents vote Labour. I regard her with a mixture of pity and amazement.

When I leave home for Oxford in 1956, my father's words about Suez are ringing in my ears. The only thing that was wrong with the Suez adventure, he says, is that Anthony Eden did not go far enough. In my ignorance and conformity, I thought that sounded OK. Later, we have monumental battles about politics. He dislikes my radicalism and I his Conservatism. For a time I am aware that I disappoint him. Not only am I involved in left-wing politics, but my adult life is not orderly in the way he would like it to be, and I can see that he doesn't think I'm fulfilling his hopes or my potential. Things change when I become a mother, but even more so when I and my colleagues create and run a successful publishing company, Virago. I suspect he is pleased above all that I am a chip off the old block – a good businesswoman.

Later still my father mellows politically – and perhaps I do too. He fiercely opposes the Falklands war. By this time he has returned to Germany to spend his old age there with my stepmother. Given his history, I find it hard to understand this decision at first. He claims that it's because he can't find old people's homes in Britain with anything like the standards of comfort of homes in Germany. But it can't be an accident that he chooses the area where he grew up, where as a child he walked in the hills with his parents. And, of course, he goes back to speaking his first language, though when we visit he spontaneously breaks into English.

*

When I leave home, I decide that I am going to reinvent myself. I will be free of difficult family circumstances and uncertain cultural messages. I will create myself from scratch. Oddly enough, this crazy project helps me to gain confidence. Spontaneity has not been my strong suit so far but I begin to feel freer to discover things. And I no longer feel so responsible to others for my behaviour.

I arrive at Oxford in 1956. Within a week I have met people

who are passionately opposed to the Suez attack, to Soviet tanks in Hungary. They argue about the Welfare State, about banning the bomb. I am easily excited, unclear as to what I believe myself, and above all I am happy to be among people who seem to accept me, who are interested in my foreign family, my outsiderness. Their views are sympathetic, they make sense to me. They are also passionate, and I am longing to be passionate about the world, to escape from feelings about myself and to respond to the outside.

At nineteen, my vocabulary is not large. I don't know, for instance, what the word opaque means. I have read science. Using language has not been a major part of my school work, and talk between my parents and us takes place in a rather chaotic bilingualism. In English my parents manage perfectly well with a small range of words. My teens have been spent thinking about emotions too much. Now I hear people getting angry, stirred up, about *ideas* – and the world is transformed. I have never heard anything like it. My chameleon nature absorbs it all. I still want to be part of the mainstream, but here is a stream that is something to do with me as a separate person. Some part of me decides that reinventing myself will involve using language. I begin to talk less tentatively, to try out new words more confidently. I become intoxicated with words, discqver what I think by saying it out loud, worry less about getting things wrong. I feel I might have a place in the scheme of things.

In my first year I go out with all the men that ask me. I am more confident about men than about my opinions. I never go out with Jewish men. I have Jewish friends, but never a Jewish lover. (Other children of Jewish refugees report the same thing.) When I bring my future husband home to meet my father, the occasion is a catastrophe. He is too quiet, inward, not formal enough, doesn't rush to help my father on with his coat. He is, in his quiet intensity, rather frightening to my father. Though he never says it to me, it is clear that my father can't make any sense of who this person is, and this frightens him too. My father is a powerful patriarch, and he expresses disapproval without saying the words. I am young and in love, and in a way there is no serious competition. But there is conflict. I am living in borderlands, where the two cultures encounter each other, and make no sense to each other. I am the go-between.

I tell my future husband (does he ask me?) that the two most important men in my life are my father and Albert Schweitzer. I am still trying to be a Good Girl. This, of course, becomes a family joke. But two years later, in 1958, there is another scene. My three closest women friends at Oxford and I are walking down the Banbury Road. We are discussing whether we want to be good or happy. It is partly a conversation about whether we want to do good in the world or marry – a conversation that dates us: it would be inconceivable a few years later. My friends conclude that they want to be good. I, nervously but not too nervously because I have come to trust these friends, say I want to be happy.

My position is hardly that of the outsider. Marriage in the fifties is still most women's idea of the next step, the way forward. At that time it doesn't seem a debate to me. Nothing in my upbringing, even my parents' by now evidently unhappy marriage, makes me ambivalent about the happy-ever-after scenario of marriage and children. I want to get married, I say. My friends are amazed. For a moment the old fear returns. I have made a mistake. I will be cast out of the magic circle. But we simply go on arguing. And ironically, it is I, not they, who later become involved with feminism and the second-wave women's movement.

Somehow my opinions and feelings begin to belong to me. There is still a sense of danger: if I let go of the opinions I think I ought to have, it would be to acknowledge that I can never be an insider, ever. But even that begins to seem an acceptable possibility.

*

There is this turning point in my apprenticeship. I am beginning to break the burdensome part, the listening out to how things are, the fitting in, the need to belong (though I will go on being famous for saying sorry until my mid-thirties, and I only really deal with being disliked when I am running a publishing company and see that pleasing people is not a good basis for doing the job properly). I start to recognise advantages in a sense of displacement, though it will be a long time before I revel in my difference. And even longer before I can look objectively and take a real interest in how my family has coped with living in a new world.

But as I write about this change I wonder whether taking on one's own past can ever ring true. My retrospective understanding of my apprenticeship in assimilation seems to teeter on the edge of a fiction. Perhaps it's because I am putting together this story from fragments. My memories come in fits and starts. It is often the briefest, oddest incidents which stand out, sharp and powerful, and which seem to me to demonstrate larger truths about the past. I am comforted by what Salman Rushdie says: 'Meaning is a shaky edifice we build out of scraps, dogmas, childhood injuries, newspaper articles, chance remarks, old films, small victories, people hated, people loved; perhaps it is because our sense of what is the case is constructed from such inadequate materials that we defend it so fiercely . . .'

Perhaps the difficult part comes later. What became of this person who tried so hard to belong and who begins, in complicated ways, to like being an outsider?

*

When I am in my forties, I live with a journalist who has spent a lot of time in Germany. He is that rare person, without a single un-English gene in him. He has fallen in love with Central Europe, and understands it in some ways far better than I do. I begin to take an interest in the German part of myself, something I have avoided up till now. On a holiday in France one year, we have been reading and talking about Nazi Germany, and in one of those small Parisian hotels, five floors up, we have a row. I am weeping with pain and rage, and suddenly I am convinced that the hotel is surrounded by Gestapo officers, and we won't be able to escape. It is a hallucination of sorts, and it lasts for about twenty minutes, until I allow myself to be calmed down and convinced that it can't be so.

Some years later, he takes me to Berlin, where I have never been. I love it immediately – who could not? It is so dramatic and vivid, with a stroppy vitality I respond to. I imagine how it might have been if this was where I had grown up. For the first time I feel a real sense of loss. We go to Dahlem, the suburb where I lived with my parents for those first eighteen months. I walk down Königin Louisen Strasse, past the post office, where my mother took me in my pram. Is it possible that I actually remember it? It looks terribly familiar. Did they describe it to me in this much detail?

I hear German all around me, and it sounds like the language I belong to. We reach the place where the house was. I had been warned that it was no longer there – bombed in 1944. There is a nondescript one-storey laboratory in its place. I walk up the side of it, and my lover takes a photograph of me. I begin to sob, and I can't stop. The past feels like home. I feel an urge to reclaim it, but I don't know how. I am overwhelmed with anger that our exile was involuntary, that we were forced out. It would have been better to have chosen it. Walking up the street to the Protestant church I am reminded of my mother's account of hearing Pastor Niemoller preaching there, speaking out against the Nazis, with an SS officer standing on each side of the pulpit. I weep again.

I have seen where my parents lived that other life. I feel proud of those two people who were only in their twenties when they had to cope with that disruption, that fear, and then to work out what was best for their children in a new world that was not theirs. This is the first time I have wept for roots which I now feel are mine, as are the pleasures, difficulties and freedoms of that strange double perspective with which I grew up.

The Tabloiding of Britain

I once had the pleasure of meeting Kelvin MacKenzie, the editor of the *Sun*, and believe me, it was a pleasure. The encounter took place at one of those posh London hotel lunches when journalists award each other prizes. Mr MacKenzie and I were placed at the same table. I thought I should introduce myself – with some trepidation, since Mr MacKenzie is not a known admirer of the *Guardian* and since there have been times when I have written about him in less than respectful terms. He beamed warmly as we shook hands, and I retreated to my seat somewhat relieved. Suddenly a raucous voice broke out across the pre-lunch murmur. 'Fuck me! We've got a few scumbags on this table then.' This turned out to be the merest appetiser for the entertainment ahead. Seated at the next table was one David Banks, a florid, rotund man with a droopy moustache who had just been appointed editor of the *Daily Mirror*. His arrival at the *Mirror* had been accompanied by the departure of nearly a hundred casual journalists. There were those who had expressed surprise at Mr Banks's appointment and who wondered whether he was ideally suited to the task of preserving the *Mirror*'s left-wing credentials. It rapidly became apparent that Mr MacKenzie was amongst the doubters. He had, in earlier life, worked with Mr Banks and, by all accounts, Mr Banks had concealed his leftist leanings with considerable panache.

Barely had we finished the soup than Mr MacKenzie was shouting at Mr Banks a good twenty yards away.

''Ere Banksie! What's socialism, then?'

Mr Banks stared back lamely.

'Banksie! Been to socialism classes, yet?'

Mr Banks giggled glumly.

And so on and so on. It was no way to behave in polite
society, but it was screamingly funny.

Very much like the *Sun*, in fact. It goes without saying that
the *Sun* is loutish and ill-mannered. But those who don't read
it fail to appreciate the fact that, like its editor, the paper is often
extremely witty.

The humour has two purposes. The first is straightforward
enough: the paper is a good deal more enjoyable to read than
the *Mirror* or the *Star* or the *Express*. Most (all?) of its readers
do not want detailed analysis of foreign affairs or macro-
economics. They want to be entertained. The *Sun* is often very
entertaining. It reads as if it was put together on a tide of
alcohol. Behind each headline you can hear the raucous laughter
of the editor. The second purpose of the humour is more devious. Mr MacKenzie seems to have divined early in his career
that even *Sun* readers experience the pricking of tiny scruples
while reading some of the more intrusive stories with which he
likes to entertain them. If faced with a straight presentation of
this adultery, or that phone tap, or such a snatched lens-over-
hedge, the averagely sensitive reader is likely at some point to
feel a bit squeamish. The feeling of grubbiness will eventually
interfere with the enjoyment of the voyeuristic act in which he
is involved. Mr MacKenzie's genius is to make the story funny.
Once you have caught yourself laughing it is difficult to feel
too censorious. The battle is won. One example will suffice. In
the mid–1980s the then chairman of Burtons, Sir Ralph Halpern,
had an affair with a nineteen-year-old model by the name of
Fiona Wright. Ms Wright correctly supposed that there was a
market for her story of the affair, and found a willing buyer in
the *News of the World*. Such an arrangement is much cleaner
than straight blackmail since you get the money *and* the story
comes out – *and* you can't even be prosecuted. The *News of the
World* treatment of the story was more explicit even than the
Sun could cope with. Ms Wright told how Sir Ralph had
demanded sex five times a night. Among her revelations was
the following: 'He got a banana and used it on me before

unzipping it and scoffing it down at the crucial moment.' The next day the *Sun* managed to allude to this by the liberal use of a logo with the legend, 'Fyffe Times a Night'. Okay, it isn't humour in the Swiftian or Woodhousian sense of the term, but a lot of *Sun* readers thought it was pretty funny. This is a million miles away from the old style *News of the World* we-name-the-guilty-man exposé. No moral judgements here, Sir Ralph. It's just a bit of fun.

So should we just laugh off the *Sun*? It is not quite that simple. There is, sadly, a severe shortage of randy retailing magnates, dirty choirmasters and adulterous soap opera stars. In between such frolics life goes on. Political life, economic life, sporting life, artistic life, emotional life. The *Sun* writes about all these areas too.

This is where the trouble starts. You can't laugh off the *Sun* the way you can laugh off the *Sunday Sport* or the *Daily Star* or the American supermarket rags. Those papers cater for the freak-show market and the tit-and-bum fetishists. The *Sun* is the most influential newspaper in Britain.

It has achieved this position in a relatively short time. No one considered the *Sun* very influential when it rose out of the ashes of the old *Daily Herald* on 15 November 1969. 'The new *Sun* will still be the paper that cares', it announced implausibly. 'The paper that cares passionately – about truth and beauty and justice.' In those days the important papers were considered to be the broadsheet papers: *The Times*, the *Guardian*, the *Telegraph*, the *Sunday Times* and the *Observer*. They didn't sell in huge numbers, but they mattered. Well into the seventies the news agenda filtered down from above.

It was Margaret Thatcher who first appreciated the illogicality of all this. Simple mathematics alone demonstrated that all the broadsheet papers between them sold little more than three and a half million copies a week. The *Sun* managed that every day. Add to that the *Mail* and the *Express*, use the standard multiplier – three readers a copy – and you were reaching nearly eighteen million voters a day. These were the papers that mattered. It helped that Mrs Thatcher's mind worked on tabloid lines. She thought in slogans. She spoke in headlines and soundbites. Things were either black or white, never grey. She bypassed the grandees of Printing House Square and formed an alliance with the *Sun*. They spoke each other's language. Together, they won.

But it was not purely in terms of electoral politics that the *Sun*'s influence became paramount. Over the years its world view became the dominant one in British society. I suspect that its world view is very close to that of Mr MacKenzie himself. It is simply put: anti-foreigner, anti-intellectual, anti-homosexual, anti-black and anti-toff. If there is a further philosophy it is that by and large those who rule over us are a bunch of hypocrites, that our so-called betters are no different from the rest of us and that the great are separated from us only by money. The outstanding virtue of the Royals in *Sun* terms is that they encapsulate so many of these themes within one family – and go in for a great deal of legover as well.

Jeremy Seabrook captured *Sun*think rather well in a remarkably prescient essay published shortly after the paper's launch. 'No nonsense here about the virtuous poor or idle rich. The paper is full of idle confessions and scandals that show the wealthy to be just as single-mindedly rapacious as we are . . . To live for the moment is the great commandment. This urgency of living in the present is maintained by a poignant insistence upon the fragility of life, the pathos of omnipresent crashes and pile-ups and sudden accidents, the fickleness of fate, the remorseless turn of the wheel of fortune. Sex roles and race stereotypes offer something tangible to cling onto in the real world of bleak de-industrialised Britain . . . It should be taken very seriously indeed as a bearer of ideology, particularly by those who would offer a wider and more generous range of human possibilities to the people. For, whatever the *Sun*'s limitations, it does listen and respond in a way that the Left seems to have forgotten.'

We now have a country in which, to a large extent, the news

agenda filters up from beneath. This is a subtle process which has been at work over more than twenty years and in a number of different ways. The coverage of the Royal Family is as useful an indicator as any of the process. Twenty years ago it was simply not acceptable to write about the Royals in less than respectful terms. That approach had little attraction for Rupert Murdoch. Whether he is a secret republican or not is in a sense beside the point. The Royal Family had a more profound significance for him – as a vast, untapped commercial opportunity.

It is perfectly reasonable to argue that the Royal Family had it too obsequious for too long. It is less easy to argue that they merited the outright declaration of war that the Murdoch papers launched. The next two decades were to see an unprecedented invasion of a family's privacy: their mail intercepted, their holiday snaps stolen, their phones bugged and their servants bribed. Other papers watched this process and realised that they could not afford to stand fastidiously by. By 1992 the resultant coverage saturated Fleet Street and television from top to bottom. Even the *Independent* could no longer sustain its affectation of being a Royal-free enclave.

Or take Mike Gatting and blonde bar-girl Louise Shipman, aged twenty. Mike was captain of the England cricket team at the time. Two days after the end of the First Test against the West Indies in 1988, the *Sun* told how Mike and Louise had indulged in sex romps – including oral sex – in an oak four-poster bed. ('Mike was not kinky – just rough.')

This was not a story that any other paper would have touched – particularly given its source (a second unnamed woman). The question with these things is always what to do on the second day. The allegations are now in the public domain. The Test and County Cricket Board will be meeting to discuss the affair. The England cricket captain may well be sacked by the end of the week. And thus the following day the story of Mike and Louise makes it to the front page of *The Times* and *Telegraph* and onto the BBC and ITN news. Oh, and Mike Gatting is sacked.

The influence is negative as well as positive. Around the same time as the Gatting affair the General Synod held a debate on whether homosexuality was compatible with priesthood. I went to the debate, which was an impressive attempt by sincere and sensitive people to get to grips with a painful issue. It was made considerably more painful by the fact that for weeks beforehand the tabloid papers had been running a virulent crusade against what they called (usually in 144-point type) Pulpit Poofs. The papers competed with each other to see how many pervy priests they could 'out' before the Synod met. The debate thus took place in an atmosphere of some fear. Any vicar speaking out in favour of homosexual priests knew he was issuing an invitation for the boys from Wapping to come and doorstep him.

The question is why Mr Murdoch chose to dump on Britain. There is nothing as relentlessly brutish in other parts of his far-flung empire. The *New York Daily Post* has lurid front pages; it also has three or four moderately erudite political columns, arts pages, books pages and city coverage. When I last looked it even had a ballet critic. So is it that the soil in Britain is simply more fertile? It is a well-worn chicken and egg argument. Do you go along with the words of Joseph Pulitzer inscribed in bronze over the front door of the Columbia School of Journalism: 'A cynical, mercenary, demagogic press will produce in time a people as base as itself?' Or do you go along with the author, Michael Lewis, who suggests flipping Pulitzer's epigram to read: 'A cynical mercenary, demagogic people will produce in time a press as base as itself'?

It would be nice to blame it all on Rupert Murdoch. Alas, life is rarely that simple.

Finishing

'*The eschatology of the Greeks . . . was singularly primitive for so quick-witted a race*' TLS (1926)

The present is so difficult to relish,
ever changing like the man I watch
who locks his car, scrapes his shoe
along the gutter's edge and hosting
a plastic bag walks towards the corner,
turns and disappears from view.

Each of the minutes I have lived
has gone with him. We are always finishing
things we didn't know we'd started –
as for Heaven, perhaps it lies behind us
or we are engaged in making it.
The glory of the Greeks was in their needing
only shadows pacing on the farther shore.

Alas, our eschatology
serves merely to fan a discontent
made in the present. Prayers however gentle
rise on smoke of sacrifice, and though
God 'plays upon the harp of stupendous
magnitude and melody' to keep Smart listening,
the price is madness for the orphaned notes,
our fleet bombarding distant, palm-lined towns.

The man is back and gets into his car –
his purpose sure, he drives off down the street
and leaves me with another sight

to file away. My dreams have been
of murdering my enemies and now
they'll be these self-same hated faces
telling me they love me. We've got to get
this done, say my communicators,
ready to enrol the smallest life.

A huge inclusiveness came from
the Creation, no single particle
was authorised to break the rules.
But this is just philosophy
or physics: I am on the blunter edge
of calibration – time now to think
of what a change may signify.
Windows warn me this is Heaven
or Hell, a moment for repentence as
a car draws up, celestial omnibus.

A Thanet Bank Manager Speaks

One time

three guys come up on the island. Mission?
To off, to ice, to waste, to cold-cock the Vicar
accounta that Ecumaniacal
Service the boy done done.

They stake
St Saviours.
What they don't know,
the Vicar's hip, got one dude up in the belfry,
fuckin' big magnum,
two more over the road by the Foamburger Tearooms,
smokin' the walls.

So what it is, they're lookin' to hit the Vic
in the porch when he's walkin' the dork
with the congregation. But listen:
the Vicar's got heat.
Blows out one cheap jive-ass right on the step.
WHAM goes the tearooms,
WHUMPH goes the belfry.
Jesus, the guys are just part of the road.

So that's how it is here, son.
Ecumenicalism. Name's Crossthwaite,
holdin' the bank here. Now just how long
you figure to *stay*?

Sad Pantomime of Lust

This poisoner has made me eat bitter meals,
dyed my food the most bizarre colours.
I thought she loved me, but no
it was all part of our lustful little pantomime.

The doctor prescribed pity and tears.
What it boils down to is this:
> lose your pep and you lose your luck too.

I don't see how I got this way
why should I worry about making a living
I can live cheaply, my needs are small
I can live cheaply, I require no fag money.
If I had the nerve to follow my inclinations
I could live quite naturally and at no great expense
(and that would explain those dreams about
> running on all fours).

When I gave notice I said I had to go
because a glorious future was waiting
(it is for most of us, it's just a question
of how long we're going to put it off).

Take a glass of milk
and one or two biscuits
don't you see that there is no need
why you should ever pass from the earth?
I plan to forage for chestnuts next year
I shall contrive an ingenious breakfast cereal,
live alone and learn how to make acorn pie.

Ice

At Richmond the ice is crooning
under the tentative weight of sticks and pebbles
we lob and slide across a frozen pond. A marvel.

Strangers exchange troubled smiles,
never dreaming before that ice had its own song,
a dull forgiving echo for those who stand at the side

watching for cracks, those who don't know how to
   skate,
and those who try to read the hieroglyphs
under the soft muzz of scurf the dancers' heels kick up.

On Being Eaten by a Snake

Knowing they are not poisonous,
I kneel on the path to watch it
between poppies, by a crown of nasturtiums,
the grey-stripe body almost half as long
as my own body, the formless black head
rearing, swaying, the wide black lips seeming
to smile at me. And I see
that the head is not a head,
the slit I have seen as mouth
is not a mouth, the frilled black under-lips
not lips, but another creature dying; I see
how the snake's own head is narrow and delicate,
how it slides its mouth up and then back
with love, stretched to this shapelessness
as if with love, the sun stroking
the slug's wet skin as it hangs
in the light, resting, so that even the victim
must feel pleasure, the dark ripple
of neck that is not neck lovely
as the slug is sucked backwards
to the belly that is not belly, the head
that is merely head
shrinking to nameable proportions.

The Olfactors

I
Nostril:
Once spelt 'nosethrill';
A double quiver packed with nasal arrows,
Those hairy old foresters.

II
Plants and clothes according to the weave and colours
Drink up the vapours, redistil them;
We walk in and through non-terminable laboratories.

III
Whatever the home, it is a palace when perfumed.
Smells deepen the mirrors to corridors of yonis,
Polished tables to abyssal wells –
Chin-in-hand like the stars in the long galleries
Of night we peer over the abysses,
For we are back in the yoni now, and can prophesy.

IV
Old Chinese sages living on air,
Growing immortal whiskers, eternal tooth-enamel,
Spiralling nails, on nothing but air!

V
The magical odours of the smithy –
Shooting ammonia steam and hammering iron –
The *corpus astrale* of living horsesweat,
The hammer the beat
Of a red pulse held in the iron volatilised by it.

VI

The lovers like a smithy together
Raising wonderful smells, these clear smokes
That spread charged with their hammering heartbeats.

VII

The mother milking happy smiles from her child,
Happy smells;
Grown-up she brings Mother her birthday present,
And knows it is right,
Her pleasure smells right.

VIII

We give each other flowers because
They are both visibly and invisibly beautiful;
We give the invisible to the visible,
The visible to the invisible girl.

IX

If you accept an animal smell you will send one back;
The visitors snuff up draughts of the subjected animals,
Quaff up the essence of lion, inhale
The elixir of hippopotamus; out of the rhinoceros-pats
The Zoo All-ghost stalks through the summer air
Enrolling Mother, Father, Child, evaporated passengers
In their howdahs of air studded with flies.

X

Paint the snakehouse scarlet and azure
Like the heart-centre of things;
Let the crowds gather there among the skin-shedding
    exemplars
To exchange their sliding skins, sly potions
The people compound from their flesh and zoological
    air.

XI

Your pebble thrown skittering across the lake
Is a delicate heat-and-perfume process
Performed between reflecting surfaces, while the birds
Trail their long dresses streaked with calls,
And there are in every cloud dynamos of mesmeric
   fluid –
See, your very denial of this diminishes your smell.

XII

She has buttoned her bosom inside a linen flask,
A linen perfume bottle with a lip for pouring;
As I lie on my back she pours from the open neck of
   her shirt
This invisible cream all over me.

XIII

The mists
Of the graveyard and the marsh,
One flesh
With the greenhouse and the grove.

XIV

Quietly reading, she has a Jane Austen spoor:
Ginger and geranium. I will not disturb her now;
Everything she reads alters the manners of her smell.

XV

Night floats out its white laboratories of clouds
Equipped with millions of droplet-bottles
Containing the semiochemicals of the land;
They fling them to the ground
Where they shatter into two truths:
Perfume and electricity.

XVI
Each cloud is a white-coated laborator
As full of laboratories
As white-coated chemists are, from under their skirts
Pouring their nectars.

XVII
Who is it then? I speak of the doves
Beating off the masonry across the gardens,
Driving perfume into the crowds, and how it is
The women drop their nectar down
Their legs in long streams that turn
To perfume as they spin their skirts; it is
Whoever conjures up the dew, whoever
Breezes the whiter tracks across the dew, across
The sea, that outdoors writing.

XVIII
He tore his white coat off, plucked his tie away,
He would never again, he swore, cover his throat;
And when she spoke her desire in the dark bedroom,
The kiss of she who breathed it forth
Tasted of the warm field and that thundery shower –

XIX
For clouds she walked under day and night
Gathered night and day inside her like one rain
Which when he was inside drenched them both.

Harvestman

Take beings. Beings need happiness. True? Take me. I am a being. I want salt. I want air. I want happiness. These are essentials for each and every day. Picture life without them. Life would be not as it should.

Take me dumping my scraps. The bin in my cooking section gets full, so full no more scraps fit in. This is natural. This is pile-up. Things pile up, things spill out. I am just explaining the essentials. Dump the bad is an essential. Healthy and clean. I am in my cooking section.

You can share in today's thought. First I will depict my surroundings. Close your eyelids. Try to see it. Evening. I wash up. Sticky smell – to my shame. Lorries ramming along on the motorway below. Bit of sky. Me. Bit of light hovering in the flat colour of perfume which I compare to a young lady's perfume. I call this 'atmosphere'. I stand thinking on my feet. I stand by the big pane. I am washing up by the sink. The spoon is a utensil. For a utensil the spoon is one of the things for which I have a lot of time. I shall say something by the by. Spoons are relative. Spoonful of love. Take your time and enjoy that saw. I rub the spoon. I stand liking it. Consider them. Together we can all appreciate the feminine touch, black man, white man. Below are voices. I look down from the window.

Sometimes I do get a very filled-up head. I stand and think. One of the things I think is as follows. 'This room is a disgrace.' I get filled up with being furious at me. I am looking at my kitchen bin. It is overdue to dump. I am getting my jacket. I am just doing what has to be done. Start and finish. I am not getting into extremes. We need balance. I look for shoes. I find them. Getting into shoes is all I am doing. Going down to dump my kitchen's bin is the extent of it. People say, 'Moderation in all things.' The simple bare necessities. I sit with my shoes. My neck is hot. I unbutton my collar. I listen and soak in the atmosphere. Not too much noise is now happening out there. I inspect the air. That is rain coming. That is called 'murk'. That is distinct wet 'murk'. Pessimistic. I am thinking for a bit. That is a long way down. I sit whilst thinking. Traffic swooshes. By the by, that traffic is a vulgarity. That traffic is vinegar on chips. Those stairs can take it out of you. Definite. They can take it out of me. Do you understand? I take off my jacket. I will dump it later. I replace my shoes. Tell me this. Do you understand? I just want to get on with tidying, that is all. Put a face on the place. I wipe my pipes. Rebrillo the tap. There is not much more to say. I do those things and I do my necessaries.

*

An hour later I am in my cooking section. I will be open with you. The feeling is mutual. I am talking about share. Share and share alike. I will tell you about what is happening. I have dished out the blancmange now being in process of swallowing it. Not so much enjoying it as so–so. Blancmange is a question of economics. Milton Keynes. Inevitably I smell the tin cans. I smell old vegetables. This is rubbish. Scraps. I look at my bin supposing I should dump it. How can I have clean surrounds with a smell? That is what I am thinking when all of a sudden what is on the lino? Guess. Share today's thought. I will tell you. What is beside my bin's rim in a tea spill on the lino? My last blancmange is in the dish. Guess. A being. I can describe it. A ball. From that ball go five-and-a-half legs to different directions. I counted them whilst eating. He cannot move. Long pokey legs like spokes which are damaged. It no longer is the true shape of a windmilliform invertebrate. You can use the term 'windmilliform'. Use your Collins. Do you know the name for this 'asteriskous' creature? You can use the term 'aster-iskous'. I happen to know the name of this creature. But I need not say it. I know the word. And so? Why boast? It has no importance. I feel like eating. I look down at my remaining blancmange. I think the following. Please follow this. He is having it rough. Please do not stand on top of him. I think it is humiliating to be such a fellow trying to hobble out of a tea spill under a rotten bin on bits of snipped legs. Can you follow? I am trying to put it across to you. A being needs legs. A home. Flies. Independence. Try to follow this. I glance at my blancmange. A being needs a lifestyle, a partner. Love. I am explaining so you can consider. Is that fair or is that not fair? I hear your thoughts. You would call him a no-big-deal being. Wrong. Let yourself be corrected, sir. Do not stand on him. What use would a bit of bitty spokes and juice be? Do not judge. God's creatures creep and God's creatures crawl. Egalitarian. Give him a break. A good time is coming. That is not just juicy waste for the dump. That might be thinking of Heaven. That is no dead soul. That is 'a harvestman'. Which happens to be the name so you now know. I am going to clean up the flat. But I am not going to squash him. He can live for a better day. The vicissitudes of life. I feel like eating. My flat is all over the shop. Stack of rubbish on the floor. Creatures. Your home is your castle. Agree? A lady is calling outside. I stop thinking.

I ask myself where I was. Blancmange perfection. My bin is a problem. I am getting my shoes. I could make it down, dump, get air, change of scene. I pinch my shoes on. I get the laces in my fingers and thumbs. I lace up. I make bows. Danglings. Nice ones. In the style of pear shapes. People can say, 'You are your own shop window.' I am standing up. My jacket is on now. I am going over to my bin. Careful of being. Good fellow. I am about to bend in order to lift my bin. That is what I do when, all of a sudden, I lift my bin.

Some of the contents drop, being awful. Easy does it. I can go all the way down, dump, come all the way up. Now I walk to the door. I open the door. Now I go out onto my floor. I go onto my stairs. Now I am going down the stairs with my stinking rubbish bin. It stinks, to be honest. It is my rubbish. I am descending. Families live in these flats. I need to stop. Let me breathe. I am recovering. My legs are bloody stiff. I am descending again. I take the steps one by one until I get to the bottom. Now I am at the bottom.

I stand in the doorway. I look at the court. I breathe, thinking. Darkness spreads out on the court. It is full as dye. Sometimes young fellows and young ladies walk along. But there are hints of the stirrings of plops. There is not a person. Rain could plop down. Lying at my foot is something, a pink bangle. I have come a bloody long way down. I am the only one who did not know it was dismal. Bloody hell. No point going out in that, I consider. Not even clean air, so why do it at all, I consider in balance. Later is the time to do it. I turn round. I am going back up. I am going bloody well back up. I will have the last of my blancmange. I start up the stairs. Going up, I have to put up with that smell up my nose. It is a difficult way up but eventually I make it with my rubbish all the way up. I have impossible hips. At the top I need to sit. I get in my door. I must sit. I plop down. I must recover. Breathe in, breathe out is the way.

After a bit I am a bit recovered. Now what to do, I smile. I am peckish, I know. I can resume. Where I left off. Now I get to my feet. I go to the dish by the window. I look at it. I enjoy a yawn. I look out. I can see a cloud the shape of a wisp. People live in these flats, I remind you. A Muslim hates a white. A white hates a Muslim. Why? Change the planet. I can see the powerhouse in that plum-flavoured smokiness. Powerhouses are identical. Here is a thought. I will share a thought with you. Blancmange in a minute. Powerhouses have souls. Why not? Spirits can easily hover in airports so why not in a powerhouse? In a second I shall eat. All things worship God. You take a block like this. I look at the blancmange. Blocks like Pondicherry Tower can be holy places. Why not? Here is a mouthful of a word: 'transubstantiation', I think. But now, suddenly, I lift the blancmange. What do you think? Are you saying we are just sophisticated matter? Cells. Database. This is what I am asking you. Give me an answer. I am asking you it. Are you saying I am a fool? Like hell, friend. Let me get something across very clearly to you. I know what I am talking about. I am just getting on with my life. Do you mind? Who are you anyway?

*

Take you. You have got your own ideas. Correct? You are entitled. I am me. I am a separate person. Autonomy. Keep things civil. Why not? I have my life. I have my pleasures. I pray. I enjoy the little things. I am busy. I have cleaned the whole flat. You have to be decent. I work too. I wash my clothes and clean the flat. A big job. It is not true that I do not work. I work. I work my testicles off. Pardon my casual words. Looseness. Outside things are less moist. I open the windows. I can hear voices down there in the handcream-coloured night. Definite. Be kind to your hands. People are out. Evidence of courting. I can hear loud footsteps of young ladies. I am a disgrace. This cooking area stinks. I am on my way to dump my dirty bin, once and for all. I am on my way. I am getting down those stairs no problem. Good for me. My lungs. Pulmonary. Careful not to dunt my knee. It is a long way down. I am not afraid to fall. Soon I will be at the bottom. I get there.

Now I am at the bottom. I am going out onto the court with my dirty bin. Breathe the dark. We are in smoky juice. There is a fire. That is light abuse. Come on light, perk up. I go slow and take it easy. A must. Anything could happen. Voices are invisible. Ignore them. I start to walk with my rubbish. The powerhouse hums. This is my chance to get bundles of air. I walk and enjoy. Up there are grubby stars. Proceed at a civil pace. I could whistle. The point is not why but why not. Accent on the positive. Dump the rubbish. Why not? Temperance. Eat well. I do not choose to go through the tunnel to the back of the flats, preferring instead the long way round and get exercise.

The air is heavy on the head. The air is soft except for the powerhouse. Cables and bars. Still I walk. A cluster of youths is climbing on an erection. They better not. I will kick their heads in. I pass ignoringly with my rubbish. Bunch of fives.

I walk under the moon. I think, lovely moon. I think, slender disc. The moon stays the same as the world is getting increasingly computerised. Bare cheek high above a computerescent globe. I get feelings. I get feelings as I walk. There is cold on my cheeks. Distantly a lorry sounds the horn. Sometimes I get mixed up. I turn round the back of the flats with my bin.

No one is here. It is still. The rotting factory stands behind hedges. Still I walk. I walk and carry. I carry and think. What happens next? I will tell you. Now something occurs. What it is is this. I think I hear a call.

I stop. That affects me. I am sensitive. Naturally my heart is pumping. I hug my rubbish. I look around. It is a mild night. I listen. I see no one. Do you want to know what happens next? I will tell you. I look up. I scan the tower. I see no proof of a call. The night is autumn handcream or facecream. It is quiet. I notice no one in the quiet facecream. There are so many souls in that tower block, I am thinking when then something catches on the heel of my eye. I stare. I continue to. All at once, nothing happens.

I breathe out. That was interesting. I turn round. Illusions. I start to walk on smiling as it was interesting. My walking can be like politics. The rise of China. This was an interesting day. Harvestman. Sweet blancmange. Now I come to the big bin. I am there.

I set my little bin down with a little tap. I straighten up. I lift up the big lid. What is this? I say. But it is full up. Brimful. Brimful of people's dirty stinking crap. There is no room for mine. You must be joking. How I am supposed to dump? Waste products. I set down my bin. Nice and easy. I stand. I think. I have walked a good bit. A hedge shimmers in the breeze. Dumping is a natural rite. Dumping is essential for each and every day. Take an example. I put the lid down again.

Bloody hell. Rights of man. I am getting my breath. This is not fair. Is this fair? Take an example. Consider private parts for example. Why not be blunt. A man's private part fills up with warm milky love. Find no one to give that love and that milk spills out. Must. Cut the crap. Picture the alternative. It going yellowy, curdley, stinking out the part. That does not happen. An unnatural thought. Then the whole would suffer. Do not think that the part is not part of the whole. Dump and be healthy and clean. A car screeches out on the road.

I bend down and lift up my bin. Easy does it. I do not value those screeches. They do not add to the night. Two trashy lines. Why? I have to take my rubbish back again. Bloody hell. I turn and aim for my room. This is no joke. I am not in the best mood. To tell you the truth, why am I telling you things at all? I smell my rubbish as I walk. To tell you the truth, I am in two minds about if you are worth it. This dyey air is weighing me down. I come out to the court. There are mixed-up feelings in the breeze. Human beings dream. Their grimy dreams are blowing off the concrete of the tower block. I come back to the entrance. The child's pink bangle is still there. It is lying. Disregarded. People do not care one iota. It is in my way. I could crush that bloody thing. I just walk past it. I matter. I go into my stairway. What I do is I just start back up the stairs to my room hugging my rubbish. There are too many stairs here. Do you know it is easy to meet a young lady round here in the flats? Normal. It could happen. A young lady with good manners could be standing about. 'Good evening,' I would say. She smiles. 'I have seen you about.' She bobs her head. The stairs are steep. I rest, leaning. Do you say God does not love his creatures? Load of balls. God loves his creatures. My collar is clinging to my neck. It makes me hot. I need advice on how to clean my lino. I am exhausted carrying. I unbutton my collar. I wonder what I should do if this situation with a lady comes up. Be prepared. 'Do you know about lino?' I would say. Let your conscience be your guide. She would come up with me to examine my lino. I am filling up with warm milky love. I

restart up the stairs. I would show her into my flat. I would
close the door. Switch on the switch. We examine the lino. I
can smell her Lifebuoy. She could do with money. I am reaching
my floor now. She need not show me her boobies. Simply talk.
Share. Inspect the lino. 'Dirty lino,' I say. Tip. Brush her
bottom. I am hugging my rubbish under one arm. 'You are a
lovely person,' I say. Healthy and clean. She shrugs. Now I am
getting my key out. Warm sticky loveliness. 'What is your
name?' I am wiping my feet. I am going into my flat. 'Linda.'
I have to get rid of my pool of warm love. I brush her pear
shapes. 'No one will know.' I have needs. I slip my rubbish on
the settee now. I take off my jacket. I go behind her. 'Linda,' I
say. 'Panties down.' I need to lie down. We need happiness.
'Need your bottom soaped.' This is natural. Nothing wrong. I
do not need to tell you my business. Why should I be truthful?
Do you think you are the dream squad? You do not love this
tower. I love the world. You do not matter to me. Irrelevant.
I love her.

The Phone Would Ring

Sometimes, late at night, the phone would ring. He would wake easily, if he were not already awake, and would wait a moment before leaving the bed. He would check the time and switch the alarm clock off, and then he would go downstairs in the dark and answer the phone. Occasionally, not often, he would listen and talk for a few minutes, his voice helpful and calm, barely above a murmur, then go back to bed and settle for sleep. On such occasions it was as if he had never woken. But mostly he would talk briefly, return to the bedroom, dress, and go out into the night.

If the voice on the phone was distressed he would talk soothingly; he talked quietly anyway. He would listen more than he talked. When he talked he would ask questions, then he would listen to the answers very carefully. He would listen to the voice as well as the answer. Then he would ask another question. He would listen and talk until the person on the phone had said what she wanted to say and he had understood it. Sometimes the person on the phone was a man. Sometimes he would ask questions because there were things that the person on the phone had forgotten to say. Sometimes the man or woman did not know the answers to his questions. Sometimes they did, but not until he asked. He knew these people well. He knew who would ring and who would not. He knew which questions he would have to ask, sometimes even before the call was made. It only took a few minutes.

When he returned to the bedroom, his wife was awake. She had taken his pillow and put it on top of hers, or maybe hers was on top of his, and she was sitting leaning against the pillows and the headboard. He walked in and she said nothing, and in the dark he didn't at first notice that she was not still asleep. He was looking for some clothes in the dark when she spoke.

'Who is it this time?'

He turned but he couldn't see her. He could tell from her voice that she was sitting up so he knew about the pillows. It was always like that. He had almost stopped noticing.

'Go back to sleep,' he said. 'It's late.'

'Ohhh,' she said, and he thought that was all she would say. Then she said, 'I'm awake now. It's early anyway. Nearly.'

'You need to sleep,' he said.

'You'd know all about that, of course.'

Sometimes he would pull some clothes on over his pyjamas but this time he stripped off and put on a cotton shirt and a thick sweater and cord jeans.

'Dressing up,' she said. 'Must be special.'

He said nothing, but he stopped and listened.

'What would you do if I phoned you up one night?' she said. 'Not you necessarily but someone, anyone. What would you do?'

He looked at the wall in front of him but could not see it. It was empty, but for a photograph of a Mediterranean village whose name he no longer knew. He often thought about this picture, he liked the jumbled angles of the roofs.

He knew what he would do. He would tell her his first name and would invite her to tell him hers. She might or she might not. If she did it was a good sign, but if she didn't it was not a bad one. He would listen to what she said, and his replies would show her that he listened. This would probably surprise her. He would say as little as possible, but enough. He would take her through a checklist, but she would never know it was anything other than a conversation. Nothing she said would surprise him, and this, too, would probably surprise her. At the same time she would be reassured by this. When he had finished she would no longer have any secrets, but she would not regret it.

The truth was he would never talk to her, she would talk to someone else.

'Do you want to phone up?' he said.

'Not really. But what if I did? I might.'

Then she said, 'I could.'

'Yes,' he said. 'You could.'

'Not that I would,' she said. 'But if.'

He found his shoes by touch and sat down on the bed. 'I'd tell you to go back to sleep,' he said.

'Christ,' she said. 'Oh Christ.'

He could hear her trying to locate the glass of water on the table beside her bed, then she drank from the glass.

'Have you seen my tablets?' she said.

He tied his shoes and moved towards the door.

'You couldn't get me some fresh water as well,' she said.

In the dark he held out both hands and took the glass from her. She didn't let go of the glass until both his hands had closed around her hand and the glass, and then she moved her hand away very slowly, her fingernails hard against the inside of his palm. His fingers were cold against the glass. A shiver touched his head.

In the kitchen he would throw the remaining water away and rinse out the glass. First he would put on the light. Then he would let the water run for a long time. He would stand at the sink with the water running and he would do nothing. He would stand there until he no longer knew why he was there. He would hold his fingers under the flow of cold water until they became numb. Then he would fill the glass and return to her bed, switching off the light as he went.

His eyes no longer accustomed to the darkness, he had to take the stairs slowly. He was aware of time passing. It was like a pressure inside his head, behind his eyes.

He brought the glass of water back to his wife's bed. When he entered the room she switched on the light that was also on the table beside the bed. He placed the glass of water on the table, then opened the bottle of tablets and shook two onto his hand. He gave them to his wife. She swallowed them down with little sips of water, after breaking each tablet in two. He put the glass and the bottle of tablets on the table. She watched him while he did this but said nothing.

Normally he would have gone by now.

'It's only a headache,' he said. 'It'll go.'
  'Yes,' she said.
  He was about to leave, his hand on the door.
  'June rang,' she said.
  He couldn't remember who June might be.
  He listened carefully to his wife's voice.
  'She talked for ages. Gerald's away again.'
  He knew he should know these people, but the names were just part of a jumble. One day, he thought, he would unravel the jumble, but not now, not now. Yet they were important, these names, they were attached to people after all.
  'Off on his travels,' his wife continued, 'making more money.'
  'Sorry,' she said. 'Sorry, sorry, sorry.'
  She looked as if she meant it but he looked away. He knew he should have done something, touched her hand perhaps, but he hadn't and now he wouldn't.
  'What did she talk about?' he said.
  His wife said nothing. He looked up but she was no longer looking at him.
  'Please,' he said. 'What did she talk about?'
  'She talked about nothing much. She just talked. I think she was lonely. *I* think *she* was lonely. Sometimes it's like that. She talks, I listen. Then we arrange to have coffee. Nothing ever happens.'
  'You have coffee.'
  'Oh, droll,' she said. 'True wit.'

'I'll be back soon,' he said.

She turned away. 'Not soon enough,' she replied.

He hesitated, then sat on the bed beside her and took her hand in his. She turned back and looked at their two hands as if they didn't quite belong, but she didn't take her hand away. Then she smiled.

'I went to the circus once,' she said.

'You didn't tell me.'

'It was a long time ago. When I was a child. It was the circus of cruelty. That's what I called it.' She looked up at him. 'I can't have been much of a child then.'

'Not much,' he said.

'I hated it. Every act was based on suffering and humiliation. First the clowns, the knockabout clowns. Then the bareback riders, pounding round and round then turning and swirling and pounding round again. The elephants and the seals. Even the acrobats. We all wanted to see them tumble. I thought if I closed my eyes it would all go away, but I couldn't close my eyes. I had fallen into a black pit and at the bottom of the pit there was a tiger, but it wasn't wild and savage, and it wasn't tame. It was nothing at all. It was like the remnant of something which had once been alive, yet it was still living.'

He knew what she meant. He thought he knew, he was no longer sure.

'Sometimes,' she said, 'that's what it's like.'

'Tell me,' he said. 'Tell me what it's like.'

She put her hand over his. It was like a kiss.

'No,' she said. 'You go. I'll still be here in the morning.'

He believed her, but he picked up the tablets anyway.

When he went out into the night, he would drive through the city until he found the phonebox he had been directed to. It was never the same phonebox. Sometimes it was a phone in a private house. There he would find a young girl (usually; sometimes an older woman, rarely a man). She would be slumped on the floor, holding the phone. If she was sleeping he would rouse her. If she was anxious he would calm her down. He would talk and he would listen. Then he would take her in his arms and he would hold her for as long as he was needed, until the sun rose or until she died. Each time he left the house he never knew which it would be.

Stonework

'Doug?'

Doug turned and I could see his age suddenly. You know that? That kind of omen of age? Jeeesus, he said, under his breath. I'm not putting it in quotes, that one, because he didn't really even say it under his breath. He more kind of mouthed it and you could see all of his bottom teeth, practically. He looked a bit like a really old string puppet that used to frighten me half to death when I was a kid. We left that behind, too, when my folks went out.

'Christ, Doug,' I said, 'you've got a load and a half on there!'

It was true, what I'd said. There were more breeze-blocks than you could count, unless you wanted to be a heck of a time counting. Bloody huge piles of cement breeze-blocks! I banged the door of the van shut and it swung open again. I didn't kick it because Alabaster was in there and I don't like to show a kid violence. Anyway, it was hot. Like a bloody oven, in fact. There was dust all over. Doug's face was kind of talced, like my old Mum slapping it on after she hit sixty. At least in Sydney the rain lays the dust now and again, I thought to myself.

'At least it rains in Sydney,' Doug said then. Amazing. Sometimes we didn't have to talk. That's what the palmist in Wollongong'd pointed out. You're chalk and chalk, she'd said, making a joke out of it but with a mica of truth, as Doug'd say. Granite was always his favourite stone.

Come to think of it, it was really that palmist's fault we came out in the first place. Or *went* out. Depending on your personal geography. 'Your personal geography's a fuck-up, Linda,' Doug'd say. 'You're a has-between, Linda.'

Well, now we're both bloody has-betweens. Get out of that

one, Dougie! The thing is, that loopy palmist was so *hazy*.
About the future, not about us. Handling dressed stone's never
that. Hazy, I mean. If you're hazy handling dressed stone, you
get a bum wall and probably a crook toe. Doug never dropped
a single rock. If you think the Ancient Gyppos were classy,
with all that pyramid stuff about not slipping a razor in the
joints, then you ought to've seen Doug in the good old days.
Doug was bloody *obsessive*. He'd get a spalling hammer and a
lump of limestone ('limo', Doug'd call it) and it'd be rough-
dressed in, well, about as long as it takes to say 'it rains in
Sydney', slowly. And then he'd stroke it, sort of fondlingly.
Great big hands, Doug had, the kind that can hold a couple of
tree-trunks with room to spare. Yet he'd stroke that stone like
it was a new-born baby or something.

I stood there and blinked a bit after Doug'd said that about
Sydney. It was like the real low. Only I felt it could get worse.
He could clout some local guy and get hauled off by the local
gendarmerie and leave me high'n dry. Or whatever. Not knowing a word of the lingo. ('All French to me, mate,' Doug'd
say.)

Then Alabaster started to scream and I couldn't even go get
her, I was so depressed. I could see her banging the window
and I couldn't even go get her. She was only, what, two and a
half then but she never stopped. Talking, I mean. Questions.
Like life was a quiz-show or something.

There were others on the site: Moroccans, Doug'd said. They
were whistling and laughing and they all seemed to have one
tooth that was silver or something. Doug was just about as
dark but he was a yard taller it seemed like and of course his
hair was blond as a beach, done up in his pig-tail Indian squaw
look with the little scrap of ribbon he'd filched from the Hopis.
Well, not filched: he'd found it by their temple thing with that
great big ladder stuck out and reckoned it must've got torn off
a mask or something. Looked like a scrap of Barbie ribbon to
me but it meant a lot to Doug. Doug collected bits from all
over, especially in his nomad days. Carted them all out with us

in an old tin from out his Dad's lock-up, the one his Dad did himself in in. (Ugly as it sounds.) Even in the tent all through that first lousy summer I'm trying to get over to yoú right now, he'd yank open the tin at sundown and lay them out neat as his stonework tools. You know what I mean – that kind of classy authentic junk your Mum'd want to chuck if you were a kid. A heap of really old pot bits you'd still see the antique nail scratches in, birds' bones from the Great Sandy, flint spear-heads that weren't, a smatch of grass from out the Himalayas, way up, and of course all the flaming pebbles. My favourite was the little blue glassy tear-drop, off a beach in Guam or something. It was the shark's tooth for him. Reminded him of surf, the big classy Aussie surf he practically lived in after leaving college early. He never wore a lot round his neck, though. Only the snake-skin thong from the camp at Tennant Rock. He used to kid me mad about my feldspar. I was kind of touchy about that.

It was the Moroccan guys had the stuff, but we didn't have the francs. Clean and dark it looked too, nice thick cakes they'd cut with a fancy bone-handled knife and wait for the campers to stroll over. That was the worst of it: sitting outside that tent in over forty degrees with it sort of wafting over all sweet and tender from the German bike gang. If it hadn't been for the vino we'd have gone mad, I reckon, though neither of us'd ever been ones for the booze. That's one reason why we left Sydney. 'Come on over and crack a tinnie, Doug and Linda!' But they didn't really want your soul. You could leave that behind for a start off, mate.

In the old days even the sauerkraut-munchers would've given us a flake or two for free, we both agreed, Doug and I. In the good old days. Just enough to get the dust blown off.

Times they are a-changing, all right. (Christ, we're so bloody antique!)

Doug didn't work, canned. I don't mean he couldn't hold a hammer steady or smooth out a curve or get a polish off granite that'd blind you when the sun came out – cos he could, even after an all-night barbie on Palm Beach, once. I mean his rhythm didn't work, with booze. He'd end up with this sort of snarly dog-in-a-teacup mood each night, and the booze'd leave a kind of tarty smile on his upper lip, like the shit the surf dumps up onto nice white Bondi. Wrack, to be posh about it. He'd sit with his wrists on his knees and his head hung down, like a pissed-off Buddha, and do these really loud sniffs that started out in his chest and finished up practically in his hair, hunching his shoulders high then hawking it all out. Mainly towards the sausage-munchers.

But actually, I reckon in a funny kind of way it was really at his Linda. And Alabaster. He'd look at her like she was a piece of garbo, and she'd scream so big half the flies on the camp site'd fly right into her throat. I reckon now he was getting at his dependants. As the admin guys called us – in French. 'You'd think they'd learn some bloody English,' Doug'd say, and then tear the papers up. 'You'd think they'd fuckin try!'

Anyway, there was Doug and these thousands of breeze-blocks and it almost made me want to cry, seeing him just stand there holding one like it was burning his hands to a blister. He held Alabaster like that in the first few days, but that was a kind of fear of something so bloody soft and slippy and frail he didn't know where to park himself. This was different.

I mean, Doug handling breeze-blocks. Lousy cement breeze-blocks a kid could pick up with one finger. I ask you!

Some huge new barn or something. It was in the middle of a whole load of vineyards so I think it was meant for those really huge grape-pickers, the same as they have back home. It was depressing, stuck out there with a whole load of vines stretched out as far as the eye could see, even without Doug holding his breeze-block, and him turned to me saying at least it rained in Sydney. I really wanted to scream like Alabaster had started doing in the van, a real tonsil-whacker. Only I couldn't. And the van wasn't ours, either. Just in case you think we could've hitched up in it, instead of the camp site. The van was bloody Marcel's. It was about as bad as you could get. I

said to Doug, the flaming Flintstones did better. It was like a
jerry can on wheels, I said. Doug said you can't be choosy and
Marcel joked about the string. It was done up liké a parcel in
string. Cut one knot and you'd have a nice pile of spare parts,
he said. At least, that's what I think he said, his English was so
bloody half-cock. We all laughed, at any rate. Laughed like
there was no tomorrow or something.

The thing about Marcel, was that he gave us hope, the bastard. He fooled us stupid. Doug'd got his folder out about a
minute after Marcel'd got talking to us, because it was early
days then. Doug and his folder were like body and soul. They
were real mates! I used to get jealous. Cross my heart, I did.
Doug'd flash his folder before he'd flash me and Alabaster, if
you get what I mean. We were kind of extras, while Doug's
folder wasn't. It was his soul-mate, that thing.

Anyway, Marcel parked himself down on the dirt and flipped
right through. This was by the camp site taps. He'd been getting
some water for his jeep, he wasn't pitched there or anything
like that. His jeep turned out to be one of those plastic types
that shouldn't come off the beach, with no treads and about
half a brake, a kind of dune buggy or something. Still, he was
friendly enough, was Marcel. A native who spoke our lingo, at
least, and about our vintage. A pair of rainbow thongs, cheese-
cloth kind of shirt, cut-away Levis. Well, he might have been
one of us except he was short and scrawny and had a kind of
wily French look you never see back home. And scent. Doug'd
rather be dead than after-shaved, though he had a turn for
patchouli oil once, behind the ears. But that was way back,
when I first knew him. We were just bloody kids then, thinking
the future'd be all surf and strumming. Night stars, crackle'n'
pop of gum branches, cool gusts out the west, hot skin out the
sea? Christ, it makes me want to weep and bloody laugh all at
the same time! Doug's hair stiff and salty and loads of it then,
his big hands laid on my breasts, like he was keeping them
warm, zonked-out Wayne in his grandfather's bathers doing his
cartwheels into the dunes and cutting his wrists on spinifex, the

good dark dope, the red chunks of meat sizzling, Nan walking
stark naked so the surf kind of creamed her thighs in the moonlight, then me having my visions and making up the songs, and
that Tibetan wind thing of Bru's we lost one day out on Palm
Beach. And it was always Doug who'd raise the tone, as my
posh sister'd say. He'd always keep it kind of sturdy. The whole
thing. Not just spaced out and stupid, like the Macquarie gang.
But my old folks never took to Doug. He was just too Aussie
native, I reckon, for them. Apart from not being mad about
Jesus and all that. They'd still got half of their flaming toes
in Gloucester, England. Has-betweens. Bloody has-betweens.
Yeah, yeah.

   Marcel had a gun, dogs, the whole works. That was weird.
When we walked back with him to his vehicle the dogs barked
like crazy, and it wasn't even the season. Anyway, he got Doug
going at first by coming on real crazy about the stuff in the
folder. He kept slapping the pages and shaking his hand all
floppy at the wrist like the Frenchos do when they think something's bloody marvellous. He really seemed to go for the fancy
limestone cornices on that City Council pile and the granite bits
Doug did for the Stock Exchange in '83, the ones that had to
be curvy like billowing waves or the Opera House or something? He kept blowing on about a friend of his called Pierre
and thumping his chest, so I reckoned Pierre was a bosom mate
of his. I thought perhaps he was into guys, this Marcel. Then
Doug went on about Pierre as well, thumping his chest like he
was mad about this geezer, too. I thought, Christ, this is rather
heavy – and they weren't really speaking any lingo now, only
this kind of love-in for this guy Pierre. Then we went back to
the jeep, as I said, and Marcel's Anglo kind of warmed up, and
he was saying all the time how he could find Doug work.
'No problems,' he said, and kept jerking his hand at this huge
farmhouse over the road, and another the other side of the camp
site, and a big old rubble-stone barn way off over the grapes,
like he was saying every stone building this side of the Med is
crying out for Doug to handle it, while those bloody dogs of

his were wanting us for tucker and practically pulling the vehicle over, they were that keen.

I suppose we'd been about a month out by the time we met Marcel. A month's a heck of a duration, when the cash isn't coming through like you thought it would. I mean, we'd left home kind of on the hop, on a one-way ticket, just like that. You have to do this kind of thing when the energies are still high, we reckoned. We kind of woke up one morning and decided to go run for the whole thing before we could change our minds, and I suppose we'd thought the house would sell real quick, being an antique clapboarder from the time of the chain-gangs practically and the yard stuffed full of Doug's originals, the ones he'd make for his own healing, as he'd put it. I guess now people aren't as heavy on sundials and totems and runes and so on as we'd kind of thought, and the house'd got some worm or something, they said, some worm that gets really high on old timber.

Well, I reckon the real estaters were bloody Macquarie crims. Just wanted the land or something to build a poshie villa. Stuff the hippies or something. Hippies, Abos, beach-bums: it's all the same to a feller in a fancy tie and scent who hangs his shirts up. Anyway, these bloody egg-suckers did us. Just like Marcel did. And he wasn't even in sneakers.

He said he had this old van he could lend us but it wasn't for free. Oh no. Doug had to do a bit of, well, *work*. Just a bit. Like moving half a ton of slate to do up some Swiss geezer's huge vacation place near St Jean du Gard, way up in the hills.

'Fuckin splendid, Linda,' Doug'd say, real knackered, 'splendid fuckin view, Linda! And boy, that slate – you should see it gleam after a soak! Blue and kind of purple – no, kind of green, kind of mulga green. Big hunks of first-class flaming slate. Snaps off the side of the hills like old bullock-shit.'

He would've laid the roof, Doug would, like a shot, but some Moroccan'd got there first and was doing it for smick, to use the French. Doug'd not had a lot to do with slate back home. It kind of gave me the heebies-jeebies, slate, the way it broke up flat as a pancake every time. I'm a limestone person myself. I think kind of soft and pale. Why Alabaster's called Alabaster, I suppose, though alabaster isn't exactly soft. Suits her, anyway, the way she talks back at me sometimes. She's, what, nearly ten now. Christ. Nearly ten. Doug'd say Doug was granite. Him and his twinkly eyes. Like mica in a block of granite.

Well, I don't know.

Doug just kind of delivered the slate and hauled it up in a bucket. That was his first job, pulling on a bloody rope, thanks to Marcel. It was all downhill from there, I suppose. At least in that one he got to handle the *real* stuff. I mean, real clean rock. The rest's dirt, Doug'd say. Bloody dirt. It had almost murdered him to see Sydney every day. All her bloody concrete and glass. 'I'm a shark in a sandwich here, Linda. A shark in a bloody sandwich.' Then there was that TV doc on the Med and Doug going crazy because every house seemed to be rock, like they'd never heard of bricks, and then the palmist.

Funny – I can't even remember what she said now, it was so vague. But we hung on to it like a hat in a buster.

I suppose we'd still be kind of intact if we'd stayed. It's like the whole bloody thing's just kind of split open. It's like nothing could break us back home, down there. Out here we went and got our faces at the wrong angle, as Doug'd say. Life just cleaved us straight through every bloody time. That's what Doug'd start to say, anyway, flat out in the tent. Then he'd get his hammer and big blue chisel and duck through the flap and bash away at the dirt, just smack away and raise a huge plume of dust. He'd make a hole the size of a bloody rock! Then he'd put his head in. The hole, I mean. Alabaster'd squeal like a pig. She didn't understand, really. She thought it was a joke. She'd bang her little plastic spade on his bum, but he didn't move. Like an ostrich, Doug looked. The sauerkrauts'd frown. They thought he was sick, I suppose, or canned. Them and their large bikes. They'd give us a yell sometimes: 'Aussie Aussie Aussie, one two sree!' Or something. They were making a joke, I suppose. He'd stay up to half an hour like that, would Doug. Just like an ostrich.

That was before he went on walkabout every other bloody day.

Marcel. I was on about Marcel. Well, after that slate job it was kind of blank for a few weeks, and Doug was going around in the van showing his stonework folder and using his hands. I mean, using his hands instead of words. He'd stop at a builder's or a stonemason's or wherever he could hear a spalling hammer at work and get out the van and find the boss and sometimes the boss wasn't there and sometimes they thought he was a tripper trying to find some place and some of them didn't like what they reckoned was the hippy look (Doug wasn't what you might call a regular user of the showers) and some of them just kind of ignored him as some type of spaced-out maniac or something and one or two looked at the folder. I reckon the stuff was too good in there, that was the trouble. It kind of freaked them out. That was stupid. I mean, it hurt Doug real bad to see a ruin. 'Look at that, Linda,' he'd say, 'it's crying out to be healed, Linda.' Or the dry-stone stuff. There was a heap of those tumbling down at the edges of fields and suchlike. Doug could've got every stone in the South of France back into place if he'd been given the chance – and enough dinero for all three of us to live on. But the stuff in the folder was too fancy, y'know? Limestone curvy cornices and billowing granite and inscriptions, that kind of stuff? Either that, or the photos had got really faded, and leaving it outside the tent one time didn't help. The sun was worse than Sydney in bloody March. It kind of just bleached out two whole pages, and one of them was that basalt deco stuff Doug did for the University Library frieze in '85. Real nice detail work with the small chisel. All those teeny weeny toes on Isis and the others. I forget their names. And the Four Elements. And me up there where it went behind the Linguistics part for a couple of feet. My face. 'Like they did on the cathedrals, Linda,' he said. 'Where no one but God could see it.' My arms out wide, in a billowing dress. Behind Linguis-

tics. He was really proud of that one. The whole frieze, I mean.
He showed me my portrait in the workshop, before he fixed it
up. 'Guess who, Linda,' he said, with a twinkly look. Brushing
the stone-dust off it like it was a diamond or something. Me
with my arms out wide, and a third eye on my forehead.
Looking kind of wise, I suppose. That's when we decided to
conceive. We just stood there and hugged each other like we'd
only just met, and I said, 'Let's have a baby, Doug.' Christ!
Tears dripping off my earlobe into the stone-dust like it was a
funeral. Him with his chisel digging into my back, big and
silent. Then feeling him nod. Yes, Linda. Yes yes. I bloody
loved him, then.

I wouldn't have minded being seen, but there you go. Poke
in the eye with a burnt stick and all that.

No, Doug's stuff was just too fancy. They could see that. It
hurt their pride, I reckon. Out of their depth! Heck, just about
every house out here looks as if it's kind of grown up all on its
own, like a bloody cliff or something. Well, the old ones
anyway. But that was what Doug went for, what he was kind
of searching for all his life, really, that organic look. He'd never
been one for straight lines!

Then Marcel pops up again like a bad smell. I can see it all
now, of course, like it's hitting me in the face. I mean, see what
I couldn't see then. The jeep sweeps up and scatters a few
Norwegians or something and there's Marcel in a cloud of dust.
Jesus, it was hot. I was feeling pretty stuffed off with the whole
thing, really. Well, I'd kind of imagined the Frenchos all dusted
over with stonework and waving their chisels or something and
hugging Doug like an old mate and us gazing at the Med from
a café table like they showed in the TV doc, with all these
houses like cliffs in the background, making Doug feel he'd
come home. But all we'd got so far was a lousy camp site and
a whole load of bikers and you couldn't see the beach for the
ten-berthers parked and anyway, the first time we went Alabaster picked up a syringe instead of a nice shell. And no bloody
work. And only Marcel seemed to have what you might call

the international lingo. We'd never have believed it. I mean, even the Krauts could say, 'We have a good laugh, yes?' Or something. But the Frenchos spoke French liké they were fucked if they were going to speak anything else, mate. They made you feel like a real dag. Well, that's what I felt, anyway.

'Good on yourself mate,' said Marcel, with his kind of slippery grin, and kissed me on each cheek about ten times. Doug'd been teaching him a bit through that slate job. The lingo, not the kissing.

'Mates aren't Sheilas,' I said, checking up on my cheeks because Marcel wasn't what you might call a close shaver.

'Where ees your darling Dog?' said Marcel, glancing around and fiddling with his little wrist-chain thing like I was about to grab it or something.

'My Dog's gone walkabout,' I said. 'You've come for your van, I suppose.' I heard Alabaster start to scream then and I had to go over to the Danish family. They were kind of really helpful looking after her but they had this whole load of fancy picnic stuff, all royal blue china and so on, and Alabaster just couldn't handle it. It would've been better had they kept right out of it, really, because I just got so tense, watching them trying to keep Alabaster from yanking off the tablecloth – all of them trying to kind of distract her in a really nice way, which she always reacts badly to. Not that I'm strict or anything – it's just that I don't have any classy breakables around. People make life really hard for themselves.

Anyway, Alabaster had just smashed a Danish coffee-pot or something, and they were all kind of trying to calm her right down, bending over her and kind of flapping their hands like they wanted her to waft up like a feather and I could see the adults were really freaked out but trying not to show it. So I came up and started tickling Alabaster under the armpits and she let go of the cloth and stopped screaming. So that was all right.

Then I looked up and there was Marcel, standing right next to me with an arm out and a couple of dineros flapping on the end of it (there was a bit of a buster at the time, blowing the dust about). He was kind of like Napoleon or someone, looking real important. The Danish mother (Kristin, or Kursten, something like that) looked at the francs and then at Marcel and then at me, real puzzled. Then she shook her head and raised her hands up and laughed while Marcel kind of waved these notes around and kept on jerking his head.

Now this was a real sticky one, because our cash wasn't exactly what you might call fluid. I didn't want Marcel to bale us out, but I didn't want us to pay for the coffee-pot and go without a feed for a week or so sooner. So I just kind of walked out of it. Lousy, I felt, doing that. A real scumbag.

At any rate, I didn't see what happened in the end. I didn't want to know. But the funny thing was that the Danish crowd packed up that day and left without saying cheerio. I reckon they'd taken the money and felt kind of scummy as well.

Anyway, Marcel came straight back and sat down on Doug's little canvas fold-up.

I didn't say thanks or anything. I just left it.

He lit up a French smoke, the type that Doug reckons smells sexy, and did some coin flipping to get Alabaster laughing or something. He'd slap his wrist and the coin'd go right up, and Alabaster'd try to catch it. She'd be really whingy all day long, and then Marcel'd do his coin flips and she'd be like honey. He had a real way with kids. Anyway, I was folding up loads of clothes after the last wash. Well, it was hell to keep anything even half bloody clean then, with all the flaming dust around and the camp taps always looking like they'd just come out of a swamp or something. So we didn't say a thing for a good while and then he cleared his throat and spat and said he'd got a number one job for Doug.

'Oh yes?'

'*Oui oui*,' he said, which always made Alabaster split herself. 'Zertenlee, Linda.'

I looked at him and I could see his hand was trembling, the one with the smoke in it. The other one was pushing back his

hair, which looked a bit tinted, actually. He was a real scrawn,
Marcel was. He had rings in both ears, too, now I think of it.

'What kind of job, Marcel?'

Marcel coughed and pulled on his cigarette and said it was a
Doug kind of job, some big barn in a vineyard or something,
with smoke coming out of his mouth as he said it, kind of
crawling out. I really hate that, I don't know why. It's probably
to do with my parents being far-out Christians or something.

'*Ouvrage de pierre*,' he said. Never any mention of bloody
breeze-blocks, I can tell you.

That bloke again, I thought. Even Marcel couldn't speak
straight Anglo for more than ten seconds. Well, I hardly knew
a word then.

'Who's this Pierre, Marcel?' I said. 'Who's Pierre?'

Weird, isn't it? – but I'd not asked Doug before. I forget
things. Doug blames the crazy days out in Adelaide, when we
used to take the little round white Bus Australia, as he used to
put it. My mind kind of hits blank patches. It kind of lets go
now and again.

Marcel laughed like a bloody hyena.

I asked him what was so bloody funny. Then Doug came
round the corner from wherever he'd gone to, first thing that
morning.

'Good on you, mate,' said Marcel, putting his hand out. At
least he didn't kiss Doug. Quite a few of the French guys do
that, even the old ones.

Doug just stood there. He was carrying a load of peaches in
a big brown paper bag. I could tell they were peaches because
of the wet kind of red patches where Doug'd held the bag a bit
too tight. Peaches were practically free just then, and there were
a whole load of stones around the tent. Peach-stones, I mean.
Doug'd just sit there and work his way through peaches each
night like he was going for a competition or something. I mean,
you only had to blow on those peaches and the skins'd kind of
wrinkle away from the flesh, they were so bloody ripe!
Anyway, he held the bag against his chest with his left hand

and the other one took Marcel's and it was amazing – it was
like Marcel's kind of disappeared for a minute while Doug gave
it a good jerk. I thought that's how people see Doug and me,
probably: I just kind of disappear next to this bloody huge
monument. I've always been kind of small, but anyone would
be small next to Doug. Doug was built too large for this world,
that's what I reckon. That was half the problem, probably.
France was like the Danish family's fancy picnic table or something, for Doug.

So Marcel's hand comes out again looking kind of stunned
and then Doug says to him, 'Marcel, you're a fuckin sleazebag.
Do you know that? A fuckin sleazebag, Marcel.'

Marcel kind of spreads his hands out like the Crucifixion and
his lips go all pouty ready to say something I suppose but Doug
says, 'Here, have a bloody peach, Marcel.'

And Doug plops a really huge peach onto Marcel's head, so
it kind of sits there like a fat type of red toad or something,
juice dripping off the end of Marcel's earlobes. Or rather, off
the end of his nice gold rings. Alabaster gets kind of hysterical,
of course, and Doug goes into the tent while I think: heck, this
Marcel's going to have to handle this like bone bloody china.
Though Doug's hardly ever swiped a soul before. I mean, he's
only hit me once in his life, and that was after a really bad trip
way back in the Adelaide days.

But Marcel just takes the peach off his head real slow and I
think: Hell, he's not quite such a dag after all, this Marcel. And
he kind of looks at the squished-up peach in his hand, real
sticky, and he just goes 'hm'. Just like that. 'Hm.' Almost like
he was *agreeing* with Doug. I thought: I wouldn't like to be
Marcel's barber right now. I really thought that! Stupid. Then
Doug appears again with our pail half-full of frothy old smelly
water from my clothes wash and says to Marcel, 'Heck, Marcel,
you look as if you need a real good shower.' And I thought:
Christ, he's going to tip the whole lot over Marcel's head. We're
going to have a real heavy blue on our hands if this goes on
much further. And Marcel must've been thinking this too,

because he was already sort of half off the canvas fold-up grinning like a maniac while Doug's raising up the pail and Marcel
ducks and sort of waddles away a bit with his arms right out
and he's not got that far when Doug lets him have it – with all
that smelly old water shooting out the pail and most of it hitting
Marcel's back, smack! Making him look even scrawnier than
usual.

'Why'd you do that, Doug?' I said, kind of lightly.

Doug said, 'I don't like pervs.'

Marcel was looking really hard at his cigarette. I think he
couldn't give a fuck about his wet clothes, because it was real
hot, but he was kind of upset by his damp smoke.

'What d'you mean, Doug?' I said.

'What I mean,' said Doug, 'is I don't like pervs.'

'I don't think he wants the van back, Doug.'

Actually, the van'd just gone crook, and sounded like it had
a pregnant elephant instead of a carbie, but we weren't telling
Marcel that just yet, or he might've gone funny and blamed us.

Doug sat down on the canvas fold-up like he wanted to flatten
it. Some of the other campers were glancing over. I guess things
over our way looked kind of interesting. Marcel started to walk
away without looking back, which rather surprised me. I didn't
like him much, but he was kind of our one and only friend.
Well, if you didn't count our neighbours and the weird old
French guy with the mangy goat on a rope we were always
trying to shake off by the telephone booth, he was the only
bloody one! Marcel was the only one who'd got Doug a job,
anyway. And he'd lent us the van. I mean, you've got to start
somewhere. As Doug'd say: 'We're on a one-way ticket, Linda.'
Which was literally true.

I gave Alabaster a banana and parked myself down by Doug.
We heard the jeep start up and leave like he had to get somewhere yesterday.

'He was only saying hello, Doug. Hello there. *Bonjour*. I
know it looked like he was making love or something, Doug,
but it's not like it is back home, out here. Anyway, I reckon

he's into guys, Doug. That scent. Earrings. And all that Pierre stuff, Doug.'

I put my hand on Doug's knee. It looked bloody stupid, I thought, my teeny weeny hand on Doug's really huge knee. I wanted to cry. I started to wish we'd never bloody left Australia. Alabaster'd finished her banana and she started to whinge again, so I gave her a tiny slap and she went off screaming. I put my face in my hands. I felt depressed, actually, but I couldn't let myself go under. I had to support Doug. I screwed up my eyes and thought of that figure behind Linguistics. That was me. In basalt. Real strong and all that, arms out wide. It didn't matter if no one could see her. I was still there, fuck it.

Doug just kind of stared out at the vineyards, like a monument.

I stood up and spread my arms out wide and stayed like that for about a minute. Then I sat down again on the ground next to Doug. I felt better.

'He came to say he'd got you a first-class job, Doug. Stonework. A big barn. Some really huge barn for a vineyard or something. I feel this is it, Doug. I feel you've got to swallow your pride and phone Marcel, Doug. That's what I feel, anyway.'

He did. That was what was so big about Doug. He never kind of rested on his pride or anything. He got up and phoned him. Phoned Marcel.

Partial Eclipse

Extract from a novel in progress

There they go again. Watching me. I say 'they', I should say she. However she is one of them. Eyes seen through a slit. Identikit. Eyes seen through a slit are never kind eyes. Eyes cut from a face. A rectangle; eyebrows, eyes, bridge of nose. Glasses sometimes. Eyes seen thus are cold eyes, mean. Take the roundest, bluest, kindest eyes and view them through a slot from inside a cell and they will seem cruel. Be cruel.

Slap and the slot closes. Reminds me of a letter flap. Slip slap letters on the mat. Cards at Christmas and parcels. The postman called in the afternoons on the special days before Christmas, laden down with good things: robins, snowmen, chocolate, scent.

No letters for me in here, however. And I have not the faintest idea of the time. The last meal was, I think, tea. Grey soup, white bread, grey apple pulp between two pastry squares. A cup of tea. Lukewarm. After every meal I vow to starve myself. But there is simply nothing to do and eating – even this colourless crap – is something to do.

I call them meals! I should not dignify them so. I long for proper food: breakfast, lunch, dinner. The comfortable rhythm of ingestion and digestion. Afternoon tea on Sundays after a roast lunch. 'Meal' meant something special. *He asked me out for a meal*, candlelight and whipped cream and silver forks glinting.

Nothing glints in here, nothing glistens and glows. The light is dim. It is never dark and never light, only dim. Perpetually dusk, perpetually the bleak moment before you'd draw the curtains, bank up the fire, flood the room with light.

I do not say I do not deserve it. Or rather, that what I have done deserves it. Or what they say I have done. Prison is what they do to you. The confiscation of liberty. They take something you never really knew you had. That is the worst they do. I should be grateful. I am still alive. People have died. I am alive and I am fed and clothed – though this canvas thing I have to wear is scarcely becoming. No one to see me though. Just the eyes through the slot. I have a bucket and the air in here is acrid and it is not just my smell. There is an accumulated smell of despair, of desolation.

The walls are the same colour as the floor. That is the worst of it. What I would not give for a splash of brightness. But it is all somewhere between grey and beige, a fungal colour, and so is my dress and so is the food and so is my skin in the dimness. Women bite themselves. Bite their arms until they bleed. Self-mutilation it's called, evidence of deep disturbance. Perhaps they simply want to see some colour, the bright luxurious glossy red of blood.

But I could never hurt myself. Strange how I hate violence. Strange I mean that *I* hate violence. I could never bite my arm to see the blood flowering. No, I could not.

Mama died when I was in my final year at university, reading English, doing well. It was only after she'd died that I saw that the doing well was all for her. To make up. Up for what?

She took me away for Christmas the year before she died. To a hotel in Scotland: Pitlochry. We travelled by coach. The wheels shushed along the motorway, through pouring rain, and even at midday it was almost dark, with sharp reflected flakes of light thrown up from the wetness, glittering on the windows.

Mama was dressed up. She wore a soft blue fuzzy hat, doughnut-shaped on her soft grey fuzzy hair and pink lipstick that had spidered into the lines around her mouth. She had her tatting on her lap. She was making a lace collar. A lace collar for what? In creamy thread. But the motion of the coach and the smoke drifting forward from the back seats made her feel sick and so she closed her eyes instead.

'Who'd have thought it?' she said.

I'd been gazing at the dull greenness that had risen into hills. The rain drops jiggled and streaked down the glass.

'What?'

'*Us*. Off for Christmas. And to an hotel.'

'Mmmm.'

'Not stayed in an hotel since . . .' Her memory failed her.

'Did you and Bob? I can't imagine Bob . . .'

'Honeymoon.' She smiled reminiscently.

I laughed, at the thought of my grandfather as a honeymooner.

'A *naturist* hotel.'

'But of course.' I closed my eyes against the memory of Bob and the hideous embarrassment of his naked body. 'Were you in love?' I asked.

'Yes. Very much.'

'Was it a naturist wedding?'

'All these questions! You know very well it wasn't.'

And she was right. There had been almost no photographs in our house, but I do remember one, a wedding photo framed in rippled walnut on their bedroom wall. Mama and Bob, young and strange. Bob, handsome but for a certain look, a look that hardened over the years until it became the shape of his head, his whole attitude. Inturned aggression, was it? And Mama, startlingly girlish with fine bones and eyes, a soft young hand on Bob's arm, a white bird against the black sleeve. Her hands were in her lap now, clutching and fidgeting with her handbag strap. They were broad hands, made coarse and stubby with the years, veins risen like soft blue worms on their backs.

How I crave softness now that all is hard. Here, alone, I touch my own breasts. They are miraculously cool and soft against my hands, the nipples like the blunt noses of docile pets. The pleasure is all in my hands as if they were not my breasts at all.

The hotel was what Bob would have called genteel in a tone of voice midway between admiration and scorn. It was built like a castle, set back from the road down a long sweeping drive between dark shrubs and trees. The lighting – it was after dark when we arrived, late afternoon on Christmas Eve – was discreet, puddled gold on the thick carpets, drizzling finely from the Christmas tree, a tree all forest-green and silver. No lovely tasteless, meaningful tat. No fairy on the top, but a tailored silver bow.

Mama was servile before the servile porter. They were almost competitively deferential and I had to insist that she allow the porter to lug our cases upstairs.

In our room was a Christmas card from the management – sheep lit to a dusky apricot by a low winter sun. It invited us to a festive sherry reception in the lobby at 7 p.m.

Mama raised her shoulders in anticipation. She removed her hat, smoothing down her wispy perm.

'Isn't it lovely Jenny,' she asked, anxious that I should be pleased, grateful, impressed.

I sat on the edge of my bed, bounced a bit to test the springs. 'Yes,' I agreed. 'Lovely.'

She found the bathroom. 'Look! Little soaps . . . little bubble baths . . . little shower caps!'

'Why not have a bath?' I suggested. 'There's time before seven.'

'Oooh, I couldn't.'

I shrugged. I would not be irritated. This was her attempt, brave attempt, to make things good for Christmas. The truth is, it had never been right at home since Bob died. Seven Christmases where no matter how we arranged the table there was still a gap. And now Auntie May had died, at 106, a brown and shrunken relic of herself, and Christmas with only the two of us was too much to contemplate.

Yes. It is like touching someone else's breasts. I have nothing soft to wear. This garment – strong-dress, shift – is stiff canvas, ugly, it chafes my armpits. The ends of my fingers are soft and

blunt. They clip your nails in here, if you do not bite them
yourself, snip and snip them down hard so there is no scratching
edge. It feels so childish. We line up, hold out our hands. And
along the warder goes with the clippers, clipping so low it snags
the cuticles. With no edge my finger ends feel blunt and numb
as rubbers on the end of pencils. Neat pink stubs.

Possibly it is the loss of control that is worse than the loss of
freedom. And the loss of privacy. Oh you might think I'm
private enough here, in this grey box. But at any moment the
slot can open and the rectangular eyes stare in. It is not a
communicative look. It is all one way.

I caught his eye over the sherry. Or he caught mine. Our eyes
met, anyway. At first I didn't notice his wife and child. Our
eyes met and there was such a warmth flowing from him that
I smiled, a real, budding, blooming, flower of a smile. And
then Mama spoke and I turned away. But as I listened to Mama
I could feel his eyes on me still, feel the warmth across my
shoulders, trickling down my back. A waiter circulated with
bright things in aspic on a silver tray. Mama was ecstatic at the
beauty of the food: pink shrimps like babies' fingers, asparagus
tips and tiny fish all decorated with sprigged herbs and glowing
under their viscous aspic skin.

'Don't ruin your appetite though,' she warned.

We had yet to be introduced, and the room was full of shy
couples and groups and one ostentatiously lone woman, tall and
white-haired in a floor-length kaftan encrusted with strange
designs. I looked round for the man. He was deep in conversation with the woman beside him, a beautiful woman, his wife.
But when he felt my eyes on him, he turned and once again
there was this tangible warmth. Beside him a small toothy girl
pulled at his sleeve. 'Da-ad.' He spoke to her distractedly, hardly
breaking the look between us that was like some sort of gravi-
tational pull, something irresistible, inevitable. I studied him.
His hair was brown, thinning, pushed back from his face. He
had a clipped beard, dark with two badgerish grey streaks. He

was old around his eyes, much older than me. The beautiful woman's look broke my own. Her eyes met mine and she smiled quizzically. She had a neck like a stem and hair piled high and soft, blue-black hair, black eyes, a rose-brown skin.

Dinner was called and Mama and I took our places at a small table by the door. The lone woman had an even smaller table beside us.

'Poor thing,' Mama whispered. 'All alone on Christmas Eve. What do you suppose she'd got on her frock?'

'No idea,' I said.

The man and his family were across the dining room by the window. The electric light was low, and red candles with holly leaf bases were all lit so that the room was suffused with a watery waxy light. The man had his back to me and I quenched a flicker of disappointment. He wore a Fair-Isle sweater and his hair curled over the neck of it, a bit unkempt. He was not as well groomed as his wife. The child had blue patches under her eyes, a tired fractious child who should have been in bed. I caught her voice now and then throughout the meal in little whining snatches.

Mama read the menu. 'Exquisite calligraphy,' she remarked. 'Pheasant soup, goujons of smoked duck or melon and Parma ham. What, do you suppose, is a goujon?'

'Excuse me,' said the lone woman leaning towards us. 'Excuse me, but might I peruse your menu. After you, of course.'

'Of course,' I said.

'The same old story,' she continued stridently. 'A woman alone, shoved at a rickety table in a draught. Look!' She wobbled the table to demonstrate its ricketiness so that the glasses slid and the candle leaned dangerously.

'Shocking,' Mama agreed, looking round apologetically.

I got up and handed the woman the menu. 'Ursula,' she said. 'Ursula Glass. How do you do?'

'Well thanks,' I replied. 'I'm Jenny and this is my grand-mother.'

'Lilian,' Mama added. She was looking curiously at Ursula's kaftan.

'Marine artefacts,' Ursula explained. She rose from her chair, wobbling the table again so that the candle actually tipped and singed the edge of her paper serviette. She approached our table and displayed the seashells, the desiccated starfish and seahorses. I caught a whiff of rotting seaweed. '*Appliqué sauvage*, I call it.'

'*Very* effective.' I could see Mama's thoughts running ahead. She loved a new idea. Once, in a mosaic phase, she had smashed much of her perfectly good china to add their fragments to her teapot stands and lamp bases. 'Why not join *us*.' Mama said. 'There's plenty of room. And you shouldn't be alone, not on Christmas Eve. We'd love you to join us, wouldn't we Jenny?'

'Yes,' I said. It was nice to see Mama so animated. A waiter reorganised us and Ursula sat down, shifting about until she'd arranged the kaftan so there were no shells sticking in to her.

The beautiful woman was sipping something sparkling. She wore a plain black sweater just low enough to show the moulding of her collar bones, a shadowy hollow in between. The man reached across the table and touched her cheek and I looked away.

Every morning, when they have taken away the stinking mattress and blanket, I suck the skin of my inner arm, the whitest tenderest part. I suck until I make a mark – a love-bite. It is hard to do, there, near the crook of my elbow because the veins are so far beneath the surface. But I suck until there is a small risen oval of skin prickled red with broken capillaries. There is no love involved. This is simply a method of recording the passage of time. Otherwise with the sameish meals and the utterly sameish pattern, the patternless days, I might lose count, lose my bearings. And that is my fear. The light is always the same, grim grey, as if light itself could be grimy and stale. It is mean.

There are three lozenges on my arm, my calendar. One dull speckled red – today's – one purplish, one fading already to green. So I lied when I said there was no colour. I have colourful bruises too. One on my shin, a ragged, pleasing bruise, blue and purple, grey where it fades at the edges into the unstained skin. It has the look of a mountain range, far off and clouded. When there are seven love-bites lined up on my arm they should release me into a place where at least there is light, where there are faces, and work to do. Where there is a soothing childish rhythm. Bed-time at eight. Get up at six. Early to bed, early to rise. And I am healthy. Scarcely wealthy. But am I wise?

Jack Sprat's Wife

She did him in with various sorts of poison, which she bought locally – stuff for slugs, for vermin, for repelling midges, for scrubbing. She used a little at a time, adding the worst sorts to Indian food laden with jeera and cayenne or even Chinese twice-cooked dishes and heavy on the five spice. In the end, he just keeled over, a little bleeding, a delicate foam on the lips, a terrified clutch of his washboard abdominals and *poum*. Really, without the pumping Dolby, the panic music, the plot build-up, it was no horror film. She was, after all, expert at handling meat.

The local butchers jostled for her custom, because she relished the selection of the meat. They saved for her the reddest, blood-iest, most glistening, most finely veined cuts, marbled with fat. At home she had to remove the extra fat. So many kinds. . . . The yellow plastic of lamb shoulder and the glutinous jelly white of pork loin; the rubber shell of belly and the loose, melting duck fat; the efficient lard of game and the animal oil of chicken. She pictured all the fat binding onto various parts of her flesh, gripping her as it entered her mouth, travelled through her gullet and arrived. The meat she cooked was good, she made sure of that; shelves upon shelves of books she had consumed to get it right. Nothing should ever be badly done.

He loved it.

'Oh my cook. My baby cook. Delicious,' he would say, masticating.

He loved beef meat especially. He loved it casseroled, *en daube*, on the bone, *en croûte*, cold between bread slices, minced in a burger, roast with trimmings, in goulash, *paupiettes*, as tournedos, entrecôte, New York cut, cold in hanks hacked off the roast with grain mustard, with dill pickles, with pickled

onions, with relish. He never put on one ounce of the beef fat.
She had it all. She gave him her food and he gave her back the
fat. It dripped off her, through her, it never stopped cuddling
her. In this life you have to be thin, she said, hating every part
of herself.

She trod water daily at the municipal pool. While swimmers
swam laps, she squatted in the miniscus, flailing her big arms
and legs like a water boatman. She exercised in water because
on dry land she had a pungent, sexual smell from the way her
thighs met at the top and sweated. She hoped it was something
only she could smell until, one night *in flagrante*, he whispered
hoarsely how it turned him on. Sex was fine though. Sex was
OK as long as she stretched out the side he was touching so
that there weren't rolls of spare under his hand; as long as he
wasn't looking at her legs when she crooked them and the thigh
bulk swung untensed; as long as she didn't have to bend over
and show her splayed rear which was like a horse's on fetlock
ankles. When she thought about sex, she thought about other
women doing it, wonderwomen with breasts as large as hers,
but shaped with a snap and nestled on bodies of boys.

Once she had him butchered, packaged in polythene bags,
labelled and in the freezer, things changed. She found a new
skill. Now she was able to lean over the toilet bowl and insert
one finger between her lips – the middle finger, longest and
thinnest, and now for a few months past, uniquely among her
fingers, cold as ice. She would tease her uvula like a nipple until
her gullet was aroused, then pull out the finger. She would
draw a breath, then re-insert the finger, then a breath, then a
re-insertion, until out it came, coated with a caul of mucus,
pulling a string of bright slime from deeper than her mouth. In
again, and out came the thin bile and the topmost food, flowering white in the bowl. A tickle of uvula, then more slime,
digestive slime, bile slime, the inside stuff that broke down the
calories. Now she would rest, panting, hair messed, then go in
again. Some time and some few insertions later and everything

that went in that way came out that way. There was no nausea.

It was a fine development. Time was, she was condemned to follow his schedule of meals and absences. The few moments after breakfast were each day's hope, the hiatus that contained a seed of her possible self, a thin self. But every morning when he'd kissed her and closed the door, she froze, head cocked at his footfall like a hunted roe, ensuring his complete departure so she could begin. Then, oh then . . . to stand alone at the freezer door, gothic ice steam spilling, to peel the foil off a corner and take a teaspoon to the fudge frosting on a frozen gateau, oh yes . . . To pull white chicken in strings off its hollow bones and cram it in her mouth, sliding a finger in the gelatinous gravy; to put her incisors to the dusky limb meat, snapping the ball and socket joint and tearing strips of tanned skin, fatty and rich – yes, oh yes.

It was awful when he came back, weary and glad to see her, and she had to pick publicly at morsels without the sauce and be fat anyway. She was anxious that he might appear in the kitchen any moment to dry the dishes or kiss the back of her neck. She saw the things he did to show his love as those old-fashioned flashbulbs that make a metallic *whump*, catching her spoon-in-mouth, chocolate-lipped.

Weekdays, when he'd gone, it was only by eating that she could tame time. However many loops she added to her daily round, time was always draped in loose fronds, dripping off the ends of the vacuuming, hanging from the ironing board, lying in ambush as she lugged the shopping inside or scrubbed the chlorine from her skin in the pool shower. If she didn't eat often, she felt, her ropes would come unguyed like a balloon's or a tent's and she'd drift like a cloud or else her giant summer dress would billow and ripple and sink to the ground, empty, and nobody would know she'd been inside it. As long as she was alone indoors, unchilded, unseen, jobless, her molecules had a tenuous grip. But eating made an animal of her, fleshed the day. Surely somebody should see this, she thought, hand pumping from cereal box to mouth, cereal box, mouth, box-mouth, box-mouth. It didn't seem to bear any relation to her shape.

The freezer well stocked with him made her feel secure. It took the best part of two days to accomplish, sweating through the Indian summer heatwave in an ill-lit kitchen, abuzz with flies. On the third day she made an *estouffade*, enriching the sauce with anchovies, kalamata olives, half a bottle of his prized '82 Châteauneuf du Pape and mauve-skinned garlic from the organic shop. She deserved it.

Afterwards she slept. Time now was a kindly old thing, softening the hours and presenting them pillowed as a reward for her diligence. And when she came to, the gorge was rising and she fled to the bathroom and hid her head in the bowl and vomited for the first time, spirits soaring as her calories plopped into the sewage. Kneeling and leaning over like that, she could detect perhaps an inch less of midriff, that little bit more waist already. And in the pool later, she allowed herself a lap or two, dodged by the athletic girls in frog goggles and racerback suits, but not minding. Oh no, soon she too would be selecting a flimsy slip of emerald nylon and fitting her rubber skullcap, the envy of fat ladies. Soon, with his love inside her, she was going to be thin too.

On a Monday or a Tuesday after some while had passed, it was his birthday, but she forgot until the phone rang.

'No,' she said to his mother, 'he had to go on a trip.'

'That's not like him,' said mother, 'to go away on his birthday. Where is he?'

She thought fast, distracted by a pinch of dirty lard that happened suddenly above her pant rim.

'Bath. He went to Bath.'

'Goodness. Well, he might have rung to tell me. You know, actually he hasn't rung me in a long time. Why didn't you go with him, my dear? Are you two all right?'

'Oh yes yes yes. It's fine. Fine fine.'

'Well, if you're sure. But you usually make such a fuss of each other for birthdays. How long is he staying in Bath?'

'Er, it depends,' she stretched an arm experimentally and the roll of fat pulled tight. 'He went to close a sale. It could take another week.'

'Oh dear. Oh what a shame . . .'

'Why?' she said.

'Well, I was coming up to town and . . .'

She tried very hard to mind what she'd done before his mother came, but she really couldn't, not with his love inside her. He would have rented a flat in Bath, she knew. He would have been ringing every evening. He would have been telling her he misses her and that he isn't eating so well and he is losing weight.

'My you've lost weight, dear,' said his mother at the door, presenting her with a pound box of Quality Street. 'Are you eating properly?'

She took the sweets and smiled without exposing teeth.

'Yes. It's a special diet.'

'Well, you must tell me your secret. The battle of the bulge is never won.' She patted her own portion of stomach flab. 'I could stand to lose a little too.'

Naturally, they talked about him at dinner, which was special to make up for his absence. She'd roasted garlicky potatoes and buttered parsnips alongside a loin joint, reduced the *jus* with a splash of marsala wine and served this with steamed kale and a herb salad dressed with lemon-dijon.

'This obviously wasn't how you got so slim,' said his mother, smacking her lips. 'It's soft as butter. How long did you marinate it? Oh no no no, I mustn't. Well, perhaps just a tiny slice.'

When the platter was polished, over some bitter chocolate sorbet with puréed raspberries and *crème fraîche*, she looked at his mother's contented face and sighed.

'He's good to me, you know. He gives me everything I want. He's the antidote to what ails me.'

'Yes, he loves you more than life itself. You're very lucky to have him.'

She beamed.

'We both are.'

The Chinese Lobster

The proprietors of the Orient Lotus alternate frenetic embellish-
ment with periods of lassitude and letting-go. Dr Himmelblau
knows this, because she has been coming here for quick lunches,
usually solitary, for the last seven years or so. She chose it
because it was convenient – it is near all her regular stopping-
places, the National Gallery, the Royal Academy, the British
Museum – and because it seemed unpretentious and quietly
comfortable. She likes its padded seats, even though the mock
leather is split in places. She can stack her heavy book-bags
beside her and rest her bones.

The window onto the street has been framed in struggling
cheese-plants as long as she can remember. They grow denser,
dustier, and still livelier as the years go by. They press their
cut-out leaves against the glass, the old ones holly-dark, the
new ones yellow and shining. The glass distorts and folds them,
but they press on. Sometimes there is a tank of coloured fish in
the window, and sometimes not. At the moment, there is not.
You can see bottles of soy sauce, and glass containers which
dispense toothpicks, one by one, and chrome-plated boxes full
of paper napkins, also frugally dispensed one by one.

Inside the door, for the last year or so, there has been a low
square shrine, made of bright jade-green pottery, inside which
sits a little brass god, or sage, in the lotus position, his comfortable belly on his comfortable knees. Little lamps, and sticks of
incense, burn before him in bright scarlet glass pots, and from
time to time he is decorated with scarlet and gold shiny paper
trappings. Dr Himmelblau likes the colour-mixture, the bright
blue-green and the saturated scarlet, so nearly the same weight.
But she is a little afraid of the god, because she does not know

who he is, and because he is obviously *really* worshipped, not just a decoration.

Today there is a new object, further inside the door, but still before the tables or the coathangers. It is a display-case, in black lacquered wood, standing about as high as Dr Himmelblau's waist – she is a woman of medium height – shining with new-ness and sparkling with polish. It is on four legs, and its lid and side-walls – about nine inches deep – are made of glass. It resembles cases in museums, in which you might see miniatures, or jewels, or small ceramic objects.

Dr Himmelblau looks idly in. The display is brightly lit, and arranged on a carpet of that fierce emerald-green artificial grass used by greengrocers and undertakers.

Round the edges, on opened shells, is a border of raw scallops, the pearly flesh dulling, the repeating half-moons of the orange-pink roes playing against the fierce green.

In the middle, in the very middle, is a live lobster, flanked by two live crabs. All three, in parts of their bodies, are in feeble perpetual motion. The lobster, slowly in this unbreath-able element, moves her long feelers and can be seen to move her little claws on the end of her legs, which cannot go forward or back. She is black, and holds out her heavy great pincers in front of her, shifting them slightly, too heavy to lift up. The great muscles of her tail crimp and contort and collapse. One of the crabs, the smaller, is able to rock itself from side to side, which it does. The crabs' mouths can be seen moving from side to side, like scissors; all three survey the world with mobile eyes still lively on little stalks. From their mouths comes a silent hissing and bubbling, a breath, a cry. The colours of the crabs are matt, brick, cream, a grape-dark sheen on the claw-ends, a dingy, earthy encrustation on the hairy legs. The lobster was, is, and will not be, blue-black and glossy. For a moment, in her bones, Dr Himmelblau feels their painful life in the thin air. They stare, but do not, she supposes, see her. She turns on her heel and walks quickly into the body of the Orient Lotus. It occurs to her that the scallops too, are still in some sense, probably, alive.

The middle-aged Chinese man – she knows them all well, but knows none of their names – meets her with a smile, and takes her coat. Dr Himmelblau tells him she wants a table for two. He shows her to her usual table, and brings another bowl, china spoon, and chopsticks. The muzak starts up. Dr Himmelblau listens with comfort and pleasure. The first time she heard the muzak, she was dismayed, she put her hand to her breast in alarm at the burst of sound, she told herself that this was not after all the peaceful retreat she had supposed. Her noodles tasted less succulent against the tin noise. And then, the second or the third time, she began to notice the tunes, which were happy, banal, Western tunes, but jazzed up and sung in what she took to be Cantonese. 'Oh what a beautiful *morn*ing. Oh what a beautiful *day*. I've got a kind of a *feel*ing. Everything's *go*-ing my *way*.' Only in the incomprehensible nasal syllables, against a zithery plink and plunk, a kind of gong, a sort of bell. It was not a song she had ever liked. But she has come to find it the epitome of restfulness and cheerfulness. Twang, tinkle, plink, *plink*. A cross-cultural object, an occidental Orient, an oriental Western. She associates it now with the promise of delicate savours, of warmth, of satisfaction. The middle-aged Chinese man brings her a pot of green tea, in the pot she likes, with the little transparent rice-grain flowers in the blue and white porcelain, delicate and elegant.

She is early. She is nervous about the forthcoming conversation. She has never met her guest personally, though she has of course seen him, in the flesh and on the television screen; she has heard him lecture, on Bellini, on Titian, on Mantegna, on Picasso, on Matisse. His style is orotund and idiosyncratic. Dr Himmelblau's younger colleagues find him rambling and embarrassing. Dr Himmelblau, personally, is not of this opinion. In her view, Perry Diss is always talking about something, not about nothing, and in her view, which she knows to be the possibly crabbed view of a solitary intellectual, nearing retirement, this is increasingly rare. Many of her colleagues, Gerda Himmelblau believes, do not *like* paintings. Perry Diss does. He loves them, like sound apples to bite into, like fair flesh, like sunlight. She is thinking in his style. It is a professional hazard, of her own generation. She has never had much style of her own, Gerda Himmelblau – only an acerbic accuracy, which is an *easy* style for a very clever woman who looks as though she ought to be dry. Not arid, she would not go so far, but dry. Used as a word of moderate approbation. She has long fine brown hair, caught into a serviceable knot in the nape of her neck. She wears suits in soft dark, not-quite-usual colours – damsons, soots, black tulips, dark mosses – with clean-cut cotton shirts, not masculine, but with no floppy bows or pretty ribbons – also in clear colours, palest lemon, deepest cream, periwinkle, faded flame. The suits are cut soft but the body inside them is, she knows, sharp and angular, as is her Roman nose and her judiciously tightened mouth.

She takes the document out of her handbag. It is not the original, but a photocopy, which does not reproduce all the idiosyncrasies of the original – a grease-stain, maybe butter, here, what looks like a bloodstain, watered-down at the edges, there, a kind of Rorschach stag-beetle made by folding an ink-blot, somewhere else. There are also minute drawings, in the margins and in the text itself. The whole is contained in a border of what appear to be high arched wishbones, executed with a fine brush, in Indian ink. It is addressed in large majuscules

TO THE DEAN OF WOMEN STUDENTS
DR GERDA HIMMELBLAU

and continues in minute minuscules

from peggi nollett, woman and student.

It continues:

I wish to lay a formal complaint against the DISTIN-GUISHED VISITING PROFESSOR the Department has seen fit to appoint as the supervisor of my dissertation on *The Female Body and Matisse*.

In my view, which I have already made plain to anybody who cared to listen, and specificly to Doug Marks, Tracey Avison, Annie Manson, and also to you, Dr Gerda Himmelblau, this person should never have been assigned to direct this work, as he is *completley out of sympathy* with its feminist project. He is a so-called EXPERT on the so-called MASTER of MODERNISM but what does he know about Woman or the internal conduct of the Female Body, which has always until now been MUTE and had no mouth to speak.

Here followed a series of tiny pencil drawings which, in the original, Dr Himmelblau could make out to be lips, lips ambiguously oral or vaginal, she put it to herself precisely, sometimes parted, sometimes screwed shut, sometimes spattered with what might be hairs.

His criticisms of what I have written so far have always been null and extremely agressive and destructive. He does not understand that my project is a-historical and *need not involve* any description of the so-called development of Matisse's so-called style or approach, since what I wish to state is esentially *critical*, and presented from a *theoretical* viewpoint with insights provided from contemporary critical methods to which the cronology of Matisse's life or the order in which he comitted his 'paintings' is *totaly irelevant*.

However although I thought I should begin by stating my theoretical position yet again I wish at the present time to lay a spercific complaint of *sexual harasment* against the DVP. I can and will go into much more detail believe me

Dr Himmelblau but I will set out the gist of it so you can see there is something here *you must take up*.

I am writing while still under the effect of the shock I have had so please excuse any incoherence.

It began with my usual dispiriting CRIT with the DVP. He asked me why I had not writen more of the disertation than I had and I said I had not been very well and also preocupied with getting on with my art-work, as you know, in the Joint Honours Course, the creative work and the Art History get equal marks and I had reached a *very difficult stage* with the Work. But I had writen some notes on Matisse's *distortions* of the Female Body with respect especially to the spercificaly Female Organs, the Breasts the Cunt the Labia etc etc and also to his ways of acumulating Flesh on certain Parts of the Body which appeal to Men and tend to imobilise Women such as grotesquely swollen Thighs or protruding Stomachs. I mean to conect this in time to the whole tradition of the depiction of Female Slaves and Odalisques but I have not yet done the research I would need to write on this.

Also his Women tend to have no features on their faces, they are Blanks, like Dolls, I find this sinister.

Anyway I told the DVP what my line on this was going to be even if I had not yet writen very much and he argued with me and went so far as to say I was hostile and full of hatred to Matisse. I said this was not a relevant criticism of my work and that Matisse was hostile and full of hatred towards women. He said Matisse was full of love and desire towards women(!!!!!) and I said '*exactly*' but he did not take the point and was realy quite cutting and undermining and dismisive and unhelpful even if no worse had hapened. He even said in his view I ought to fail my degree which is no way for a supervisor to behave as you will agree. I was so tense and upset by his atitude that I began to cry and he pated me on my shoulders and tried to be a bit nicer. So I explained how busy I was with my

art-work and how my art-work, which is a series of
mixed-media pieces called Erasures and Undistortions was
a part of my criticism of Matisse. So he *graciously* said he
would like to see my art-work as it might help him to
give me a better grade if it contributed to my ideas on
Matisse. He said art students often had dificulty expresing
themselves verbally although he himself found language
'as sensuous as paint.' [It is not my place to say anything
about his prose style but I could] [*This sentence is heavily
but legibly crossed out.*]

Anyway he came – *kindly* – to my studio to see my
Work. I could see imediately he did not like it, indeed was
repeled by it which I supose was not a surprise. It does
not try to be agreable or seductive. He tried to put a good
face on it and admired one or two *minor* pieces and went
so far as to say there was a great power of feeling in the
room. I tried to explain my project of *revising* or *reviewing*
or *rearranging* Matisse. I have a three-dimensional piece in
wire and plaster-of-paris and plasticine called *The Resistance of Madame Matisse* which shows her and her daughter
being *tortured* as they *were* by the Gestapo in the War whilst
he sits by like a Buddha cutting up pretty paper with
scissors. They wouldn't tell him they were being tortured
in case it disturbed his *work*. I felt sick when I found out
that. The torturers have got identical scissors.

Then the DVP got personal. He put his arm about me
and hugged me and said *I had got too many clothes on. He said
they were a depressing colour* and he thought I ought to take
them all off and *let the air get to me*. He said he would like
to see me in bright colours and that I was really a *very
pretty girl* if I would let myself go. I said my clothes were
a statement about myself, and he said they were a *sad
statement* and then he grabed me and began kissing me and
fondling me and stroking intimate parts of me – it was
disgusting – I will not write it down, but I can describe it
clearly, believe me Dr Himmelblau, if it becomes

necesary, I can give chapter and verse of every detail, I am still shaking with shock. The more I strugled the more he insisted and pushed at me with his body until I said I would get the police the moment he let go of me, and then he came to his senses and said that in the *good old days* painters and models felt a bit of *human warmth and sensuality* towards each other in the studio, and I said, not in my studio, and he said, clearly not, and went off, saying it seemed to him *quite likely* that I should fail both parts of my Degree.

Gerda Himmelblau folds the photocopy again and puts it back into her handbag. She then rereads the personal letter which came with it.

Dear Dr Himmelblau,

I am sending you a complaint about a horible experience I have had. Please take it seriously and please help me. I am so unhapy, I have so little confidence in myself, I spend days and days just lying in bed wondering what is the point of geting up. I try to live for my work but I am very easily discouraged and sometimes everything seems so black and pointless it is almost hystericaly funny to think of twisting up bits of wire or modeling plasticine. Why bother I say to myself and realy there isn't any answer. I realy think I might be better off dead and after such an experience as I have just had I do slip back towards that way of thinking of thinking of puting an end to it all. The doctor at the Health Centre said just try to snap out of it what does *he* know? He ought to listen to people he can't realy know what individual people might do if they did *snap* as he puts it out of it, anyway out of what does he mean, snap out of what? The dead are snaped *into* black plastic sacks I have seen it on the television body bags they are called. I realy think a lot about being a body in a black bag that is what I am good for. Please help me Dr

Himmelblau. I frighten myself and the contempt of others is the last straw snap snap snap snap.

Yours sort of hopefully,

Peggi Nollett

Dr Himmelblau sees Peregrine Diss walk past the window with the cheese-plants. He is very tall and very erect – columnar, thinks Gerda Himmelblau – and has a great deal of well-brushed white hair remaining. He is wearing an olive-green cashmere coat with a black velvet collar. He carries a black lacquered walking-stick, with a silver knob, which he does not lean on, but swings. Once inside the door, observed by but not observing Dr Himmelblau, he studies the little god in his green shade, and then stands and looks gravely down on the lobster, the crabs and the scallops. When he has taken them in he nods to them, in a kind of respectful acknowledgement, and proceeds into the body of the restaurant, where the younger Chinese woman takes his coat and stick and bears them away. He looks round and sees his host. They are the only people in the restaurant; it is early.

'Dr Himmelblau.'

'Professor Diss. Please sit down. I should have asked whether you like Chinese food – I just thought this place might be convenient for both of us – '

'Chinese food – well-cooked, of course – is one of the great triumphs of the human species. Such delicacy, such intricacy, such simplicity, and so *peaceful* in the ageing stomach.'

'I like the food here. It has certain subtleties one discovers as one goes on. I have noticed that the restaurant is frequented by large numbers of real Chinese people – families – which is always a good sign. And the fish and vegetables are always very fresh, which is another.'

'I shall ask you to be my guide through the plethora of the menu. I do not think I can face Fried Crispy Bowels, however much, in principle, I believe in venturing into the unknown. Are you partial to steamed oysters with ginger and spring onions? So intense, so *light* a flavour – '

'I have never had them – '

'Please try. They bear no relation to cold oysters, whatever you think of those. Which of the duck dishes do you think is the most succulent . . . ?'

They chat agreeably, composing a meal with elegant variations, a little hot flame of chilli here, a ghostly fragrant sweetness of lychee there, the slaty tang of black beans, the elemental earthy crispness of beansprouts. Gerda Himmelblau looks at her companion, imagining him willy-nilly engaging in the assault described by Peggi Nollett. His skin is tanned, and does not hang in pouches or folds, although it is engraved with crisscrossing lines of very fine wrinkles absolutely all over – brows, cheeks, neck, the armature of the mouth, the eye-corners, the nostrils, the lips themselves. His eyes are a bright cornflower blue, and must, Dr Himmelblau thinks, have been quite extraordinarily beautiful when he was a young man in the 1930s. They are still surprising, though veiled now with jelly and liquid, though bloodshot in the corners. He wears a bright cornflower-blue tie, in rough silk, to go with them, as they must have been, but also as they still are. He wears a corduroy suit, the colour of dark slate. He wears a large signet ring, lapis lazuli, and his hands, like his face, are mapped with wrinkles but still handsome. He looks both fastidious, and marked by ancient indulgence and dissipation, Gerda Himmelblau thinks, fancifully, knowing something of his history, the bare gossip, what everyone knows.

She produces the document during the first course, which is glistening viridian seaweed, and prawn and sesame toasts. She says, 'I have had this rather unpleasant letter which I must talk to you about. It seemed to me important to discuss it informally and in an unofficial context, so to speak. I don't know if it will come as a surprise to you.'

Perry Diss reads quickly, and empties his glass of Tiger beer, which is quickly replaced with another by the middle-aged Chinese man.

'Poor little bitch,' says Perry Diss. 'What a horrible state of mind to be in. Whoever gave her the idea that she had any artistic talent ought to be shot.'

Don't say bitch, Gerda Himmelblau tells him in her head, wincing.

'Do you remember the occasion she complains of?' she asks carefully.

'Well, in a way I do, in a way. Her account isn't very recognisable. We did meet last week to discuss her complete lack of progress on her dissertation – she appears indeed to have *regressed* since she put in her proposal, which I am glad to say I was *not* responsible for accepting. She has forgotten several of the meagre facts she once knew, or appeared to know, about Matisse. I do not see how she can *possibly* be given a degree – she is ignorant and lazy and pigheadedly misdirected – and I felt it my duty to tell her so. In my experience, Dr Himmelblau, a lot of harm has been done by misguided kindness to lazy and ignorant students who have been cossetted and *nurtured* and never told they are not up to scratch.'

'That may well be the case. But she makes specific allegations – you went to her studio – '

'Oh yes, I went. I am not as brutal as I appear. I did try to give her the benefit of the doubt. That part of her account bears some resemblance to the truth – that is, to what I remember of these very disagreeable events. I did say something about the inarticulacy of painters and so on – you can't have worked in art schools as long as I have without knowing that some can use words and some can only use materials – it's interesting how you can't always predict *which*. Anyway, I went and looked at her so-called Work. The phraseology is catching. "So-called." A pantechnicon contemporary term of abuse.'

'And?'

'The work is *horrible*, Dr Himmelblau. It disgusts. It desecrates. Her studio – in which the poor creature also eats and

sleeps – is papered with posters of Matisse's work. *Le Rêve. Le
Nu Rose. Le Nu Bleu. Grande Robe Bleue. La Musique. L'Artiste
et son Modèle. Zorba sur la Terrasse.* And they have all been
smeared and defaced. With what looks like *organic matter* –
blood, Dr Himmelblau, beef stew or faeces – I incline towards
the latter since I cannot imagine good *daube* finding its way into
that miserable tenement. Some of the daubings are deliberate
reworkings of bodies or faces – changes of outlines – some are
like thrown tomatoes – probably *are* thrown tomatoes – and
eggs, yes – and some are *great swastikas of shit.* It is appalling. It
is pathetic.'

'It is no doubt meant to disgust and desecrate,' states Dr
Himmelblau, neutrally.

'And what does that matter? *How can that excuse it?*' roars
Perry Diss, startling the younger Chinese woman, who is lighting the wax lamps under the plate-warmer, so that she jumps
back.

'In recent times,' says Dr Himmelblau, 'art has traditionally
had an element of protest.'

'*Traditional protest, hmph,*' shouts Perry Diss, his neck redden-
ing. 'Nobody minds protest, I've protested in my time, we all
have, you aren't the real thing if you don't have a go at being
shocking, protest is *de rigueur, I know*. But what I object to
here, is the shoddiness, the laziness. It *seems to me* – forgive me,
Dr Himmelblau – but this – this *caca* offends something I do
hold sacred, a word that would make that little bitch *snigger*, no
doubt, but sacred, yes – it seems to me, that if she could have
produced *worked copies* of those – those masterpieces – those
shining – never mind – if she could have *done some work* –
understood the blues, and the pinks, and the whites, and the
oranges, yes, and the blacks too – and if she could still have
brought herself to feel she must – must *savage* them – then I
would have had to feel some respect.'

'You have to be careful about the word masterpieces,' mur-
murs Dr Himmelblau.

'Oh, I know all that stuff, I know it well. But you have got to listen to me. It can have taken at the maximum *half-an-hour* – and there's no evidence anywhere in the silly girl's work that she's ever spent more than that actually *looking at* a Matisse – she has no accurate memory of one when we talk, *none*, she amalgamates them all in her mind into one monstrous female corpse bursting with male aggression – she can't *see*, can't you see? And for half-an-hour's shit-spreading we must give her a degree?'

'Matisse,' says Gerda Himmelblau, 'would sometimes make a mark, and consider, and put the canvas away for weeks or months until he *knew* where to put the next mark.'

'I know.'

'Well – the – the shit-spreading may have required the same consideration. As to location of daubs.'

'Don't be silly. I *can* see paintings, you know. I did look to see if there was any wit in where all this detritus was applied. Any visual *wit*, you know, I know it's meant to be funny. There wasn't. It was just slapped on. It was horrible.'

'It was meant to disturb you. It disturbed you.'

'Look – Dr Himmelblau – whose side are you on? I've read your Mantegna monograph. *Mes compliments*, it is a *chef-d'oeuvre*. Have you *seen* this stuff? Have you for that matter *seen* Peggi Nollett?'

'I am not on anyone's *side*, Professor Diss. I am the Dean of Women Students, and I have received a formal complaint against you, about which I have to take formal action. And that could be, in the present climate, very disturbing for me, for the Department, for the University, and for yourself. I may be exceeding my strict duty in letting you know of this in this informal way. I am very anxious to know what you have to say in answer to her specific charge.

'And yes, I have seen Peggi Nollett. Frequently. And her work, on one occasion.'

'Well then. If you have seen her you will know that I can have made no such – no such *advances* as she describes. Her skin is like a *potato* and her body is like a *decaying potato*, in all that great bundle of smocks and vests and knitwear and penitential hangings. Have you seen her legs and arms, Dr Himmelblau? They are bandaged like mummies, they are all swollen with strapping and strings and then they are contained in nasty black greaves and gauntlets of plastic with buckles. You expect some awful yellow ooze to seep out between the layers, ready to be smeared on *La Joie de Vivre*. And her hair, I do not think her hair can have been washed for some years. It is like a carefully preserved old frying-pan, grease undisturbed by water. You *cannot believe* I could have brought myself to touch her, Dr Himmelblau?'

'It is difficult, certainly.'

'It is impossible. I may have told her that she would be better if she wore fewer layers – I may even, imprudently – thinking, you understand, of potatoes, – have said something about letting the air get to her. But I assure you that was as far as it went. I was trying against my instincts to converse with her as a human being. The rest is her horrible fantasy. I hope you will believe me, Dr Himmelblau. You yourself are about the only almost-witness I can call in my defence.'

'I do believe you,' says Gerda Himmelblau, with a little sigh.

'Then let that be the end of the matter,' says Perry Diss. 'Let us enjoy these delicious morsels and talk about something more agreeable than Peggi Nollett. These prawns are as good as I have ever had.'

'It isn't so simple, unfortunately. If she does not withdraw her complaint you will both be required to put your cases to the Senate of the University. And the University will be required – by a rule made in the days when university senates had authority and power and *money* – to retain QCs to represent both of you, should you so wish. And in the present climate I am very much afraid that whatever the truth of the matter, you will lose your job, and whether you do or don't lose it there will be disagreeable protests and demonstrations against you, your work, your continued presence in the University. And the Vice-Chancellor will fear the effect of the publicity on the funding of the College

– and the course, which is the only Joint Honours Course of its
kind in London – may have to close. It is *not* seen by our profit-
oriented masters as an essential part of our new – "Thrust", I
think they call it, our students do not contribute to the export
drive – '

'I don't see why not. They can't *all* be Peggi Nolletts. I was
about to say – have another spoonful of bamboo-shoots and
beansprouts – I was about to say, very well, I'll resign on the
spot and save you any further bother. But I don't think I can
do that. Because I won't give in to lies and blackmail. And
because that woman *isn't an artist*, and *doesn't work*, and *can't see*,
and should not have a degree. And because of Matisse.'

'Thank you,' says Gerda Himmelblau, accepting the vegetables. And 'Oh dear yes,' in response to the declaration of
intent. They eat in silence for a moment or two. The Cantonese
voice asserts that it is a beautiful *morn*ing. Dr Himmelblau says:

'Peggi Nollett is not well. She is neither physically nor mentally well. She suffers from anorexia. Those clothes are designed
to obscure the fact that she has starved herself, apparently,
almost to a skeleton.'

'Not a potato. A fork. A pin. A coathanger. I see.'

'And she is in a very depressed state. There have been at least
two suicide bids – to my knowledge.'

'Serious bids?'

'How do you define serious? Bids that would perhaps have
been effective if they had not been well enough signalled – for
rescue – '

'I see. You do know that this does not alter the fact that she
has no talent and doesn't work, and can't see – '

'She *might* – if she were well – '

'Do you think so?'

'No. On the evidence I have, no.' Perry Diss helps himself
to a final small bowlful of rice. He says, 'When I was in China,
I learned to end a meal with pure rice, quite plain, and to taste
every grain. It is one of the most beautiful tastes in the world,
freshly-boiled rice. I don't know if it would be if it was all you

had every day, if you were starving. It would be differently delicious, differently haunting, don't you think? You can't describe this taste.'

Gerda Himmelblau helps herself, manoeuvres delicately with her chopsticks, contemplates pure rice, says 'I see.'

'*Why Matisse*?' Perry Diss bursts out again, leaning forward. 'I can see she is ill, poor thing. You can *smell* it on her, that she is ill. That alone makes it unthinkable that anyone – that I – should *touch* her – '

'As Dean of Women Students,' says Gerda Himmelblau thoughtfully, 'one comes to learn a great deal about anorexia. It appears to stem from self-hatred and inordinate self-absorption. Especially with the body, and with that image of our own body we all carry around with us. One of my colleagues who is a psychiatrist collaborated with one of your colleagues in Fine Art to produce a series of drawings – clinical drawings in a sense – which I have found most instructive. They show an anorexic person before a mirror, and what *we* see – staring ribs, hanging skin – and what *she* sees – grotesque bulges, huge buttocks, puffed cheeks. I have found these most helpful.'

'Ah. *We* see coathangers and forks, and *she* sees potatoes and vegetable marrows. There is a painting in that. You could make an interesting painting out of that.'

'Please – the experience is terrible to her.'

'Don't think I don't know. I am not being flippant, Dr Himmelblau. I am, or was, a serious painter. It is not flippant to see a painting in a predicament. Especially a predicament which is essentially visual, as this is.'

'I'm sorry. I am trying to think *what to do*. The poor child wishes to annihilate herself. *Not to be*.'

'So I understand. But *why Matisse*? If she is obsessed with bodily horrors why does she not obtain employment as an emptier of bedpans or in a maternity ward or a hospice? And if she must take on Art, why does she not rework Giacometti into Maillol, or vice versa, or take on that old goat, Picasso, who did things to women's bodies out of genuine *malice. Why Matisse?*'

'Precisely for that reason, as you must know. Because he paints silent bliss. *Luxe, calme et volupté.* How can Peggi Nollett bear *luxe, calme et volupté*?'

'When I was a young man,' says Perry Diss, 'going through my own *Sturm und Drang*, I was a bit bored by all that. I remember telling someone – my wife – it all was *easy and flat*. What a fool. And then, one day I saw it. I saw how hard it is to see, and how full of pure power, once seen. Not *consolation*, Dr Himmelblau, *life and power*.' He leans back, stares into space, and quotes:

> *Mon enfant, ma soeur,*
> *Songe à la douceur*
> *D'aller là-bas vivre ensemble!*
> *Aimer à loisir*
> *Aimer et mourir*
> *Au pays qui te ressemble!*
> *Là, tout n'est qu'ordre et beauté*
> *Luxe, calme et volupté.*

Dr Himmelblau, whose own life has contained only a modicum of *luxe, calme et volupté*, is half-moved, half-exasperated by the vatic enthusiasm with which Perry Diss intones these words. She says drily, 'There has always been a resistance to these qualities in Matisse, of course. Feminist critics and artists don't like him because of the way in which he expands male eroticism into whole placid panoramas of well-being. Marxists don't like him because he himself said he wanted to paint to please businessmen.'

'Businessmen and intellectuals,' says Perry Diss.

'Intellectuals don't make it any more acceptable to Marxists.'

'Look,' says Perry Diss. 'Your Miss Nollett wants to shock. She shocks with simple daubings. Matisse was cunning and complex and violent and controlled and *he knew he had to know exactly what he was doing.* He knew the most shocking thing he could tell people about the purpose of his art was that it was designed *to please and to be comfortable.* That sentence of his about the armchair is one of the most wickedly provocative things that has ever been said about painting. You can daub the whole of the Centre Pompidou with manure from top to bottom and you will *never* shock as many people as Matisse did by saying art was like an armchair. People remember that with horror who know nothing about the context – '

'Remind me,' says Gerda Himmelblau.

' "What I dream of, is an art of balance, of purity, of quietness, without any disturbing subjects, without worry, which may be, for everyone who works with the mind, for the businessman as much as for the literary artist, something soothing, something to calm the brain, something analogous to a good armchair which relaxes him from his bodily weariness . . ." '

'It would be perfectly honourable to argue that that was a very *limited* view – ' says Gerda Himmelblau.

'Honourable but impercipient. Who is it that understands *pleasure*, Dr Himmelblau? Old men like me, who can only just remember their bones not hurting, who remember walking up a hill with a spring in their step like the red of the Red Studio. Blind men who have had their sight restored and get giddy with the colours of trees and plastic mugs and the *terrible blue* of the sky. Pleasure is *life*, Dr Himmelblau, and most of us don't have it, or not much, or mess it up, and when we see it in those blues, those roses, those oranges, that vermilion, we should fall down and worship – for it is *the thing itself*. Who knows a good armchair? A man who has bone-cancer, or a man who has been tortured, he can recognise a good armchair . . .'

'And poor Peggi Nollett,' says Dr Himmelblau. 'How can she see that, when she mostly wants to die?'

'Someone intent on bringing an action for rape, or whatever she calls it, can't be all that keen on death, will want to savour her triumph over her doddering male victim.'

'She is *confused*, Professor Diss. She puts out messages of all kinds, cries for help, threats . . .'

'Disgusting art-works – '

'It is truly not beyond her capacities to – to take an overdose and leave a letter accusing you – or me – of horrors, of insensitivity, of persecution – '

'Vengefulness can be seen for what it is. Spite and malice can be seen for what they are.'

'You have a robust confidence in human nature. And you simplify. The despair is as real as the spite. They are part of each other.'

'They are failures of imagination.'

'Of course,' says Gerda Himmelblau. 'Of course they are. Anyone who could imagine the terror – the pain – of those who survive a suicide – against whom a suicide is *committed* – could not carry it through.'

Her voice has changed. She knows it has. Perry Diss does not speak but looks at her frowning slightly. Gerda Himmelblau, driven by some pact she made long ago with accuracy, with truthfulness, says, 'Of course, when one is at that point, imagining others becomes unimaginable. Everything seems clear, and simple, and *single*, there is only one possible thing to be done – '

Perry Diss says, 'That is true. You look around you and everything is bleached, and clear, as you say. You are in a white box, a white room, with no doors or windows. You are looking through clear water with no movement – perhaps it is more like being inside ice, inside the white room. There is only one thing possible. It is all perfectly clear and simple and plain. As you say.'

They look at each other. The flood of red has subsided under Perry Diss's skin. He is thinking. He is quiet.

Any two people may be talking to each other, at any moment, in a civilised way about something trivial, or something, even, complex and delicate. And inside each of the two there runs a kind of dark river of unconnected thought, of secret fear, or violence, or bliss, hoped-for or lost, which keeps pace with the flow of talk and is neither seen nor heard. And at times, one or both of the two will catch sight or sound of this movement, in himself, or herself, or, more rarely, in the other. And it is like the quick slip of a waterfall into a pool, like a drop into darkness. The pace changes, the weight of the air, though the talk may run smoothly onwards without a ripple or quiver.

Gerda Himmelblau is back in the knot of quiet terror which has grown in her private self like a cancer over the last few years. She remembers, which she would rather not do, but cannot now control, her friend Kay, sitting in a heavy hospital arm-chair, covered with mock-hide, wearing a long white hospital gown, fastened at the back, and a striped towelled dressing-gown. Kay is not looking at Gerda. Her mouth is set, her eyes are sleepy with drugs. On the white gown are scarlet spots of fresh blood, where needles have injected calm into Kay. Gerda says, 'Do you remember, we are going to the concert on Thursday?' and Kay says, in a voice full of stumbling thick ill-will, 'No, I don't, what concert?' Her eyes flicker, she looks at Gerda and away, there is something malign and furtive in her look. Gerda has loved only one person in her life, her schoolfriend, Kay. Gerda has not married, but Kay has – Gerda was brides-maid – and Kay has brought up three children. Kay was peaceful and kindly and interested in plants, books, cakes, her husband, her children, Gerda. She was Gerda's anchor of sanity in a harsh world. As a young woman Gerda was usually described as 'nervous' and also as 'lucky to have Kay Leverett to keep her steady'. Then one day Kay's eldest daughter was found hanging in her father's shed. A note had been left, accusing her school-fellows of bullying. This death was not immediately the death of Kay – these things are crueller and slower. But over the years, Kay's daughter's pain became Kay's, and killed Kay. She said to Gerda once, who did not hear, who remembered only later, 'I turned on the gas and lay in front of the fire all afternoon, but nothing happened.' She 'fell' from a window, watering a window-box. She was struck a glancing blow by a bus in the street. 'I just step out now and close my eyes,' she told Gerda, who said don't be silly, don't be unfair to busdrivers./ Then there was the codeine overdose. Then the sleeping-pills, hoarded with careful secrecy. And a week after Gerda saw her in the hospital chair, the success, that is to say, the real death.

The old Chinese woman clears the meal, the plates veiled with syrupy black-bean sauce, the unwanted cold rice-grains, the uneaten mange-touts.

Gerda remembers Kay saying, earlier, when her pain seemed worse and more natural, and must have been so much less, must have been bearable in a way:

'I never understood how anyone *could*. And now it seems so clear, almost the only possible thing to do, do you know?'

'No, I don't,' Gerda had said, robust. 'You *can't do that* to other people. You have no right'.

'I suppose not,' Kay had said, 'but it doesn't feel like that.'

'I shan't listen to you,' Gerda had said. 'Suicide can't be handed on.'

But it can. She knows now. She is next in line. She has flirted with lumbering lorries, a neat dark figure launching herself blindly into the road. Once, she took a handful of pills, and waited to see if she would wake up, which she did, so on that day, she continued, drowsily nauseated, to work as usual. She believes the impulse is wrong, to be resisted. But at the time it is white, and clear, and simple. The colour goes from the world, so that the only stain on it is her own watching mind. Which it would be easy to wipe away. And then there would be no more pain.

She looks at Perry Diss who is looking at her. His eyes are half-closed, his expression is canny and watchful. He has used her secret image, the white room, accurately; they have shared it. *He knows that she knows*, and what is more, she knows that he knows. How he knows, or when he discovered, does not matter. He has had a long life. His young wife was killed in an air-raid. He caused scandals, in his painting days, with his relations with models, with young respectable girls who had not previously been models. He was the co-respondent in a divorce case full of dirt and hatred and anguish. He was almost an important painter, but probably not quite. At the moment his work is out of fashion. He is hardly treated seriously. Like Gerda Himmelblau he carries inside himself some chamber of ice, inside which sits his figure of pain, his version of kind Kay, thick-spoken and malevolent in a hospital hospitality-chair.

The middle-aged Chinese man brings a plate of orange segments. They are bright, they are glistening with juice, they are packed with little teardrop sacs full of sweetness. When Perry Diss offers her the oranges she sees the old scars, well-made *efficient* scars, on his wrists. He says, 'Oranges are the real fruit of Paradise, I always think. Matisse was the first to understand orange, don't you agree? Orange in light, orange in shade, orange on blue, orange on green, orange in black – I went to see him once, you know, after the war, when he was living in that apartment in Nice. I was full of hope in those days, I loved him and was enraged by him and meant to outdo him, some time soon, when I had just learned this and that – which I never did. I never did. He was ill then, he had come through his terrible operation, the nuns who looked after him called him *"le ressuscité"*.

'The rooms in that apartment were shrouded in darkness. The shutters were closed, the curtains were drawn. I was terribly shocked – I thought he *lived in the light*, you know, that was the idea I had of him. I blurted it out, the shock, I said, "Oh, how can you bear to shut out the light?" And he said, quite mildly, quite courteously, that there had been some question of him going blind. He thought he had better acquaint himself with the dark. And then he added, "And anyway, you know, black is the colour of light." Do you know the painting *La Porte Noire*? It has a young woman in an armchair quite at ease in a peignoir striped in lemon and cadmium and . . . over a white dress with touches of cardinal red – her chair is yellow ochre and scarlet – and at the side is the window and the coloured light and behind – above – is the black door. Almost no one could paint the colour black as he could. Almost no one.'

Gerda Himmelblau bites into her orange and tastes its sweetness. She says, 'He wrote "I believe in God when I work." '

'I think he also said "I am God when I work." Perhaps he is – not my God, but where – where I find that. I was brought up in the hope that I would be a priest, you know. Only I could not bear a religion which had a tortured human body hanging from the hands over its altars. No. I would rather have "The Dance".'

Gerda Himmelblau is gathering her things together. He continues, 'That is why I meant what I said, when I said that young woman's – muck-spreading – offended what I called sacred. What are we to do? I don't want her to – to punish us by self-slaughter – nor do I wish to be seen to condone the violence – the absence of *work* – '

Gerda Himmelblau sees, in her mind's eye, the face of Peggi Nollett, potato-pale, peering out of a white box with cunning, angry eyes in the slit between puffed eyelids. She sees golden oranges, rosy limbs, a voluptuously curved dark blue violin-case, in a black room. One or the other must be betrayed. Whatever she does, the bright forms will go on shining in the dark. She says, 'There is a simple solution. What she wants, what she has always wanted, what the Department has resisted, is a sympathetic supervisor – Tracey Avison, for instance – who shares her way of looking at things – whose beliefs – who cares about political ideologies of that kind – who will – '

'Who will give her a degree and let her go on in the way she is going in. It is a defeat.'

'Oh yes. It is a question of how much it matters. To you. To me. To the Department. To Peggi Nollett, too.'

'It matters very much and not at all,' says Perry Diss. 'She may see the light. Who knows?'

They leave the restaurant together. Perry Diss thanks Dr Himmelblau for his food and for her company. She is inwardly troubled. Something has happened to her white space, to her inner ice, which she does not quite understand. Perry Diss stops at the glass box containing the lobster, the crabs, the scallops – these last now decidedly dead, filmed with an iridescent haze of imminent putrescence. The lobster and the crabs are all still alive, all, more slowly, hissing their difficult air, bubbling, moving feet, feelers, glazing eyes. Inside Gerda Himmelblau's ribs and cranium she experiences, in a way, the pain of alien fish-flesh contracting inside an exo-skeleton. She looks at the lobster and the crabs, taking accurate distant note of the loss of gloss, the attenuation of colour.

'I find that *absolutely appalling*, you know,' says Perry Diss. 'And at the same time, exactly at the same time, I don't give a damn? D'you know?'

'I know,' says Gerda Himmelblau. She does know. Cruelly, imperfectly, voluptuously, clearly. The muzak begins again. '*Oh* what a *beautiful morn*ing. *Oh*, what a *beautiful day*.' She reaches up, in a completely uncharacteristic gesture, and kisses Perry Diss's soft cheek.

'Thank you,' she says. 'For everything.'

'Look after yourself,' says Perry Diss.

'Oh,' says Gerda Himmelblau. 'I will. I will.'

First Winter

She knows even before she opens her eyes that it has snowed again in the night. She knows by the smell, and by the light in her eyelids.

In their first house she woke almost every morning to this, the peculiar light, peculiar silence, relentless snow. She woke up first, like this, as if the stillness disturbed her sleep. Once, when she was still amazed that he could continue to sleep, still remain heavy in air that seemed weightless to her, when every room they were in together still seemed like his room, because it was his house – she leaned over the edge of the bed, half-asleep, and wrote something on what she remembers was a bookmark. She no longer has the bookmark, but what she wrote, some part of a poem she never finished, floats to the surface when she is dozing now, so she is almost speaking it by the time she realises it has snowed again.

> I wake to the delicate chain of early morning,
> snow-light barely through the blinds
> you never raise –
> I have been dreaming . . .

She can't remember what she has been dreaming about, but as always with snow, it feels like a beginning, urging her awake and moving before she is really ready.

She opens her eyes and sees the white-blue light of new snow, perhaps of snow still falling, coming in around the red velvet curtains. The room is still dark because of the curtains, and she misses the blinds which let in the light in their first house. She would change the velvet if she could, but she can't, because this isn't her house, or even her husband's, but his mother's.

She gets up and dresses, all in one movement, freezing. She bends close to her husband, touches his back. It is cool, and she pulls the covers up around him.

She goes through to the sitting room. The curtains are open in here all the time, even at night, to keep the condensation from being so bad, and this morning the white light is blinding. She stands at the bay window; outside, the houses of the village are dotted down the hill, rounded, still sleeping, shut tight against the weather. At the bottom, she can just make out the two parallel marks of a single car's wheels which passed in front of the church sometime in the night. And beyond, on the other side of the valley, silent white hills echo those behind her.

She takes her jacket from the banister, puts it on, and walks through to the kitchen, closing the door behind her. She coughs from the cold, her chest hurting. All of the windows in here are wide open, so the paint can dry; her breath comes out white like the snow and the paint. She fills the kettle, puts coffee and milk in a cup, and steps into the next room.

What she sees there makes her catch her breath, painfully. Snow has blown in all night, depositing itself in pyramids and deserts under the large windows, drifting into lips and cliffs on their shiny sills. She tips her head back, surveys the walls, ceilings, windows, all newly painted brilliant white, now covered. For days they have painted in the cold, practically outside, their fingers red and slowed, their torsos bulky, hardly bending in their jackets. The wind has blown on them day after day, threatening, and at last it has made its way in. She imagines that this could be the beginning of the end, would be, if the rest of the house didn't exist. First the snow, then the rain, then the building of nests and moss on stone and soft wood, the eventual return to dust.

She realises the kettle is boiling, and when she goes back, it is steaming on and on, turning the air and the glass of the window bright white too. The china cup seems cold enough to break at the slightest heat, and she warms it in her hands before pouring the water in. She stirs it, turns and walks through to the tiny spare bedroom at the back, the first room they finished painting. She sees that the snow has avalanched in through the window and tumbled into the sink. She sits down on the plastic-covered bed. Now they will have to clean everything up, their days of work, it seems, wasted. She reaches out her hand, knocks some snow off the edge of the sink. It is surprisingly light, easy to clear away. One day, she thinks, relieved, that's all it will take.

She is suddenly tired, and stretches out on the bed, her cup on the floor. In spite of the cold, she feels oddly warm. What is it they say, she thinks. *Don't let yourself get sleepy*. She closes her eyes for a while to see if she can feel it, the cold that is really warmth, the sleep that is really dying.

Her husband's mother was buried less than a year ago behind the house, in the cemetery at the top of the hill. Last summer, everything there bloomed bright colours and grew; in the winter, they know now, all they see is the valley, the road, and the houses through leafless trees.

The morning after the night she died, the builders came to the front door. The foreman had his cap off, holding it in front of him, even though it was drizzling. The top of his head glistened.

He apologised. *If it's going to be done*, he said, *it has to be done before winter*.

As the eldest, her husband had the final say. He went into the bedroom and thought about it, leaving the foreman out front in the rain.

She drew up the plans herself, the foreman said. *She wanted the house to be bigger, so everyone could sleep under one roof if they wanted. That's what she said.*

Her husband came out and told the foreman it was all right, he could start after the funeral. It was what she would have wanted, everyone knew it, but still.

The high-pitched sounds of the children playing downstairs

kept them from having to talk to each other for a while. Finally
her husband said, *Let's just finish what's been started, then think
about it.*

After the funeral everyone went back home, to their separate
houses, all miles away. In late autumn the foreman telephoned
them to say it was done. She could hear her husband talking to
him on the phone in the next room. He hung up, and walked
back into the kitchen.

He says it's done, it looks good. Her husband looked tired,
strained. *I told him I thought we would go ahead and paint it – before
Christmas, before the damp comes in.*

She agreed. It was something he needed to do.

The next week they went out and bought the paint on sale,
white to avoid decisions, they thought, not realising that when
they came to do the job, it would be snowing, or that her plans
had called for so many windows, latticed and difficult, where
every mark showed. For a week they progressed quickly, the
rooms turning bright white, but the last few days had been
different, the careful white gloss on the windows and doors
slowing them down, stopping conversation. They stood with
tiny brushes in one hand and damp cloths in the other, the
ancient transistor radio playing the same Christmas carols over
and over, endlessly.

She goes to the back door, puts her boots on, and walks up the
hill to the cemetery, careful to keep her footprints neat in the
snow. The frozen gate won't open, and she climbs over it, her
feet in the boots swinging like pendulums, too heavy.

The stones are white, smoothed over with snow like everything else, drifted, so the side of the hill looks decorated, spread
with white icing into a regular chain of peaks and valleys,
unrecognisable.

She picks her way around the edge of the patch, aiming for
the underneath of trees where not so much snow has fallen.
After a minute she reaches the far corner, where his mother's

gravestone, indistinguishable from all the rest, lies rounded, filled out like a rock, like part of the landscape.

She crouches next to it, peering at it, trying to make out the words she knows are carved there. Then she brushes the snow off with her bare hands, easily. She reads it, and the grey slate of the stone is bright, almost black, the darkest thing she can see, darker even than the tree trunks.

Her hands are red, wet with melted snow. She puts them in the cold pockets of her jacket, and bites her lip from the pain. She knows they will be leaving soon, right after Christmas, because they are almost finished. The house will be done, as big and clean and white as a new one.

She looks at the stone. His mother would be glad, glad to have it done, glad that everyone can be together, finally. In a way, she is glad too, because something that's important will be complete, and she longs to tell his mother about it. But she can't bring herself to speak in the quiet, and leans forward instead, pressing her cheek against the stone, the remnants of the snow melting into water and running down her face. She stays there as long as she can, until her face and feet grow numb, and until she remembers the house full of snow.

As she starts back down the hill, carefully retracing her steps so the snow stays even and flat, she hears a few birds, but their songs stay muffled, travelling only short distances, to the next tree, like messages.

Back inside, she puts the kettle on again for more coffee. She is surprised he isn't up yet, and when the water boils, she carries two cups into the bedroom.

Sleeping like this he looks like nothing bad has ever happened to him, his hair spread across the pillow, eyelashes touching the light purple circles under his eyes. He is breathing heavily, like a small child with a fever, mouth slightly open, trembling with each breath. His fingers twitch under the covers.

She breathes on her hand to warm it up, and places it on his back lightly; he sighs, rolls over. She sits on the edge of the bed and rubs his arm until, finally, he opens his eyes. Almost immediately, he closes them again, presses his lips together, then says thickly, *I was dreaming.*

She squeezes his shoulder. *You've been sleeping hard.*

He reaches up and pushes some hair out of his face. *Freezing.*

Yes. She hands him the coffee and says, *It snowed against last night. Reminds me of when we were first married, remember, when every other day we woke up to this, started that car . . .*

He sits up slowly, carefully negotiating the coffee. *Good Lord,* he says, *yes. Seems like forever, absolutely years ago.* He takes a sip of coffee, then looks at her. *You never think any of this is ever going to happen, do you. There's just no way to think about it.*

He twists around to the window, where sunshine is coming in around the edges of the curtains now. She goes over, opens them, and a flood of light makes them both squint.

Harsh, he says.

Then he gets up and dresses quickly, in the same rush of movement she did.

He gets his coat, and they walk out into the kitchen.

Good Lord, he says again, stopping in the middle of the room. She knows he has looked through into the next room. *This is awful.*

She glances at him, but his face is turned away. She follows him into the other room, where he sees one of the big windows like she did, the snow coming in everywhere. He lifts his arms away from his body, then lets them fall back with a soft slap. He walks over and pulls a chair in front of the window.

We might as well be outside, he says, sitting down, *just let the whole place go. It's all buried, anyway.* He rests his hand lightly on the snow on the window sill. *I'll bet the gloss under here is ruined.*

She stands still for a moment, then goes over to him.

No, I don't think so, she says. She brushes some of the snow next to his hand off the sill, and the paint shines through, unmarked. *I think the snow just freezes everything.* She brushes off more, and it floats down onto the carpet. *See, it's all powdery, real cold-weather snow. It won't even melt anywhere and make a mess if we're careful, if we don't bring any heat in here. We can just sweep it up, like dust.*

He is quiet, staring out of the window, his chin in his hands. She puts one hand on his shoulder, and looks out the window too. The sun is still shining.

It doesn't mean anything, she says, *it's just natural. It settles on anything cold enough, that's all, like we're a tree or a frozen pond, anything like that.*

They make some toast, the toaster's coils disturbingly out of place, and have breakfast in the sitting room. Outside, they see smoke curling from chimneys now, and snow beginning to slide silently off eaves.

The snow is easy to clear up, as easy as she said, and they sweep it into enormous piles in the middle of each room, then into dustpans and out the windows, before it melts. They polish everything with soft cloths, until nothing is even damp or misted over.

Then they return to painting, doing the little things, the finishing touches, working faster than they had imagined. Hours pass with only the radio in the silence.

Late in the afternoon, after dark, a song plays for the third time that day. It is one they have both laughed at, country and western, about reindeer and drinking. She looks up at him through the glass of a huge partitioning window he is finishing, ready to laugh. But the expression on his face makes her stop: it is drawn, white with concentration, as if there is nothing more important than this moment, then the next, and next. He doesn't hear the song, doesn't see her looking at him.

She sits back on her heels and puts down her brush. She senses he hasn't noticed it, but she has. There is something pushing them forward, something they don't have any choice about. It breaks over her like wind and rain. She knows that even if she went back up the hill, even if she made a snow angel to lie in, her own quiet place next to his mother's grave, even if she lay face up to the sky, trying hard to learn something about time, another snow would just fall and melt around her nose and mouth from her breath, for her to breathe. She could never be covered. And it would be a sleep, perhaps, her sleep close to death, but not really dying.

She looks back up at her husband, who has not wavered, she knows, a moment from his task. With a cloth wrapped tightly into a point around his fingertip, so tightly she sees the blood gathered purple above it, he is wiping over and over at the glass of the window he has just finished. It looks clean, but he is persistent, cleaning up smears of white paint, flecks which must be too small to see. She has no idea how long he has been doing it, or how long he will continue, but now watching, her arm aches for him. His arm will hurt him when he stops. But she stays like this, sitting back on her heels, at the same point in time, it seems, forever. Only it can't be, because with each of his movements she feels they are closer to the end of something, to some time when they won't be able to do anything else, anything but leave.

Iphigeneia in Hampstead

I am Christine Grainger. All in a breath, as one announces oneself among strangers. As much as to say, Look, after so many larval stages I have risen to the surface, these are my eyes, this is my voice, seeking inflections that might get me through.

After that, choosing a place to begin seems easy. A day in mid-October 1953, when Ronald Seymour rang to ask me to dinner. A month or so after my Attempt.

I was in the spare bedroom of my flat in Hampstead. I was listening to Bach's 'St Matthew Passion' on the Third Programme and trying to paint a landscape with figures. Those days of my convalescence all seemed the same, they flowed together, they were borderless, dreamlike and in a way frightening. I spent the time working on my picture or walking about on the Heath in the hazy autumn weather.

In spite of this sameness of the days I saw everything with unusual particularity. Formations of cloud, the look of a face, the posters on hoardings. There was a staring, arrested quality in things, a sense of faintly glittering suspension, which I wanted to get into my painting. Summer was slow to leave that year. The beeches on the Heath were rusting over but the ash trees were green still, their clusters of seed-cases raw yellow and full of violence, as if bursting asunder.

This eagerness of vision was taken by friends as a hopeful sign. But in the days before I tried to end my life I was noticing things in the same driven kind of way, and everything I saw then confirmed the need for my death. It was like collecting evidence for something known to be true but needing to be proved.

What needed to be proved now I had no idea. The motions of wielding the brush afforded me frequent glimpses of the scar

on the inside of my right wrist. The wrist seemed too slight,
somehow, for the wound – I am a small-boned woman, though
rather tall. My scars had not paled at that time, it was still not
possible to see their final shape.

I was trying to get these clumps of raw yellow into my
painting. In the hazy, glimmering air, the seed-cases were like
underwater shell-bursts. Beyond, lower down, the light was
thicker. Inhabiting these lower regions were rudimentary
human figures, men and women. I remember quite well the
moment the phone rang, as it rescued me from some feeling
of apprehension or anxiety about these figures. They seemed
accidental, but weren't.

'Rachel and I have been concerned that you are left too much
on your own,' Ronald said. He sounded, however, more
reproachful than anything. 'We have both been rushed off our
feet lately. What is that music? What are you doing?' This was
said suspiciously, as if he thought I might be planning some act
of self-outrage at a high point in the oratorio.

'I am painting,' I said. 'I have taken up painting again, I don't
quite know why. It is kind of you and Rachel to think of me,
but – '

'We'd like you to come to dinner on Saturday if you are free.
We are asking a few other people. You could stay the night and
I would drive you back the next day. I have to come into town
on Sunday morning in any case.'

This last remark, in its candour and lack of grace, was typical
of Ronald, he always made you feel part of some schedule. 'We
would have to leave soon after breakfast,' he said now, as if it
were an added inducement.

I said I'd be delighted, which was overstating it. Then I went
back to my painting. It was no scene that I could positively
remember and yet I felt I knew it intimately: the ground sloping
down towards a stream with a rustic bridge, trees thinly
grouped together, the spaces between the trees opaque with
mist and shafts of sun, and figures moving in these depths,
mere smudges, indeterminate, amphibious creatures. The

undergrowth of the trees had a trailing look, like weeds under water. . . . A memory came to me of swimming underwater in a warm sea, in Greece, when I went to see the place where Iphigeneia was sacrificed, Aulis. Opening my eyes under water, a gingery light stirring into yellow then darkening to amber, touch of ribbon-weed on my shoulders, the water deepened from these trailing, glinting weeds down a shaft of pale rock, below the touch of the weed the water grew cold suddenly. . . .

The people in the painting were again beginning to disturb me, they were people who existed. I held off knowledge of who they were as one would hold off terror, keeping it vague. There was one I had done in black. Leggings and a flat projection on his head, who was this wavering through the spaces between the trees? In haste to forestall fear, I charged my brush with ochre and dabbed at face and head. Now he swam headless, armless, black like a tadpole. But I knew it was Spencer, my father's chauffeur, whom I had not seen for twenty years. And the creature was not headless, after all; that daub of ochre made a face. It was Iphigeneia in a close-fitting black evening dress. Iphigeneia, whose throat was cut for a favourable wind.

A Neo-Northerner

It seems my best hope is that my record will speak for me
and that my customers will too. I am, after all, a law-abiding
businessman, not some escapee from a film with Al Pacino.
Respected. Respectable. Doreen's Mum sent a message of support. That made me blub, but now the lawyer is not sure he'll
call her. It seems she thinks it was a *crime passionel*. Poor thing,
she dopes herself with valium and novelettes.

Doreen used to say that all I ever read were comic books –
and I ask: why not? For years I worked a twelve-hour day.
And who profited? Who skedaddled with her swag like some
weaselly creature in a comic book? A professor I know wrote a
history of cartoons and comics which he claims are a significant
form of popular culture. He promised to give me a copy. Then
he forgot. That made Doreen laugh.

'It's a book!' she jeered. 'He knew you wouldn't read it!'

Books impress her. So do plays. She dragged me once to see
the Royal Shakespeare Company. It was one of my early-to-
market days so, having been up since dawn, I fell asleep. I was
sorry about that because they were showing *The Duchess of
Malfi*. Amalfi is up the coast from where I was born, and I
would have liked to know if the play put its citizens in a bad
light. I couldn't tell, though. My eyelids kept dropping and
each time I got them open someone was being seduced or killed
– like in a horror comic. The language, though, was beautiful.
'Cover her face. Mine eyes dazzle!' *Aúlico*. Almost as fine as
Italian!

My English, my professors tell me, is positively aulic – *aulico*
– unlike Doreen's. She has a Greater London accent but I learned
mine from them. I call them 'my professors' because, though
they're really my customers, they *are* also professors: French,

‹

English, North American. Some are men of eminence. The
snack bar and restaurant are close to the British Museum and,
times being what they are, younger readers cannot afford our
prices.

Several professors used to come for breakfast. I think their
wives sent them out unfed, for in they'd pop like clockwork,
just after nine. By then they would have dashed to the reading
room to bag places before coming to us for a cappuccino and
brioche. Later, they'd be back for elevenses. While savouring
my *crostini di milza* – I never let on what *they* were made of! –
they sometimes held quite elevated discussions and claimed,
more than half seriously, that our snack bar was like the old
Academies of Rome and Naples. 'See you at Carlo's,' these
eminent men would tell each other and, even though one or
two had appeared on TV, they treated me as a friend. Only the
Italians were standoffish. When the others brought one in,
saying 'Meet our friend Carlo,' I'd see the visitor stiffen. He'd
see, you see, not what I meant to become, but what I'd been.
That's what it comes down to. Don't get me wrong. The
English have their own prejudices – but the ones they have
about the South fizz with romance.

To a Milanese, 'the South' means the Mafia, migrants, laya-
bouts, and murdered magistrates. But for my BM profs it's all
Pindar and Pirandello, pedigreed crime (Tiberius), dolphins and
wild asphodel. You see why I don't need to read books! I hear
about them as I chop my salads, just as I could see the temple
of Paestum, when I was small, without having to join a package
tour.

Doreen and her Mum came on one of those and the first time
I saw them was at lunch in my uncle's trattoria. I was waiting
at table and some local men began making off-colour remarks.
This annoyed me because, working with tourists, I could tell
the decent ones from the other sort. I'd picked up some English
too, so when the men sent me over with a message, what I told
the two was to steer clear of oafs who took every foreign
woman for a rich blonde bombshell. I didn't add that they

thought the bombshells came south because their own men couldn't satisfy their lusts. Perhaps the women guessed.

'Maybe then,' said Doreen's Mum, 'we need protection? Why don't you join us when you get off work?'

It was the sort of friendly banter would-be Latin lovers can't assess. These were independent women. Something might happen. Or not. They weren't tarts. Nor rich. Nor bombshells. Just nice to look at. I liked that. I'm not Marcello Mastroianni either and by the end of that day I knew Doreen was the sort of woman I could marry.

One of our 'Accademia' debates was about the march of the hungry South upon the North: a very old march, noted one of the professors.

'Carlo knows that,' he told his friends. 'His part of Italy was colonised by Greeks and later, just south of it, came the Arabs. Now it's starting again on a vaster scale . . .'

I had to put on my food processor to make mayonnaise so I missed the next bit. So I fantasised about a go-getting Greek ancestor's spirit rising in me. His enterprise and vim. Greeks in their day were like the English in theirs! Venturesome! Resolute! With balls! Think of Ulysses sailing past Gibraltar and the confines of the known universe! Business had recently been brisk and it was while watching the processor blades whirr and the mayonnaise thicken that I decided to expand. I had my eye on premises that would be just right for a small restaurant and knew a man from home who might go shares with me. Doreen could take over here while I started up something new. We'd hire someone to do the donkey work.

'We need places like this in England,' she'd mused that first evening, as we dined on cuttlefish in a clifftop trattoria. All across the bay, a skin of moonlight quivered like shaken mercury and, from below, came the groan of ropes, yielding then tugging at invisible boats. 'You should come and open one!'

'Maybe I will,' I said. Then we toasted the thought in Falernian wine.

It was just chaff, but by Christmas I'd joined her in London.

Why not? I was twenty-three and she was nineteen. Her Mum liked me and in no time I was a regular Sunday-lunch guest with the family. Soon Doreen and I began making cheap, interesting sandwiches which we peddled to office-workers at lunchtime. Then we hired a place no bigger than a stall. Then one with a few chairs. Then . . . a moral tale. We worked and prospered and were mates and partners and, along the way, got married. She learned Italian as I did English, and in those years she didn't mind my failing to provide any *dolce far niente* at all. She could soon cook as well as I, who, if I say so myself, worked as hard as three Englishmen, which is why five years later we already had our snack bar and a big clientele. We bought a house on the edge of the city and furnished it. Once a week I got up extra early to go to the market, and every morning was here by seven to prepare sauces, grate cheese and cut sandwiches. I thought she – my entrepreneurial Northern bride! – would be thrilled by my plan to expand. After all, since we had no children, she might as well be the businesswoman she's cut out to be. I kept expecting her to see the thing as an adventure.

But no! My pace, it seems, was too precipitate. Wham! Dada-dadà! Whizzo! That's me reading my comic books, or, alternatively, flattening garlic bulbs with my spry and trusty knife. Stabbing, boning, slicing, skinning, whisking, blending and so delighting in my busyness that, having savoured what I'd created in my mind, I rarely ate more than the sip or spoonful needed to test the result. Result: I grew as thin as my own boning knife, whereas Doreen now began, very fetchingly I may say, to wax plump. Also, I sometimes felt, lazy. Had she succumbed to that English indolence which made our professors waste my time discussing unusable recipes from something called *De Re Coquinaria* by Apicius, photocopying Napoleon's nephew's book on *Fauna Italica*, so as to show me the plates, and gossiping about each other while, absentmindedly, nibbling so much of our complimentary *ciabatta* that its doughiness showed up in their figures? They didn't jog, as their foreign colleagues did, nor spend nearly as much time in the library.

Instead, they slacked off and this, I came to see, was what
Doreen wanted too. Life for her – as for them – is more hobby
than challenge, and it peeved her to find me a spoilsport. Unless
it was something else?

Had I hurt her by mentioning our lack of children? My sisters
have them to spare and I took it for granted that, one day, a
bright nephew would take over our business. Did Doreen mind?

Talk of the South marching North came up again. Or, rather,
I brought it up myself. We'd had a run of hot summers. I'd put
three tables out on the pavement with a sunshade, and was
moved to remark that we immigrant Italians were the new
Northerners. We had relinquished the delights of idleness to
which the English were now addicted. I nodded at my three
tables where lolling, bare-chested men and girls in sundresses
were turning a dangerous pink.

'You,' I flattered my professors, 'have inherited our charm
and we your industry. We have swopped characters!'

Their laugh was doubtful and I, as if doubt were contagious,
wondered whether Doreen felt I'd sold her a bill of goods? On
that first evening, when we'd said London needed a place like
the one we were in, had she been thinking of the moon and I
of the menu?

Later, I promised myself, later on, I'll make it up to her. For
now, though, my new scheme absorbed me. There is romance
to planning – even if it's only a restaurant kitchen. First there's
nothing there. It's all in your head, whirling and shifting like
primordial particles and then, miraculously, there it is! Firmed
up and final! The end of a dance! It's almost sad.

The new restaurant was to be called The Paestum and I'd got
an art student to paint a fresco of the main Paestum temple on
one wall. Already I'd posted photos of it to my family in
Campania. I was, as the English say, over the moon: a precarious situation, which made it seem wise to organise some luck.
There are rituals for this – blessings, etc. – but I didn't use
them. Instead, my attention was caught by an Oxfam ad in the
daily paper showing a naked Peruvian waif. Here, imploring

patronage, was a needier South than my own. *Noblesse oblige.* I
sent off a cheque and, when hiring help for our two establish-
ments, picked a small Colombian couple with long straight
eyelashes who would not have looked out of place in the Oxfam
ad. They were illegal immigrants and, philanthropy aside, I
knew they'd work harder than the English applicants.

Gustavo, the husband, looked fifteen but was twenty-three.
He had never seen a dishwasher and, on his first day, spent an
hour cleaning ours out under the impression that it was a fridge.
His aim, in coming to London, had been to study Veterinary
Science. It had not occurred to him that he would need certifi-
cates to enter the university – nor that a rich country like
England would require him to pay fees. Grounds for hope, in
his own mind, were his experience with animals and his skill at
ascertaining the gender of a goose. Neither he nor his wife,
Ana, spoke English. Italian, however, is friendly to Spanish and
Doreen called our pidgin 'Spitalian'. Like a wobbly bike, it
could carry us for long confident stretches then pitch us over
the handlebars. In some ways it turned out to be the perfect
vehicle for Gustavo's brand of sly, crooked innocence.

Shortly after starting with us, he was assaulted late one night
on the platform of Finsbury Park underground station. It was
the weekend. Unknown to us, he had been moonlighting, doing
a dishwashing job in Soho, and was waiting for a connecting
train, when three unknown Colombians appeared from
nowhere, knocked him down, and might have kicked the life
out of him, had not a fourth one rushed up shouting, 'It's the
wrong man!' They fled. An ambulance was called and the next
morning Doreen – ours was the only telephone number found
on him – got a call from the hospital where he was concussed
with three broken ribs.

Apart from the inconvenience – the incident left us short-
handed – there was something tenebrous, not to say ill-omened,
about this. After all, the Colombians had been meant to bring
us luck and instead, if Gustavo's assailants were the strangers
he said they were, then his own country's violence was in

fortuitous pursuit of him. *Was* it a fatality or might he be lying? How had he found the money to come to England anyway? By smuggling? Colombia suggests drugs, as Southern Italy does the Mafia. I upbraided myself. Dodgy immigrants! Don't think that way, Carlo!

Some of my customers who knew Bogotá now described the wretchedness from which Gustavo must have emerged. They talked of street vendors touting trays with maybe three items for sale, the cardboard box beside them with a baby in it, the rabbit-sized rats which ate the babies' faces if they were left at home, the gangs of abandoned children who lived in the sewers so as to escape the killer police. . . . It was cartoonish and unsettling : a leaking, sewerish contagion from a South which seemed like a nightmare version of my own.

After some weeks Gustavo was back working for Doreen in the snack bar, while Ana worked in the restaurant with me. I considered that we had behaved generously. After all, they were not exactly old family retainers and, as illegals, could simply have been fired. Ana, however, was moody and often on the edge of insolence. Why? Never mind, I told myself. Colombia is another South. Distant. Different. Get on with the day's work.

Though Doreen assured me that Gustavo was turning out well, I suspected her of coddling him and not getting as much work out of him as she might. But I didn't press the argument. We had other bones of contention and I let this one be.

She wanted a holiday, arguing that we had not had one for two years. This was true, but how could we take time off? The Paestum was barely launched and who would take over the snack bar? Doreen was being unreasonable. At the same time, I understood her restlessness. Here she was in the flowering of her years – just turned twenty-nine, bloomy, languid, prettier than ever before, better dressed, jingling with jewellery, lively and lovely, and where could she display herself? In our tiny snack bar? In the Paestum? She needed a broader stage. But, for the moment, our lives were confined by work. The professors

went home in the evenings to worlds we never saw. Once we
went out to dinner with two of them, an American couple,
then back to drinks at their flat. I saw the experience unsettle
her, as she looked at their prints and books, taking in the
difference between their decor and ours. She's quick, you see,
and sensitive. It was what I'd sensed on that first evening when
she was admiring and coveting *my* culture. Falernian wine and
the dolphins! Mediterranean moonlight! Paestum! Now, she felt
I'd left it behind. We argued. She asked what good money was
if you never had time to enjoy it? I said wait. Give me a chance.
She said she was tired of waiting. She wanted to go to the
theatre, the ballet, the opera. She bought tickets to something
wildly expensive and again I fell asleep. Next time, I told her,
she should take her mother. But her mother caught a cold so,
in her place, she took Ana to the bad-luck play, *Macbeth*. I asked
Ana next day what she'd understood and she talked of murder
and said it was too much like Colombia and that she liked
cheerier things. Love. Pretty songs. Style. The clothes in *Macbeth* had been all tatters. She preferred the cinema. No she hadn't
liked it. Doreen took Gustavo the next time and Ana sulked.
But I couldn't waste time worrying about that. Then they went
to the opera. Then. . . .

I'm like a man looking in one of those trick mirrors and
wondering if this is me? Or was the me I thought I knew false?
How many people knew by now that my wife was sleeping
with the help? When did it happen? How soon? After that first
play? Did they even go to the play? Were Ana's sulks always
because of this? How soon did she know it, cause it, guess it?

And did Doreen see him as a substitute for me? Another
Southerner? A *meridionale* from a Third World which evokes
neither dolphins nor asphodels but attracts anonymous assaults
by thugs! Who, maybe, came into this country as a smuggler,
after swallowing a plastic bagful of cocaine. That's what they
do. Sometimes, I'm told, it bursts inside them and they die in
agony. Have I really something in common with that Oxfam

waif – who, by the way, was now fattened up on my food and no longer looked waifish.

It was Ana who told me and I didn't believe her. I even scolded her, told her she was mad and sacked her there and then. I couldn't, I said, in my Neo-Northern way, put up with this sort of hysteria. I had a restaurant to run. I replaced her with a docile Filipino. Then she told the Home Office, denouncing Gustavo for working illegally. Hell hath no fury, said Doreen, quoting some play, like a woman scorned. Cartoons! Cartoons! The wisdom of the world is in them and I didn't want to believe it! Gustavo was threatened with deportation and – three guesses what happens next. Do I beat him up? No. He was, despite his new plumpness, as slight as a greyhound and I could have broken his neck. But I am no *Mafioso* 'man of honour'. No, what happened next was that Doreen said she wanted a divorce so as to marry him and enable him to stay in the country. I, she said, neglected her and had, morally speaking, deserted her. I had not been a companion to her for years.

I insisted that we see a marriage counsellor. This, I argued, half mad with shock – it was her going from me to *him* which undid me – was, *must be*, maternal frustration gone mad. A uterine fixation. Hysteria! He was seven years younger and looked more. And childish! Remember his talk about guessing the gender of a goose? Well, he'd managed that all right! And she was the goose! I'd been warned and – oh hell! I stormed out of the counselling session. What in God's name sort of a companion could he be to anyone? A Third-World primitive! A barbarian at our gates! No, not at the gates. This barbarian had slid inside, helped – I could have kicked myself – by me.

Doreen's mother couldn't believe it either and her shock added to my humiliation. At first she wouldn't even meet Gustavo. Clearly someone had told her too about Colombian shanty-towns and babies cradled in cardboard boxes. Could he, she asked me, read and write? He could? But no English? And what were we doing about the property? Her eyes were wide with anxiety. Doreen, I told her, would keep the snack bar and

I the restaurant. Ah. Then, despite her distress for me whom
she claimed to love like a son, I thought I caught a faint glint
of relief in the depths of her sad orbs. I was growing deeply,
sadly cynical.

'I won't see her,' she said of Doreen. 'I'm ashamed of her!'

And talked of a cat in heat. But, knowing how pained she
must be, I decided to stop visiting her until the two had made
their peace. Fair play is an ideal of mine.

Summer came back and a man from home turned up at the
Paestum asking for me. At once I imagined my mother – who
knows nothing of what has happened – showing him photos of
me and Doreen holding hands in front of the restaurant and of
having to explain to him about Doreen. I told the Filipino to
say I was away and – something I never do – gave him the keys
to lock up later if I didn't return. Then I slipped out the back
and began walking at random. It was a hot night and soon I
found myself outside Covent Garden, where loudspeakers were
relaying the singing inside the Opera House to a second audience
in the streets. Luciano Pavarotti was belting out old favourites
from my childhood: *Sorrento, Santa Lucia, Funicoli Funicolà*, all
the consoling, syrupy, sentimental numbers. I was starting to
surrender to them, when I saw Doreen and Gustavo with their
arms around each other and an ice cream in each free hand.
They were singing along: a picture of childish, stolen bliss. I
went stiff with anger. Rage. I turned, raced back to the restaurant and spent the rest of the evening inventing work for
myself. When Gianni, my partner, dropped by, I had to tell
him. I had to tell someone how murderous I had felt when I
saw them there. As I left, Pavarotti had started on *La Donn'è
mobile*! And I wanted to murder *him*!

'Well that's one way to get your name in the papers,' laughed
Gianni. So I got over my mood – but the thing is he made a
story of it, telling people that I'd talked of murdering Pavarotti,
not to speak of my wife and her lover. And, now, this could
count against me. It's extraordinary the way I've lost my luck.

The divorce went through. We divided our property down

the middle and I began to recover. After all, as Doreen complained, I am wedded, first and foremost, to my work.

Then Ana came to see me. She said that she had received no compensation for the loss of her husband and her job. She had some story too about being pregnant and needing help. Pregnant by whom? I couldn't work it out. She said it was by Gustavo but the implications of that were distasteful and I refused to listen. How could he still be sleeping with her?

'Well, he left some stuff in my place,' she told me, 'and I don't want my new friend seeing it. He's jealous, which is why I can't go into the snack bar. Could you drop it off with him?'

I was just leaving for my afternoon off, as no doubt she knew, so, to be rid of her, I said yes. Then I walked past the snack bar and saw Gustavo through the windows. It was a quiet time and he was sitting reading the *Sun*, or rather looking at the cheesecake on the third page. I remember thinking, well, he's no workaholic. Doreen must be pleased. Then I opened the door, handed him the parcel from Ana and left. I was maybe ten yards away when I heard the explosion and saw the glass shatter. Foolishly, I ran back. You'd think, I told my lawyer, that that would be in my favour. A real bomber wouldn't hang about. But he says I have to contend with the image of Latin jealousy in the minds of an English jury.

'They might think you wanted to gloat,' he said, and quoted something from one of those unseemly English plays which Doreen likes so much. Sick stuff! I've been wondering if Ana's Colombian bloodiness might have been stirred up by being taken to see one? She has now disappeared as, it appears, thousands of people do every year: poll-tax dodgers, illegal immigrants and the like. Also, I imagine, murderers.

Gustavo died outright. At first they thought it might be the IRA but the trail quickly led to me. Doreen, to give her her due, said I'd never do it. That I lacked the passion and the guts. I don't know whether she was trying to help me or speaking out of bitterness. Either way, the lawyer thinks she'll be a more useful witness than her Mum and that I should do my best to keep her sweet and myself steady.

I do. I do try. Night after night now I concentrate on clearing my mind so as to get some sleep. But then the dreams come and, later, a muddled interlude when I can't tell whether Gustavo ever existed outside them because he seems like a shadowy incubus summoned by Doreen's need. He was so alien to us and his coming – and going – so chancy that even when I am awake disbelief lingers and with it an unexpected pity. Like the smart-Alec men in my uncle's trattoria, all those years ago, I now see her as wild with neediness, and this has softened my feelings and made me hope – mad as this sounds – that if only I can get out of the trouble I am in, we might perhaps get back together. Oh shit!

Pisgah

Remember the tunnel at Fonthill Gifford, a tunnel for the road under a wooded hill, and my father sounding his horn halfway through, for the echo.

My cousin Sarah at her father's funeral, easing herself back off her knees onto the pew in front of me, and leaning down to massage her foot.

The buzz of a car bringing light to my barred bedroom window. The light intensifying as the car approached, and the swipe of a barred stripe of light across the ceiling and down the wall behind my bed.

Two Welsh dressers. The one running the length of the larder, opposite the marble-topped table on which stood butter and cheese and the tray of milk waiting for the cream to rise, the dresser of scrubbed grey ash, with cupboards and drawers full of treasures, an old lace tablecloth made by my grandmother, old liqueur bottles, attachments for the Hoover, a broken thermos flask, a silver and glass epergne, the silver hooped to hold the glass, the glass fluted and conical, shaded green at the base, white at the top, in approximate imitation of a lily, the shelves hung with hooks, on one of which my Uncle Philip, according to legend, had fallen and slit his nose. The second in the room that was first kitchen, then dining room, then breakfast room, according to my mother's fancy, the wood indeterminate under layers of paint, the shelves hookless and piled with plates and books, dictionaries, anthologies and atlases, which my mother used for her crossword puzzles, its cupboards full of mustiness, darkness and old shoes, and I swinging from the doors, sometimes sitting on the door, sometimes belly over it, delighting in the swing, playing with the darkness, experimenting with fear.

My father on the way back from Tisbury, stopping the car at Hindon to buy apples.

After tea in the Grosvenor Hotel in Shaftesbury, listening to Dan Dare on the radio, waiting for my mother to finish her cigarette.

Hiding under the back stairs, crammed between the sideboard and the wall, waiting to leap out and make my mother jump as she came down the stairs.

Christmas tea at my Aunt Elizabeth's, laid on the covered billiard table. Slices of bread and butter, and sandwiches, jams and spreads, and fruits and jellies, and meringues, and flapjacks, and macaroons, and clusters of Corn Flakes and Rice Crispies glued together with chocolate and Golden Syrup, and spongecakes, and Madeira cakes, and ginger cakes, and Battenberg cakes, and chocolate biscuits, wafers, fingers, and marshmallows, and a Christmas log, frosted with icing sugar, and topped with a robin and a sprig of holly, and the Christmas cake, sodden with brandy, encased in marzipan and royal icing, and we, in the brief pause between Christmas lunch and a supper of tranches of cold ham and turkey, with bread, pickles and cheeses, and cold mince pies and cream to follow, all of us, tucking in to it.

Going down to the river at Norton Bavant, the crunch of stones giving way to the squidge of mud under the water, the nuzzle of fish against naked thigh, the turbulent rush of water over the weir, the swag of Keith Dredge's cock in his trunks as he poised himself to dive from the weir into the turbulence.

A group of us at Downside, circled round Johnny MacCormack, begging him, Ah now Johnny, come on Johnny, give us a Cork one, and he gave us a Cork one, and I heard again the accents of Father O'Sullivan as he gave us his deathbed sermon, the anxious cluster of relatives round the bed, the ticking of the clock on the wall, and we, the congregation, fidgeting in the pews, twisting our hands, not knowing where to look.

My brother Matthew and I, sent uniquely down to my Uncle Philip at the cottage for tea, the tea prolonged beyond pleasure, and walking home eventually in the dark to find my father jubilant, my mother smiling, in bed, with a baby.

How my grandmother gave me sixpence to buy ice cream on the front at Bournemouth and I bought two threepenny cones.

Sister Mary Anne in the bathroom at Abingdon showing me a box of lead cowboys and Indians, frozen in attitudes of conflict in a sheet of cardboard, which my mother had left to console me for her absence, and me reaching out to touch one, an Indian crouching in a war bonnet, and the box closes and I don't see it again.

Sister Mary Rose and Sister Mary Francis working their way up the dormitory to my bed and stopping at my pillow and Sister Mary Rose saying. He's not asleep. He's just pretending.

My first nanny, an Italian, Valeda, whose nose I broke, whom I remember only from photographs.

Spending the night at my aunt Kathleen's house at Long Ivor, and my aunt asking me if I felt all right, if I didn't maybe feel sick, was I sure I didn't feel sick? and I didn't, but later in the night I woke to darkness and a rattling window, and my pillow ice cold and no matter how I twisted or turned it, wet with vomit.

Sitting in the window embrasure between the curtain and the glass, reading *Jane Eyre* and watching the velvet fall of snowflakes.

The men lining up at my father's study window on Saturday morning, to be paid.

My father rubbing a pear from his Christmas store, chuckling and saying, Luscious fruit, Luscious fruit.

Riding my pony through Southleigh wood, saying to myself, A hundred yards more and I'll meet somebody.

Mr Turnip on the television who frightened me so much I had to close the doors of the set.

How the grandfather clock in my father's study, which had so often swayed from the perpendicular and back again this time didn't, and fell, and smashed.

Standing at the gate at Whitelands, looking down over the newly baled field and the village, looking forward to the first episode of *Good Wives* on the television that evening.

Afternoon walks with Jenny, how we once walked all the way round, that is from home down to Tytherington and on to Heytesbury, down again to Norton Bavant, and from there back to the village and home.

How Nurse Latimer fell down, tripping tray-laden over the carpet-concealed step in the corridor outside the breakfast room, and my father found her sitting dazed in a pond of spilt tea.

Waking up at All Hallows, the dormitory dark behind its blinds, and going to the lavatory, and seeing from the window senior boys running, talking, playing tennis, working in their gardens on a summer evening.

Mixing milk and salt in a screwtop bottle, and shaking the bottle till the milk turned to butter.

Working on a loose tooth, pulling, twisting, biting, pushing, cracking, till it snapped and came out.

How I didn't know what water was, lying in the bath, watching the transparent membrane creep up my body.

The asparagus ferns in my grandmother's garden.

My father telling his favourite story of Dougie and the Old Crone, how Dougie hit someone at the cricket match and knocked him out, and said, I just lifted my arm, I might have touched him, and the Old Crone wailed and said, Aah, he'm goin', he'm stiffenin' on.

Walking after school at Mrs Poor's to my Aunt Elizabeth's at Greenhill and reading *The Sleeping Beauty* while I waited for my mother.

How my mother said, Don't touch the glass, you'll leave a fingermark, and I touched the glass and left a fingermark, and my grandmother smiled.

My father's corgi, Josephine, put nightly to bed in the corn bin.

Cupboards. One in the hall by the back door into the front garden, deep, a walk-in, where drinks were kept. Two in the breakfast room, one in the embrasure where the Aga had stood, packed with silverware, dinner services and assorted tableware, tins of biscuits, tins of cakes. And one in the wall by the back stairs, full of missals and mantillas and gloves and Palm Sunday palms. Three in the sitting room, one by my mother's chair where she kept her sewing things, needles, buttons and scraps. A mysterious curtained cavern behind the television, full of old boxes, tubs of grapes and the fireguard, and a corner cupboard above the telephone where copies of the *Swift* were kept for me to read on exeats from school. Two in my parents' L-shaped bedroom, one by the fireplace, full of hats, wraps and shawls, and an oaken wardrobe at the dark end of the L, where my father's dress suits hung, my mother's evening dresses, and a fur. A giant press in the bathroom, full of blankets, old clothes, spare sheets, fancy dress costumes, and an old leather truss for someone with a broken rib. And a dressing table in the large spare bedroom, the room sparsely furnished and ice cold, the table empty, the cupboard empty, the whole swathed in crisp, cold chintz.

My mother's laugh, aspirate, fricative, voiceless.

The old baking oven in the kitchen, walled away now, but hollow sounding when you tapped it.

How my mother once threw down the sink the juices from the turkey which Christmas ritual demanded be used to make gravy, and how it became part of the Christmas ritual to recall this accident.

My father, early in the morning of my birthday, leading me to the window to show me the new swing in the garden.

How I didn't know what cars were. How I would sit in the front passenger seat while my father drove and wonder at the strange floating beings that accompanied us, half animal, half machine.

In my grandmother's bedroom, reading my favourite book, a story of a kitten and a swan and how their necks got mixed up, with pictures of a kitten with a swan's neck, a swan with a kitten's neck.

Running into my bolthole at Abingdon, my mouth full of stolen sugar, and finding it full of nuns cleaning their shoes.

Getting into my cold bed, lying curled up tight, tight in the glacial sheets, and gradually unknotting, slowly inching my legs straight, my feet to the bottom of the bed.

How the fox came down the garden path. How I stood in the back kitchen listening to the click, click, click of the fox's claws on the path, and how, when it rounded the corner into the kitchen, it was only Sal, the spaniel.

Standing at the paddock gate, waiting for the bus to take me to Mrs Poor's at the top of the village, and the bus was late, and my mother came out into the garden and called back to Dorothy in the house, Good Lord, is that child still there?

How, when I spent Sundays at my grandmother's, lunch was

at one o'clock instead of the home time of midday, and how not even my grandmother could make the extra hour pass quickly.

The rack of rifles and shotguns in my father's study, and my own first gun, an airgun, with which my brother and I murdered a robin.

How I didn't know what a fart was, how the only reasonable explanation seemed to be a turd that came halfway out and went back in again, and how my aunt Lilian said to her dog, You've farted, Benny, I know you have, I saw you, and how I looked and looked but couldn't see.

Working for Sykes' Chicks one summer, creosoting a barn door, and looking up at the surrounding country and thinking, That field is my uncle John's, those fields are my uncle Garfield's, that hill is my father's.

Riding my bicycle round the garden, starting at the back door and up the path past stone troughs full of flowers and a flowering plum trained up the side of the house, past the front door steps, the stomach-turning drop down over the lawn outside my father's study to the hard turn by the garden gate, along the path past espaliered pear trees to the staddle stone by the swing, and up under the sycamores to the back door again.

The night light in my bedroom, the shadows in the orange light.

Picnics in the cornfield, in the distance the pulse and dust of the combine harvester, the scratch of wheat stubble against my calves.

Two cocker spaniels, Sal and Lil, Sal the daughter of Lil, and how Sal whelped in the hay barn and I found Lil chewing, with a double-dotted champ, her grandchildren.

A point-to-point at Lark Hill, all mackintoshes and gumboots and headscarves, shooting sticks and flasks of hot tea, and how

I turned to look at a passing horse and when I turned back my family had gone.

How the corn lay in sacks on a perforated cement sheet in the drying barn, and how you could crawl in underneath them into the dark, oatsmelling warmth.

My cousin Erica carving her name on one of the beech trees that divided the paddock from the fields, and how the roots of the trees formed a bank, and you could climb down into the gap between the bank and the fence into another world, and how my cousin Gregory and I once found and caught a snake there.

Standing in the clump of bamboo at the end of the orchard and pressing the leaves against my thighs.

My father sitting on the edge of my bed, saying that I wouldn't go to hell, only very wicked people went to hell, go to sleep now.

How I hated lavatories, how I would shit in the woodshed.

Duck shooting down by the Wylye, where our fields bordered our neighbour's, and a stretch of water so covered with weed that it looked like another field.

My father angrily kicking at the distended bag of guts protruding from a dead sheep, and bursting it.

How my brother Mark fell into the chicken shit, up to his eyes in chicken shit, over his head in chicken shit, and I pulled him out.

Hanging my head out of the passenger window of the new Austin and throwing up fountainously down the door outside Curry's in the High Street.

Castrating piglets in the old barn, their mother a bale barrier away, frenziedly rooting through the straw for the balls we threw her.

How we all left church slowly and stood outside on the pavement talking, going the rounds of family, my parents talking with my aunts Joan, Elizabeth, Kathleen, my uncles John, Alan, Bernard, Peter, Roland, and I with my cousins, while we all waited for the taxi for my great-aunts Winifred and May.

Lying in the cornfield by the Dutch barn, staring at the sky, supine in the ripening wheat.

Dorothy at the back door, polishing shoes.

How I woke in the middle of the night and it was impossibly dark. How I went to my parents' room and it was empty and impossibly dark, the only scrap of light the night reflected in the dressing-table mirror.

Sitting in a tree above the rhododendron bank with my cousin Gregory at Botany, behind us the sunlit road across the fields and through the woods to Crockerton, in front of us lawn and house and yard, and depending over all the enormous sweet creamy smell of cow shit.

My first pony, a skewbald Shetland called Merrylegs, abandoned in the paddock, crippled with laminitis, walking on his heels.

How my mother drove first the Austin, then the Singer, both cars my father's size, either leaning forward to see over, or back to see under, the steering wheel.

How, on Good Fridays, we would climb a hill.

A green headland overlooking the sea, my parents wear overcoats, drink tea from a flask, sitting on the grass by the open car door, and the wind blows their hair.

In the back seat of the car, driving to Sandbanks, my cousin Gregory and I, melting boiled sweets in a bottle of water.

The year my mother made a herbaceous border in the front garden and my father manured it with agricultural fertiliser:

bushes of lobelias, clouds of hydrangeas, antirrhinums like lupins, peonies tall as a tall man.

How I kept my head bowed during the Elevation of the Host lest I see the moment of transubstantiation, not even peeping out of the window from the corner of my eye lest I see God descending in glory over Warminster.

An esplanade of moss-grown bricks in a suntrap corner of my uncle Bernard's cottage at Norton Bavant, and a circular pool in the middle, with plants and fish, and my uncle's Jack Russell terrier, Topsy, standing trembling on the verge, fixed on the fish.

Snow-on-the-mountain on the garden wall.

How my brother and I stole the fruit press from the kitchen cupboard and took it to the orchard to press Beauty of Bath apples, hoping that if we left the juice long enough it would turn into cider.

How I collected a jam jar full of caterpillars from the underside of cabbages in the vegetable garden, and then filled the jar with hot water.

The old hen coop in the orchard, how dark and warm it was, its ammoniac solitude and silence.

How bales were kept above the batteries and how, if you climbed up one end you could push through to a darker clearing, and if you moved through that and climbed up its far wall you would find yourself on the brink of a third, pitch dark, hollow.

The weeping ash tree in the front garden whose enclosing branches if you crawled through them tented you in a green shade.

The water reservoir at the bottom of the batteries, still, cool, dark, distant, full to the lip and immeasurably deep.

The attic above the bathroom, how empty it was, how it smelled of dust.

Treasures in the main attics, pictures of horses and dead uncles, rattan chairs and cracked picture frames, an art nouveau portrait of a pensive lady, worked on wood by my grandmother with a hot poker, a picture of the beach at Weston-super-Mare by my Great-aunt May, leaves for the dining table, boxes and trunks and old hats and clothes, and once three volumes of Hume's *History of England*, the 1836 edition, Vols III-V.

How I was sitting reading in my mother's armchair in the drawing room, and someone came to the front door. How they opened the door and walked into the house. How they walked into the hall and down the corridor, opening doors, looking round rooms, and then went away.

How the roots of the fir tree next to the front garden wall had bulged the wall so out of true that it hung over the road, and the tree had to be cut down.

How gradually, one, two, three, four, the old barns disappeared, leaving scars and stumps, and how one full corner of the yard was full of rusting, antiquated machinery, reapers, binders, and piles of rotting harness.

How I rode down the second drive to the river fields in winter, my pony up to her belly in mud.

How we excavated a barrow, and how on the day the body was exhumed, my mother and I rode down to inspect it, a black skeleton curled up in the earth, and away to the side another one, and that night my father saw a ghost in the farmyard, a white corporeal mist, in the space where the old sack barn had stood.

How once the cellar door was opened and I saw the steps leading downwards.

The back outhouses, four of them, one after the other, off the kitchen. The first full of tack and saddlery, old dog leads and walking sticks, saddle soap and grooming kit and bicycles. The second, the window glassless, the ceiling unplastered, cobweb-veiled rafters, the floor flagged, used for storing logs. The third dark, the light bulbless, full of old oil bottles, broken radios, electric fires and damp. The fourth a stable, accessible only from outside, with a half door and straw, a place for the dogs to whelp. And behind it a place never visited, never even accurately located, an old outdoor lavatory hidden behind a bed of nettles, and an ancient cesspit full of immemorial slime into which, according to legend, my Uncle Philip once descended to retrieve an errant puppy.

How a man would come after the lambing and burn off the lambs' tails and balls, the heat of red coals in their midwinter brazier, the smell of burned wool and flesh, and how you held the balls under the cold tap and squeezed and popped them out of their outer membrane, prior to rolling them in breadcrumbs and frying them.

How my brother and I, home from school for my grandfather's funeral, walked along the hither nut grove, cracking and eating unripe hazelnuts.

Bovie gutting and plucking chickens by the back door, and my mother later dousing them with flaming methylated spirits to burn off stubble.

My first Communion, how I returned from the altar to kneel at my place, replete with God, and laid my face in my hands, how I turned round and saw my grandmother smiling at me, and Sister Mary Aloysius gesturing to me to turn back again.

How the rain came through the roof.

How I would wake up in the middle of the night to the sound of the horses blowing, whinnying, galloping in the paddock.

How my uncle Austin sent us every year from Kenya the *Karamoja Times*.

How I slept under sheets, blankets, eiderdown, and over them my duffel coat, my head in its hood.

How I used to lie curled on my right side, reading in the light from the landing, my book held out to the open door.

The clunk of the latch on the garden gate.

How my grandmother and I made a crib out of an apple box.

My first confession, how I knelt in the dark, and confessed: I have told lies, I have stolen, I have been disobedient, I have been rude, I have used bad words.

How on winter nights a paraffin chimney stove was put in the upstairs lavatory and the trapdoor in the ceiling opened over it so that the water tank in the rafters would catch the heat and not freeze, and how it was a nice balance when you visited the place in the middle of the night between the comfort of warmth and fear of the dark hole above you.

The way my father looked over his glasses, the way he compressed his lips after drinking.

Cutting out patches for holed sacks, spreading them with Copydex, hammering them tight into place.

My Uncle Philip and I in the misty morning, hunting mushrooms.

The sheepfold on the top of the hill, and how the sheep ran out of it, every third one bounding high in the air, bleating loud, frisking away.

How I would wake early in the morning and climb into my mother's bed after my father had left it, how I would brush my mother's hair while she slept.

My brother and I out for a walk, and I slipping as I climbed over a barbed wire fence and opening my leg from thigh to calf on a barb, how I cupped my hands round my mouth and bellowed *Fuck!* to the answering hills.

The avenue of beeches between Tytherington and Corton, and the rampart at its end, where the road turned under the hill past the oakrooted slope and out into the valley. The furthest point of our afternoon walks.

Standing on a chair in my Uncle Roland's kitchen, singing *Angels from the Realms of Glory*.

The cathedral avenues of trees on the road to Salisbury. The lights of Bath as you drove down into the valley.

The flagstones on the kitchen floor, their unevennesses filled with plaster of Paris.

My Uncle Philip searching his black labrador for fleas, and popping them when found between his fingernails.

The smell of horses. The feel of their lips against your palm.

How my Great-aunt May and I, out for an afternoon walk, met an old gypsy woman who reached out a dirt-mottled hand to stroke my curly white hair and begged my aunt to give I thic babby, mam. Let I have thic babby.

Sneezing in bed, lying on my back and sneezing upwards, and the fine cold mist descending on my face.

Coming down the hill astraddle the tractor-drawn watertank, shifting water sonorous beneath me.

The ruined church of Saint Leonard's down the back lane, surrounded with daffodils and unkempt graves, where once I hid something in a hole in the wall.

The mirror in the changing room at All Hallows which was too high for me when I came, too low when I left.

A party in a hall in Warminster where the girls formed an

inner circle and the boys an outer, and revolved clockwise and counterclockwise respectively till the music stopped, and your partner was whoever stopped in front of you.

Five Ash Lane. Lord Bath's woods on one side. Major Walker's on the other.

Spending the night at my grandmother's, sleeping in a dark double bed, and dreaming of a bright wide river at the foot of the bed, and on the other side wild animals at graze, zebra, giraffe, gnu.

How the sheep went into the sheepdip, head high, floundering plunge, total immersion, a scramble up the slope.

Hammer strokes in Mrs Poor's garden, making you blink.

My cousin Erica beating me hollow at sums.

Penholders and inkwells, and how your fingers, no matter how hard you tried, got covered in ink.

The clearing in Eastleigh woods where we would picnic, a green rutted track led from the road to a bowered sward under an overgrowing beech branch to which we would tether our ponies, my cousin Susan and I, and devour sandwiches: jam, fishpaste, bacon, banana.

How Ronnie Graham told me Mrs Poor's was on wheels, square wheels so you couldn't see it move.

A spike in the batteries and Flossie Graham's hand grasping it, working up and down.

Cobwebs brushing my face on the attic stairs.

My Aunt Joan suckling my cousin Jane in the sunshine at the kitchen door.

The distance from the cottage where I was born and lived my first three years to the big house where my uncle lived. How it didn't seem so far at first, and got longer and longer.

How there used to be five shops. Mrs Ewen's where I bought chocolate and sherbet lemons, pear drops and jamboree bags. Mrs Waylen's up the road where I bought exercise books and pencils and elastic bands and soap for blowing bubbles and balloons and an imitation slate made of plastic film and carbon paper from which it was possible to erase what you had written and start again. Shepherd's the bakers opposite Mrs Ewen's. The post office at the top of the village, opposite the garage, where I once put a bicycle repair kit on my father's account. And McCracken's down Duck Lane, the off-licence where I bought illicit cigarettes.

Galloping my pony through the pigs' field, pursued by grunting, charging boars.

How there were two ways up the hill. The normal way and a second, much steeper way, a chalk road from which, if you sat on the back of the ascending tractor, the rapid passing of the overgrown hedges on either side made it look as if the hill on the other side of the valley was following you.

How I used to wake up early in the morning and sneak down to the kitchen for the biscuit tin, take it back to my bedroom, and eat Rich Tea biscuits before breakfast.

Cycling home across the common at night, how no matter how fast you pedalled down Bishopstrow hill it never gave you quite enough impetus to make it up the long slow slope past the Eastleigh turn-off, how you always had to get off and push, through the jittery dark, under the soughing trees.

Lying in my bed at the cottage, under my wallpaper with its pattern of trains, and hearing a train whistle on the Salisbury branch line across the fields.

My Uncle Philip's library, and how he gave me the complete set of the *Waverley* novels.

The sound of passing cars, passing trains, aeroplanes overhead.

How, when you walked at night from the garage to the back door, the night was here and there overlaid with milky vapours, and it was all you could do not to run.

Moving chicken coops with Flossie Graham, his naked feet in the clover, the hair on his toes.

The three ways down to McCracken's. Right at the gate, down past Miss Keith's house, down Duck Lane past the Goodalls' and along the ditch to the shop. Through the farmyard and left, past the cottage, up the lane to Saint Leonard's, the tunnel between the churchyard and Miss Alexander's garden, and down past Ayres' dairy. Across the wire fence at the bottom of the vegetable garden, a quick dash across Miss Alexander's field to the cottage opposite Goodalls', and you were almost there.

A picnic near Branksome Chines, and my aunt Joan in her new low-waisted dress.

How you could look out of an upper window of the piggeries on to an overgrown path past the batteries and an unhinged iron gate.

Night-time in the forty-acre field, shooting rabbits caught in the tractor's headlights, the whine of high-speed bullets fired at random through the dark.

My grandfather on his deathbed, his hands like claws, his face mottled, his cheeks gone, his nose a great beak.

My father and I in the paddock chicken coop. The uproar and the sudden silence as Bovie wrung the chicken's neck for our lunch.

The terror of Punch and Judy shows.

How I was watching television at my Aunt Joan's, a suspense thriller in which a character watchfully climbed the stairs and peered out onto an empty landing, and my cock hardened into its first erection, which seemed still to be there in the car on the way home and I wondered when and if it would ever go away.

At a Hunt Ball at Cortington Manor, Adrian Legg loosening, then untying, his bow tie.

The two bridges over the Wylye between Bishopstrow and the Boreham Road. How you always left your stomach behind when you drove over the first one, but never the second because you had to slow down for the junction.

How one of the houses in the village had a door on the first floor, a green-painted, pine plank door, opening onto the air.

How the water at Mount Mill fractured the reflections of the windows.

How we went on an outing to see *Reach For The Sky* and I fainted ten minutes into the film.

How sometimes I would get mixed up about where I was and genuflect in the aisle of the cinema.

How with each pass of the field the harrow had to be lifted and a thick mat of couch grass pulled away.

How a fine cloud of dust motes under the plane tree turned into a choking cloud of midges.

Lying on the Nicholls' lawn at Tytherington, reading the *Arabian Nights*, with the Dulac illustrations, the story of the prince who was turned into marble from the waist down.

Walking back from the swimming pool with a crowd of cousins along Imber Road and seeing my aunt Kathleen on the other side of the road. How I called out and waved, and it wasn't my aunt at all.

Cycling back at midday from my Saturday job, listing the items I would lay out on the bath tray. Soap, flannel, shampoo, nail brush, back brush, and the parts of the body I would wash and the order in which I would wash them.

How a fox ran under my horse's legs one day out on the Ranges and I didn't dare shout View Halloo. I watched it run through the grass and away till my cousin Erica saw it and shouted.

My father's photographs of his parents, dead in the year I was born, high on the wall above a shelf in the breakfast room.

The changing light over the watercress beds at Sherrington.

How I was ill and broke a fruit bowl, and when I confessed to my mother she smiled and soothed and I confessed some more and she still smiled and I went on confessing.

The meals. Breakfast of either bacon and eggs with fried bread or a couple of boiled eggs on alternate days, followed by cereal with milk, sugar and cream, and toast with butter and marmalade. Tea and biscuits at eleven o'clock. Lunch of meat, gravy, vegetables and potatoes with a pudding, stewed fruit usually, with junket. Tea of bread and butter with jam with cakes and biscuits, when it wasn't hot toast in front of the sitting room fire. Supper of soup, bread, fruit, pasta. A cup of tea and a biscuit before bed.

My father outside my door, head down, looking back at me and waving.

My mother in her armchair with cigarette, paper and crossword, looking up at the sound of my opening the gate and jumping up to open the door for me.

My grandmother at the top of the hill at the back of her house, and I walking with her, asking her to come on, to come down the hill with me, and she declining, saying that she would be able to get down well enough, but getting up again, that was another matter.

How at my mother's funeral my niece Rosie left a bunch of

daffodils on her grave, and how I came down later and took one of the daffodils from the bunch and put it on my father's grave behind her.

Barbed Wire Blues

Hear that wild dog hollering?
Keep him out with Two-Staple Wing,
Roll me some Two-Staple Wing, yes, and make it
   plenty,
My baby has ten fingers and a throat to croon and sing.

No ways he going to reach you, girl.
Keep him out with Merrill Twirl,
Roll me Merrill Twirl, yes, and keep it rolling,
My baby has a mile of hair and starlight every curl.

Roll me Brink Flat, roll me Buckthorn,
Roll me Baker Perfect.
Never know what I'm expecting,
Post and wire is for protecting,
Still more fences to be pegged.

Pray that if he leaps he'll miss.
Keep him out with Oval Twist,
Roll me Oval Twist, yes, and make it bristle,
My baby has a tongue that moves like a contortionist.

What makes him think he's getting down?
Keep him out with Wrap-Round,
Roll me Wrap-Round, yes, and make it double,
My baby has a couple of legs that reach right to the
   ground.

Roll me Old Square, roll me Half Round,
Roll me Haish and Glidden.

Tug it, turn a loop and bend up,
Where I start is where I end up,
Ripped-up hands is all I get.

Tell that dog to take a trip.
Keep him out with Scutts Clip,
Roll me some Scutts Clip, yes, and pack it thick,
My baby has a low-slung rear cracks like a rawhide
 whip.

How's that wild thing getting in?
Keep him out with 4 Point 1 Between,
Roll me 4 Point 1 Between, yes, and nail it clean,
My baby has the tightest little snatch I ever seen.

Roll me Stubbs Plate, roll me Sawtooth,
Roll me Kelly's Knife Blade.
Plugging staples, three days riding,
Bodies never made for hiding,
Still they find her where she lies,
Still they find her where she lies.

Driving

Tracer
The cat's-eyes' tracer:
I drive too fast
and play my latest
cheap cassette full–blast
to clear my head
of the soured past
I drive away from
this week, like last.

Pelt
The flash of fur
the wheels' soft jar
the half-heard, half-felt
bump not stopped for
and the ruptured pelt
rapidly dwindling
in the mirror –
something limp
and useless on the road,
a gritty lump
I meet again
week after week.

If we rescued it
from the passing tyres
I too could hold it up
and point to scars.

It was a mutt
it was lame
it had only one eye
but you loved it
just the same
whatever it was
with its piebald fur
its ticket-punched ear –
and it loved you
when not licking its wounds
or inflicting more
with one paw
or the other paw.

Bee

'There's a bee in the car.'
Anxious love in the mirror,
but there was no danger,
nothing to stop for,
just the dancing medallion
my watch set swinging –
summer's reflection
lasering the interior:

something precious
and non-existent
lasting only
as long as the sun
or the journey
or my having
my hand on the wheel.

Dash

And if, one of these tired nights,
lost in a reverie of loss,
I lose my way in the oncoming lights,

and free-fall through a pail of stars
to rest among crossed elbows on the dash,
I'll rise above the slowing, curious cars
to contemplate the fairground flashes,
the sirens and the walkie-talkie static,
the maze of cones through which an armband waves
the hesitant and seemingly reluctant traffic,
and hug myself with armless sleeves,
exulting in the emptiness
your back-seat seat-belt hugs like
life itself, like a reprieve.

Night Fishing

From a distance – twilight's distance, which is
   measureless –
they stand identically bulked out, coat on coat,
stubborn-stumped as breakwaters watching the sea
creep fawning to their feet, retreat again. And he is
   there

among them, indistinguishable from the rest; no one
   would guess
how frail, how warped his frame is now, how inside
the woollen gloves red blooms on his knuckles, veins
surface from the netting of each hand. He has escaped
   me,

joined this camaraderie of men who come to test
the dark, each bivouacked beside a tilted half-shell
sheltering a flask, a stool, spread ammunition:
weights spiked round like spurs, the crawling bait;
   trawling

from this long unfeatured beach for the treasures,
   wrecks
of childhood. Night will hang a curtain over what he
   does,
the night which rolls in with the tide and lights
a hundred lanterns springing white along the coast,
   unblinking,

inventing the lie of some vast road; along its route, as
   far

and further than the eye can see, they loom, rods
    straining,
lines stretched taut into the opaque hopefulness
of space. Distant sandbanks, shifting, tempt them: We
    are here,

they whisper, rising to be picked out palely by the
    moon,
altering the water's weave; this is where
the fish lie, softly waving their tails from side to
    side . . .
My father threads his hooks, adjusts the pendulum,
    leans back,

and casts. His shoulders, knees, crack out a warning in
    my ears –
he is so brittle beneath his camouflage of clothes;
I wait for it to happen, the overanxious throw
which sends him clattering down, rod leaping from his
    hands, his face

fish-white and small, bleached in his own lamp's light,
    and no one there
to see; and I am flying, struggling to return him
to familiarity, to drag him back
with me into any of the windblown weekend afternoons

of all the years we scoured the emptied beach together,
    my hand
in his and warmer and more real than any lure
the sea tossed at our feet – which we threw back,
    laughing:
snares of tangled line, the silvered cold of a lost weight.

Avoirdupois

The weight of mercury and frost
or the plover's weight of remorse
at the root of my tongue

when I stood in the polished hall
and my grandfather died by ounces
a door's breadth away.

No one could measure his house:
the loads were too subtle, too fine:
the weight of hooks, the swish of gaberdine,

his ghosts come in to tea, still damp with rain,
stains in the books Aunt Eleanor had read
the year she died,

and where he lay, the weight of riverbeds:
the tide of shadows under Fulford burn
where fat trout swam like phantoms in the weeds

and where I saw him once, big and alive,
dabbling his hands in the water, as if he would lift
the fish of our dreams, the catch that would break the
    scales.

Lud's Church

A chasm roofed with ferns was our assembly room.
Whimsical spiders landed on our skin,
And droplets of week–old rain
Pulled by a magnet to their secret pool
Like spies called to a conference,
Altering course, arriving severally.

We knew the niches where our lamps would stand
Arched in their spluttering constellation.
Settling, we felt against our bones
Familiar knobbly places, as when
A vagrant husband holidaying at home opens
His arms to the brain-flood of memories.

Damp leaked into our lungs, like the soft wedge
Of autumn in the trees. Long-suffering, we sifted
Sense from sound, and only then spoke out,
Clothing new sense as best we could
Around a skeleton of borrowed eloquence,
To shape another soldier for the cause:

As our lives were treated, so we would treat their laws.

Worse Things than Divorce

I was helping Dancey lift his wife April by her ears into
   the sky
(he was round today like someone a fish might imagine)
when a gang of blue-jeaned mothers, each with a tiny
   snuffling baby
floppily-strapped to her bosom, rushed us and rescued
   her.
That evening I surprised Dancey buttoning himself into
   one of her gowns.
Swathed in the soft bondage of her perilously-frail
   undergarments,
he said with a regal glare, 'Obviously I seek to detain
   her spirit,
Carol. But her perfumes are fading, minute by minute!'
He avoided red the least of all the colours in her
   wardrobe.
'Oh why did they take her from me!' he wept, his
   moustache
dripping with tears. 'Now I am just like everyone else.'
   (Despairingly
he pulled one of her stockings down over his face.)

We parted friends, sometime in late summer, early
   autumn.
It rained and rained as he legged it past the Lloyd's
   Building,
lovely bright rain, you know?
so that everything had this golden-wet alchemique
   glitter,

especially the sky rainbowing high over the city of
   fierce mothers
and tiny babies and disappeared wives, the sky
where Dancey longed to reign with April.
'Darling,' he shouted, scampering along. 'April,
   darling!'
As he splashed away, he grew taller and taller,
like somebody a spider or a baby might imagine.
   'Darling!'
His yells grew fainter, his head nudged the clouds . . .
And me? Here I am, ironing shirts, yawning,
   grumbling,
grinning at the whiff of sex that sneaks into the room,
just as if Dancey were here, saying, 'Lo, it is I . . .
   Everything is OK.'

Teashop '92

O superfluous sprays of light on an esplanade!
The winter urn is cooling, the girl is closing:
I'm sorry, she says, *We are closing now*.

But the customer asks about tea with such hopeless
   charm
That the girl is not resentful she cannot
Go home quite yet; perhaps go home any more.

This one can charm the birds down from the trees
So they thud to the ground in dozens, and the girl
Is second by second feeling wingless

And she drops down behind the counter, behind
The fridge of coloured ices, small plastic skips
Full of scraped-at choices of lime, or tangerine,

Or rum-and-raisin. It drones while he drums his fingers
(Little finger up to thumb) and smiles and smiles.
The girl lies there and thinks, *Do I have a choice?*

With my head against the cartons of UHT?
With my eyes trapped by shelves lined with newspapers
Full of photographs of terrors I hadn't really

Ever noticed 'til this moment, one leg straight out,
One leg bent under, one thin arm free to move?
Could I lie here and hope he leaves, and closes

The door? she wonders. *I shall know if he's gone*

When the bell rings. Or should I push
The panic button, fast, for living help?

Or should I serve him? Over the sea, the sun
Goes through the bottom-line horizon, far away,
Below three colour-choices of January cloud.

The Crossing of Herald Montjoy

A piece of ground near Agincourt. October 1415.

He does not have far to ride.

The distance between the two encamped armies is little more than a mile. They are so close that at night-time, in the cold stillness, each can hear the laughter of the other, and the swearing and the cries. They're like neighbouring farmers, eavesdropping in the moonlight.

The French are noisier than the English. There are far more of them, they have more liquor and they seem to know more songs.

Herald Montjoy walks out from the French camp, through the wood on the right towards Maisoncelles, and stands among the trees and listens to the English. He can hear a lot of hammering. He thinks the exhausted soldiers may be trying to make cabins out of elm. He remembers his little nephew, Roland, who has made a tree-house. He loves Roland. Having no children of his own, he's tried to describe what he is to Roland. He has told him: 'A herald is a watcher. It's important to understand this. He oversees the conduct of armies, but doesn't really belong to them. He's not a man-at-arms, but a man apart.'

Then, a morning comes, salt-white with frost, when Herald Montjoy is summoned to the Dauphin's tent. The Dauphin instructs him to ride out across the fields to the English camp and inquire whether the English King is ready to ransom himself, to save his ragged army from certain defeat. The Dauphin's tent is sumptuous with blue and gold hangings. The Dauphin is doing body-building exercises all the while he is talking. As Montjoy leaves the tent, he hears him say to the Duke of Alençon: 'God, I'm fit.'

Herald Montjoy gets on his horse. The land he must cross
has been ploughed and he's worried that the horse is going to
stumble on the icy ridges of earth. A mist hangs on the fields,
milky and dense, and the herald wishes that this, too, wasn't
there. This and the hard frost give the day such strange singu-
larity.

A piece of ground near the manor of La Vallée. April 1412.

He did not have far to ride.

The distance between his parents' house and the manor where
Cecile lived was little more than two miles. He and his horse
knew every step by heart. It was mostly downhill. And he
would see the house long before he reached it. And always his
thoughts flew ahead of him and landed, gentle as birds, on
Cecile's head and on her shoulders and on her feet in coloured
shoes.

She was so . . . *exceptional*. He tried, on these journeys to
and from her house, to decide what, if anything, she resembled
– in nature, or in man's inventions. He wondered whether he
could compare her to a lake of water lilies where silvery fish
glimmered deep down. Or was she like a sundial, unerring, yet
always speaking, in her adoration of ephemeral things, of time's
passing?

He decided there was nothing and no one as strangely beautiful as her. Not even the landscape through which he and his
horse had to pass, with its flowering meadows, its clear stream,
its silent woods and its perfumed air. Not even his dreams, in
which he sometimes gave himself wings and flew up into the
sky and floated above France.

No. Cecile was more to him than any of these things. She
kept honey bees in tall hives in her father's orchard. Her bee-
keeping hat had a gossamer veil that fell to earth all round her
and whenever Herald Montjoy dreamed of flying above France,

there below him walked Cecile in her bee veil with nothing on underneath.

He knew he had to marry Cecile. He had to possess her: her body, her soul, her petticoats, her bees, her shoe cupboard. He couldn't wait much longer.

He was a handsome man, with dark soft hair and a curling lip, and he had no doubt that when he proposed to Cecile he would be accepted. He would say to her father: 'Sir, in two or three years' time, I aim to become Chief Herald of France. I don't think that is an unrealistic boast.'

Agincourt. October 1415.

His hat is a strange confection, indigo blue with loops of velvet that fall just above his left eye and bounce up and down as the horse canters.

This bouncing of his blue hat as he advances into the icy mist makes him fret. It's as if everything is conspiring to blind him on this frozen day. He finds himself wishing it were night, with a round moon to light the field and the songs and the hammering of the English to guide him on. He feels that under these conditions, he would see and think much more clearly; whereas, in this fog, with the forest petrified and silent close by, he feels confused and half-afraid.

He reins in his horse and turns him into the wood and dismounts. He sets down the weighty standard by an oak tree. He ties the horse to the tree.

He takes off his hat, runs a hand through his curly hair. All around him is the tracery of the night's frost, fingering every spine. He asks himself: Why afraid, Montjoy?

He is thirty years old, three years older than Henry of England.

Is everyone on this piece of earth afraid of the battle that is there and not there in every mind? Of the future battle that is coming or may never happen – there and not there, departing like a lover, returning like a fever . . . ?

The Dauphin isn't afraid. 'Afraid? Bunk!' And then he admires his leg. 'The English won't last more than half an hour. If that.'

His instructions reveal his nonchalance: 'Just tell the King to give himself up for ransom, all right, Montjoy? Then that sack of bones he calls an army can go home and litter up Southampton.'

He's been told to ride fast, to return quickly. The Dauphin's getting impatient with all the waiting. Montjoy has never disobeyed an order in his life, yet now he's in the wood, scratching his head, standing still, staring at the trees. He feels as if he can't make this crossing, but he doesn't know why.

La Vallée. April 1412.

He felt weightless on that April morning. He felt as if he could swing himself up off his horse and into the air. He was wearing a sky-blue tunic. The sun shone on those soft curls of his.

He was riding to La Vallée to ask for Cecile's hand. His mother and father had waved and grinned as he'd set off: 'Such a *beautiful* girl, son. So striking! We wish you joy and success.'

His thoughts, as always, had already landed on Cecile. They caressed her shoulder. They lay trapped like butterflies under her lavender-coloured cloak as she put it on and walked out of the house carrying a basket.

What was she going to put in the basket? Branches of blossom?

A thought is seldom trapped for long. It can travel anywhere. It can make decisions.

Montjoy's thoughts escaped from under the cloak. They walked with Cecile through the damp grass. They hid in the shadow of her skirts, high up in the darkness between her legs. They were touched in a caressing way as she took each step.

So then he had to slow his horse, dismount, walk to a stream, try to clear his head. 'You're running too fast,' he told himself. 'You're not her bridegroom yet.'

He knelt over the stream and cupped icy spring water and splashed his face. He gasped. There were days in a life so momentous they seemed to alter the size of the world. His heart felt as colossal as a cuckoo bird. The sky above his kneeling figure expanded and expanded, wider, fatter, closer to heaven than it had ever been.

He sat down on the grass. His horse grazed and flicked his tail at the spring flies. There *are* splendid lives, he thought. There *is* bravery and there is luck. There is ingenuity. A woman's shoe can be yellow. . . .

There were yellow flowers at the stream's edge. Montjoy wasn't good at the names of flowers, but he sat there for a long while, admiring these particular ones.

Agincourt. October 1415.

In this desolate wood, Montjoy looks for something green, something that will be soft to the touch.

This fear that he can't name has seeped from his mind, down and down all through him and touched his heart like a ghost and then his sphincter, and now he's crouching down and defecating onto the dry bracken.

He can see nothing green, nothing soft to the touch to wipe his arse with. He has to scrape up handfuls of harsh bracken and fallen leaves and clean himself with these. As he pulls up his stockings, he feels like weeping.

The wood oppresses him. He'd come into the wood to find a moment's peace before he has to complete his ride to the English camp. But the wood feels dead.

Leaving his horse tied up and the standard leaning against the tree, he makes his way back towards the ploughed field under its curtain of mist.

He walks forward, his feet unsteady on the frosted ridges. He can sense, now, that the mist is going to clear and that the day may after all be fine. Already, there's more light on the field.

He looks down at the earth. He wonders who works this land, what crop he has in mind for the year to come. The loops of Montjoy's indigo hat fall over his eyes. He is standing now on the place where the very centre of the battle will be. Here, where his feet are, an English soldier will fall, his lungs pierced with a lance, blood bursting from his throat. All around him will lie his doomed compatriots, souls vanished into the air. This is the crop to come: in an ecstasy of death, this land will be seeded with the English. And it will be his task to count them – his and the English heralds' – to make an orderly tally, even if limbs or heads are severed and fall some way from the torsos. All heralds must be precise. They mustn't look away. Afterwards, he will say to his nephew, Roland: 'I saw it. It took place near the castle of Agincourt. But you couldn't call it a great battle. It was too one-sided.'

He is aware, suddenly, that a lot of time has passed since he set out. Far ahead, he can hear the English resume their pathetic hammering. And this comforts him, somehow. His fear has lessened.

He strides back into the wood and unties his horse. The horse is trembling with cold. He slaps it gently to warm it.

He mounts and takes up his standard. He faces his horse towards the light soaking through the rising mist and rides on.

La Vallée. April 1412.

Sitting by the stream with the sun quite warm on his nose, Montjoy rehearsed his declaration of love and his offer of marriage.

He imagined Cecile standing with her back towards him, looking out of a window. He went down on one knee, but she hadn't noticed this. Her shoulders were very still. He said: 'Cecile, I think it must have been apparent to you for some time that I consider you to be the centre of my universe . . .'

He imagined her smiling – *so now he's going to propose to me!* – but trying to conceal the smile.

He said: 'And really so it is. Or rather, it's more than this: you have actually altered the way I see the world. Before I met you, my life seemed so small, so circumscribed. But together, you and I could become masters – or rather, I mean, master and mistress – of a fine destiny!'

He decided it was wise, or at least diplomatic, to ask Cecile at this point whether she, too, felt the earth transformed by *his* presence at her side. And he imagined that she turned from the window and came running to him and pulled him to his feet and said: 'Yes, Montjoy! Yes. I feel the earth transformed!' And then he kissed her.

The kiss was so heavenly that Montjoy, alone by the stream, let it last for several minutes. His eyes were fixed on some vacant spot, unseeing. Above him flew thrushes and finches. Fleets of minnows sailed by him in the water.

When the kiss was over, Montjoy looked around him. At dusk, he would ride back this way with Cecile's promise to be his wife locked inside him like money locked in a box. And always, after today, when he rode this way, he would feel that this was hallowed ground – the spongy grass, the yellow flowers, the icy stream – because it was here that his future came to meet him.

A bee buzzed by him.

He got to his feet. He and the bee were moving to the same enchanted, perfumed destination.

Agincourt. October 1415.

One of their scavenge-parties, sent out to gather nuts and berries and firewood, sees him coming with his flying banner from far off. Two of the party stand and gape at him; two others start running back to the English camp.

They make him feel smart, these bedraggled English, carrying bundles of sticks. His blue hat no longer feels ridiculous, but slightly stylish. He bounces high in the saddle.

He is memorising the Dauphin's instructions: 'Look,

Montjoy, the thing is perfectly simple. The English can't possibly win. We outnumber them five to one. If they can't understand this simple arithmetic, do a demonstration with pebbles or coins or any damn thing that happens to be at hand. They are about to be overwhelmed. What a marvellous word! *Overwhelmed*. I love it. Right?'

And now, as the mist disperses, he can begin to see the English camp. It huddles in among some thin trees. Just as he'd envisaged, the men have made themselves hovels from sticks and bracken. There are a few threadbare tents. Smoke rises from a dozen small fires. He can see soldiers grouped around them, trying to warm themselves. They turn their white faces towards him.

Montjoy has never been to England. He has been told that one corner of it lies under water, but that elsewhere there are great forests, older than time. And these men that he sees look half drowned to him, or else, with this pallor they have, appear like people who live perpetually in a wooded darkness.

He slows his horse. Like grey ghosts, English soldiers have crept out of the trees and stand staring at him. What honour for France can there possibly be in slaughtering people already half dead? What honour for the heralds to oversee such a massacre? He thinks of Roland. In the tender privacy of the boy's tree-house, Montjoy had once said to him: 'Roland, there are two things that have counted with me in my life and one of them is honour . . .'

But his thoughts are interrupted, because now he realises that a group of men-at-arms is approaching him. They have formed themselves into a square. In the middle of the square, Montjoy can glimpse something bright. It is the crown on the King's head.

Montjoy takes off his hat. He dismounts. Carrying the standard and leading his horse, he moves forward on foot. And in this moment (he can't say why) a fragment of his earlier fear lodges in his heart and he sees coming towards him, as if in a dream or a vision, not Henry of England but his beloved Cecile, wearing a garland of yellow flowers round her hair.

He falters. Then he urges himself on. He is aware, now, that hundreds of the English ghosts have come out of the trees and are gazing at him.

He bows to the King. When he looks up, he sees a squarish, bony face and a complexion less pale than those around him. The regard is soft and the voice, when he hears it, is gentle.

'Well, herald?'

'Sir,' says Montjoy, 'I've come from the Dauphin. He and all the nobles with him urge you to consider your position. They estimate that your army is outnumbered by five to one and they feel that, to save your men from certain death, the best course you can follow is to give yourself up for ransom . . .'

Montjoy sees one of the men-at-arms belch silently. He decides that two things keep these people from fleeing back to Calais: drink and the presence of their King.

'What is your name, herald?' asks the King.

'Montjoy, Sir.'

The King smiles. The men-at-arms appear to stare through Montjoy to the piece of ground over which he has just travelled.

Still smiling, the King says: 'Montjoy, say this to Prince Dauphin. We would like to remind him that there are very few certainties on earth. Extraordinarily few. When I was a boy, I kept a stag-beetle in an ivory box. I used to speak to it. And one evening, it spoke back to me. Until that time, I'd been absolutely certain that a stag-beetle was unable to talk.'

The King laughs. The men-at-arms turn their anxious eyes from the field and look at their monarch. 'So you see,' says the King. 'One never knows.'

'What did the beetle say, Sir?' asks Montjoy.

'Oh, I don't remember. Just a word or two. It was the unexpectedness that struck me. So there you are, herald. Your Dauphin can believe in his certainty or not as he pleases. It makes no difference to us. We will not be ransomed.'

The ghostly faces have clustered near to the King and are

trying to listen to what he's saying. They stare and blink in the sunlight so foreign to them. They scratch their bodies through their clothing.

'God go with you, Montjoy,' says the King.

Montjoy bows. The King and his men-at-arms turn round and walk away. Montjoy replaces his blue hat on his dark head.

La Vallée. April 1412.

There was the house. There were the doves, like winged thoughts, on the roof. Smoke drifted up from one of the stone chimneys.

Montjoy was still rehearsing his proposal as he dismounted and handed the reins of his horse to a servant. Then the servant informed him that Mademoiselle Cecile and her parents had gone to visit a cousin struck down by a tumbling weathercock. They were not expected back until late afternoon.

In the tableau Montjoy had seen in his mind, there had been morning light at the window where Cecile stood while he told her about the alteration to his world. And he liked things to proceed as he'd imagined them. So now he hesitated: should he leave or should he wait?

He decided to wait. The servant led his horse away. He sat on a stone wall and stared up at the sky. Then, he walked to the orchard where the apple blossom was in flower and stood near to Cecile's beehives. The traffic of bees to and from them absorbed his attention for a long time. He kept picturing the honeyed world inside. He decided that the thing in nature Cecile most closely resembled was a cluster of bees. She moved in ways that he couldn't fully understand and yet all the while there was purpose in her.

Cecile discovered him in the orchard. He'd fallen asleep in the sun and was dreaming of the sea. When he woke and found Cecile standing above him, he believed, for a fragment of a second, that she was a ship in sail, moving past him and on.

She was laughing. Montjoy realised how ridiculous he must

look, asleep in the grass like a peasant boy. He scrambled to his feet, straightening his tunic, running a hand through his hair. Desperately, he searched for words.

Before he found any, Cecile held out her hands for him to take. He noticed then that her face was very pink and her eyes wide. She was wearing a white dress.

'My friend!' she said, 'I'm so glad to find you here! So happy! That you should be here – and sleeping like a child! – is somehow perfectly right. Because I'm in such a state! You can tell just by looking at me, can't you? I'm in such a state of pure joy!'

'Are you, Cecile?'

'Yes! And you are just the person I want to share it with. You've been such a sweet friend to me and now I can tell you my wonderful news! What day is it? I'll always remember this day. Always and always. Now ask me why!'

'Why Cecile?'

'Because I'm going to be married! Monsieur de Granvilliers proposed to me this afternoon. I'm going to have a wonderful life!'

Cecile let go of Montjoy's hands and went dancing off round the orchard, twirling her arms above her head. Montjoy saw that the shoes she was wearing that day were also white and it occurred to him that the grass would soon stain them. The grass appeared dry, but it wasn't. He could feel its dampness on his buttocks and against his shoulder blades and all down his spine.

Agincourt. October 1415.

Returning at a canter, Montjoy soon leaves the smells and sounds of the English camp behind. He doesn't stop to look at the field or the wood. He isn't thinking about the battle to come, but about the kind of voice a stag-beetle might possess. Up in his tree-house, Roland makes up different voices for the wind and the stars. Some of the stars don't speak, only yawn.

The Dauphin is at lunch with all his favourite counts and dukes. They're eating blackbirds.

'God, Montjoy,' says the Dauphin, 'you've been an age. What happened?'

Montjoy is very hot after his ride. He can feel sweat in his hair.

'I'm sorry, Sir,' he says, 'I did explain to the King how far he's outnumbered, but – '

'But what?'

'He refuses to be ransomed. He seems willing to fight.'

The Dauphin picks up a blackbird and bites it in half, crunching the little bones. He speaks with his mouth full. 'Did you explain it properly? Five to *one*. Did you show him?'

'There wasn't an opportunity to show him, Sir. His mind is made up.'

'Well then, he's a fool,' says the Dauphin. 'A bumptious fool. It means that he's now going to die. Simple as that. Every single one of them is going to die.'

The Dauphin eats the second half of his blackbird. He spits out a piece of bone and wipes his mouth. 'Get me the Constable of France, Montjoy,' he says. 'We'll get all this over with tomorrow. I'm tired of being here. And the food's ghastly. Off you go.'

Montjoy backs out of the Dauphin's tent. He feels tired. He feels he could lie down anywhere and sleep.

La Vallée. April 1412.

Out of politeness, he had to pay his respects to Cecile's parents before he could leave. They told him that Monsieur de Granvilliers had hinted at his intention to marry Cecile back in January. Cecile's mother said: 'We're very flattered. This is a very good match.'

Montjoy wanted to say: 'I love her better than Granvilliers. She alters my earth. I'd sleep with her in my arms. I'd buy her

any number of pairs of shoes.' But he kept silent and only
nodded.

Then he rode back along the way he had come. The sun was
going down and glinted red in the fast-running stream. He tried
not to think of anything at all. When he got to the clump of
yellow flowers, he looked the other way. His horse stumbled
on a stone and he wished he could become that stone and feel
nothing.

Montjoy's parents were eating dinner when he arrived back
at the house. They looked up expectantly from their soup and
put down their spoons.

Montjoy stood in the doorway and looked at them. For the
first time in his life, he envied them with an aching, fathomless
envy. They had lived side by side contentedly for thirty-one
years. They still shared their bed.

He put a fist up to his mouth. Through the clenched fist, he
said: 'Cecile's not in my life any more. So please don't mention
her again. She's in the past and I don't want to speak about it.
It or her. I don't want to talk about any of it. Ever.'

He turned and left the room before either his mother or his
father could say a word.

Agincourt. October 1415.

He has been summoned by the English King, three years his
junior.

It's getting dark. The rain that came in the early morning has
stopped and a white moon is rising. And under the white moon
lie the French dead.

He and his horse have to pick their way among corpses.
There's a shine on them and on the fouled earth where they lie.

For the second time in Montjoy's life, he asks himself, as he
rides on into a gathering dusk: 'Why was something as terrible
as this not foreseen by me?'

He remembers the Dauphin's mockery: 'They won't last half

an hour!' He remembers his own imaginary words to Roland: 'You couldn't call it a great battle. It was too one-sided.'

He's a herald. Heralds ride in the vanguard of events. They announce. They watch and assess. They bring the expected after them. But not him. Despite his eminence, despite his optimistic name, the unimaginable follows him like a shadow.

He doesn't know precisely how this day was lost. He tried to follow what was occurring. He kept weaving in and out of the wood, trying to see, trying to get a picture. He heard the English arrows fly. He saw a cloud of arrows fall on the first line of cavalry, heard them clatter on helmets and backplates, like hailstones on an army kitchen. He saw some horses go down and their riders fall, helpless as saucepans in their armour, kicked or trampled by hooves.

Then he saw, as the first line rode on, the English men-at-arms fall back. They fell back in a ghostly way, just as, before, they emerged from the wood – one moment there and the next moment not there. And where they'd been standing, facing the French cavalry, on the very place where they'd been, now there was a line of stakes, newly sharpened, pointing out of the ground. There was a thick fence of them, a thousand or more, three or four deep with room in between them for only the most insubstantial men.

He knew the horses would rear, would try to turn, would do all that they could not to be thrown onto the stakes. But many of them couldn't turn because in their massed charge, flank to flank, they were coming on too fast and so they exploded onto the fence and the riders were pitched forward into the enemy's arms.

One of the other heralds had told him at dawn: 'The English are eating handfuls of earth. This means they accept their coming death and burial.' And he'd felt pity for them, as violent as love. Now, Montjoy's horse carries him awkwardly, slipping and staggering in the mud, through the field of the French dead. The dead appear fat with this white moon up, casting bulky shadows. Montjoy covers his mouth with his blue glove and tips his head back and looks for stars. There is one in the west, yawning, and he thinks again of Roland in his tree-house and then of all the souls of the French struggling to cross the chasm of the sky.

He won't give an account of the battle to Roland because then he would have to answer too many unanswerable questions. Why did the first line of French cavalry turn round and collide with the men-at-arms coming forward? Does this mean that some of the French foot soldiers died before they even reached the English line? And then, when they reached the line, what happened that so many died so quickly? Were they packed together so tightly in a mass that they couldn't fight properly? Was the mass, shouting and pushing and afraid and confused, soon walled up behind its own dead?

It had rained so hard all through the battle, the heralds' task of seeing had been impeded.

All Montjoy can hope now, as he nears the English camp and hears voices singing, is that time will bring him understanding.

He rides on. He must make a formal acknowledgement of defeat to King Henry. He hopes that his voice is going to be strong, but fears that it may sound weak and small, like the voice of a stag-beetle in an ivory box.

He feels exhausted. In his exhaustion, he aches to be no longer a man apart, but a man going home to his wife with a gift of crimson shoes.

Wild Duck

'They will come from over there,' the man pointed at a red volcanic hill.

He and the boy both had guns resting across their knees. They sat facing each other in a small motionless boat with the oars tucked in.

'Are you ready?' he asked his son.

'Yes.'

'They come in clouds, huge clouds moving very fast.' He moved his arm in a wide sweep, rocking the dug-out boat. 'You have to be quick. Shoot fast.'

The boy ran his finger down the cold blue barrel. Minute by minute the light changed on the flat surface of the water. Orange, red, mauve seeped from the sky. It was late afternoon. A lake in a wilderness.

The man checked his gun; there were six cartridges in the magazine. He opened a knapsack and took out a fresh box of ammunition. 'Loading is what takes the time.' He placed the open box on the wooden slats between them. The fat brass rings of a dozen cartridges stared out: bright, neat, hard, with purple pupils.

His son was cradling the other gun: a .22 rifle he had given the boy after the revolution. He had won it at a poker game. The Colonel had claimed it was the deposed dictator's own first gun, a weapon of some considerable notoriety used to dispose of early opponents through fictitious acts of heroism. The moment he heard the story he had wanted the gun. He pushed his whole pile of Taiwanese chips – blue and red – to the centre of the table. 'Here. The whole lot against the gun.' The sweat burst out of his forehead but he won; he had four jacks in his hand.

His son had been pleased with it and quickly learned to puncture bull's-eyes and empty cans strung up at the end of the field. This was the first time he had taken it out to kill.

'You loaded?'

'Yes.'

'Remember, aim well ahead. You have to imagine the flight path. With just one pellet, you've got to be dead-on.'

'I know.'

The boy didn't waste words. He sometimes wished his son was bigger – taller and wider – with a bigger tongue; maybe that might have made him talk more, be more open and share his view of the way things were. He wanted the boy to get a feel for the whole world and their place in it. *You have to move out of your corner.* But the boy had his every nerve always concentrated between the *v* and the *ball* of his rifle sights: his narrow shoulders hunched to drive a bullet into the centre of its target. He wanted total control. Nothing left to chance. The man wanted to tell him total control was impossible. Even God sometimes misses. He had learned over the years how little is ever fulfilled. Nothing is ever certain. If only the lessons of life could be handed on. But time passed too quickly. The boy was growing fast. The years slipped by even as he reached out. He had wanted someone, his son, to *know* someday what he was really like inside. To touch his deepest nerve and connect him to another. But sitting in the boat watching his son check the smooth action of the gun-bolt he wondered what could a boy ever know of his father. His son had grown up under a wretched regime; the boy had no idea of the hopes of his father's youth and the compromises by which they had been eroded. Their lives were moulded by a dictatorship of vanity.

Suddenly the boy looked up. 'Is that them?' A ribbon of black dots billowed out of the horizon. The boy was spellbound: breath whistled out of his small round mouth. 'There must be millions.' Half the sky was covered by teal. Huge clouds of them banked one way, then another, changing the shape of the sky and blotting the light. The sky deepened, the water turned black. Small groups broke away: diving, then rising in perfect formations. 'Will they all land here, on the lake?'

'They look too high. I think they're aiming for somewhere else.'

'Who decides?'

'They know.'

Then they were overhead. The sky filled with arrowheads of duck, masses in flight. A crescendo of bird calls. Father and son looked at each other.

'Here goes,' the man undid his safety-catch and started firing, throwing buck-shot at the sky. The explosions shook the boat. The lake rippled. He pumped the gun empty. 'Too high, they're flying much too high.'

His son slowly raised his rifle; he had a more patient and steady hand. He picked a single speck out of the mass in the sky: the leader of a formation flying towards them. He aimed and fired and fired and fired. He worked the bolt rapidly, loading fresh bullets and discarding old shells without removing the gun from against his shoulder. The speck plummeted.

'You got the leader,' the man cheered. Another bird swiftly took its place; they were all leaders by instinct.

'I want to find it.' The boy put down his rifle and took the paddle. 'Did you see where?'

'He fell just behind the bulrushes. Go round that way.'

The boy moved the boat against the tide of teal still wheeling overhead; his arms trembled as he pulled the paddle through the black water.

Last Sunday he had taken his rifle apart, cleaned and oiled every inch of it. At that same time the teal, with his victim among them, would have taken to the skies: bird and bullet propelled towards each other by some inner compulsion.

The man imagined his son squeezing the trigger when he had *already* in a sense hit the duck; the intersection of the two flight paths – bullet and bird – was preordained in their two lives, it was only a matter of inking in the lines. He felt a delicious sense of destiny. 'I think I can see it,' he said, leaning forward.

There was a lump floating on the water. A broken wing pointing at the sky like the ragged sail of a toy boat. The boy lifted the paddle and they glided up to it. He bent over the side and scooped it up.

'Well done!' the man said.

His son was silent.

The duck was big; helpless. There was nothing it could have done against the bullet. It would not have known what was coming, when or where from. Touching its soft feathers and its thin bony neck, the boy looked frightened at what he had done.

Then the duck lifted up its head.

'Look, it's not dead.'

The blood seemed to flow again in the boy's arms. He breathed in relief.

'You must have winged it.' The man examined the bird, 'No. The wing's broken from the fall.' He looked up at his son and laughed, 'You know, I think you *missed* it. You must have just shocked it. The sound of your bullet whizzing by.'

The duck looked blank. The boy stroked its head. 'I want to go home.'

'You'll have to look after it.'

'I know. I want to.'

*

At home the boy bandaged the wing and learned to feed the maimed duck. He spent hours watching it waddle about the back yard. Sometimes it would stretch its neck and try to flap its lopsided wings but it could never fly again.

One day the man asked his son, 'Where's the gun?'

The boy said nothing.

'Where's the two-two?'

'I threw it away,' he said defiantly.

'You *what*?'

'It was mine. You gave it to me.' He looked much bigger

than he had ever looked before. His feet were set determinedly apart.

'But it didn't *kill* your duck. It gave you your duck.' Even as he said it the man realised that this did not absolve anything.

'It made me sick. I could smell that killer's breath, his sweat on it.'

The man felt the blood pumping in his head. Over the months he had seen his son's face being shaped by the wooden stock of that gun; he found he was now relieved the gun had gone. He was grateful to discover a lost fragment of his past gleam in the boy.

Intemperate Latitudes

Extract from a novel in progress

New Zealand 1964

'Here,' said Isobel's father, denting the map with a thick nicotine-stained finger. 'Mount Toe . . . Toe-hurrah.'

'Mount Tauhara,' said Isobel, who had decided Maori pronunciation was common sense. The others seemed incapable of grasping this simple fact. They had fumbled their way north – Mangaweka, Utiku, Taihape, Waiouru – distorting vowels, putting emphasis in all the wrong places. Her father had even adopted some sort of stupid French accent.

'Oh-*tack*-ay,' he said with assurance, as the car swished down an endless abandoned high street. Isobel ground her teeth in the back of the car.

'It's an I on the end, not an E acute,' she said.

'Daddy was in France, darling, in the war. He ought to know,' said her mother.

'This isn't France,' said Isobel. 'Or the war.'

Her father braked hard. A big man, slumped on a horse as if it were an armchair, held up a hand. A herd of black and white cows was swaying towards them like a great ship, jaws working, udders and tails swinging, manure splatting.

'No, it certainly isn't,' said her mother. 'Cows on a main road. Whatever next? Look at the man, kiddies. He looks like a Mar-i. A half-caste, anyway.'

'Maori,' snapped Isobel.

She and her father knelt on the bald carpet, studying the map. The floor of the cottage ran downhill towards windows with a

dirty view over the back garden. It was hopelessly overgrown,
scarcely a garden at all, with the lawn waving seedheads around
the window sills and rampant yellow roses bumping the glass.
In the middle was a tree. A tree with a long skinny trunk which
sprouted astonishingly at the top.

Her mother's face had dropped when their father unlocked
and shouldered open the front door. It had led straight into a
dingy kitchen with a strange mosaic draining board and cracked
brown lino.

'David,' she said, with a hand to her mouth. 'I thought you
said a cottage. I thought . . .'

Isobel knew exactly what she had thought, and there and
then, though she had hated the idea of a holiday with them all
as if she were still a child, decided to make the best of it.

'Look at the awful furniture,' she had called gaily from the
lounge, to disturb her mother still more. Somebody's cast-offs,
several people's actually. For none of the six or eight armchairs
with their backs to the wall around what passed for a carpet
matched any of the others. Some sort of map was pinned up
crookedly, browning at the edges. A calendar with corgis in a
basket – 'Look, Stubby,' said Cynthia, holding him up –
announced 1957. It really was awful, Isobel thought. And then
she saw the tree. Never in her life had she seen anything so
wildly exotic. It made her blood race. And every time she
looked at it, a little voice said, this is a foreign country, everything is different here.

By then her father was standing with his arm around her
mother in the kitchen. And her mother was muttering in a
desperate undertone, so as not to spoil it for the children, something about how was she to prepare meals with only two saucepans, and such appalling china, and what sort of a holiday
would it be for her anyway? Isobel stared at the tree and its
blades gleamed and twisted in the sun like knives.

'Not as good as ordnance survey maps, of course. Get off,
Stubby,' her father was saying. 'But not bad. Look, Izzy, there

seems to be a path up here, so if we . . . woah, here we go again.'

They glanced up at the huge bulb poking out from its nasty green shade. It was swinging with captivating grace.

'Six,' yelled Cynthia, tearing out of the bedroom. 'That's the sixth.'

'Seventh,' said Gillian, behind her. 'You missed one yesterday. When you took the dog for a walk.'

'It's stupid, counting,' said Isobel. 'You've already missed hundreds.'

Gillian looked at her without expression. 'It's not stupid,' said Cynthia. 'We're just counting from when the man said.'

The man was the man behind the counter in the shop at the corner of the street. 'Gidday, young ladies,' he'd said, 'and what can I do you for?'

'Three ice lollies, please,' Cynthia had said confidently, pushing the money across.

It was a strange sort of shop. Under the counter and piled around and behind it were not tall sweet jars but open boxes, full of unrecognisable things. The boy before them had asked for a threepenny mixture and the man had picked out one of everything and slipped them into a little paper bag. The shop also sold soap powder and candles, birthday cards and sardines, and stayed open all evening. It was called Des's Dairy, although there was no sign of a cow.

'Come again?' said the man, Des presumably.

'Three ice lollies.' Isobel was grateful for Cynthia's resilience.

Des lifted a grubby brimmed hat, rubbed one hand through his hair and replaced the hat. 'Now, we've got lollies, and we've got ice blocks. Which is it to be?'

The girls looked at each other. 'Could we just see the ice blocks?' said Isobel, as if humouring the little ones.

'Help yourself. Over there in the freezer. On holiday are you, from England?'

Isobel, thinking they might as well be carrying a sign, chose raspberry. Gillian copied her. 'We've come here to live,' said

Isobel, tearing off the sticky wrapping, 'but we're on holiday too.'

'In a bach, are you?' said the man.

Isobel licked and thought quickly. Perhaps he meant beach. But how could you stay *in* a beach, even if the lake had proper beaches, which it didn't, just feeble little waves flopping onto narrow strips of pebble, worse than Brighton. The only good thing about the lake, which was a great barren puddle as far as she could see, was the way strange rocks bobbed on its surface, defying the laws of nature.

'One of the places up the road?'

Isobel nodded. An ice lolly was an ice block. A bach was a holiday cottage. She would not be like the others, exclaiming about everything, parading their ignorance, making fools of themselves. On the other hand, she was fairly sure she would never be able to say gidday.

'Here for a coupla weeks, are you?' said the man. Cynthia was still peering into the depths of the freezer, taking stock of the new possibilities. 'Picked a beaut time.' He leaned forward, about to share a secret. 'Bet you didn't know there'd been two hundred and thirty-eight shakes in the last two weeks. Bet you don't get those, back in the Old Country.'

'No,' said Isobel politely. A handwritten sign over his shoulder referred to shakes – vanilla, banana, chocolate and strawberry. 'Come on, Cynth.'

'Heard it on the news this morning. Two hundred and thirty-eight. Some bloke was saying the mountain might blow too. Better keep your eye on it, girls.' He chuckled and picked up a newspaper that claimed, redundantly Isobel thought, to be the *Truth*.

She dragged Cynthia, who had finally chosen a livid lime, out of the shop. Gillian untied Stubby from the lamppost and watched her own ice block tumble into the gutter. Typical, thought Isobel. Typical, and even more disgusting, was Gillian's stoic acceptance of her loss. They walked back to the bach, Isobel trying to stride ahead of the others.

'He was talking about earthquakes,' said Gillian helpfully, catching up.

'I know,' snapped Isobel. 'I'm not stupid.'

She looked at the map. 'Stubby,' she shouted, 'get off,' and then ran her fingers through his furry chest to show she wasn't really angry. To the south, the contours clustered around three peaks. She traced them with her finger.

'Gar-a-ho,' said her father.

Isobel sighed. 'It's a volcano,' she said. And felt a thrill similar to the one induced by the tree. Imagine living on the edge of a volcano, knowing any minute your house might be swept away, your life blown to smithereens. It made the English look pathetic.

'Mount Toe-hurrah is an extinct volcano,' said her father. 'The one we're going to climb tomorrow.'

'How do they know?' said Isobel scornfully. 'Just because it hasn't blown up for ages doesn't mean it won't. Maybe soon.'

Her mother dumped several plates of baked beans on the table. 'Anyone'd think you wanted us all swept away by red-hot lava,' she said sharply.

They fell on the beans. Their mother chewed fastidiously, putting down her fork between mouthfuls. Her little finger didn't quite stick out, but it wanted to. Isobel tried not to watch. No sensible person would eat beans like that in a broken-down house. Her father chewed with an aggrieved expression, and when he pushed his plate away, asked if there wasn't some ham in the fridge for a sandwich.

'I don't know,' said their mother, wiping the corners of her mouth. 'Why don't you look?'

*

'Oh David, it's lovely,' she said, tucking her hand through her husband's arm and giving him a delighted smile. Her father grinned back as if he had bestowed a great treat, and patted the hand, baked beans forgiven.

They were walking through a field dotted with buttercups. Breezes stirred the long grass. Drab little moths flitted about their heads, and dogs were barking a long way off. Now and then, an odd musical chirrup piped up from the grass. They leaped a narrow stream. 'Look at that wonderful watercress,' said Isobel's mother. Cynthia and Gillian had run ahead, with Stubby yapping at their heels. Isobel maintained a dignified distance from her parents.

'Look at that sky,' said her mother, turning to include Isobel. Isobel grudgingly glanced upwards, and was nearly struck down by the fierce blue. 'It's going to be hot,' said her mother in her Mrs Runciman-Brown voice.

Her parents reached the top of a rise and turned. 'Oh,' breathed her mother. 'Look at the mountains.' Isobel stomped past, wishing she had a radio, although what was the point when Rita had given her 'Twenty-four Hours from Tulsa' when she left and it hadn't even got here yet.

The path climbed a ridge, then disappeared into dense woods. As she approached, Isobel became aware of a noise which began as a ringing in her ears, building in volume and intensity until her legs and arms seemed to vibrate like violin strings. She stopped on the path, unnerved. It was coming from the woods.

'Grasshoppers,' said her father. 'Rubbing their back legs together.'

Isobel shot him a scornful look. She peered up the hill, shading her eyes. 'All the way up there? Oh God' – 'Language, Isobel,' said her mother – 'Do we have to? What's the point?'

'Because it's there,' said her father, who brought mountaineering books home from the library. 'It's not far. We'll be back in time for lunch.' He held apart the fence wire for her mother to climb through.

'They don't believe in making things easy, do they,' said her mother. 'Come along, Isobel. You helped plan it. The exercise will do you good.' Isobel scowled and followed her through the wire.

The gloom was deafening, and unnaturally still. No wind. No birdlife. She gazed fearfully around, dreading the sight of millions of shrieking insects. But nothing flickered. The air itself seemed to scream, to press in around her head, and then, just when she could stand it no longer, it stopped. The path was steep and rough, and wound disconcertingly through the tangled trees. Sunlight spattered at their feet, but mostly the deeply littered ground was dark and dank. She felt shut in, shut out. Ferns sprouted from mossy banks at her feet, like Miss Dodds' conservatory. Overhead, rope-like vines arced from tree to tree, making her think of Tarzan. It isn't woods at all, she thought. It's jungle.

'Whew,' panted her mother, sitting on a tree trunk and wiping her brow, trying to look jolly. 'You'd think it would be cool in here, out of the sun, wouldn't you?'

Her father stood with his hands on his hips, gazing about with satisfaction. He hasn't noticed, thought Isobel. He thinks this is like England. 'Come on,' called Cynthia and Gillian.

Her mother heaved herself up. 'Well, so long as there's a nice view from the top.'

The path became steeper still. They stumbled, and in one place had to haul themselves up with their hands. Her father was studying the map at the top. 'Mmm,' he said, peering along paths that plunged away in several directions.

'Well. No view. That's a bit disappointing,' said Isobel's mother, brushing twigs and leaves from her arms. She was very red in the face. 'Isobel, I told you you should have worn your wellingtons. Look at your shoes.' Isobel didn't.

'No, Irene' said her father. 'This isn't the top. Look . . .' Her mother ran her eyes uncomprehendingly over the map.

'How much further then?' she asked, not bothering to hide her dismay.

'Hard to say really.' He squinted at the map.

'Only, you said not to bring lunch and it's half-past one already. And the children must be getting very tired.'

'I'm not,' said Cynthia. 'Neither am I,' said Gillian. 'Just hungry.'

You see, their mother's look said. But their father didn't catch it. He was folding the map and stuffing it into his pocket. 'Onward and upwards, then.'

Isobel strode ahead with him. 'It's strange, isn't it?'

'Mmm?' he said, without looking at her. 'Edmund Hillary was a Kiwi, Izzy.'

Sometime later there was a cry from behind like an injured bird. Isobel turned and saw her mother sink to the ground. 'It's Mummy,' she said, and the long-unused word clogged her mouth.

'What?' Her father turned dreamily.

'David, I can't go on,' her mother gasped. She held her forehead in a portentous way. 'I feel . . . most peculiar. I really do think we ought to turn back. And the children . . .'

'I'm not tired,' said Cynthia. 'Neither am I,' said Gillian. 'Just bored.' Stubby panted enthusiastically.

And what about me, wondered Isobel? I'm tired and bored and hungry. Why do I want to go on? Her mother made a strangled sound, hinting at profound but bravely borne suffering, and hauled herself to the side of the path.

'Come on, Irene,' said her father, as if they were playing French cricket on the beach. Stupid, thought Isobel. Anyone can see she isn't going to move.

'Not far now,' he said, patting the map in his pocket.

'You haven't a clue how far,' burst out her mother. 'And it's so selfish of you, bringing us all this way when you don't know where we're going and how far it is. Well, I'm staying here. If you insist on going on, I'll wait for you.'

Isobel looked down at her with disgust. Never had she seen someone so ill-equipped to wait several hours on the side of a jungle-covered volcano.

'. . . and I'm sure Isobel's had enough, too, haven't you, darling? She'll wait with me, won't you?'

'No,' said Isobel. 'I want to go on.' Because I'm not going to be like you.

'I'll stay, Mummy,' said Gillian.

Her mother managed a martyred smile. 'No, that's all right, darling. You go on if you're enjoying it.' Gillian looked crestfallen and took a few steps backwards up the path.

'Fine,' said their father. 'We shouldn't be long. Just . . . er, try to make yourself comfortable. And enjoy the trees.' He's pleased, thought Isobel. Pleased to be free of her. Me too.

Another twenty minutes up the track, the trees began to untangle from around the path, shrinking to shrubby growth that brought to mind Miss Dodds' garden again. The path was a tight gully carved into the hillside. Cynthia and Gillian ran their hands along the banks, exclaiming. The sun beat on their heads. They were exposed to it now, climbing steadily in a way that struck Isobel as foolhardy, ignorant. They were the only people on the hill. She could feel it. Yet it also felt as if they were disturbing someone, or something, clomping up and up in their stupid English way. Forgive us our trespasses.

Cynthia began to whine steadily. She was thirsty. She was tired. She wished she'd stayed with Mummy. She wished she'd stayed at the cottage. 'Bach,' said Isobel. 'Come on. We're nearly there.' She sounded like her father.

The growth become sparser, tougher. The path broadened, and they clambered over huge smooth rocks, blotched with lichen.

'Yes,' shouted their father. He was standing on a plateau the size of half a hockey pitch. At their feet brooded the dark jungly green. Beyond, everything dissolved into blue, except far to the south where a snowy peak glistened.

'Marvellous,' he said. 'Isn't it, kids.'

But Cynthia and Gillian were running wildly over the flat ground, and Isobel was dismayed. By the terrible rolling vastness that had nothing whatever to do with her.

'One of your mother's cheese and tomato sandwiches'd go
down a treat,' said her father, squatting happily on a rock.

Isobel shifted her weight from one foot to another. 'We ought
to go down.' She grabbed her father's wrist and frowned at his
watch. 'It's half past four. We left her hours ago.'

'Well, let's just enjoy it for a minute, Isobel. Mummy would
want us to.'

Isobel waited impatiently, squinting into the sun at Cynthia
who was hiding behind a rock, waiting to jump out on an
unsuspecting Gillian. Behind them a succession of hills ranged
away to the sky. Some of the closer ones exhaled puffs of steam
from their flanks like sleeping animals. She was gripped by a
terrible ache for England, a conviction that she could surely see
it from up there. But which direction? All of them, she realised,
in panic. England was in all directions. Which made it worse.
Put it more utterly beyond her.

Cynthia limped over, whining again. Blood dripped disconsolately down her leg.

'Come on,' said their father, giving her an absent-minded
pat. 'We've left Mummy long enough.'

They seemed to tumble down the hill. In no time they had
plunged into the trees again. The sun had gone from this side
and it was darker than ever. But the hot afternoon was trapped
in the knotted growth. They moved silently, without stopping,
as if all driven by the same anxiety.

Isobel got there first, but maybe she had made a mistake.
'No, Izzy, I think this is where we left her. See, there's the log
across the path. She must have gone back to the car.'

They flew on. The shrieking on the edge of the woods had
abated slightly, and by six-thirty their shadows were stretching
over the golden field. Cynthia and Gillian whooped and
plunged, arms like wings. Isobel's father said, 'I suppose we
were gone rather long. You know how she worries. Can you
see her down there by the car?'

'No,' said Isobel.

'Perhaps she's sitting in it,' he said. She didn't point out that the keys were jangling in his pocket.

The heat rushed out of the car like a caged beast. Cynthia and Gillian lay flat on the grass, their faces red and shiny. Stubby sank the three inches between him and the ground and sighed deeply. 'Can we have an ice block?' said Cynthia, as though it was an entirely reasonable request.

Their father was leaning on the car roof, gazing back up the hill. The gullies seemed to darken before their eyes. 'Stay here,' he ordered. 'I'll have to go back up.'

Isobel stared in disbelief. But he was already striding across the field. She lay in the grass and closed her eyes. There was a blank which she realised had been sleep when she heard Cynthia's piping voice.

'We've lost our mother. She's up the hill.'

The man frowned. He had a leathery face, eyes buried in deep furrows. An over-excited black and white dog was licking Gillian's hand.

'Ged-in,' thundered the man, and they all jumped except the dog. Stubby whimpered and crawled under the car. The man poked the ground thoughtfully with a long stick.

'Be dark soon,' he said. Isobel knew he was right. In New Zealand, night fell suddenly out of the afternoon sky.

'Our father's gone to find her,' said Isobel. 'She must have gone the wrong way.'

'Ged-in. Bloody well hope not,' he said. 'You know the bush.' Apparently it wasn't obvious to him that they didn't. She was gratified.

'Not going to eat that watercress, are you? There's a dead ewe upstream.'

'I'm cold,' said Cynthia.

'Get in the car then,' said Isobel. She wished the man would either say something more or move off. He was leaning on his stick and poking the dog with the toe of a huge unlaced boot. The dog looked grateful. There was a silence as long as the shadows.

'They're coming,' cried Gillian.

Two figures appeared at the top of the rise, the smaller almost limping, leaning into the bigger. Isobel's heart sank.

'I'm all right, kiddies, really,' said their mother, as soon as she was within earshot and it was quite apparent that she wasn't. 'Don't worry. Just a silly mistake.' She wiped her eyes and blew her nose in a charade of self-control that made Isobel want to slap her.

'Gidday,' said the man without expression. 'Thrown a bit of a wobbly, has she, squire?'

Isobel's mouth fell open. Never had she heard such an apt expression.

'Er . . . yes,' said her father. 'Just a misunderstanding. You know how it is.' And he smiled man-to-man.

Her mother drew back from his protective arm. 'No, it wasn't. Not a misunderstanding.'

'But you just said . . .'

'Don't you dare talk about me as if I was a child. You left me up there. For hours and hours. I was worried sick. And you had no idea, no idea at all where you were going.' She was shouting into his face. 'The children . . . no lunch . . . getting dark . . . and the trees . . . those awful trees . . . everywhere . . .' She sobbed.

The girls shuffled, alarmed and embarrassed. Their father grinned sheepishly over her head.

'Righto then,' said the man. 'Ged-in.' And they watched him shamble off. 'By the way, squire,' he called, turning, 'private property here. Not a public path. If it was lambing season, I'd've shot you.'

A Regular Thing

I'm confused. For years I hoped Emily would stop charging me. Now she has I find I don't want it. I feel the bottom has dropped out of my life. I feel threatened, insecure.

I'm thirty-six. I first met Emily when I was twenty-one. At my work in Astley Central Library.

I started in the library at sixteen. A natural step: I've always been fond of books and during schooldays was nicknamed 'Boff'. But I'm not intellectual. Most books are beyond me. Like the books Emily reads on advanced economics.

I'm just comforted by books. Well-thumbed books with cheesy pages and broken spines. Like the paperbacks in the Romance section. At sixteen I kept away from Romance, thought it sissy. Now I'm Section Head.

I met Emily two months into my promotion. I was rummaging behind the Loans Counter for the most recent edition of the *Romance Writers Quarterly* when I heard coughing. The coughing was accompanied by a voice. Such a voice, husky but efficient. 'Excuse me,' it said. 'But I'm in a rush. Can you stamp my books now?'

Used to disappointments I expected the voice to belong to an elderly spinster with a smoker's throat. So I was abrupt. 'Sorry,' I said. 'I don't work on the Loans Counter. I'll get Miss Pedi to deal with you. MISS PEDI!'

Then I saw Emily. My eyes worked upwards from her girlie breasts, to her face with its cold eyes, its bob of oily hair. My heart somersaulted, and my penis began to stiffen. I rubbed it casually against the Loans Counter. 'Hello,' said Emily. 'I'm called Emily.'

'Steven,' I replied.

'Steven,' she said. 'Nice name. Before Miss Pedi comes can I ask a question?'

I nodded, flushed. Something told me the question wouldn't be about books.

I'm not usually daring. I tend to stand back, watch others walk into the lions' den. But Emily bewitched me. She has tremendous power. She knows how to make a coward brave.

When we met at the fountain she looked like a lonely man's dream: tight black jumper, skirt, and those little lace-up booties with pointy heels made from shiny plastic. I felt ill-equipped. 'I haven't much money,' I said. I clutched my thin wallet; even as Section Head I make less money that my father who sweeps for Astley Precision Tools. 'I can stretch to a Chinese and a couple of beers.'

Emily smiled, an amazing smile, the lips pulling back to show the fleshy pink underside. 'What do we want with a Chinese?' she said. 'Let's make our own entertainment.'

Emily took me to her home, a flat above a baby-wear shop. A small flat with one main room painted white. Two archways led from this room. Through one archway was a kitchen; through the other, the bathroom. Swinging bead curtains hung from each archway. They were identical, depicting an American usherette wearing a Stars and Stripes bunny outfit. Around the usherette's neck hung a tray. The tray rested on her large breasts. She smiled a big smile, and a bubble led from the smile. 'Peanuts, Sir?' she asked.

I didn't really know what to make of the flat. It was so sparse. The bead curtains provided the only real decoration, and they seemed to be deliberately over the top. Like they'd been chosen as a statement. But I couldn't work out the statement. They hung there, shimmering, threatening. And instead of asking Emily about them, I turned to her bookcase.

The bookcase ran between the curtains. It was huge. Filled with books. For a while, I examined the books. They were all on finance. 'What's wrong, Steven?' asked Emily. She slid a thin arm round my shoulders.

'There's not a novel in sight,' I said.

'Or a book about women's troubles,' she laughed. 'I'm a practical girl, into what makes the world go round.'

'Money,' I said.

'And sex.' She took my hand and led me to the only other piece of furniture in the room – her bed.

I'd dated before Emily. Mostly nice girls with soft bodies and big eyes. Willing girls. But unadventurous. No costumes. No games. No dirty talk. No slapping, kicking, punching, or spitting. That first time with Emily showed what I'd been missing. She made me feel like a king, a conqueror. 'Emily,' I said. 'That was wonderful.'

I was unprepared for what followed. I thought we'd have a drink, swap stories, relax with each other, feel our way. But no. Emily sat astride me, bending her arms behind her back, making her small breasts point forwards like individual jellies, and made plain what was going to happen.

'This one's for free,' she said. 'Charging first time is counter-productive. You'll not come back for more. Not unless you're desperate. And I don't want you if you're desperate.'

I don't think myself an idiot. But perhaps I am. Perhaps Emily saw me coming. Sometimes I check myself in the mirror, to see if it's written over my face. But there are no clues. Only my spectacles, my thin mouth, my blondish hair, my bad skin stare back.

'But Emily,' I protested. She placed a finger upon my lips and hushed me.

'Don't knock it,' she said. 'It's a good deal.'

My body was hungry for Emily so I began to see her on a regular basis, once a week, twenty pounds a time. But I wasn't swept along. Mentally I kept distant, tried to sort out the situation. I took to spying on her.

Early mornings, library lunch-times, dinner-times and most evenings I waited outside her flat to catch her at it. But no men in dirty raincoats, no young boys anxious to lose their virginity, only a small woman dressed in a suit and carrying a briefcase.

'So Emily, you're not a prostitute?' I asked, casually as I could. She lay on her bed, looking wonderful: her top half naked, her legs covered with a wrap of black silk.

'No,' she said in her husky voice. 'I'm your lover.'

'But then why do you charge me?'

Emily explained. She said men had treated her badly. They had taken her love and used it against her. So now she charged. Because charging meant she was in control, charging meant she was safe. She spoke matter-of-factly, like she was reading a shopping list. But I believed her. It made sense to me.

The confession strengthened our relationship. We began to see more of each other, took the test, and stopped using condoms, and though Emily continued to ask for money I felt encouraged, hopeful. I imagined a day when we'd be like any normal couple, exchanging our love freely.

After a year we bought a flat together, and I took Emily to meet my parents. They hated her. On sight. They wouldn't admit to it. They were polite. They talked to her about her job, gave her ham and boiled beef sandwiches, iced fancies and a cup of weak tea. But you could see it in their eyes. My mother looked Emily up and down. As she took in Emily's thigh boots, hot pants, and lycra top, her face was blank, her pupils marked with distaste. She actually said, 'A word in your ear, Steven. Is this the right kind of girl for you? Isn't she a bit unclean?'

I replied, 'I love her, mother. We get on well together.'

Then I began to feel less positive. There were days when I'd look at our relationship, and see nothing. Emily and I would meet after work, go out for a meal or to the pictures, return home, and yet still seem separate. It knew it wasn't my fault. I offered myself; told her my history, my likes and dislikes, my longings. But Emily was so closed, only gave out at night when we touched. And she spoilt that by charging.

At one point I nearly cracked. Her charges rose above the rate of inflation. They began to cripple me. And I had to take an extra job, collecting pools monies from Astley's nastiest estate – Craigheath. It wasn't a pleasant job. I had a couple of dangerous customers who once got me in a back alley. They beat me. They took off my glasses, stood me against a wall, and pushed ring-covered hands into my face. 'Poor poor Steven,' cooed Emily when I returned home.

'You could stop it, you know,' I said to her as she dabbed a cotton-wool ball over my cheeks, nose, ears. The ball was soaked in Dettol. It stung. To take my mind off the pain I concentrated on Emily's breasts which moved across my chest, tickling.

'How can I stop it?' she asked, innocent. 'Should I take up karate, go out for revenge?'

I squeezed her hand. The Dettol trickled brown down her skinny wrist.

'Getting ready to thump me now, are you?' she said. Her eyes were strangely bright.

I went to the doctor. I told Emily it was because my wounds were infected. It wasn't a total untruth. Blue-green pus lined the cut which ran across my cheek.

I chose a locum. I didn't want to confess to my regular, who'd seen me grow, who'd watched my testicles drop. The locum traced her gentle finger along the cut, then asked me what I'd really come for. 'Sexual problems?' she asked.

'Sort of,' I confided.

The locum listened carefully. She nodded her head, made notes. 'I think you should approach the mother,' she advised. 'You shouldn't blame the mother, mothers get blamed for too many things. But I think you should have a chat. Mothers can be very helpful.'

Emily's mother dresses like a man. She favours double-breasted suits made from merino. Beneath which she wears a white shirt and a yellow or black tie. She sports cufflinks, Argyle socks, and brogues. Her hair is cut to the scalp, her face free of make-up.

Emily introduced us at the flat warming. I recognised her immediately. 'You used to visit Emily at her old place,' I said. 'Tuesdays and Thursdays. I saw you.'

'Yes,' said Emily's mother. 'I know all about your spying.'

I hated her then. Now not at all. She speaks her mind, and, beneath the macho stuff, has a heart. Emily loves her too. The flat seems to lighten when her mother's around. There's more laughter, and Emily opens up, tells stories I've never heard before.

It took me a while to confide in Emily's mother. I was reticent because I suspected she wasn't straight. I imagined her as a lover of women similar to herself. Of course I couldn't ignore the evidence. But somehow I thought of Emily as a one-night stand: Emily's mother lying back and taking it because she wanted a child. But no.

Emily's mother loves men. My boss, Mr Brudly, confided in me. 'She's a real fire-cracker,' he said. 'A rare and dangerous woman. Our affair lasted five months.'

'Yes,' said Emily's mother when I faced her. 'It ended badly. I told him it was over whilst waiting my turn at the Outpatients.'

Then I learnt that Emily's mother knew about her daughter. About how she charged me. 'Emily has told me all,' she said. 'But there's little I can do. My daughter's headstrong, opinionated. She'll always approach life her own way. You could try to make her jealous. But that's a crude device. I suggest if you love her, then just persevere.'

'But,' I said, lifting my head off her fly-buttoned lap. 'But I don't even know if she cares for me. She's so controlled.'

Six months ago, Emily made the spare room into an office. She left her job as financial adviser for Dryson, Dryson and Sons to go it alone. I was worried. For a while I thought it'd cost me more for sex. Extra revenue to cover loss of earnings, or to fund the computer, desk, headed notepaper, filing cabinets, photocopier and electronic pencil sharpener. But she didn't seem to need it. Emily poached clients from her old firm. She ran an advertising campaign which promised personal service; a promise headlining beneath a profile shot of Emily looking her best. Soon her desk diary was full and she was having to turn away clients.

She now has a host of regulars. Mostly men, though some are women. The women power-dress and carry briefcases. They snub me. The men wink.

I was jealous of the men. I took a fortnight off work to check Emily was giving them financial advice and nothing else. One evening she came to me and said, 'This business is kosher, Steven. I only want to sleep with you.'

That night Emily and I had our first real row. From opposite sides of the bedroom we slung insults, grievances. Emily said I was a typical chauvinist. I told her she was a typical whore. We made our demands: Emily wanting to be loved for herself, me wanting free sex.

That argument may have been behind Emily's change of mind. That and my decision to become celibate. Though I still desired her, I turned my back on her.

Eventually she confronted me; complained that her incomings from our sex were at an all-time low. 'Why, Steven?' she asked.

She looked confused when I explained. 'This isn't normal, Emily,' I said. 'My paying you has to stop. It puts a barrier between us. I've lived with you for years and still I don't know what you're thinking. Since I met you I've been on an emotional roller-coaster. I'm tired out.'

She watched me closely. Her cold blue eyes, unsympathetic, searching. I began to cry. I lifted my hand to my face, and that was when she changed. The eyes stayed the same cold blue, but her chin, her cheeks, her mouth lost their hard edge. She wasn't my Emily.

A week later she handed me a letter to read on my way to work. I slid it in my jacket pocket, fearful of the white envelope, the bold 'STEVEN' on the front. I entered Elder Park, found a bench by the pond. The sun shone, gardeners raked stray twigs and Coke cans from the murky water, the boat-keeper untied the paddle boats. I listened to the sound of rope dragging across wood. Then I opened the letter. At first I couldn't read the writing. It seemed to blur, and inside I felt sick, imagined Emily saying goodbye. When I could focus I was surprised to see her words stretched across the page gigantic, urgent, saying something very different. '*Dear Steven, I've decided to stop charging you. It doesn't make sense. We've been together for so long. Let's start afresh. Emily.*'

I read the letter three times. Each time I felt more elated, felt my future advancing – hopeful, warm, blessed.

Now I'm not so sure.

Emily hasn't charged me for a while. In the early days it was glorious. Real pleasure. I found my wallet growing fat. I treated myself to new clothes, bought Emily finance books and sexy underwear. We made love whenever and wherever. The foreplay was exploratory. Our caresses not governed by how much I could afford. And after sex we would open up, reveal our fears, desires. Emily had some terrible tales to tell. A man had once tried to set fire to her, threw a lighted box of matches into her hair. Another man had kept her locked in his room, chained to his bed. I would hug her as she spoke of these things. And she was generous. When I spoke of my past, and my petty difficulties with girls who'd behaved too nicely, she never condemned, never claimed her experiences more important, more painful. Then she flipped.

I should've seen it coming. Emily is a professional. If she chooses to do something she does it right. She does not skip corners. She began to borrow books from my section of the library. She would devour the slim pink volumes, jot down endless notes on Romance. She would take these notes everywhere with her, consulting them when washing, eating.

She wears rose-print dresses now. Puts a large silk ribbon in her hair to soften it. She's talking of selling her business. She wants me to be the breadwinner, while she stays at home. She wants to get married. She wants to have children. She's become submissive, her conversation punctuated with phrases like 'Whatever you think, darling', her love-making conventional. She's lost her cold cold gaze.

Last night, I telephoned her mother. 'Please do something,' I begged. 'I can't stand this. It's torture.'

Emily's mother laughed. 'I've told you before, Steven, I have no control over my daughter. She's stubborn. Besides, why are you complaining? Isn't she giving you what you've always wanted?'

I was silent.

'Well, isn't she?' pushed Emily's mother.

'I suppose,' I replied. 'I really don't know.'

This morning I wake, raise myself on an elbow, watch Emily as she sleeps. She is very beautiful. Despite the little-girl ribbon. Despite the flannelette nightie. I touch her upon the shoulder, brush a hair from her mouth. I am so confused. I wonder whether I should've let things be, not forced her to change. I have no answer. I feel like the floor has been taken from under me. That I have nothing solid to stand on. I feel desperate.

In Defence of the Short Story

'The short story', wrote Elizabeth Bowen in 1959*, 'is at an advantage over the novel, and can claim its nearer kinship to poetry, because it must be more concentrated, can be more visionary, and is not weighed down (as the novel is bound to be) by facts, explanation, or analysis. I do not mean to say that the short story is by any means exempt from the laws of narrative: it must observe them, but on its own terms. Fewer characters, fewer scenes, and above all fewer happenings are necessary; shape and action are framed for simplification. As against that, there are dangers and can be penalties: essentially, at no point in the story must the electrical-imaginative current be found to fail.'

Not all short story writers would go along with all Elizabeth Bowen's rigorous tenets here (Alice Munro, for one, notably and marvellously breaks Bowen's 'fewer' rule in the three categories cited, and is not averse to facts and explanation either); nevertheless, coming from one of the finest exponents of the form this century, Bowen's prescription still serves as a pretty unbeatable guide, reminder and warning. Put a full stop, however, after 'The short story is at an advantage over the novel', and you'd probably elicit hollowish laughter from practitioners in Britain today. For although our history in the story is as distinguished as any, and while the story continues to flourish in the United States and Canada, in South America, in Eire and in other places besides, it must be true to say that notwithstanding a small band of supporters and enthusiasts in all corners of

* In her introduction to a selection of her stories published by Vintage Books, New York.

the book trade, the literary short form is no longer paid much (or serious) attention here.

If anyone requires proof for the statement, they need look no further than the first volume of *New Writing* (to which, it should be said, I was a contributor and which fact makes me, of course, an 'interested party'). *New Writing 1* contained five critical essays and three 'overviews', each concerned with a separate aspect of current fiction, yet not one of these treated the short story in any but the most glancing way. It seemed to escape both the editors' and the essayists' notice that although the anthology contained a few extracts from novels-in-progress, the bulk of the fiction on display *was composed of short stories*. As a result, perhaps, the reviewers of *New Writing 1* took their lead from the anthology's editors and essayists and, while making passing reference to individual stories, failed to discuss the form itself: the novel, and the state of its health, was what concerned them. (At a reading to promote *New Writing 1*, I mentioned the irony of all this to an author – an academic – of one of the 'overviews', and he said, not unkindly: 'Yes, well – but there's not much, critically, that can be done with the short story, is there?')

I'm an interested party, as I say. Even so, there must be others, readers and writers, who would be unhappy to see the short form in this country fade away through neglect. If, in recent years, we haven't had too many practitioners (Pritchett out on his own in England) in the class of Cheever, it is in part because of the negative attitude I've just described – an attitude held by publishers, literary editors and booksellers, no less than critics – and in part because the traditional showcase for the story, the weekly or monthly literary/general magazine, has all but disappeared. (Since the demise of *The Listener* and Judy Cooke's *Fiction Magazine*, story writers seeking a first home have fared even worse than poets – *Stand, London Magazine, New Statesman & Society, Panurge* and *Critical Quarterly* being, I think, the only periodicals left which consistently publish new work of any length.)

Of course that's not to say there are no outlets for the story at all. For the writer who's comfortable with the 2,500-word limit and who's prepared to curb any leaning towards the experimental, or any ambition to treat the explicitly sexual (the 'f' word rare on radio, even as an adjective), the BBC does sterling stuff in providing a daily fifteen-minute story slot on Radio 4 and in accommodating slightly longer stories in 'seasons' of selected writers on Radio 3. It is anthologies, though, that over the past decade have increasingly replaced magazines as the chief outlet for short fiction. Of these, the 'theme' variety (*The Faber Book of This*, *The Chatto Book of That*, *The Virago Book of the Other*) can have a manufactured, 'gift book' feel and there are signs that it may soon have had its day, since even if there isn't a limit to really interesting themes, there is, maybe, a limit to really first-class stories to fit them. Some 'theme' anthologisers choose to commission pieces rather than to give the tried and trusted, or the unjustly neglected, another airing: a good idea, one would think. But it isn't everyone who, faced with the invitation: 'Write me a story on Greed/Pink Elephants/Smoking; limit 4,000 words and let me have it by Wednesday', can come up with the goods – as is evident from some fairly mixed results.

One of the most useful and rewarding types of anthology must surely be the one, exemplified by *New Writing*, that in encouraging submissions from both established and unknown writers (on subjects and themes of the author's own, and written, in so far as is realistic, to his or her preferred length), acts as a forum for what is new and interesting in fiction and/or poetry. I wish there could be more of these.

It's a solo collection, in hardcover or paperback, that the story writer is hoping for, of course. But solo collections, on the whole (or unless you're Jeffrey Archer) don't sell and publishers, not unnaturally, are wary of them. The publisher who rates a collection enough to publish at a loss is most likely to be doing so in the expectation that the story writer will reinvent him or herself as a novelist second time around – a trick, if successful, that will not only give the writer a higher profile but also

improve his or her chances of earning out the publisher's next
advance. Some story writers will be able to work this trick.
And many will want to anyway, having been novelists at heart
all along, and needing only the publisher's encouragement to
trigger them. But what of those who don't want to write a
novel or who, having made several attempts, find they can't?
What of those whose vision and concentration are more suited
to the short form; whose heroes are the masters of it; who
would, given the chance, be content to spend a lifetime (as V.
S. Pritchett, in his fiction, most notably has done) exploring its
possibilities; and whose driving force is the hope that one day,
and by some stroke of fortune, they'll come up with the 'big
one' – a story, in power and resonance, to stand comparison
with Bowen's 'Mysterious Kor', say, or Delmore Schwartz's
short masterpiece 'In Dreams Begin Responsibilities'? Is there,
in what are difficult times even for novels, any hope for more
than superficial critical attention, for anything approaching half-
decent sales, for the short story?

Well maybe there isn't. Maybe, as someone once said, 'you
can't buck the market', especially in a recession. Or maybe
readers in Britain don't want short stories. There's no point in
pretending they've ever had anything like the appeal that the
novel has always had. (Though if there are no readers for them,
just who are all those anthologies for, I'd like to know?)

One thing's certain: it can't help at all that short story collections are, except in a very minor way, excluded from the award
system. Because whatever we may think about the whole concept of attempting to judge what's 'best' in literature, prizes,
and a writer's potential to win one, play an increasing part in a
publisher's decision to take on a new author; added to which
there's no doubt that the Booker and the Whitbread Prizes, in
particular, along with the speculation and controversy that they
generate, do help to sell books. The prizes that do exist for
story collections – the Macmillan Silver Pen Award, for
example, (won in 1993 by George Steiner for *Proofs* and *Three
Parables*); and the Geoffrey Faber Memorial Prize of £1000,

awarded, in alternate years, for fiction and poetry (won in 1993 by Will Self for *The Quantity Theory of Insanity*) – although in themselves prestigious, are virtually unknown outside a tiny literary/book trade circle.

Some might argue that a 'small' literary form that doesn't enjoy a huge popular following doesn't merit big prizes. My answer to the prize money part would be that the struggling young story writer is likely to need it more than most. As to the rest – could anyone call the contribution to literature of, say, Chekhov, Flaubert, Mansfield, Kipling, Joyce, *small*? I know, before anyone points it out to me, that some of the writers I've cited were novelists too, but that doesn't take away from the fact that much of their finest work was in the shorter form. Pritchett (that name again), who has been described by Frank Kermode as 'by such a margin the finest English writer alive that it hardly seems worth saying so', is the present-day example of a writer whose genius has found best expression in the story. That there should be no provision in the Booker or the Whitbread for the form in which he excels and in which his greatest contribution has been made seems extraordinary, if not as ridiculous as declaring a world-class sprinter unworthy of Olympic gold on the grounds that he performs less well in the marathon.

Even if we're to accept that, within its present terms, and despite evidence that novellas can make it onto the shortlist these days, the Booker can't accommodate the short story collection, what about the Guardian Fiction Prize? And what about the Whitbread? Its categories include biography, a children's book, a first novel and poems – so what have they got against short stories?

I've no way of proving this, but I've a suspicion that if short story collections were in with a chance of winning a major prize, publishers would be more positive about publishing them (and less tempted to try to turn their 'geese' story writers into novelist 'swans'); reviewers about reviewing them; booksellers about selling them; and so on. Unless that happens, the best efforts of those who do support and promote short stories are likely to remain largely unrewarded. Which won't stop the committed short story writer writing them. For, in the words of Elizabeth Bowen:

> '. . . literature is a compost to which we are each contributing what we have. The best that an individual can do is to concentrate on what he or she can do, in the course of a burning effort to do it better.'

Those Silly Novels by Lady Novelists

It is a well-known fact that women read more fiction than men and that the fiction they read in greatest number is what is labelled slush, schlock, S & F. The very tags bristle with the derision that the romance, the family saga, the domestic novel, the woman's blockbuster – and inevitably their readers – elicit from the custodians of the nation's literary culture.

As a writer of women's popular fiction, but otherwise a more or less respectable member of the literary classes, I have long been intrigued by what it is that lies at the root of this largely British critical contempt. It is a peculiarly stubborn phenomenon and one which until recently has refused any notions of better and worse within the domain of the popular novel – as if all these many individual books were uniform simply because they fell into recognisable categories.

'He who burns a romance purifies the human mind,' Richard Carlisle, the radical nineteenth-century publisher, remarked, capturing the authentic tone of puritan revulsion which has shadowed popular romance ever since *Pamela* appeared on the literary stage.

George Eliot may not have been a book burner, but she was hardly less scathing in her mockery of the popular women's fiction of her day. Her tone has a note of defensiveness, which I recognise. After all, the discourse of criticism is public and hence male.

> Silly Novels by Lady Novelists are a genus with many species, determined by the particular quality of silliness that predominates in them – the frothy, the prosy, the pious, or the pedantic. But it is a mixture of all these – a composite order of feminine fatuity, that produces the

largest class of such novels which we shall distinguish as the *mind-and-millinery* species.
Westminster Review 1856

Mind-and-millinery has given way to sex-and-shopping, the pompous and purple religious flights Eliot scorns to more mundane information about career prospects, but the tenor of critical ridicule has remained constant between the 1850s and the 1990s. Even the advent of postmodernism – which has made an eclectic wandering between high and popular culture more or less 'politically correct' – has only dented it slightly.

I used to think the contemporary derision was in part fuelled by envy and inverse snobbery. The more copies a book sells, the worse the book, unless it has been jet-propelled into best-sellerdom by the motor of a Booker prize. The American writer John Irving has humorously noted that critics used to applaud his novels when they sold some 2000 copies, but when his books catapulted onto the bestseller lists the very same critics scoffed at them mercilessly.

Yet envy can't be the whole answer. True, Jilly Cooper, Catherine Cookson, Rosamunde Pilcher, Barbara T. Bradford and their less established sisters regularly appear amongst the year's bestsellers. But they appear side by side with their male counterparts – Wilbur Smith, Jeffrey Archer, Dick Francis, Frederick Forsyth. With the possible exception of Jeffrey Archer, whose sins extend beyond the writing of popular fiction, male writers of thrillers or adventure or horror stories rarely suffer from the same quality of snigger. Nor do they regularly find themselves transported, like the now iconic Barbara Cartland, into numerous literary novels where they feature as the batty and dangerous purveyors of boy's own tales of distant peaks and subterranean money vaults.

Women's popular fiction is relegated to the very bottom of the great class divide of culture, the white trash in the critical hierarchy, and wrongly sexed to boot.

Don't get me wrong. I am not about to make a daft case for

the outstanding literary value of women's popular fiction. A proportion of it is fatuous and badly written – though it is difficult to sink to the depths Barbara Cartland has reached and few have achieved it. Sally Beauman, Maeve Binchy, Rosie Thomas, Susan Howatch, on the other hand, use language well and characterise with sensitivity. The point is that there are as many differences *within* the popular novel as there are between it and the literary novel in its present guise.

A homely analogy may help. Scrambled eggs and lemon soufflé are both foods composed of the same basic ingredient, yet they are impossible to confuse. Though it undoubtedly takes greater panache to bring off a soufflé, it can flop disastrously. Scrambled eggs, too, can be made well or be inedible. Yet one would hardly cover scrambled eggs with moral opprobrium or sneer at them for not being their more subtle kin. And one would like to be permitted to eat one or the other depending on one's mood, without having to look guiltily over one's shoulder.

Language and form are the basic ingredients of the novel. Unlike those of some of the more adventurous literary fictions, the language and form of the popular novel do not call attention to themselves. They are on the whole transparent, there to be put to traditional nineteenth-century novelistic uses, to move plot, create character and atmosphere. As for storylines, as Goethe told us long ago and the structuralist Propp more recently reiterated, repetition with variation is the name of the fictional game. The literary novel at its best strives for originality and subtlety in language, thought, form in order to rupture or play with or ironically distance itself from that repetition. The popular novel shuns any structural ironies, and stays within the codes of repetition with variation, since it is precisely the compulsion and comfort of repetition, the reconciliation of the happy end, that readers most seek from the story. And if this weren't the case, the popular novel would be unpopular with more than critics.

But these formal differences between the popular and the

literary novel apply across the genres and the sexual divide. If we are to locate the reasons for the particular contempt which the women's novel elicits from the guardians – both male and female – of our literary conscience, we shall have to look further.

Virginia Woolf in *A Room of One's Own* provides us with a starting point:

> Speaking crudely, football and sport are 'important'; the worship of fashion, the buying of clothes 'trivial'. And these values are inevitably transferred from life to fiction.

But that is only a beginning.

Women's popular fiction today finds its immediate antecedents in the novels of Jane Austen and the Brontë sisters. No scaling of the jagged irony-clad heights of modernism has broken the trajectory. Its subject is, in the first instance, love. Love of the girl-meets-boy, Cinderella variety; love which transforms or destroys; love which necessitates a deluge of introspection; love which is passion and sexual feeling; grand melodramatic love which permits a fantasy of escape from the banality of the everyday or from the difficult everyday love of husbands and wives, parents and children. Whether domestic or romantic, dressed in historical garb or in the comedy of manners, these women's novels are novels of sentiment and often of sentimental education.

The gamut of emotions explored in these fictions is broad. Perhaps broader in many instances than in their hard-boiled male equivalents where the predominant emotions are anger or fear or a sense of triumph in puzzles solved and battles won. Indeed, a portion of women's popular fiction seems to address this very problem. Thick-skinned men, through their love for the heroine or through the experience of the novel, are schooled in sensitivity, railroaded and wooed into confronting feeling. As such, the books fulfil what is patently a female desire.

Female desire. Female fantasy. It is the blatant or more sophisticated play of these in women's mass fiction that I suspect in part accounts for the puritan moralist's wish to burn such books and the male critic's revulsion which masquerades as scorn.

Whereas it seems to be all right for men to have male fantasies of murder, often of women, of colonial wars and heroism on earth or in space, of penetrative detective work and boardroom coups, it is certainly not all right for women to have female fantasies – *en masse* – which include families, friendships, sex, love and varieties of male who ultimately succumb to their power or good sense. It almost makes one think that there is something fundamentally subversive in women's popular fiction.

Can it be that we are still suffering from a residue of that old preacherly fear which warns that once women's imaginations, their fantasies, their desires are let loose in unpoliced privacy, anything may happen? They may get ideas above their station. They may begin to despise their menfolk. And worse, much worse: they may experience pleasure. Virtue and fidelity and compliance will go out the window. Lives will be ruined.

The discourse of the susceptible woman, of women as potential victims of fiction, may seem exaggerated and out of date. But it is still, sadly, with us. It hides, I suspect, a fear of what women may want, as well as a discomfort with emotion in its more or less naked state, lacking the stylish trappings of irony and elegant prose and literary panache.

Woman's sphere has traditionally been that of personal relations. Her morality, her way of being in the world, as Carol Gilligan and other feminist theorists have argued, is less guided by abstract principles of justice and mechanical absolutes, than it is by a sense of responsibility to others and a sensitivity to others' needs and desires. This, of course, is the terrain of the women's novel. In an age when all the grand narratives of justice and political philosophy seem to have played themselves out, it seems odd that once clothed in the critic's mantle, we should still defensively despise these smaller narratives in which the sentiments are engaged in the dance of personal relations.

Sigmund Freud, certainly as stern a patriarch as the next man of his generation, nonetheless managed to suspend moralising prejudices when it came to his work. In interpreting *Gradiva*, a popular novella of his day, he shows how the hero of the tale is cured of his delusions, and of his inability to engage with a living sexual being, by the love of a woman, the heroine metaphorically turned physician. Arguing against his sceptical and 'logical' interlocutors, Freud is keen to point out that the author of *Gradiva* did not tack on 'the usual happy ending of marriage' simply to please his 'female readers'. Freud, indeed, is on the side of the female readers. The process of cure, he argues, is only accomplished

> in a relapse into love, if we combine all the many compo-
> nents of the sexual instinct under the term 'love'; and
> such a relapse is indispensable, for the symptoms . . . are
> nothing other than precipitates of earlier struggles connec-
> ted with repression or the return of the repressed, and
> they can only be resolved and washed away by a fresh
> high tide of the same passions.

I am not trying to make any grandiose claims for women's popular fiction as therapeutic texts or tools. However, it is interesting to note how often the theme of incest in whatever mediated guise fuels family sagas and romances; how often the repressed returns to be liberated in love. In the large and often simple brush-strokes of these novels, as in fairy tales, childhood fantasies and hurts play themselves out, sometimes though not always to be resolved by love. The very repetitive nature of some of the stories by the bestselling authors in the field are perhaps part of the 'cure'.

It would be hard to find much in common between Henry James and Sigmund Freud except for a chronological overlap. But the wily old inventor of high modernism in English fiction observed in a 1914 review of Mathilde Serao, a popular writer of his day, that there had been enough fiction describing man's relationship to 'the pistol, the pirate, the police, the wild and tame beast'. It was time, he said, to turn to the ladies, since, 'It is the ladies, in a word, who have lately done most to remind us of man's relations with himself, that is with woman.' James did, giving us heroines as romantically headstrong as Isabel Archer and as tragic as Milly Theale, who dies of lack of love and deception.

One, perhaps fanciful, way of looking at the effects of high modernism on fiction is to say that James hijacked the woman's novel of personal relations and transformed that loose baggy monster into art, an art of rigorous selection where the word recaptured all the sacral aspects of its earlier biblical emphasis. With James, the professional writer becomes an Artist, not a concept women have ever been particularly at home with. And the woman's novel of personal relations, of the peaks and pitfalls of love, of the vagaries of the Oedipal triangle and the buried secrets of the family romance, has after James to aspire to at least some of the subtlety, the high seriousness of *The Golden Bowl*; and to the saintly resignation of his heroes and heroines. Or be damned.

Meanwhile the boy's own story with its pistols, pirates and police, its rapacious though tight-lipped heroes, goes its own merry way.

Not altogether merry, of course. For the popular novel as a whole gets a rough ride from the critics. It's odd. As readers we are adept at differentiating between fictions which, like their counterparts on the small or large screen, set out in the first instance to entertain through story and others which make larger claims. But when we don the public mantle of the literary critic, a kind of Leavisite pall of high-mindedness takes us over and we feel we have to judge fiction not only aesthetically but in moral terms as well – does it edify? is it good for the soul? Bye-bye the values of entertainment which often the same critics are prepared to apply to film and television: is it gripping? does it compel you? is it enjoyable? And only after that do shades of thought and meaning come in.

So what is it that characterises these fictions, apart from their subject matter, and draws women in their millions to them? A few capacious generalisations are perhaps in order despite their inevitable fallibility.

A compelling story, effectively told, is, of course, a primary given. Beyond that, I would say that the immediacy and the intimacy of the narrative voice play a central part. There are no barriers here of irony or verbal fireworks or density of thought to distance the reader from the characters. It is almost as if there were no shaping authorial presence strutting its hour upon the stage. As a result, the reader can 'sink' into the novel, allow herself to be taken over, to disappear into the fiction. For women, there is a particular pleasure to this sinking. As numerous commentators have pointed out, women suffer from a sense of being constantly surveyed, either by the evaluating male, or by the surveyor they have internalised. Unlike women's magazines, which they otherwise sometimes resemble, these fictions do not harass with endless strategies for self-betterment. Call that escapist if you like, but I have never been able to see why the occasional escape is less than salutary.

Which brings us to the proverbial 'happy ending'. The reader's pleasure in the happy ending is not simply in the arrival of what is anticipated or in the daydream fulfilment. Since the general contours of the end – the 'sealing with a kiss', the 'walking hand in hand into the sunset' – are in a measure known from the start, what is pleasurable is the participation in a knitting process which will bring the sometimes precarious threads of narrative together. Tangles will have to be unpicked, obstacles overcome, patterns stitched, so that the garment takes on the expected shape. The grip, the speed with which one turns the pages of these novels, is in part due to the suspense involved in finding out how exactly it is that we are going to arrive at the known end. And sometimes, there are surprises even there.

I have to confess that as a reader I like the happy ending: not because I'm too dim to recognise that life entails a great deal of suffering and that we don't live happily ever after. But nor is it the single task of the novel to mire one in bleakness. We are not dealing here with a matter of realism: by that logic, all fictions would have to end with death. Like fairy tales, popular novels cut at a point before that end and it is usually at a point of hope rather than despair. Whatever the trials and tribulations contained within the narrative, the resolution breathes something of hope.

During the greedy eighties one strand of these fictions drew their characters only from the very rich. Designer labels tripped off the pages in equal time to yachts, grand houses and gourmet dinners in three-star restaurants. These are not my preferred fictions, but then, like all popular culture, bestselling novels reflect the aspirations of their time. It was that kind of time.

Tycoons and glamorous career superwomen are the eighties version of the dukes and duchesses, princes and princesses of yore. What is interesting about this recurrence of the grand and great is that it signals not only the topology of the fairy tale, but the psychological sphere in which these books ultimately play themselves out – despite their naturalistic idiom. Henry James once remarked that the reason so many of his characters were very rich was that it was only the rich who had the necessary time to pay attention to either moral niceties or the refinements of sensibility and personal relations. Now, I am hardly suggesting any direct comparisons, but there is a sense in which the very grandness of the characters in these kinds of novels gives them the time to focus on the life of the passions.

It is something of a gross over-generalisation, but one could say that while one dominant strand of the British literary novel grew increasingly minimalist over recent decades and found its subjects either further and further down the social scale or in the extremes of behaviour, the popular novel grew more capacious and occupied what to many readers was a more recognisable middle ground with its attendant aspirations. The recent bestseller status attained by Joanna Trollope and Mary Wesley, whose comedies of manners hark back to the cosy values of traditional English village life, is perhaps not only a sign of an ageing readership, but an indication of readers' desire to find the familiar in fiction. The novel can offer comfort and solace as well as disturb.

What attracts me as a writer to the popular novel is its closeness to its loose and baggy nineteenth-century kin: the large canvas which is a world, the span through generations which allows history to reverberate through characters' lives. The challenge is to write a good story, a story that keeps the pages turning; and somehow to embed in that story what may be more serious considerations. Yes, even popular fictions can have aspirations – not perhaps to the Art of the novel with its subtleties, its desire for originality, its stylistic signature; but to its more modest craft, the craft of creating an intelligent entertainment. Silly novels by lady novelists can sometimes be that as well.

It would be refreshing if the guardians of the great tradition occasionally shed their armour and leapt over the great literary class divide to take note of what readers have known for a long time.

Dégustation Domestique

Fish and chips for two

2–3 fillets of fish
1–2 scoops of chips
1 lemon cut into wedges

Pre-heat oven to 200°F. Place fish and chips in newspaper in centre of oven to keep warm. Plates in warming drawer. Serve with lemon wedges.

This, from *Recipes for the Busy Bride*, a wedding present from Mrs Oliphant, fills me with fury. Can she have forgotten the cheese soufflés I used to make when I was seventeen and visiting? 'Amy will run up a cheese soufflé,' they used to say. Too furious to add lemon wedges. Anyway fish and chips are best consumed in a car by the sea.

Cheese soufflé

roux sauce
3–4 eggs separated
generous amount of cheese, pref. parmesan .
salt and pepper
375° 20 mins

The bare outline in my seventeen-year-old handwriting on a smeared piece of paper like a love-letter. As sure of the recipe as I was hopeful of love. The smugness of mastering the roux: that liaison of butter and flour in which the starch grains burst like the popped braces of a passionate gentleman doing the tango. Then the milk is added slowly. And if the liaison comes unstuck there is always the eggbeater.

Gravy

A different matter. No amount of eggbeater or Marmite can get the colour right. It turns out like the two-toned shoes of a gangster. Phoned Mother who comes within half an hour bearing a cupful. I know she doesn't like Jasper. She processes along the narrow path through the long grasses, sets the cup in my hand like a chalice and says 'Here you are, dear,' before turning on her heel. Fancy walking 3 miles (1½ miles each way).

Pavlova

Well, it's no use tackling Pavlova, even if it is the national dessert. A national dessert that resembles a hat to wear to the races, with gloves. A meringue on tight curls and a fierce grip on the purse strings. The sort of woman who would beat a jockey for not winning. Perfect for leading the winner in though, keeping well clear of the foaming and frothing horse. And yet a touch of froth to show solidarity, to share the effort.

Instead on winter's nights I make little individual upside–down treacle puddings which we eat by firelight. Even Jasper, being an engineer, has no idea how the treacle crumbles like asphalt on the top and soaks into the sides. Like a treacle well. Elsie, Lacie and Tillie. I never think of the recipe, just throw it together. Margarine because the butter is hard in July, brown sugar, an egg or two, self-raising flour, raisins if I feel like it, generous pool of treacle at the bottom of each little dish with crimped sides. Then *voilà*. Out they slide with the treacle still congealing and sinking into the soft, golden, cake–like flesh.

Was it the same winter I took to inserting a whole pumpkin in the centre of the oven to blacken and soften ready for soup?

Pumpkin soup

Place pumpkin, leaving stalk on if desired, in centre of oven on moderate heat until softened and charred. Remove cautiously with oven gloves. When cool, remove seeds. Reserve flesh. Blend with chicken stock, seasonings, in blender. Reheat and just before serving add dollop of cream and scatter of parsley.

Feel as proud of this as if I had invented Hallowe'en!

First dinner party and a ferocious argument among the guests about *Nouvelle Cuisine*. Men firmly ranged on one side. One of the guests, Angela, has learned how to do a wing design on a sauce. 'Bird passing island', her husband calls it. Luckily the meal is almost over when this occurs.

Menu★

cheesy pear (p. 19)
hot curried vegetables (p. 69)
served with rice
            tossed green salad
            bowl of apple slices
            bowl of cucumber yoghurt
            cubes of banana in coconut
watermelon sorbet (p. 22)

I advance the argument, trying to reconcile both sides, that *Nouvelle Cuisine* suffers more from demolition than a meal in a railway station cafeteria. Angela bursts into tears. Robert recounts how he has been practising dry Martinis and throwing most of them down the sink.

Jasper complains the coffee is awful. Hurt, I go back to

★ from *The Taste of Life* by Julie Stafford. Greenhouse, 1983. Based on the concepts of Nathan Pritikin.

making it in a saucepan (open-pot method). Bring water to boil, then let it cool for a minute or two. Toss in the coffee (2 tbsps Blue Mountain moderately fine-ground), stir gently and allow to steep, covered, for two to four minutes. Pour into heated mugs through a fine strainer. In the same week he mentions the dearth of flowers in the house. Add a few nasturtium leaves to a salad. Should I go further and become a fruit bottler, stripping entire trees, carefully gathering the windfalls for tarts and jellies? Decide this is in the category of Pavlova. Buy a pizza dish instead and practise making the base: 12oz white bread flour, 1 tsp salt, 1 tsp castor sugar, 2 tsp dry yeast, 1 egg, 6 fl oz warm water (approx).

Chicken fricassee

whole cooked chicken
roux sauce
salt and pepper
pinch nutmeg (optional)
2 egg yolks
juice ½ lemon
chopped parsley
grilled bacon for garnish (optional)

Pull chicken to pieces (discard skin) and add to sauce. Stir in egg yolks and cook for 1–2 minutes. Add lemon, parsley, and garnish with bacon. Serve on a bed of rice with creamy mashed potatoes.

Fond of this bland-tasting dish, reminiscent of childhood and convalescence. Wouldn't like to have it too often, is Jasper's verdict. When I counter that it makes a chicken go further he brings up my lack of skill with gravy. The thick white sauce *is* the gravy, I shout.

Another hilarious/disastrous dinner party, depending on your sense of colour. This is Suzy's and my third attempt to cut expenses and surprise ourselves. She does the soup and dessert, I do the mains and after-dinner nibbles. The men provide the wine. White wine because neither Suzy nor I like red. There is no consultation, no synchronising of recipes. So we get (from Suze) a chill whitish-green cucumber soup; from myself chicken fricassee, creamed potatoes and broad beans; a lemon sorbet (Suze) and, instead of chocolate mints, I have scooped up a bag of frosted caramels.

'It's a wonder you don't cover both of us with whipped cream and be done with it,' Andrew, Suzy's husband, groans.

'You'd be a sight more colourful, old man,' Jasper joins in.

We laugh so much we might have drunk half a dozen bottles of claret instead of two modest Gerwürztraminers, a Matawhero and a Villa Maria. As she kisses me goodnight, Suze suggests an all-red dinner. Bortsch, raw beef platter, raspberries, drinks with red cherries floating.

Years, cycles, now of carrot, silverbeet and potato – one potato, one silverbeet leaf (not the outer ones) one young yellowish carrot – cooked and puréed. Stewed apple, rice (2 tbsp in a pie-dish, lump of butter floating on the surface like a golden boat, left for hours and hours at 200° F). Icecream, fruit, crackers, cheese. Muffins, pizzas, shepherds' pies, poached egg on spinach nest, macaroni cheese with diced ham, nursery cum adult like two languages: one simple, the other simple enough to contain deceit. 'Give the children a sausage wrapped in bread with tomato sauce and send them to bed early. Be waiting with an intimate dinner for two with candles.' Measure the energy level of both partners. In the morning, toast, egg, cornflakes, a small destroyed encampment on the table top. Plain food, bland food, carrot, potato, green leaf with white light shining in the stem. Why not mash *everything*? Why not *pills*?

A little herb garden by the back steps, raised for easy picking, was salvation. The very names – if the herbs were never cut or dried or used – were enough. Balm, basil, chives, chervil, endive, fennel – how beautiful they sounded, like planning a holiday in Tuscany. Garlic, of course, hanging or rubbed into salt, *à la* Colette, parsley, cut fine or coarse, watercress growing where the pond overflowed and nasturtiums (young) for salad. Today when we go to restaurants and a feathery frond of fennel lies alongside Sole Bonne Femme* or a purple and yellow pansy beside Marquise au Chocolat** Jasper and I are unfazed thanks to the little herbarium.

Liver Provençale

2 oz bacon	2 tbsp flour
1 lb onions	½ pint stock
2 tsp salt	1 lb sheep's liver
pepper	chopped parsley

Cut the bacon in small pieces and fry gently. Remove. Slice and fry onions until they begin to colour. Add seasoning and flour and mix well. Add stock and stir until boiling. Return bacon and liver cut in small pieces. Cover and simmer for ½ hour. Serve with chopped parsley.

Jasper has severe indigestion and disappears to the golf course. Feel Liver Provençale is the beginning of a coolness between us. Loses tournament and vomits behind a tree at the thirteenth hole. N.B. Did think 2 tsp was excessive for salt.

Leafing despondently through *Marie Claire*. The children are at boarding school, Jasper has just phoned to say his business trip has been extended. Bar-room noises in the background; he sounded slightly flustered. On the first page of *Marie Claire's Cuisine Ordinaire* is a most extraordinary illustration. A black

* Good wife's sole
** Chocolate Marchioness

glossy background and an oil- and herb-drenched (I should be able to recognise the herb) lettuce leaf. It looks, drifting towards two partially-shown edges of lettuce leaf at the bottom of the page, like a great cloud unfolding. Or it could be an exquisite piece of lingerie in the act of floating through the air.

'French cookery, despite its very traditional base, is constantly changing. While welcoming and reflecting innovation, we do not ignore the charms of the past.' I turn quickly over *The French Larder* and say the names of the sauces like a litany: Crème Fraîche, Cèpe, Béchamel, Mornay, Velouté, Soubise. Then, since I haven't eaten, I imagine myself at Maxim's and order in perfect French:

> *Soupe de soles
> Salade tiède de verdures aux foies de volaille
> Tournedos aux herbes du jardin de monsieur le curé
> Choux rouge à l'Alsacienne
> Persil frit
> Crêpes 'veuve joyeuse'

The very sound is enough to produce happiness. Happiness and sadness, as in Velouté sauce. So soft and full does it sound one imagines a starving man in prison – a chef perhaps – dining on memories. Then, since I am dining on memories myself tonight, I open a can of baked beans, set one egg in the little poacher which gives such a perfect appearance and plug in the toaster.

Marie Claire has a broccoli and cauliflower terrine (Terrine de chou brocoli et chou-fleur), a slice of which resembles a landscape. The puréed broccoli stalks make the grass, two whole broccoli perfect little green trees with crushed pink peppercorns for fruit, crème fraîche and puréed cauliflower make the sky and clouds. The most perfect touch is one large cauliflower floret which makes a perfect cumulus cloud.

* Sole soup, Warm salad of chicken livers and mixed greens, Tournedos with herbs from the curé's garden, Alsace sweet and sour red cabbage, deep-fried parsley, 'Merry Widow' pancakes

Shopping list for a solitary weekend

4 pkts instant noodles (pork, chicken, oriental, beef)
2 croissants
1 Danish camembert
500g muscatels
3 slices ham
1 avocado
2 tomatoes
Betty Crocker cheesecake (small size)
1 can Dairy Whip (medium)

Now that term has recommenced and Jasper is in Europe I am reading more and more and discovering the links between food and literature. Not discovering them exactly, since I am still an amateur, but beginning to associate certain books, certain characters, with certain dishes. I noticed it first some years ago when I was reading *A House for Mr Biswas* and felt an almost irresistible desire to eat rice off brass dishes. I even found myself in the kitchen boiling a large quantity of rice which had the next day to be made into a cold rice salad. I used to imagine that those writers who introduced recipes and descriptions of food were simply filling up space, in the same way two or three drafts of a letter may be shown and the reader invited to select the one posted. Thos and I had quite a good discussion when I was packing his tuckbox and he was suggesting what I might add. It seems it is important to have a good quantity to share as well as a private hoard and the one conceals the other. We talked of priest-holes – he is studying the Dissolution of the Monasteries and the thought of secret caches of chocolate bars seems very like a priest-hole. Also I was convinced by something he said that he regards the hamper as a kind of surrogate mother. He tells me he hates Jane Austen who is on his reading list. No mention of food and not enough about sailors. I pointed out that Elizabeth Bennet does walk up an appetite in *P & P* but I have to agree with him that mostly exertion results in a storm of nerves. When he had gone back I suddenly thought of the cold spread in *Emma*.

Mrs Tancred, the new housekeeper and treasure, has left

> Lamb and vegetable hotpot
>   and
> Pear and walnut upside-down pudding

Last week she brought a Dundee cake.

Thos has sent a quote from John Betjeman on a postcard:

> 'I know what I wanted to ask you,
> Is trifle sufficient for sweet?'

Can we have trifle next hols and lots and lots of sherry?

Two new pies from Mrs Tancred:

> Bacon, leek and apple pie (scrumptious!)
> High-rise apple pie.

I've decided to give her a raise.

Collect toll call from Benjamin. Tuck box seriously depleted. Then, obviously put up to it by his elder brother, he reads out with much guffawing:

> 'It's a very odd thing –
> As odd as can be
> That whatever Master B eats
> Turns into Master B.'

I gather this is from Walter de la Mare (adapted) and he regards me as responsible for girth, height, muscle tone, attractiveness to girls. Capitulate but insist he studies harder.

Over a candlelit dinner at *Bellissimo* Jasper tells me he wants a divorce. He has ordered his favourite Fettucine Alfredo⋆ and after toying with Trenette al Pesto⋆ or Cannelloni all' Laziale⋆ I have decided on two entrées: Calamaretti Fritti⋆ and Carciofi alla Romana.⋆ This gives a slightly refined impression, not exactly invalidism but a related kind of discernment. In a way it is a compliment to the chef. Jasper has been known, in certain moods, to send a half bottle of Barolo with his compliments. Two entrées allows room for dessert: I am already anticipating Gelato all'Anguric⋆ or perhaps Cassata alla Siciliana.⋆

'And to think I have always considered Italian food as the food of love,' I hiss angrily. Naturally I am not going to finish squid or artichoke now. I'd like to seize the carciofi and throw it at Jasper's face. He's just toying with his fettucine.

It seems he blames me for not recognising the pattern of his absences or a certain *frisson* between himself and his secretary Jill when he brought her to lunch last year (tinned soup and toasted sandwiches). I try to summon up a face and I come up with dark wavy hair, dark unplucked eyebrows and the faintest trace of a moustache. It is the moustache that undoes me. It conjures up an Italian Mamma cooking pasta for the midday meal, pasta casalinga or pasta casalinga verde, lovingly rolling and cutting, and sifting the spinach. Then I see her setting the table, closing the shutters, sitting in her black apron with her head in her hands. I resolve never to eat Italian again or only in company of children. I throw my napkin (red with white checks, naturally) into the Calamaretti Fritti and stalk out.

Now comes a period, before the settlement is drawn up, when the boys with their tuck boxes eat better than I do. Baked beans on toast and poached egg left to frill in the water. I have returned to baby foods. Stewed apple. A canister of Dairy Whip. Perhaps there should have been one final feast culminating in a great

⋆ Fettucine Alfred, Fettucine with Pesto sauce, Cannelloni with beef, bacon and mushroom stuffing, Fried small squid, Globe artichokes Roman style, Watermelon ice cream, Sicilian cassata

Pyramide de glaces, de sorbets et de fruits:* three litres of mixed ice creams and sorbets: vanilla, mango, lime, melon, mint, apricot. A great pyramid to crash down, a gastronomic eminence that would melt away like a candle.

'Don't eat too many almonds,' Colette wrote. 'They add weight to the breasts.' I look at myself in the mirror and wonder if I have eaten too many almonds. Decidedly I am heavier. I have always been pear-shaped.

The boys have been assured we shall attend cricket matches and end-of-term concerts and graduation as we always have. Jasper will simply be spending more time in the city. Eventually I shall find something smaller but there is no hurry. Jasper will find something larger than the one-room flat we used to use for staying overnight for theatres and concerts. Where the fridge was stocked with Veuve Cliquot and pâté. Once it held a generous helping of Stilton brought home in a napkin.

French toast II

2 slices day-old wholewheat or enriched white bread
2 egg whites
2 tbsp skimmed milk
¼ tsp vanilla extract
⅛ tsp cinnamon
½ tbsp oil

In a mixing bowl combine the egg whites, milk, vanilla and cinnamon. Beat lightly. Heat a griddle or heavy frying pan until hot and grease it well with oil. Dip bread slices in the egg white mixture and fry on both sides until golden brown and crisp. Serve with jam.

Yield: 2 servings
Approx. Cal/Serv: 115

* Ice cream, sorbet and fruit pyramid

Ate one serving for breakfast; one, cold, for supper. Approx. total cals: 300.

Why, I wonder, did we never eat Looed beef (p. 312),★ Pappard-elle with telephone wires (p. 371), Chinese sausage, dried duck, and roast pork sand pot (p. 340) or Headcheese salad (p. 332)? I'm glad we missed live drunken shrimp (p. 169)! 'I hesitate to tell you about this dish, but I have decided I can chance it with you. By this time we understand one another and you know that I will try anything, any food anywhere at any time, at least once. . . . A large glass casserole is brought to your table with quite a bit of Chinese rice wine in the bottom of the dish . . . the live shrimps are dumped into the heavy wine . . . as the wine intoxicates them they begin jumping about . . . banging themselves on the lid. They are drunk! They are then removed from the wine bath and dropped into rapidly boiling Chinese Chicken Soup Stock. They die instantly of course . . . you can taste the wine they imbibed. A light dipping sauce accompanies this very Hong Kong dish.'

I am walking by the sea eating fish and chips from a newspaper. The newspaper is as warm as a muff or a hot brick. I insert my fingers, greasy and salted as the sea is, and pull out a plump golden chip and then break off, for the fish is unbearably hot, as the shrimps were before they died – I don't believe, and never will, that what dies instantly feels nothing – just a corner of fish. The fish is blue cod for which there is a small extra charge. As my hand goes deeper into the bag it feels like fire and at the same time is oddly comforting, a bandage under which healing and all that entails is taking place. I think of the absurd *Recipes for the Busy Bride* and when the bag is empty I go and dip my fingers in the sea.

★ Smith, Jeff. *The Frugal Gourmet cooks three ancient cuisines: China, Greece and Rome*, N.Y., Morrow, 1989.

Eyes Averted

I knew she'd killed herself. Before I walked in on Harold, a grubby old man in a house that was falling down around him, I'd been told his wife had committed suicide twenty years ago. I wasn't supposed to know, at least as far as Harold was concerned. None of us at the visiting centre were. But a previous visitor had found out accidentally from the social worker. 'Oh, didn't you know?' she'd said. 'She killed herself a fortnight after he retired.' So it went down in the file.

To Harold she'd 'passed away'. He said that the first time I visited him. I was sitting across from him on the bed that he never used, except for stacking old shoe boxes and carrier bags full of junk. The place was covered in the dust, grease and nicotine of twenty years. He never seemed to notice. He seemed a nice enough old man, but I'd heard he could be stubborn, even violent, if he didn't get his own way.

He lived in the middle of a terrace that had been enveloped in an inner-city renewal scheme, where they brighten it all up, paint the doors, throw on new roofs, guttering and gates, even flower baskets if you're lucky. But not Harold's place. He'd refused to move out. Said he wanted to die there and he wasn't going anywhere else even if it *was* temporary. So his house remained the soft, rotting tooth in a newly capped row. The roof was dark and sunken like the bruise on a peach, the few square yards of garden overgrown, the door and window frames a tired blue that was a mass of flakes. The glass panes were grey and cracked.

Every time I walked down the street and came to the house I'd stand at the gate and look up at the discoloured net curtains of the bedroom. The upstairs that had never been used since his wife died. Then I'd carry the gate open (one hinge was gone so it just scraped the ground), step up to the front door and push. It'd come unstuck and fly back shakily, feeble and hollow-sounding, like a balsa wood door from a film set. And then the smell would wash over me. A thick odour of dust and dampness with the sharp, almost sweet tinge of brandy-laced piss. It did this the first time, and every other time, once a week, throughout the summer.

He'd be sitting in the armchair almost on top of the gas fire, his white head down to his knees. A chair he hardly moved from, a chair that had become a bed. The bulky black and white television, coated with dust, would be murmuring to itself. Even the programmes looked old. The whole room was mean and dark, cluttered with the debris of a life.

'I have a bad heart, y'know,' he said, using his sweet-old-man's voice. 'No one to look after me since me wife passed away. That's her, up there.'

A large, framed studio portrait on the sideboard. A woman in her mid-forties, taken about 1950 from the look of the hair and jacket. It seemed the photographer had caught her at the end of a smile: lips strangely non-committal, eyes averted. Or maybe, I thought then, maybe she couldn't smile.

I couldn't get that look out of my head. What had happened to make her do that? And all through the summer, as I visited him, the question grew in my head like a tumour.

He'd always be sitting there in a daze when I walked in (he never locked the front door – burglars would be hit by the smell and retreat), then he'd crawl back to this time, this place, while I sat staring at him. Most times he'd send me to the corner shop for a bottle of brandy, and he'd sit there with his glass of gold winking in the drabness. 'It helps me chest,' he'd say, in his sorry-old-plaintive voice.

And then he'd talk.

When he was aggravated he'd complain about the Asian neighbours pushing down the barbed wire on his fence, and that their kids were climbing over to use his outside loo. It was

all rubbish. *No one* would want to use Harold's outside loo, and
the fence could hardly keep itself up; it was just a lot of old
doors, planks, bits of corrugated iron. But I'd go out occasionally and tap at it with a hammer to humour the old sod.

On other days he talked about the past and the lifetime he'd
spent in this house. I preferred that.

All through the summer I sat on his unused bed while he
pinned the scraps of his life onto me. How he'd walked into his
first job as a general hand at a local factory because he couldn't
stand his mother and sister going yap, yap, yap at him, and
when he'd walked in with his first pay packet he'd sat in the
armchair thinking 'You're in charge now, Harold', and
demanded his dinner and cup of tea. And got it too. 'They soon
got the bloody message,' he said triumphantly. He said he
always liked a good fight.

And then he told me of his wife's cleaning job. She'd taken
it on so she could have just a little money for herself. 'I allowed
it,' he said. 'But then she started yapping with all the other
women, and when we were arguing once (I forget about what,
she was always having a breakdown about something or other)
she turned and said. "You don't keep *me* any more!" '

So he marched out, telling her she'd better give up the job or
else. She cried and ran after him, down the street, shouting his
name, apologising, with him ignoring her. And she gave in.

I couldn't get her out of my head. Her face on the photo:
clouded, downcast, lips caught at the end of a smile, eyes
averted.

And then he showed me the photographs. As if he knew. He
was gazing out at the back garden through the dirty, cracked
pane.

'Eh, it used to be a lovely garden. We'd sit out there in the
summer . . .'

Before, before, before. . . .

He raised himself, taken with an idea, and his feeble legs
made it to the sideboard. He took out an old, long-used Black

Magic box, made it back to the chair and took off the lid, sifting through the mound of photographs with a bony hand. He handed one to me.

A neat spacious lawn with a straight path through it, down to the picket fence at the bottom. A man and a woman. He fortyish, smooth-featured, with slacks and white shirt turned up at the elbows. She in summer frock, hat and a half-smile.

'This is the garden?'

He affirmed it proudly, but laughed too.

Then he passed her into my hands, frozen in monochrome on half-a-dozen different holidays. The face, over and over again, but always with eyes beginning to cast themselves downwards. Except on one photograph. The one where she stood by a small aeroplane, laughing wildly.

'You see that,' he said. 'She'd just been up in that. You could pay for a five-minute ride. Look at the grin on it. And she was supposed to be having a nervous breakdown then and all.'

The distance. The chasm of decades between all of that and this time, this place. Why should it have mattered to me, some kid in his twenties; what did I know about any of that? A succession of miseries, now memories, locked away in a gallery of half-drawn moments. The past, magnetised in the dampness. Years of petty injustices primed ready for playback, with no switch marked *stop*. All of those photos, through the nineteen-twenties, thirties and forties, and then that portrait on the sideboard. Then nothing of her in the last twenty years with Harold. Twenty years of that expression. And then all it took was a fortnight of him being in the house, and the reel snapped in mid-play.

I suppose it just wasn't the right time. Any other time and I'd have been okay. But not that summer. Because every day after work I'd catch a bus to the other side of the city to our little haven, and wonder if I was going to find Theresa sitting on the stairs because it was the only place she could escape the irritating

white walls which she said were staring at her. I always knew
what would follow. That the scene was primed and ready for
playback with no switch marked *stop* and that her first word,
with her first realisation of this time, this place, would set in
motion the crackled thread of tape riding under the reels' dis-
jointed orbits. Her lips would open. My eyes would close. I'd
wait for the first word.

'Love?'

And thus it snaps. Whatever it is that keeps her holding on.
She's adrift somewhere in a cold lagoon. And a voice is whispering from somewhere above the fluid blackness, words that come
like clumsy arms to pull her out. But the grasping arms relax
because the voice has been offering its reasons to carry on, and
has run out of reasons.

We'd been dragged through the scene again and again. I'd
stay quiet, because the first word would set the scene in motion.
It was that I couldn't help her that was causing the pain. That
sometimes I wanted to say 'I want *my* nervous breakdown now.'

And I got it. In a way. Something has to account for it. I don't
believe in ghosts. Not me. I believe in magnetism, memories
and melancholia, but not ghosts.

The next time I called on him, after he'd shown me the
photographs, he was complaining about the fence again. It was
an oppressive morning, humid, and I noticed that Harold's penis
was hanging out of his trousers, a fat grub the colour of stewed
tea. I didn't bother telling him he'd forgotten to put it back in
after going to the outside loo. He would only have said *what,
what, what*, till I was bellowing 'Your prick's hanging out!' so
I just took the hammer and tacks and started banging at the
fence. He made his way into the garden with his walking stick,
tongue sticking out with the effort. A fighter. Cock still hanging
out. Stood there, grinning, white sky on his glasses. His wife's
photograph standing somewhere in the brooding house behind
him.

A young Asian woman was in the garden next door, hanging

out washing. The fence was too high for them to see each other, but I could see them both. With difficulty I said, 'He says the kids keep climbing over.'

Her face remained calm, distant, and she answered in Oxbridge English. 'Would you tell him not to throw his dirty water over the fence onto our washing, please.'

I said yes and resumed my banging. The whole exchange going on under his nose but he being so deaf it didn't matter. All he ever did was grin and say 'Arr'. His wife's photograph standing somewhere in the brooding house behind him.

I was bang bang banging at the fence, the question throbbing in my head like a tumour: *why, why, why?* And then the fence lunged at my face and something snapped in the back of my head, like a thunder crack in my skull. And I turned on him and said: 'You killed her, you bastard. You killed her.'

And he stood there grinning, nodding his head and saying 'Arr . . .' And then I didn't notice his face, because I was staring at the woman standing in the door behind him, gazing at me over his shoulder, with the same eyes as the photograph.

The house, the garden, the sky seemed to rush away past her like the landscape past a train, her face static at the centre of it all. And then I pulled my finger out of the box of tacks because it was speared. The white flesh erupted in a kiss, and when I looked up she was gone.

Harold showed me his retirement photo the next time I called. He'd found it in all the junk on the bed. All week I'd been walking round like my hand had been trapped in a car door: numb, dazed and cold.

An erect and stern man accepting a watch, surrounded by a multiracial group of couldn't-give-a-toss apprentices in overalls. 1969. She was still alive then, I thought. Waiting in this room for forty-five years of being his wife to come to a head. Twenty years older than on that photo. Another twenty years of that expression etched into her face, showing deep behind her averted eyes, and the bitter taste of it on her lips. Sitting here. Waiting.

What was it, going through her head? Did she know then what we know now (the gossip of social workers, the content of visitor's files), even though you think we don't, Harold? Did she know then what she was going to do? Did she know when? Did she know how?

Or was it just that forty-five years of being ground down was experienced all over again in just two weeks and she didn't even think about it? Was it just like putting on her coat and going down to the corner shop for a bottle of brandy?

Or was it another argument – a retort she knew you couldn't answer and that's why you hate her for it, for not letting you win your good fight?

'It was just after we were married. Brighton, it was. That's where we went for our honeymoon, my dear departed wife and me. And I remember we took a walk along the seafront just after we got there, and she had this new umbrella, parasol kind of thing. Anyway, we were having an argument. I'd wanted to stay in the room, you see, 'cause we'd only just got there, and she'd wanted to go for a walk. But she marched off and I went after her, and she was getting upset, the way she always did. Then she opened the umbrella and, heh heh. Our friends had played a trick on us, they'd filled the umbrella full of confetti. So there she was, in the middle of the street, covered in it, and all the passers-by were laughing, thinking there's a honeymoon couple. And we started laughing too. Heh heh. It *was* funny. I've never forgotten that.'

And then he was dead. Just like that. Walked in one morning, leaned over him sat in the ragged armchair, patted his hand and it was cold. Something fell out of me. I felt it physically. It dropped inside me. I don't remember how I got upstairs. The upstairs he hadn't used for years. I was just in the unused bedroom suddenly, opening the nearest wardrobe to find it full of men's clothes.

'Where are they, Harold?' I shouted, running across to the other wardrobe and wrenching the doors open, to stand facing a row of wire hangers chiming together in the empty box. 'Did you burn them, Harold? Like rubbish!'

I threw an armful of hangers across the room, stumbled and fell back sitting in the wardrobe. And she was there, where the hangers had hit the wall. Harold's dead wife. Looking through me. Calm, almost indifferent, sad and non-committal. And then she was gone. There was no one in the room with me. Her face was replaced in my mind by Theresa's. I sat there in the empty wardrobe, coat hangers chiming in the space above me, and I cried. Great hunks of sobs retching out of me, and I remember saying 'I'm not like you, Harold. I was never like you.' But the words were hollow, like I didn't believe them myself.

She feels a tug in her belly as they lift and her skin erupts in an orgy of tingling all over her body. The horizon is snatched away and the clouds and clouds in the bright sky are pulled down with it, some great male hand is ripping them down like a curtain. She is crying out with joy and fear but she cannot hear her own voice against the engine's roar. The land has been snatched away and all there is is the blueness, clouds like frail wisps of promises and the blinding sun. She is laughing, screaming with laughter, and she cannot hear her own voice.

Valentine

I hate February.

There is no natural excitement about the second month of the year. Valentine's Day makes me embarrassed.

I used to think this was a fault and covered it up. Despite me, the valentine is always there on the table when I get up, a boxful of something padded with hearts on the front and a plausible poem inside that I always scour with my eyes, trying to get below the surface and feel what it was that made him choose this one. Which parts of it are closest to what he would say himself if he ever said things like this out loud. Only he doesn't. People don't, he says. That's what the cards are for.

> You know that you will always be
> The one who's everything to me:
> Your eyes, your smiles, your heavenly touch,
> Mean, o my darling, o so much.

Sometimes the poems don't rhyme:

> One word is my essence of you . . . Forever.
> We two . . . are One.

This morning the valentine is roughly A4 size with a baby-blue background and gold border, two rabbits on the front. The rabbits have inflated faces, cheeks all swollen up like they have mumps and the bandages fell off. You can tell one is a lady rabbit because she has longer eyelashes and a pink bow round her neck. He has buck teeth. Nonetheless, their whiskers intertwine. Inside, it says:

I never thought that life could be
As wonderful as this
You mark my hours with happiness
There's splendour in each kiss
And tho it's true I sometimes fail
to say what's really true
At least I have this special day
To tell you I love you

My eyes fill up.
  They really do.

I watched a TV programme once about how they make movies. One of the sequences in the programme showed how they fix a tearjerker by shooting this terrible fragment of script about a couple who were on the verge of divorce then adding music and lighting to the fragment in such a way that you could hardly help being drawn in in the way they wanted you to be. Despite the fact that what was happening was implausible and banal. Despite the fact that it had nothing to do with anything and you knew bugger all about them. And moreover they were pretty shitty people. So I made up my mind while I was watching that I'd really use the information the programme was giving me: I would see the devices and not be manipulated by them. I sat smirking as they piled on the rising melodic line, plaintive oboe counterpoint, soft-focus rose-coloured filters for profiles against a dark background, single tear glistening on female cheek, man biting back his tears out of pride (that was the bit that nearly got me), swooping crescendo of synthesised strings. I could see how it all worked and was being really world-weary about it all. Then they did a rotten thing. Just when you thought you'd survived intact, a door behind the couple opened, flooding the foreground with white light and a child on crutches pushed himself forward out of the aura calling Daddy, Daddy in this reedy little voice. It was ridiculous, of course. They layered it on thick so you would see just how far this kind of thing could go. I saw it was ridiculous of course. But the bastards hadn't warned me it was coming. I just keeled over on the carpet and gret buckets.

Conditioning. Give me a cue and I play ball.

This is my valentine, the only one I get.

I kiss the first letter of his name, smudging the signature he has written in blue felt tip and underlined twice, imagining where his skin has traced over the card.

Blue marks on my lips in the bathroom mirror.

I sit it on the top of the TV before I go out to work.

Stella has heart-shaped sandwiches for lunch. She says she bought a cutter to make heart-shaped sandwiches as a surprise for Ross when he opens his piece-box (she can hardly eat for giggling, thinking about the surprise when he peels back the lid of the tupperware, she'd LOVE to see his face) and she thought she might as well cut her own like that while she was about it. She opens one out to let me see. Perfect pink hearts of ham, the grain of the muscle severed clean at the edges of bread. No butter. She is on a diet. For Ross. He told her she was getting fat. I imagine Ross in his factory, opening the piece-box she has prepared and trying to hide what he finds. If he can't hide it then he will talk about Stella as though she is a retard: tell the boys (maybe not overtly, but tell them anyway) how stupid she is, what an embarrassment. Some of the boys I see him explaining to have not shaved that morning. Some have tattoos. They are all glad it isn't them with the sandwich problem. Ross will eat them anyway, the shapes of the hearts hidden inside his hands, just enough to bite poking through. The boys know to laugh, irrespective of deeper, more ambiguous emotions. Maybe they would like their women to be as little-girl cute as Stella. Maybe that is why they laugh at her, encourage Ross to do the same behind her back. Maybe they're jealous: maybe they worry their women don't love them enough to do something that stupid. Stella looks up and asks me if I got a card. Her mascara is in blobs all along the bottom rim of lashes. Stella is hopeless with mascara. Of course, I say.

Boxed?

I nod. I don't tell her I think it's a waste of money. She'll think I'm a killjoy or else I haven't got one and I'm lying and being sour. I dare not admit I want something more real.

I've not had mine yet, she says. It'll be there when I get back with the roses. Yellow roses. Always gets me those. Romantic and just that wee bit different. Wee bit of imagination thrown in.

She sinks her teeth into the bread, shearing half-moons clean through the ham centre.

A big softie.

I suffer a terrible need to brush my teeth. Otherwise I will walk around all afternoon with egg mayonnaise rising up the back of my throat like drain emissions. I leave trying not to hear the noise of chewing, Stella mashing her hearts to paste.

The car drops me off and they wave. I wave too till they're out of sight then start running. I am running because I am wearing his jersey and need to get it back in the drawer before he comes home. If he finds out he gets moody and says I put his jerseys out of shape. He thinks I punch tits in the front of them just by wearing them, as though my breasts were leather darning mushrooms. I run up the stairs with the key on a keyring he bought me the weekend after I moved in: tiny, delicate keyring with a white porcelain fob and my initial in gold filigree. I tried to keep it safe by leaving it in the drawer with my earrings but he said I bought you it to use it Margaret, so I use it, knowing one day I'll have to tell him it's lost. The door never feels secure when you open it: always loose on the hinges. I keep meaning to do something about it but it causes bad feeling: if I pick up a hammer or a Black and Decker he thinks I'm trying to prove something. He's right. I'm trying to prove the door needs fixing but he won't buy that. He'd rather I asked him. He'd rather I nagged. Like his mother.

I am always last out. Last out and first back. That means any mess I don't like is how I left it and therefore my fault. Curtains not even drawn. I bump into the Moroccan table he hauled all the way back from Fez and which does not respond to cleaning as we know it, reaching to pull the curtains open and show how much dust there is on the sills. A clear view of the binstores for the whole block. Over the binstores today there is a clear stretch of sky rising up beyond the flat tops of the other buildings. Between the two furthest blocks you see hills. Birds perch on the TV aerials for a moment, then wade back into the thick blue paste up there, hovering on irregular air currents from the laundromat vent. The polarising stuff in the window always makes the view look nicer from inside than out: bright and cheery. It's the thing I like best about the whole flat. I can watch the clouds here for hours.

Two papers opened out at the TV page (old ones), a jar of brine he finished the olives out of, empty silver poke of posh crisps. Chilli with a dash of lemon flavour. I brush up slurry with the side of my hand, pick up the debris. Share he said, we'll share. I get rid of the bits and take off his jersey with one hand, haring for the bedroom.

YOOHOO.

I'm in the bedroom waving his jersey out the window hoping it's not obvious from down there in the garage space but it's only the man from the bakery. The thing must look like a bloody flag. Maybe it's visible all the way down the back road: maybe he can see it this minute as he drives along the back road home, knowing fine what I'm doing: already thinking Christ I told her not to wear my bloody stuff and veering near the centre line with his cuffs loose, folded back because it's warm. How do I know? But I wave the jersey hopefully out of the window all the same, the red sleeves catching and flicking bits of paint off the frame like giant dandruff. If I wave the jersey out the window it will cool down and lose the smell of me. I don't know what I smell like but he says it's distinctive. He says he knows when I've been in a room. I leave traces behind.

Red immersion light. The immersion is an expensive way to heat water but it gets the tank ready for him coming home. If there's plenty of hot water he'll have a bath before anything else. Like raking through his jerseys. He works in a glass office and sweats when it's sunny. That's all I know about what he does. That and the lunches: he always tells me what he's had in the canteen. I picture him in the glass office, maybe slotted into the middle floor of five, sitting at the drawing board and trying not to blink too much while the sweat burrows like insects through his armpits, the thick furze at his crotch. There are stains in ovals on his back and where the arm seams join. His tie is slewed to one side, the top button on his shirt undone showing the hair at the base of his neck. Every so often he moves one leg behind the other, widening his knees to let his body breathe. His skin bristles with the slow movement of sweat beads. He frees the watch strap and rubs the damp wrist, then goes back to what he was doing. He's holding a pen. I don't know what he's writing with the pen. Maybe it's a pencil and he's drawing. I don't know what he does all day. When I ask him he says it's not interesting: he doesn't come home to talk about work. It involves pens though. He's never done pinching mine. Sometimes he's there from eight in the morning till after midnight. Whatever it is takes up big parts of his life.

Other times, I imagine him walking along a sunned-out corridor, one hand balled into the right trouser pocket, his jacket slung over his shoulder, watching his feet as he walks. Occasionally, he kicks something on the floor that isn't there, a mimed football tackle that pulls back its power at the last minute. Just working off a little energy. People walk past in the corridor and he nods or moves his mouth a little (not a smile though:

few men make open smiles at each other) or says hello. Not
hello. AYE AYE. He says AYE AYE and keeps going. Maybe
he's going to the canteen since he's so relaxed. The canteen has
glass doors that slide back automatically when he's within inches
of slamming against them but he doesn't flinch or slow down
at all. He knows this place like the back of his

Shirt on the floor. Didn't see it this morning.

His things are always nice to touch, aromatic because he's so
clean. Even things he touches smell nice. I slip the jersey into
the wardrobe rack, shake the layers so they resettle. Mine are
in the drawer above his. My things smell of deodorant. I put a
T-shirt on over the bra. Then I'm in the kitchen with the
curtains, glad I don't have to think what to make out of two
tins of tomatoes, pickles, anchovies and yards of herb jars,
walking back into the living room with the sun coming through
the T-shirt and making goosepimples on my arms and see the
newspaper I missed first time round. I've been working all day
but that's no reason. Plenty of women work all day and have
kids and a man to run. My mother tells me I don't know what
tired is. I thought I was tired. So I pick it up: not consciously
but something always makes these decisions for you. Anyway
I should be cleaning up. I don't even normally read newspapers
but I read this. SUICIDE PACT FAILS. Two pensioners had
gone out in a car, doused themselves in petrol then run the
thing into a wall at sixty. They both survived. Not in okay
condition but breathing. Ten miles or so up the road to where
I was standing reading about what they'd done. A kind of
village with an open park and lots of trees. Ten miles up the
road.

The sound of the car braking in the parking area six floors
down.

Already he is home and safe, winding up the nearside window
and collecting his *Evening Times* from the empty passenger seat,
reaching into the back for the jacket he'll sling over his shoulder

to come upstairs. He walks with his eyes screwed up these days because his hair needs a cut. He'll be walking upstairs now with his eyes screwed up small, maybe resting finger and thumb of one hand on either side of his nose, trying to shake off tiredness, happy to be home. My heart jumps into my mouth so I breathe out, thinking about him setting foot on the stairs, coming home. Appearing on top of the landing and smiling when he sees me, making my nerve endings spring to life. I can't help it. I'm crazy about him. Wholly and terminally raddled with love.

He appears and I smile, meaning every bit of it.

He comes in grinning, presents spilling from under his arm. He gives me:

> flowers (irises since I said they were favourites)
>
> something chocolate, usually heart-shaped
>
> a bottle of wine, dry and white (a gesture: he prefers red. I prefer sweet but he can't bring himself to ask for that.)

The wine is out of habit.

We used to stay in on Valentine's Day and eat my speciality with the packet of frozen prawns and strawberry mousse, a magazine-recipe special with claims to being aphrodisiac though in a self-deprecating way so you know not to take it too seriously. My only speciality. It recurs. The magazine page is spattered with pink bits, fatty blobs that show mayonnaise has been this way but I keep it all the same.

Not tonight though. I'm not cooking tonight.

I point to his card, waiting on the sofa. He opens it while I take his jacket, puts it on the TV next to mine. They both threaten to fall off, not designed to sit upright, too full of satin and foam. I want to give him something better than that but don't know what. The options are limited. Anyhow, he seems to like it. We kiss. The tips of our tongues touch.

I've not had time to wrap it, he says and fishes something else out of a poly bag. A flat, black box. I give him an oblong box covered with stars. We open our boxes at what is meant to look like the same time but I'm holding back. I know what he has since I bought it but I want to see his face. I'm just like

Stella. He always looks the same when he opens something from me: shy. Happy and shy. It takes a minute for him to realise the folded cotton is a pair of thermal drawers. He holds them flat in one hand, not wanting to see the legs dangle, thin and empty, where I can see.

Very funny, he says.

I know something about the present has disappointed him. I interpret that he'd rather I was interested in what I've been given. Already I'm through to the pale blue tissue, trying to rustle a lot so he knows I'm thrilled. One of the pieces between the layers comes away in my hands, something soft enough to make my hand feel it's melting. I'm holding something shiny, red nylon with a black panel. I splay the pieces on the settee. It's a suspender belt and bra, a pair of knickers trimmed with fluffy stuff. Tiny feather boas. Our faces will look much the same then. Neither of us knows how to react. The evening is in jeopardy so we pretend this isn't the case at all. We just float in separate directions and begin getting ready for going out. We haven't got all night.

The water is cool but OK. I fill my bath up to the mark he hasn't washed off after his and lie back, getting sad at the sounds of him getting ready elsewhere in the house. What he has to put up with, me being such a hard bitch and everything when he just bought me a present. After all, it's the thought that counts.

The fluffy stuff sticks to my skin cream. Two strands like ferns adhere to my upper thigh. I don't look in the mirror but it seems to fit as much as this sort of stuff ever does and the feather bits don't bumphle the material as much as you'd think. I dress fast, looking over my shoulder and listening the whole time, hoping he doesn't come through. Maybe I want it to be a surprise.

The restaurant is reasonably familiar: nice intimate concern run by two Italians with Scots accents. The waiter gives me an obligatory smile when he helps me to my seat, tells me I look nice so I can't stop the simper. He sits opposite, managing his own chair, and smiles at me in a very sincere way. He likes good food. We get mildly drunk. Through the dessert and coffee we start sharing the looks that indicate sex. A particular kind of sex. I run my hand along the inside of his trouser leg with one hand under the table and he has to squirm while his brandy is being poured, barely able to stay seated while the erection forces a hump in his tight trousers or is forced to bend itself double, trapped in the flap of his y-fronts. My hand shifts to his penis. Watching his face trying not to flicker when the waitress asks him if he enjoyed the strudel gives me a real thrill of power. I'm making this difficulty, I'm altering his behaviour and it means he wants me. He wants me. I need to feel that's what it means.

On the way home, I hook the four-inch heel of one of my shoes onto the dashboard. He looks twice, undoes his fly as the car decelerates: then stops the car and fucks me in a layby till the car windows run like rain on the inside.

I get more excited by this kind of display then I'd be prepared to admit when I'm sober.

I blush hauling my breasts back inside the feather and satin contraption, ashamed for something I can't quite pin down. He clears the inside of the windscreen with the back of his jacket sleeve and looks at me. My back is stiff, eyes up to the roof vinyl. Listening. The sound of sirens. I hear sirens far away like remembered noise, too distant to know for sure. Maybe there's an accident someplace. I ask if he hears it and he says no. He says I imagine it and maybe I did. I always get maudlin afterwards: volatile. It's what I'm like.

When we get out of the car, our breaths appear. Low fog over the flat roofs on the other side of the street. There will be frost. At the foot of our steps, I find an empty box and I fold it carefully for the bins rather than do it tomorrow. He doesn't notice these things. His collar flashes white semaphore from the top of the steps and I hear him reach for the keys. He opens our door and goes inside. This is our home, how we live. He is in there taking off the tie and loosening the trouser band, trying to feel relaxed. We have already had sex. Further touch is unlikely. I stall at the foot of the stairs, not wanting to, then hear his solution. Dirk Bogarde being earnest about something in a late-night movie. We always have the TV. Tonight it has cards on top.

> And tho it's true I sometimes fail
> to say what's really true
> At least I have this special day

I can always go into the kitchen and make tea. One step at a time, my turn to lock us in for the night. The sound of actors speaking on TV, my heart bursting with wanting to give more and not knowing what it is, how to give it. And sirens. I still hear the sirens he thinks are not there coming closer.

Open Sesame

Six. One-two-three-four-five-six. Now we are six. Campbell counts the porcelain cats on the shelf while he tries to fall asleep. There are six. There were six yesterday and six the day before. Jam tomorrow and jam yesterday. John bought the cats from the Salvation Army Bargain Barn. He paid for them by the pound which meant they were expensive. More expensive than clothes. Everything at the Bargain Barn is fifty cents a pound.

Campbell can hear John and Richard laughing in their bedroom. They laugh almost all night long, until they get tired and fall asleep. Their laughter is high-pitched, screeching like their metal bed frame. Campbell closes his eyes and imagines the rust marks on the wall, like a scribble with brown pencil, above the headboard. He can see it, when he thinks about lying on their bed. Lying on the bed, staring at the headboard while John and Richard laugh hysterically, lick long stripes down his back. He can't handle it. He couldn't handle it. The warm mouldy smell of their pillows made him sick. Their sheets were slippery and soft and coated with dried sweat.

Everything in the house is damp now. The wooden TV table slouches like the back of an old horse and Richard can't see anything from his rocking chair any more. The wallpaper is beginning to separate at the seams like a shirt that's too tight. The floorboards undulate and Campbell keeps falling down on the way to the kitchen. Every time he opens the refrigerator, all the cats come running. There are only three, including the kitten. But when they all come running up, yowling and rubbing against his legs, it seems like six.

Campbell decides eating won't help. His whole body aches. It feels stretched. As if the muscles in his feet have been pulled up to his eyebrows. Every time he moves his eyebrows, his

feet yank up and jerk the muscles in his face, as if he had been
smiling too long. Every time he rolls over, he is crushing
something else. He remembers someone telling him that if you
slept on your stomach, your hips slid forwards into your intes-
tines. And if you slept on your side, your ribs kept your lungs
from expanding properly. Campbell worries that he will stop
breathing.

Campbell lies on his back with his arms crossed over his chest
like a body at a wake, the way his physical therapist told him
to. This is the most effective way to sleep and not ruin your
alignment. But his dance teacher told him the constructive rest
position meant that your knees were bent and your arms were
crossed so that your hands touched your shoulders. This releases
tension in the shoulders and lower back. It does not help
Campbell sleep.

His aunt keeps telling him he should drop out of college.
Everybody thinks a dance degree is a waste of time. Everybody
says Northern California is just full of fruits and nuts and if he
isn't careful he's going to be another one of them. She's always
telling him what everybody thinks. He tries to get her to shut
up. He tries not to listen. He hums. He thinks about pornogra-
phy, which he knows will shock his aunt, maybe keep her out
of his head for good.

The armchair he bought at Millie's in Capitola has green
mould under the cushions. Campbell never expected vinyl to
get mouldy. But the white cushions have small green shapes on
them that keep expanding. His aunt gave him the money for
that chair. She sent it to him in a flowered envelope so that
John and Richard couldn't see the money from the outside and
steal it. Then they would just say that it had never come. His
aunt warned him about that.

Whenever Kat came over, she told Campbell what a great
armchair it was. And John liked it too. No one else had a vinyl
armchair with a clean fifties look as if Annette Funicello could
have swung her legs over one arm and leaned her head back
against the other, the telephone cord wrapped around one of

her feet, the receiver dangling from her ear. No one else had a chair that would have floated over powder-blue carpeting like an ice cream throne. It had a round back like one hump of a heart. And arms that curled over as if they were hugging themselves.

John kept trying to sneak the chair into the living room. Campbell came home and found it wobbling in front of the television. He had to drag it back into his room, the legs pulling up the carpet and tripping him. John and Richard just kept toking on their bong and laughing at the television. The rockers on Richard's chair creaked in rhythm with his laughter.

Tonight, Campbell can hear the chair humming Frankie Valli and it keeps him awake. Then it starts complaining about John and Richard. It insults Kat. Campbell smells perfume. It is overwhelming. Cheap perfume that covers the scent of mildew. It doesn't take him long to recognise the perfume and the sound of the voice.

His aunt is in the chair. She is in the chair so that she can watch everything he does in his room. She thinks he's a fag. She doesn't believe that he's really decided to be straight. He had decided to be straight a few months ago. He hadn't slept with a woman yet because he wanted to wait longer in case he had AIDS. Well, Campbell is not going to give his aunt the satisfaction.

He gets out of bed and kicks the chair. It whines slightly and now he is sure his aunt is in there. He kicks her a few more times just to teach her a lesson.

He lifts the chair. It's heavy, so heavy he almost has to throw it into the living room. It hits the floor with a crash and Richard and John get very quiet. Campbell knows that they won't come out. They think he's freaking out again. He can hear them locking the door to their bedroom.

He wanted just to shut the door to his bedroom and leave the chair alone in the living room, but he can still hear it through the wood. Lying in bed, he can hear the whining complaints, slightly muffled, but comprehensible. His aunt knows he can hear her. She won't shut up.

So he gets up and kicks the chair a few more times, but it still won't shut up. It's raining outside. Thundering and raining in great crashing torrents. Campbell drags the chair out the door. It resists, hanging on the door frame and trying to bring the carpet with it. He bumps it roughly down the stairs, breaking off one of the wooden legs as he goes. The chair gives up the leg with a sharp squeal of pain. Campbell leaves the chair tottering limply in the driveway.

Now that it's gone, he can finally fall asleep. The sheets relax around him, even the clock seems to quiet its ticking.

By the end of the winter, the chair is green and bloated with rainwater. The three legs are swollen and the place where the fourth leg had been has small bugs crawling in and out of it. Campbell has to explain to Kat that his aunt is in the chair. He leaves it outside as the weather gets warmer.

By midsummer, the mould is dried up and the vinyl is cracked and tearing. He hears his aunt screaming, even from inside the house. He refuses to bring her in.

The screams are shrill, more insistent, piercing the eardrums when he walks out the door in the morning. He ignores her. That's the best way to deal with it. When he walks past her, she keeps trying to get in his head, but he doesn't let her.

She has more energy in the pale wet mornings, before the beach crowds drive in, filling the air with the scent of exhaust and suntan oil. The cars gleam in rows like a shopping centre parking lot. They honk and rev their motors, and jerk back and forth as if they're at the starting line of the drag race. Sun-blackened fifteen-year-olds sit on the back of the convertibles waving at each other in time to the radios like beauty queens in a parade.

Campbell wakes up an hour before he has to and drives to work while the streets are still cool and empty. He doesn't mind getting to the café early. He sets up the coffee pots, puts the pastries out on the counter. He likes working. Just doing things and not thinking about them. It's worth it not to have to pass the guys in the muscle shirts yelling 'Faggot!' and throwing beer bottles out of their cars as his face and ears turn red.

Lately, he keeps thinking about how he's going to have to go back to college in September. He doesn't want to see Richard in class. Richard keeps telling everyone that he's gay. He doesn't want to have to stand in the front of auditions and hear everyone in the back of the studio whispering about him. At least he's actually slept with a woman. Now Richard can't say he's a fag. He was surprised at the way Gita's body felt. He didn't expect the hard round stomach like the bottom of a cereal bowl, narrow shoulder blades like little wings. Her breasts swelled to tiny pointed nipples. When she sweated, her skin smelled of spices, like cumin bubbling in hot oil, garlic and fenugreek.

Her body felt like a boy's, like Campbell's must have felt to the men in the park when he was fourteen. The men in their grey suits and red ties, stroking Campbell's hips and unbuttoning his purple jeans, asking him about his classes in high school. He paid for his trip to Belgium that way.

Campbell goes to pick Gita up for work one day and her father meets him on the porch. He's tall and dark and wearing a turban and a thick beard tied around his chin with a stocking or something. Open Sesame. Campbell thinks of Ali Baba.

'I'm sorry, Campbell. Gita is not well. I'll bring her to work later myself, after she rests for a little while. Could you please tell the manager that she is late?' He rolls his r's like machinery and rolls the words back and forth in his mouth so that it sounds like he's speaking a foreign language.

Her mother barely speaks English at all. She comes out and wobbles nervously beside her husband. She has a doll face and her hair is oiled and wrapped into a long tight braid. She squeezes Campbell's hand with her fat little fingers. 'Hello, hello. Your name, please?'

Campbell tells her. 'Good, very good. Very nice boy.' She

reaches up and squeezes Campbell's cheeks together the way his mother used to force him to chew his brussels sprouts. 'Your mother?' she asks, 'your father?' Her fingers smell like food.

'OK,' says Campbell. 'Bye.'

When Gita comes to work, her eyes are small and red. Campbell grabs her arms and she says, 'Ow! That hurts,' but he doesn't want to stop pulling her into him so that his hot back presses against the frozen glass of the ice cream counter. She struggles and says, 'No, I can't. My father – ' and he wants to spend the rest of his life licking the raspberry-chocolate ice cream off her mouth and fingers and hair. Even her hat has shiny raspberry slashes across the stripes.

Campbell takes pictures of her with her hat on, behind the counter, holding a scoop of ice cream in the air. He takes pictures of her sitting at a table, clicking her shoes on the black and white tile floor. He paints her name on a piece of paper with watercolours and lets them run, so that all the colours drip into one Gitangali rainbow. He takes some of the hair clips she buys from the drugstore and a napkin she wrote a note to him on, with a little cartoon of herself on the bottom. Campbell hangs all the stuff on the wall next to his window. In the morning, the sunlight slashes across them and the pictures turn into squares of light. Sometimes, he tapes a flower to the wall beside them.

She saw the pictures and everything one day when she came over after work. 'Why do you have these here like this? They're terrible pictures . . .' She wants him to take them down. 'I don't know, it seems weird – ' and he says, 'OK' but it's his room and he doesn't have to.

Gita passes the chair when she walks down the driveway and says, 'Wow, what a cool chair. I wonder if you could fix it?'

A car full of surfers swerves towards her and she has to jump onto the sidewalk bumping into Campbell.

'Excuse me,' Campbell says.

'Nice tits, dot-head!' screams a surfer over the squeal of his tyres on the asphalt.

The scent of the flowers gets stronger and stronger in the sun. Then it fades and becomes papery as they dry. Eventually, Campbell takes them off and throws them away.

John is stoned and backing up his Volkswagen when he hits the chair. It releases a heavy sigh, a deflating sound. John thinks it's hilarious. He gets Richard and they reverse the car into the chair, over and over again, whooping hysterically until Campbell runs out of the house, throwing himself down the stairs so that he almost falls on the lawn, 'Stop! Stop it!'

They are laughing so hard that when Campbell jerks the door of the car open, Richard can't stop himself from rolling out onto the driveway. John just keeps laughing, 'It was just like hitting an old lady crossing the street, the sound that thing made, whoo! That sound!'

Campbell isn't going to think about Gita any more since her father told him not to come over again. The last day of summer, her brother and some of his friends came over to the café. Campbell wasn't scared of them. They were almost all small and wearing glasses. They looked like they spent all their time studying in the library. They walked in, laughing loudly and filling the café with the sour smell of old sweat. They sat around for a while, saying, 'Hey cool, man, this place is really cool. Hey, firungi-bhai, get us some drinks, shit, what do you think we're waiting for?' Most of the time, they didn't speak English, but he knew they were talking about him. Some of them wore turbans or little balls of hair wrapped in handkerchiefs and rubberbands on the top of their heads. Finally, one of them came up to him, 'So you are Campbell? You think my sister is pretty. But you are wrong. She is not pretty, she is beautiful. And she is too pretty for garbage who works in restaurants. She is a good Indian girl and she is engaged.' The other guys laughed. 'She already has a husband waiting for her in India. And he is very rich.' They all laughed again. 'So you leave her alone or we will come and beat you and there is nothing you can do.' One of the other guys added, 'And we will come and pick her up everyday, so don't think you can drive her.'

Campbell can't think about Gita any more. He hasn't seen her in three months. Not since college started. But, at night, sometimes he can hear her brother and his friends speaking in that language in his head. They keep talking about him, he can't figure out what they're saying. They keep talking. He tries not to look at the chair when he leaves the house because he can . hear it whining 'I told you so' with its last ounce of energy.

He decides he'll just have to concentrate on dance class. The best thing to do is to try and concentrate on his technique. He just thinks about being a better dancer. Lately Campbell can't seem to remember the phrase after the dance teacher shows it. He's not sure if he forgets or if they change it halfway and no one notices. He keeps stopping class and saying, 'It starts on the mirror leg, remember?' And everyone just looks at him. Like no one else would admit he was right so he has to run out of the room and scream on the balcony.

The only person who listens to him in technique class is Kat. She even ignores Richard when he says, 'For Chrissakes, Katherine!' But there's only one Kat and the six other dancers don't care what Campbell's talking about.

Walking past the Bargain Barn after class, Campbell sees his chair in the window. He wonders how they got it there. When John and Richard finally heaved the chair out of the back of the truck at the dump, all three legs collapsed, sticking out twisted and akimbo like broken limbs, and the stuffing gushed out of the gashes in its sides.

Someone must have fixed the chair, because there it is, gleaming in smooth vanilla cream, each leg straight and solid as a slab of dark chocolate. A mannequin is standing beside the chair, an American Indian girl that probably used to stand in front of a wigwam along the highway. Except that this Indian's wearing an evening dress of blue sequins and a black pillbox hat covers her head-dress. Campbell follows the curve of her long brown arm back down to his chair, and her graceful hand resting on the white arch looks like Gita's hand. As if someone cut off Gita's hand and put it on the mannequin.

Campbell knows why it's there, his aunt is trying to tell him something. He thought he killed her in the chair, thought she was going to stay out of his life. And now like Jesus Christ, don't take God's name in vain, it's a sin, but he can't help thinking it, the chair's come back to life. He can't hear her through the thick pane of glass, but he knows he has to save Gita from his evil aunt.

The girl at the Bargain Barn says, 'Oh no, sorry, that's just display, it's not for sale.' And when Campbell tells her he doesn't care, he'll buy it anyway, she shakes her head and giggles, 'I mean, how much do you think it'll weigh?' She blinks her flat blue eyes at him.

That night, Campbell can't sleep again. He can hear his aunt calling Gita a dirty Indian, telling him Gita stinks of curry, calling her father a pimp and an uppity towel-head. He should stick to his own kind. What does she mean by his own kind? thinks Campbell, getting out of bed. He drops the screen door as he leaves, letting it bang against the flimsy door frame and make the whole house shudder.

He can't wait to find his keys or start the car. He runs all the way downtown in his bare feet, getting cut by sharp stones and bottle caps and pieces of broken glass, but he doesn't care. There's no traffic so he runs in the middle of the road, the thick paint of the double yellow line smooth against the soles of his feet. Even with all the dance classes, he's not used to so much running, his breath is tearing out of his lungs and his purple jeans are heavy and stiff with sweat.

When he gets to the Bargain Barn, the chair is there, glossy and white, a shine of a smile reflected across its bloated middle. The chair's smile widens into a laugh. It's laughing and laughing. And the Indian girl is gone.

Campbell beats the window with his fists. He screams. He

kicks the window with his feet and they throb with pain. The glass is so thick it doesn't even tremble. He picks up little stones and throws them at the window, but they just bounce off like superballs.

Campbell steps back and trips over a cinderblock, chipped and discoloured, lying on the sidewalk. He hoists it up and swings it back and forth in his arms. Then he takes a deep breath and leans back. He swings again. He closes his eyes and lets go.

The cinderblock smashes through the window shooting shards of glass around it like rain. It hits the chair square in the middle and the chair falls back. It strikes the ground with a groan. Campbell holds a piece of jagged glass like a switchblade and jumps in the window. He shrieks and slices open the chair, ripping out the stuffing and throwing it around him. He stamps on the legs until they snap and splinter off. 'Is that enough?' he screams. 'Now will you leave me alone?' He kicks the chair until it's flat and deflated. When he jumps out of the window, all he can think of is Gita. He has to save her.

Now, as he's swallowed by the darkness, he doesn't even feel his body. With each gulp of salty air, the balls of his feet float higher off the pavement. Campbell feels like a cloud, a running shape, made of mist. He's so light, he can't keep himself on the ground. He's flying and spinning forward like a catherine wheel on the Fourth of July, shooting sparks of light all around him. Four months since he's been down this road, but he would know the way to Gita's house even if he were blind.

Campbell's face and hands are burning. His eyes are watering so much the flames seem like orange stripes, trembling and waving. The smoke is almost choking him, but he walks closer. He's going to walk in the door just as it blackens and crashes from the hinges onto the porch. The firemen are smashing through the porch with their boots and kicking doors and windows and shouting. Behind Campbell, it sounds like mermaids screaming or singing, hundreds and hundreds of mermaids, but maybe it's peacocks like *A Thousand and One Nights* and then he hears Kat saying, 'No! You idiot! What's he doing there?' And there are firemen all around him, grabbing his jacket and, arms, and they smell like plastic and campfires and chemicals and Kat is saying, 'I can't believe it – this isn't London or Israel, what kind of a nut has a bomb in California?'

The car is warm and Kat pushes all the junk in the back seat. She puts her arm around Campbell as she drives him home. 'Someone said it was Gita's father's mistress or something. Some woman he'd dumped. It's ironic, isn't it?' says Kat. Campbell hopes Richard and John don't think he'll let them sleep with him now.

'I mean, she throws a pipe bomb through his bedroom window, and he survives. Everyone else was dead from the smoke by the time the rescue people got there. Poor Gita.' Kat touches Campbell's cheek and her fingers feel like claws on the charred skin.

The Aunt's Progress

I

house of night whispers
between sisters
house of wasted flesh

scarred house
cut and stitched house
house of your rasping breath

hide-and-seek house
hunt-the-aunt house
cat-and-mouse house

house of the uninvited guest

II
behind your bedroom door
a roar of cold air
buffets my ears
slaps me back

who's this impostor
laid out on your bed
sheet stretched taut
from chin to toe

this sly arrival
nose in the air
so secretive

all closed up
impossibly still

who let her in
this chalk-faced mime
her eyelids as smug as eggs
implacable, dumb
under a shutter of skin

any minute now
she'll unstifle her laugh
and look
she'll speak
this fake, this replica

this scarecrow with sparse hair
who feigns sleep
this effigy, this doll

III
at 2 a.m.
your absence knocks in the roof
gurgles along the pipes
from room to room

tap tap tap
are you there

below my stiff pillow
the hum of that chill machine
the jumpy tread of the stairs

tap tap tap
are you there

IV
on the fourth day
the men in black
arrive to wheel her out
in her wooden pram

they get her as far as the hall
this impersonator of aunts
in her rotten disguise
her mask of greenish wax

she's on display
tucked up in brown nylon
quilts, incorrupt
an imitation saint
her porcelain head sunk deep
her bonnet
of white padding
narrow as a nun's

the men collect her, their prize
wadded in cotton
boxed up, presentable

whoever she is
they slide on the lid
they pull her away

V
from the house
we deliver you, Brigitte

into these men's hands
the hands of the undertakers
the grave-diggers
the priests

out of this life
we deliver you

to be churched
praised, blessed, borne off
prayed for, and buried

so that fear may finish
and grief may begin

VI
your parents were your windows
your shutters, your walls
you built yourself to their plan
on their foundation

when they removed
to death
the house shook, shivered
bits and pieces
of yourself fell off
never to be recovered

first your breast left you
then your hair
it was practical
the collapsing flesh
your life leaked out of you
into bedpans
white enamel kidney dishes

VII
in Le Havre
in the pink-floored hospital
you gagged on plastic
you couldn't speak

your great eyes
testified
made your statement
to us, your witnesses

you tried to collect yourself
your long finger wagged *no*
at the misplaced gauze
the crease in the clean towel

but the chairs jumped about
gulls from the docks
zigzagged their cries
above your bed
needy people
clopped in and out
they bristled with gifts
gladioli whose colours hurt
crème caramel you couldn't eat

we tipped into you
one drop of water at a time
between your lips
from the tilted spoon

your sister became your mother
she held on to you
throughout the night
of that lost summer

you whispered:
it's difficult to die

VIII
I skulk back
to your unhomely house

which holds my breath
these disturbances of air

the ghost moves in
close, only a skin away

she tickles my spine
through invisible swing doors
she squats my grandmother's chair
keeps watch
over peeling paint
empty picture hooks

anger packed up
with porcelain and glass
desire beaten back
by platoons of silver forks

that haunted child
for forty years
I hushed her
hushed it up
a family secret
her unnameable wish

she waits for darkness
she leans over my bed
slides in
too frightened for crying
refugee from punishment

that cold white woman below
resurrects herself
an avenger in marble
rises
jumps up the steep stairs

hovers just beyond the keyhole

crash
the mirror breaks
down, into the basin
shards tumble like water
daggers of ice
all the selves I was

IX
for your last outing
to Etretat
Margi and I hauled you
between us, frogmarched
your legs of wool
you were gleeful:
those smart people
will think I'm drunk

onto the beloved beach
propped you on the stone hill
bandaged with scarves and coats
lay back, all three
salt on our lips, into seaweed smells
sun stroked the water
the cliffs threw themselves
out, deep in, down

never before had we sat together so long
never before had we sat together so still

in silence
the blue-green sea
drawing us forward
pushing us back

till the shops had all shut
the fish for supper was not got
you sang out never mind
you wanted to stay

your life
still goes
on sliding
in and out
of mine

back and forth
the sea on these stones
rubbing itself out

repeatedly

writing itself in on me
over and over

9 a.m.

For a long time
There is sunlight in the sky, but in the streets no
light;
Then it arrives and walkers going by
Are joined to their shadows. Overhead
On a tall building a flag
Twists shadowless in the morning air:
Why so, when there are shadows everywhere?
I see a running man, dwarfed
By his shadow-legs; a man whose shadow-stick
Trails a long stilt to far-off shadow-feet:
A pigeon flies down to land
On its inverted cut-out, and the cars
Carry for a moment the shadow-shaft
Of the lamps they are passing under. Now,
Screened far above me on a single
Facet of sky-high wall, I see
The shadow-flag an hour will efface,
Passing its serpentine black rag
From side to side across a surface
Of resplendent concrete it is energetically cleansing.

Postcard from Troy

In this metropolis
death wears a sheep skin

along the freeways
the traffic never stops

beneath the side street waterfall
three coffins full

baa baa black sheep

grass grows in the taxis

who can reverse
the hour glass of gravel?

to pin down
the wall to wall carpet
wood anemones are hammered in

yes sir yes sir
the gate is shut.

only enough to wrap
dead bunting in.

Captain Lord

Captain Lord is on his sofa when the boy comes rushing
    down.
'Sir, there are rockets!' 'But what kind are they?'
Nobody mentions the trail of white stars,
distress flares from Titanic, half a mile away.

Nobody mentions. I doze on my sofa
watching the gas crackle blue upon bars.
They are many as leaves. They fall silent, like snow.
They glitter our closed lips, the millions of stars.

The Swallows Move In

You, with the new haircut, steadily
scrape birdshit from the sink, and from
the rusty washing machine, because
swallows are nesting in your outhouse

and mustn't be disturbed. Didn't you notice
lightning shake the wires where the birds
perch at dusk? While you scrub the smelly drainer
and prod at cascades of dung in the bowl, the city
    shakes

with news from Europe, with news of the minister
and the actress, with news of the prince
and the married woman. Houses subside
all over London, and dreamers swear they've seen

medieval apprentices return to frozen Moorfields.
Ever-resourceful, they tie bones of animals
to their shoes and skate across the ice.
You patiently lay old newspapers for protection

across the lawnmower and the bicycle,
the sink and the sad spin-dryer. A crumb
of shit is in your eye but you try to wink
back at the newspaper photographs of ministers,

married women, murdered women, refugees,
the mauled and mutilated of the world,
the weeping dead themselves, photographs
which make you wonder how a person

could look at that and not die of shame,
the same photos you are spreading
with care against the dirt of swallows who play
and swoop at midges in the light summer air.

Raptor

You have made God small,
setting him astride
a pipette or a retort,
studying the bubbles,
absorbed in an experiment
that will come to nothing.

I think of him rather
as an enormous owl
abroad in the shadows,
brushing me sometimes
with his wing, so the blood
in my veins freezes, able

to find his way from one
soul to another because
he can see in the dark.
I have heard him crooning
to himself, so that almost
I could believe in angels,

those feathered overtones
in love's rafters. I have heard
him scream, too, fastening
his talons in his great
adversary, or in some lesser
denizen, maybe, like you or me.

Through a Glass, Darkly

'It's by Salvador Dali,' Helen told her husband.

Andrew Lockhart made a face. 'That much I know,' he said stiffly. 'It was the title of the picture I couldn't remember.' He looked once again at the barren landscape of ants and soft watches that featured on the glossy cover of the conference folder and then returned it to her.

'I can't think why they chose it,' she said, opening the folder and searching through the sheaf of papers it contained. 'It's the sort of thing that gives psychiatry a bad image. There's nothing particularly surreal about the way the human mind works. Still, it's an improvement on Munch I suppose.'

'I've remembered it now,' said Andrew. '*The Persistence of Memory*. I think that's rather appropriate. For you more than most. What's the subject you're going to speak about?' He waved his hand in the air as if trying to draw the title back from another dimension. 'Temporal thingy – '

'Temporal Lobe Epilepsy.'

'Well isn't·that something to do with memory?'

'Something to do with it,' she murmured. 'But more to do with pseudo-presentiment, *déjà vu*, that kind of thing. Your memory playing you false.'

'Yes, well I can understand what that's like,' said Andrew. 'You know I could have sworn there was a railway station next to this hotel.' He shrugged. 'Still, the castle's where I thought it was. I might take a look at that tomorrow.'

Helen looked up from her papers and smiled at her husband with barely concealed envy. While she would be cooped up with a lot of fellow psychiatrists and neuro-surgeons he would be able to wander round Edinburgh just as he pleased.

'How long did you say it was since you were last here?' she asked.

'Twenty-five years,' he said affecting the Edinburgh accent he had somehow managed to lose at some stage during an adolescence about which Helen was aware of knowing very little. Andrew had never spoken much about his childhood. 'Seems like another life. As though I've been two people, if that doesn't sound too schizophrenic. The Scots boy and the English man.'

'Why were you never back before now?'

'Most of my relations were dead even before we moved down south,' he explained. 'The few that were left died soon afterwards. So I suppose I never found much of a reason to come back. You have to have a better reason to come all this way than just sentiment.'

'No one could ever accuse you of being sentimental,' she said. 'You know, I'd almost forgotten that Edinburgh was your home town. You never talk about it. You must be the least Scottish Scot I know. You don't even look Scots.'

He laughed and flopped down on the big double bed.

'That's what the boys at school used to say. People used to assume that I was some kind of foreigner. Because of my colouring.' Andrew was as dark as if he had lived all his life on the shores of the Mediterranean. 'I guess I was an outsider even then. Maybe that's the real reason I've never been back.'

'You were – how old when you left? Twelve?'

'That's right. June 1968. I think it was the day Robert Kennedy was shot. Or was it Martin Luther King? Somebody died anyway.'

The telephone rang and Andrew answered it. Helen hovered near the bedside until she had established that the call was for him and then went into the enormous bathroom to repair her make-up, her high heels clicking on the marble floor like two ping-pong balls. One of the advantages of going anywhere with a successful film director was his insistence on staying in an expensive hotel. She would never have stayed at the Caledonian, let alone a suite, unless Andrew had been paying. Not that it was always a pleasure to be around someone who was so used to having people do exactly what he wanted. Hollywood encouraged that kind of personal fascism. The director is always right. So she had learned to be wary of his formidable temper. It was not that he had ever struck her, or anyone else for that matter. Andrew's violence was of the verbal variety, the kind that reduced people to the sum of their inadequacies. It could be anyone. Like the man at Turnhouse Airport who told them that their bags had been left at Heathrow and Andrew had started swearing at him as though he was just dirt. But even at moments like that she suspected that he still remained in control of himself, that he was just exorcising his own frustration, taking it out on someone else. Which somehow made it worse. Helen often wondered what her husband might have been capable of doing if he ever did really lose his temper. She heard the receiver being slammed back into its cradle and called out to him.

'Who was that?'

'The airline. They've found our luggage. They're sending it on from the airport.'

'Good. I'm dying to change into some fresh clothes.'

'The stupid bastards sent the bags to Newcastle, of all places. I mean, do we look like the kind of bloody people who would be going to Newcastle?'

She came out of the bathroom, smiling encouragingly, as if she hoped to shame him with her optimism. 'It's sorted now,' she chimed. 'So let's just forget it happened and concentrate on having a good time, can we?'

He caught the look in her eye and the implied accusation in her tone and covered his face with his hand, remembering the four-letter words that had poured out of his mouth at the airport and her silence in the taxi to the hotel.

'Was I dreadfully rude?' he said.

'Dreadfully only just covers it,' she said, opening the mini-bar and selecting a packet of over-priced cashews in the knowledge that he had already booked a table in the hotel's most expensive restaurant. She wanted to test the level of his contrition.

'Sorry,' he said quietly.

'It's no good apologising to me,' she said. 'I'm not the one you swore at.' She shook her head. 'Just try and remember that it's not just the person you're having a go at who has to stand there and listen to it. It's me as well.'

Andrew sprang off the bed and folded her in his arms.

'You're right,' he said. 'Look I'll try not to let it happen again.'

'We'll see,' she said warily. He had said that before. 'I don't know what gets into you sometimes, really I don't.' Then she kissed him on the cheek.

'You're very patient with me,' he said.

'I am a psychiatrist dear,' she said and pulling away from his embrace she threw a handful of cashews into her mouth.

To avoid having to watch her spoil her appetite, Andrew moved across the room to the window and, drawing the net curtain aside, he stared up at the specially requested view of Edinburgh Castle, which seemed to be slipping, like a mess of grey bedclothes, from its great, lozenge-shaped bed of rock. As a small boy a recurring nightmare had found him stranded high on that rock, with no possible way up or down, clinging to a tuft of grass until the playful wind shook him from his precarious, nocturnal perch and he found himself recovering from his terrifying fall, in bed. Edinburgh, the bronchial Auld Reekie of thundering Knox and doppelganger Stevenson, was, he knew, brimful of such dark, nightmare places: the black cobblestones of old Rose Street with its evil-smelling public houses and granite-faced brothels; the oblique, cloacal alleys and murderous closes of Burke and body-snatching Hare; the haunted look of Greyfriars with its ancient graves and solitary cast-iron dog, a lonely memorial to an animal that was faithful to a dead master; the Doctor Jekyll and Mr Hyde who dwelled with lethal duality in one of the smart Georgian houses of the so-called New Town;

and the justified sinners, the elect and the damned who lurked up on the windswept Salisbury Crags. Even the names of Edinburgh's places he had perused in the street guide he had bought at the airport seemed charged with darkness: Crow Hill; Jawbone Walk; Windy Goule; Gutted Haddie; Blackchapel Road; Clovenstone Gardens; the Old Tolbooth Wynd; Succoth Park; Yardheads; Talisman Place. There was something about the place, something old and unspeakable that he didn't care for. He could not have said what it was, only the feeling of apprehension was there in his mind, like a nagging doubt about an unpaid bill.

'So when does this trip down memory lane get started?' asked Helen. She was worried that leaving him on his own so much during the four days of her conference might make him bored, and hoped that she might encourage his sense of personal discovery.

'A journalist from the *Scotsman* is coming to interview me tomorrow morning, over breakfast,' said Andrew. 'So after that, I guess.'

David Scobie was a small terrier of a man with a cheap suit and the peremptory manner of a man who is always rushing to meet a deadline. His questions seemed aggressive to Andrew – How much money had he made in Hollywood? Did he feel that he had sold out in any way? Was there not too much violence in his films? Did Andrew really think of himself as Scots? Why do people have to leave Scotland before they can make something of themselves? And he had to remind himself that the Scots were, after all, a rather belligerent race. He might think of that the next time he was obliged to excuse one of his Krakatoan outbursts to Helen: it was in his make-up, in his genes, that he should be aggressive; and compared to this chippy little bastard from the *Scotsman* he was, Andrew told himself, a pussycat. It was something in the air perhaps, in the cold north-easterlies that blew in from the sea and through the doors of the many churches that were dedicated to a stern and unforgiving brand of Protestantism. Or maybe it was drink, the fiery spirits, the beers, the ales and the stouts you could smell almost everywhere you went in the city centre. It wasn't just him, thought Andrew. He could see that now. It began to seem as though this tardy homecoming might explain more than he had first expected.

'You'll have seen a few changes then,' said Scobie, 'coming back after all this time?'

'Quite a few,' Andrew admitted. 'Didn't there used to be a railway station next to this hotel?'

'Oh that was knocked down years ago. Even before you left, I think.' He shrugged. 'I was just a wee boy myself at the time, so I can't be sure exactly when that was. Oh, by the way, which school were you at?'

'The Academy,' said Andrew.

Scobie grunted as if he was hardly surprised by this information. 'I was at Boroughmuir myself,' he said.

Andrew smiled politely. He could no more have said if this was a good school than he could have described where it was to be found. Edinburgh was not short of schools, many of them enormous neo-Gothic buildings that looked quite as awesome and inhospitable as any haunted Transylvanian pile, and the sort of places, he felt sure, that would leave their mark on you. Some unseen scar. Some half-forgotten trauma.

'Last question,' snapped Scobie. 'Do you think you'll ever make a film in Edinburgh?' He nodded at what looked like a small telephoto lens that was hanging on a chain about Andrew's neck. 'Or are you already making one?'

'This?' Andrew held up his Arri Viewfinder. 'I always have it with me. You can't trust your eyes as a film director. I suppose it looks a bit affected when one isn't actually making a film. But when I'm looking at things, really looking at things, it helps me to focus my mind on what I can see. Helps to make it look more like a picture. And that way I can remember what I'm looking at. You know I can remember scenes in movies I saw years ago. I've got a good memory for film and pictures. A useful thing to have if you're a director. Just as well though.

My memory for anything else is terrible. Thank God for producers. I'd forget my head if it wasn't screwed on.' He looked through the viewfinder at the businessmen seated at other tables who were working their way steadily through large plates of bacon and eggs, and polished both ends of the Arri with his handkerchief. 'I thought that it might help to have it along when I walked round Edinburgh. Stir a few memories.' He smiled. 'A case of Arri-vage, as it were.'

Scobie was scribbling furiously in his notebook, too busy to take the time to acknowledge Andrew's little pun. After a moment or two, he stopped writing and frowned thoughtfully.

'That's very interesting,' he said. 'For now we see through a glass, darkly.'

'What's that?' enquired Andrew. It sounded like a good movie title. 'Lewis Carroll?'

Scobie smiled politely and shook his head.

'The New Testament. First Corinthians, chapter thirteen.'

'Oh?' Andrew hadn't so much as seen a Bible since leaving Edinburgh. Nor been to a church service. 'How does that go then?'

Scobie leaned back in his chair and pushed his uneaten breakfast away from him as if his text needed space. Although it was a particular favourite of his, the text was only one of many he knew well, for Scobie was a deacon at his local Baptist church and every page of his Bible revealed its own strata of red marks, like a back flayed with the stripes of mortified devotion.

' "When I was a child, I spake as a child, I understood as a child, I thought as a child: but when I became a man, I put away childish things." ' He nodded at Andrew and finished the verse with even more deliberation and emphasis, as if he hoped to win a pencil for his effort. ' "For now we see through a glass, darkly; but then face to face: now I know in part; but then shall I know even as also I am known." '

Andrew smiled appreciatively. He admired anyone who could remember a quotation, even if it was one from the Bible. About the only lines Andrew was able to quote were the jingles from the television commercials he had directed before making his first feature film.

Scobie stood up. He was even shorter than Andrew had realised, perhaps no more than five feet in height, and with his black beard and largish features he most resembled a malevolent dwarf from some dreadful fairy tale. He squared his narrow shoulders, buttoned his schoolboy's blazer and offered up his diminutive hand.

'Thanks for your time,' said Scobie.

'My pleasure,' said Andrew.

'Don't leave it so long to come back next time.'

Andrew heard himself utter some platitude about roots and escorted the journalist to the door of the breakfast room.

When Scobie had gone Andrew returned to his room, collected his street guide and went out of the front door of the hotel, heading up the incline of Lothian Road and into Tollcross.

How poor everything looked, he thought. Shops were boarded up, and covered with fly posters. Buildings were browned and blackened as if trying to live up to the tourist's misapprehension that Edinburgh was still a fuliginous city. Most of the men he saw looked as if they could have used a shave or a bath. The women dressed with more expectation of rain than of being looked at, although the sun was shining brightly.

He walked onto Brougham Street and then turned left along the north side of the Meadows, a contrastingly pleasant area of tree-lined parkland that stretched for over three-quarters of a mile. He had come to see the place where he had been born: the Simpson Memorial Maternity Pavilion. His mother had often pointed it out to him as they drove about Edinburgh in his father's Jaguar. Standing in front of it now, the hospital seemed smaller than he remembered. Everything did. Even the journalists. When, the previous afternoon, he and Helen had walked along Princes Street he had been surprised at how quickly they had made it from one end to the other. There had been a time, he thought, when it would have taken him the best part of an afternoon.

'Christ,' he muttered and shook his head at what time had done. It was thirty-seven years since he had emerged from this hospital. So much had happened since then. So much that he had forgotten. It was frightening the way time passed. You were there one minute and the next you were gone. He began to realise how much of this sentimental journey would be about death.

Andrew turned left on Meadow Walk and headed north for a while. His route took him into the Grassmarket where the air was more than usually sour with the stink of beer from the area's numerous public houses and, although it was still mid-morning and the sky was bright blue, the streets seemed oppressive and threatening to him. Narrow doorways gave onto claustrophobic wynds and alleys and precipitous flights of steps that led between buildings several storeys high, like secret footpaths through some ancient terraced rock-cut city. It seemed the kind of place where a convenient short-cut might have led the hapless pedestrian into the gnarled hands and surgically sharp blade of some nameless waiting maniac. Quickening his pace he walked along Victoria Street, crossed King George IV Bridge and went down the Mound, a steep, curving road that swept round the two Greek temples that were Edinburgh's principal art galleries, to Princes Street. By now his feet were aching and so he rested for a while in the manicured gardens that nestled in the shadow of the castle rock, sitting on a wooden seat donated by some former first citizen in memory of her husband and observing, with the true film-maker's detachment, a fight between two small boys, marvelling at their bad language and their violence until a passing railwayman from nearby Waverly Station put a stop to their altercation, at which point one of the two combatants ran off in tears.

Andrew tried to recall some of his childhood scraps and found to his surprise that he could not. Had he really been such a youthful pacifist? It did not seem very likely in view of his

athletic build and uneven temper and Andrew felt quite certain
that he must have had some occasion to fight. But there was
no one opponent who sprang to mind. His best friend had been
a boy called Fergus Gilmore. Never did a boy have such a good
and loyal friend as Fergus. Until the day when Fergus went
swimming in Newhaven Harbour and was swept out to sea and
drowned. It was years since he had thought of Fergus. He was
still thinking about him when he hailed a taxi and told the brick-
faced driver to take him to Trinity. The man nodded and sped
down Leith Street.

'Where are you from?' asked the driver.

Andrew hesitated before telling the man he was from London.
To have said Edinburgh would have been to have condemned
himself to interminable explanations of how and when he had
left and how much he thought the place had changed, etcetera,
etcetera. Andrew had the misanthrope's loathing of intercourse
with strangers. He preferred to sit in silence with his own
thoughts and half-remembered memories which, although he
did not know it, is an Edinburgh characteristic.

For most of Andrew's childhood his parents had lived close
to the Granton Road, in a rather grand house several storeys
high that was typical of the well-to-do Edinburgh professional.
His father had been one of Scotland's leading architects until
more lucrative and exciting commissions had carried the family
– there were just the three of them – south, to London. Andrew
told the taxi driver to let him out on Ferry Road so that he
could retrace his own childhood footsteps up South Trinity
Road to his former home.

Trinity, with its leafy roads and solid, well-kept houses, was
a more salubrious part of Edinburgh than those older, more
central parts of the city. He walked slowly, trying to recollect
something of his time there, occasionally stopping to check
things through the Arri viewfinder in an attempt to jog his
memory. When finally he confronted the familiar frontage of
his old address it was indeed like a scene from a film.

There was a light on in the ground-floor drawing room and

for a moment it was as if he had become a child once more, as if his parents had been at home, as if his mother was cooking lunch and he had only to find his key in his trouser pocket to have gone through that black front door. Except that his parents were dead. He put his hand on the gate as he so often had done and pushed it open, wanting to go up the short path to the door, as if it were only a question of willing things to be back as they were for it to have been so. A light breeze in the front garden stirred the cherry tree that his father had planted one spring day, as if reminding him that those times were gone, and he heard himself utter a profound sigh for that long-lost boy.

Andrew stayed for several minutes until he grew worried that anyone seeing him there, looking through the Arriflex, might easily have mistaken him for a thief assessing the house's security, or lack of it, in preparation for a burglary. Reluctantly he turned away and began to retrace his steps along Stirling Road, beside the little park where he and his friends had once played football.

The park was no more than a hundred yards long and a quarter as wide and surrounded with an iron railing fence. He had hoped to see some kind of game in progress but there was only a boy of about ten or eleven years old practising his skill in keeping the ball in the air. Lacking much of an eye for a moving ball, this was the kind of footballing skill Andrew had always envied but had never been able to master. What was it they had called it? Keepy-Uppy? Not a bad little player, thought Andrew and brought the Arri up to his eye.

Slowly he turned the focus on the white opaqueness, one tube moving snugly in the other like an inverted telescope so that the light travelled more slowly than in the surrounding air, and the fog cleared from within the Arri's optically projected right angle as if it had been dispersed with a seeding of salt particles or solid carbon dioxide, to reveal a suburban scene of quiet clarity that lasted for only a fraction of a second. What happened next drew a cry of horror from deep within himself for, as his eyes converged on the boy, he saw him struck viciously on the head with a shovel from behind by some unseen assailant and felled like a slaughtered calf, its skull shot through with a sharpened bolt. Almost immediately the startled discovery that what he had seen simply had not happened, and that he had witnessed some kind of delusion, drew another even louder cry of shock.

The boy let the ball fall to the ground and looked over to where the man was standing behind the fence. He waited for him to repeat whatever it was he had shouted, but when the man said nothing the boy curled the toe of his trainer under the curve of the ball and flicked it into the air once more, bouncing it off his head onto one knee and then the other like a performing seal.

Andrew shook his head and wiped the sweat from his brow. His skin had turned cold and clammy and for a brief moment he thought he was going to vomit. He sat down on the pavement and started to breathe deeply, trying to ignore what he had felt intuitively, to explain it to himself in terms that his more rational parts might understand, although this was no more comfortable to absorb. He had read how sometimes a hallucination presaged a stroke or even a heart attack. Pressing his hand against his sternum, Andrew tried to feel his heartbeat.

Curiosity got the better of the young footballer and collecting his ball under his arm, he came over to the railings and regarded Andrew with vague concern.

'You all right Mister?' he said gutturally.

Even after his visual shock Andrew found himself reflecting that this was what he might have sounded like once.

'Er, yes,' he said. 'Just a funny turn that's all. I'll be all right in a moment.'

'You sure? You look like shite.'

Andrew expelled a large breath. 'I'll be all right, thanks,' he said and climbed unsteadily to his feet.

The boy nodded curtly, spat copiously across his shoulder and kicking his ball in front of him, he walked away, a little disappointed that he had not seen a man die of a heart attack in his own road.

'Your pulse is maybe a little high,' admitted Helen, and dropped Andrew's arm into his lap. 'Tell me what happened, again.'

Andrew was sitting on the edge of the bed. Instinctively, as if trying to relax himself for his own psychotherapist (Andrew had been in analysis since living in Los Angeles), he picked up his legs and swung them onto the bed.

'I went to see my old house,' he explained. 'Nearby there was this boy playing football. I guess he reminded me of myself at that age. Well, I was looking at him through my Arri and, as I turned the focus, I saw someone strike the boy with a shovel. Bashed his head in. I mean, really bashed his head in. There was blood everywhere. I don't suppose this lasted for more than a second. Because when I dropped the Arri from my eye, the kid was still standing there, quite unharmed and looking as if it was me who needed help and not him.'

'And you say you felt faint?'

'Yes.'

Helen nodded and went into the bathroom where she unzipped his leather toilet bag and quickly searched it for drugs. She was aware that during the early eighties her husband had had a minor amphetamine problem, a corollary of his major drinking problem. She knew that one of the most severe after-effects of large doses of amphetamines is a toxic psychosis whose symptoms resemble those of paranoid schizophrenia. But the bag contained nothing more powerful than a packet of glucose tablets, and a bottle of Aspirin.

'What are you doing in there?' he shouted.

Helen ran the tap and filled a glass with water.

'Just getting you something to help you relax,' she said and returned to the bedside. She sat down beside him, placed the glass on the bedside table next to his precious viewfinder and collected her case from under the bed where she had kicked it earlier.

He watched her tap two capsules out of a plastic bottle onto her perfumed palm and hand them to him.

'What's that?' he said, raising himself on one elbow and examining the small plastic torpedoes with suspicion.

'A minor tranquilliser,' she said and laughed when still he did not swallow the capsules. 'Do you want me to find you a Pharmacopoeia? It's Benzodiazepine. Okay?'

He nodded, swallowed the barbiturate and dropped back on his pillow.

'You know,' he said after a moment, 'if I didn't know better, I'd say I'd had a premonition.'

'Why do you say that?' said Helen.

While he considered his reasons, he lifted himself on one elbow again and swallowed the rest of the water. It tasted good after London's tap water, like water used to taste before chlorine and lead and aluminium and other people's urine got mixed in it.

'Well, at the time I had this intuitive feeling that it was exactly that: a premonition. A feeling that I was looking at something that hadn't yet happened. Even so, I tried to convince myself that it wasn't that at all. I actually remember trying to tell myself that I might be having a stroke in preference to accepting what I felt was really happening, as if I couldn't accept it. Can you imagine that?'

'Why did you say "if I didn't know better"?' she asked him carefully.

'It's what your lecture's about, isn't it? Pseudo-presentiment? Don't look at me like that. You read it to me on the plane, for Christ's sake. And once before that.' He frowned and then jack-knifed off the bed. 'Look I'm not making this up, Hels. Why should I?'

'I don't know,' she said innocently, but thinking of a good reason why he might do just that, as a way of gaining her attention. His ego needed constant feeding, like a new-born baby. He was not the kind of person who liked being in any-one's margin. When he was not working he was not the centre of attention, and when he was not the centre of attention he soon became quarrelsome and difficult, like some Third World dictator forced to flee his country and to kick his heels in an isolated villa on the shores of Lake Geneva. But she never thought that he would pull something like this. The more she considered this explanation the more she thought it was a real possibility. And he was certainly devious enough. But at the same time she was tired. It had been a long day and she had no wish for an argument. She was looking forward to a nice dinner and an early night. So she added:

'Look Andrew, I believe you. All right. I think you saw what you saw. But there could be several perfectly ordinary explanations that don't necessarily mean you're suffering from a psychiatric disorder. I wouldn't be at all surprised if it's just you being back here after all these years that's produced in you the kind of heightened emotive state in which you're much more likely to be abnormally sensitive to your own subjectivity, and more vulnerable to feelings of anxiety and perplexity.'

Andrew nodded appreciatively. This kind of jargonised reassurance was one of the benefits of being married to a doctor.

Helen continued with her explanation, aware that she too had started to accept the probable veracity of her own diagnosis. It was certainly preferable to the alternative she had first considered.

'Seeing your old house like that after all these years was possibly quite a shock to you and might well have induced a simple anxiety attack.' She shrugged. 'That might have produced a feeling of jealousy and hostility towards the small boy you saw. Perhaps you were wishing you could be young again and carefree like him, with nothing to do but kick a ball around. And this manifested itself in your hallucination.'

Andrew smiled, nearly persuaded by what she had said.

'Yes,' he said, taking her in his arms. 'What you say sounds convincing. I think you must be right.' He kissed her on the forehead. 'What ever would I do without you?'

He knew it was a mistake to go back there in view of what

Helen had said. What if she was right? he asked himself. What if he really had suffered an anxiety attack and felt hostile to the boy? Was it possible that he might actually be a danger to him? Even as the taxi dropped him on South Trinity Road, he felt he was tempting fate somehow. But the idea that he might actually have experienced a real premonition was too seductive to dismiss as easily as his wife had done. After all, Helen was a scientist, not an artist. What did she know about intuition? Real life was full of things that could not be explained, things out of the ordinary that were the very stuff of movies. His whole film career had been a celebration of the bizarre and the macabre. He wasn't called the new Hitchcock for nothing. Tempting fate he may have been, but living on the edge was what his work was all about. Who knows? he told himself: there may even be a script in this.

At the little park beside Stirling Road the boy was back kicking his ball again. His concentration was of a level that only children can attain for it was also in part a heroic fantasy in which he found himself demonstrating his impressive ball control to an appreciative Hampden crowd of one hundred thousand spectators. With his weight on one foot, the boy played the football with the other, achieving a kind of relentless rhythm so that the ball seldom rose above waist height and, apparently invested with a constant amount of kinetic energy, seemed almost permanently in the air as if in defiance of the weight of its own leathery body and the acceleration of free fall. Andrew lifted the Arri to his dark eye and turned the focus.

He was almost relieved when nothing at all happened. Nothing except the ball hitting the ground at last, as if somewhere a spell controlling the change in an object's position with respect to time had been broken by Andrew's presence. Andrew dropped the Arri on its chain and waved to the boy.

'How many was that?' he called to him.

'Thirty-two,' said the boy, and picked up his football as if somehow suspecting that Andrew wanted to take it away from him.

'Is that your highest?'

'Naw. I did forty-three last week.'

'What's your name? Perhaps one day I'll see you play.'

'Kenny,' answered the boy, confident that despite what his mother had told him about talking to strangers, he could look after himself. 'Kenny MacRae.'

'Do you live round here?'

The boy's thumb jerked back across his shoulder.

'Zetland Place,' he said. 'Number ten.'

'I used to live in Primrose Bank Road,' said Andrew. 'But that was years ago. Before you were born. I used to play football in this park.'

The boy nodded uncertainly, suddenly afraid of growing any more familiar with this man.

'Well good luck to you Kenny,' said Andrew and walked on.

Once more he found himself loitering outside his former home, like George Bailey in Capra's movie, *It's a Wonderful Life*. If only his own avuncular guardian angel had thought to have put in an appearance and returned things to how they were, twenty-five years ago. The house seemed bigger through the Arri and darker too, as if the weather had suddenly changed for the worse and, as he watched the reflected clouds drift across the windows of what used to be his bedroom, he seemed to hear someone cry out. He turned and listened carefully. What was it that he had heard? A seagull perhaps? He had forgotten how close the sea was to the house. You could have seen Newhaven Harbour from one of the upper windows at the back of the house. But somehow the cry had seemed more human than bird. A feeling of dread and foreboding possessed him and he started to run back towards the little park, worried that something might have happened to the boy after all.

The trees in the empty park bent towards Andrew, their leaves rustling in sympathy with his growing sense of danger and their branches spreading wide as though to prove that they were not hiding the boy from his sight, like a circle of old magicians demonstrating that they were concealing nothing in their hands or up their sleeves. Andrew's eyes searched the empty park in seconds. Then he looked through the viewfinder.

The child's body lay in a heap on the half-dug shrubbery at the far edge of the park, his fair hair covered with a shiny red carapace of blood and brain tissue. But when he looked a second time with the naked eye, there was nothing there. Andrew staggered back against a parked car and collapsed across the bonnet, the Arri landing loudly on the metal like a glass banged down on a garden table. This time he hardly felt faint at all. Gradually he got a grip on himself. There was just a sound like the sea in his ears as the blood forced its way among the transmitters and receivers of his temporal roaming brain and suddenly he recognised the truth of how man's psychic entity inhabits a material body in a universe that has both physical and non-physical aspects. But what was he to do about it? He felt as certain that some harm was going to come to young Kenny MacRae as he was sure that Helen would tell him that he was having a nervous breakdown. Warning the boy or, at the very least, his parents seemed a matter of some priority, but how was he to do this without alarming them and finding himself confined in the local insane asylum? He could hardly ring the doorbell and explain that his precognition had led him to suspect that Kenny was going to have his head battered in with a shovel. Sorry to have disturbed you. Have a nice day.

There was only one thing he could do.

At the headquarters of the Edinburgh City Police in Fettes Avenue, Detective Constable Muir considered Andrew Lockhart's story with more politeness than he would have thought himself capable of. You get all sorts in this job, he told himself. Even so, Lockhart hardly seemed like the usual nutcase. He was well-dressed, well-spoken, clearly he was an intelligent man and he had been suitably contrite about bothering the police with what he admitted was a weird tale. But as Lockhart had also said and Muir felt was true, stranger things have happened.

There were several precedents where psychics and clairvoyants had helped the police.

'Has anything like this ever happened to you before, Mr Lockhart?'

'Never.' Andrew shrugged. 'I can't explain it. If I could, I guess I wouldn't be here talking to you now and risking your opprobrium. Believe me, I know what you must think of me. And I don't blame you one bit. I'd probably think the same if our situations were reversed. But it was such a powerful sensation, you see. I felt I simply had to do something about it, and naturally, having no wish to alarm the boy or his parents, I came here.'

'You did the right thing, sir,' said Muir, standing up. 'If you'll excuse me a moment, I'll just have someone check that the boy's all right. Maybe that will help to put your mind at rest.'

'Thanks very much,' said Andrew. 'You're being very understanding. I appreciate it.'

Muir left the interview room and wandered along the corridor to the radio room.

'Are there any vehicles in the vicinity of Ferry Road, Sarge?' he asked the man sitting at the desk behind a cabaret-sized microphone. As he spoke he frowned at his own involuntary use of police-speak: why couldn't he just say 'car' or 'area' like any normal person? The other night he had asked his own mother if she wouldn't mind moving her vehicle onto the drive so that he could wash it for her.

The uniformed sergeant at the desk repeated Muir's question into the microphone and when a voice responded he leaned back in his chair to let Muir deal with it.

Muir explained the situation but added that he was worried in case his informant turned out to have molested the child in question. 'Ten Zetland Place,' he said. 'Boy name of Kenny MacRae. Check he's all right will you? Just tell them there's been a report of a strange man in the area offering kids sweets. You know the kind of thing.'

'Understood,' said the muffled voice.

Muir lit a cigarette and waited.

'Do you believe in it?' he asked the sergeant. 'ESP and all that Uri Geller stuff?'

The sergeant sniffed and helped himself from the packet in Muir's hand.

'My wife reckons she saw a ghost once,' he admitted. 'And she's Free Church. Won't touch a drop. Not even at New Year.' He shrugged. 'I dunno. You believe in God, you might just as well believe in all the rest of it as well. What's he like? Your headcase.'

'Says he's a film director, from London.'

'Well that explains it. Some of those boys have got imaginations like I dunno what.'

A female constable appeared with a message for transmission. The sergeant winked at her as she left and then spoke into the microphone, after which he descibed to Muir a film he'd seen on television the previous evening. 'Jings, you've got to be some kind of weird bastard to think that up, eh?'

'I suppose so,' said Muir.

A patrol car radioed in that Kenny MacRae was at home and that far from having his head bashed in with a shovel he was sitting in his kitchen having his hair cut by his mother, much to the boy's irritation.

Muir nodded at the sergeant.

'Headcase,' he said and opened the door of the radio room.

'Better get his address,' said the sergeant. 'You never know when it might come in useful.'

Muir grunted and returned along the corridor to the interview room and its peculiar occupant. What, he asked himself, was that object hanging round his neck?

Andrew stood up expectantly as Muir came through the door.

'We've checked on the boy, sir,' Muir told him, 'and he's fine. But we'll be keeping an eye on him just in case.' Muir didn't know about this. He thought it much more likely that they would be keeping an eye on Andrew Lockhart.

'Thank you,' said Andrew. 'I'm very grateful. I know how busy you must be, and having to cope with some madman who claims he's had a premonition that a child is going to be murdered is probably the last thing you need.' He moved towards the door. 'You've been very patient. Thanks for not throwing me out on my ear.'

'That's all right, sir,' said Muir. 'All part of the service. You'd be surprised at the variety of our sources, I'm sure. Where is it that you're staying in Edinburgh, just in case we need to get in touch with you again?'

'The Caledonian,' said Andrew. 'My wife's attending a conference. She's a doctor.' He neglected to mention that she was a psychiatrist for fear that Muir might take him for one of his wife's own patients. 'I'm just along for the ride. A trip down memory lane, you could say. I was born in Edinburgh, you see. Went to school here until I was twelve.'

'I'd certainly never have guessed it, sir. You've no trace of an accent.'

Andrew shrugged awkwardly.

'Is there somewhere I can phone for a taxi?' he said. 'Only I'm feeling rather tired.'

Muir wondered if Lockhart might be ill in some way. A nervous illness perhaps. From everything he'd read about these film people they were often quite highly strung. It might look bad if the man was to collapse in the station. Or anywhere near it.

Muir glanced at his watch. 'Look,' he said. 'I'm going off duty now. D'you want a lift? Only I live in Greenbank and the Caley's on my way.'

'Well, if you're sure it's no trouble.'

'No trouble at all,' said Muir and led the way to the car park.

'That's a hell of a medallion you've got there,' he observed as they drove away from the police station.

Andrew pointed the Arri at Muir and explained its use. 'Some people carry a camera,' he said, defensively. 'I carry this.'

Muir frowned at the steering wheel.

'Something the matter?' asked Andrew.

Muir stopped the car and getting out saw that the front offside wheel was the shape of a motorcycle helmet. Andrew wound down his window.

'Can I help?' he said.

'It's a puncture,' said Muir. 'You'll have to get out for a minute. It won't take very long.'

Andrew climbed out of the car and watched the young detective retrieve the spare wheel and the jack from under the bonnet. Muir made slow work of changing the wheel and it was evident to Andrew that he knew very little about his own car: it took him ten minutes just to find the jacking point and lift the car's flat tyre clear of the road. When at last Muir was finished, Andrew handed him his handkerchief. Muir hesitated. The handkerchief looked as if it had cost more than the tie he was wearing.

'Go on,' said Andrew. 'Your hands are filthy.'

Muir wiped his hands and returned the square of blackened linen with sheepish thanks. Then they proceeded on their way. In sight of the familiar red stone of the Caledonian Hotel, Muir said: 'Must be very nice, staying there.'

Andrew said it was very comfortable. Almost apologetically he added, 'But the service lacks a little imagination.'

Drawing up opposite the hotel on Lothian Road, Muir wondered if he would ever have noticed the difference.

Andrew opened his door and got out and, leaning in the still open window, he thanked Muir once again for not laughing him out of the station.

'Take it easy,' Muir warned him and watched him across the road and through the front door of the hotel. 'Headcase,' he muttered, and released the hand brake.

The traffic was slower than usual up Lothian Road and into the bottleneck of Tollcross and it was another twenty minutes before Muir reached the small bungalow where he lived with his parents on the edge of the Braid Hills. A keen golfer, Muir was looking forward to a few holes on the impossibly steep public course that butted onto his back garden, before his tea. A message from the desk Sergeant back at headquarters put a stop to any hope of touching a golf club that evening.

Kenny MacRae had disappeared. One minute he had been at home with his mother about to serve his lunch and the next he was gone, since when almost an hour had passed, and it wasn't like Kenny to miss lunch. His mother was worried that something might have happened to the boy, especially so because of what the police had told her about the strange man seen talking to children in the area.

Muir made a U-turn on Greenbank Drive and drove back to the Caledonian Hotel, considering a theory that had now presented itself to his suspicious mind: Lockhart had an accomplice, his wife perhaps; he'd used Muir to establish an alibi for himself while the wife enticed the boy away; she could have slipped out easily enough from her conference without anyone noticing; if indeed there was a conference; if indeed she was a doctor; it wouldn't have been the first time a woman posing as a doctor or a social worker had been used by a ring of paedophiles to abduct a child. And to think that he'd given the bastard a lift, that he'd even felt sorry for him. Muir put his foot down.

He hardly expected to find Andrew Lockhart at the Caledonian Hotel. He was quite sure that Lockhart had fed him a story about that as well: that Lockhart had walked into the hotel bar, ordered a drink and then left, to meet his wife at the place where she had taken the boy. Muir cursed himself for not going inside with him, for not seeing Lockhart collect his key. He left the car outside the front door of the hotel and, ignoring the doorman's protests that he couldn't park there, he ran inside.

Muir had to revise every part of his persuasive theory when the girl behind the reception desk confirmed that Mr and Mrs Lockhart were in the hotel and dialled up to their top floor suite.

'The boy's dead.' Andrew spoke with conviction. 'I know it. I can feel it.' He shook his head desperately. 'I can feel it.'

'You don't know what you're saying Andrew,' protested Helen.

'It's true I tell you,' he said loudly.

Helen sighed and turned away, directing her next remark to Detective Sergeant Porteus who was leading the hunt for Kenny MacRae. Porteus sat beside Muir facing the couple across a table in the same interview room at police headquarters in Fettes Avenue where Andrew had first told his story.

'I'm a psychiatrist,' she explained. 'I believe my husband is having a nervous breakdown. The disppearance of this boy is an unfortunate coincidence, that's all, and I very much resent us being brought here like this.'

Porteus started to say something but found himself cut short by Helen.

'From what my husband has told me,' she continued brusquely, 'it seems that he was with this Constable when the boy actually disappeared.' She fixed her eye on an uncomfortable-looking Muir. 'And, as I have already explained, I myself spent the whole morning giving a lecture to an audience of over eighty psychiatrists at St Andrew's Church on George Street. An audience that included your own forensic psychiatrist. Now I insist that you either check this out or let us go. Either way I shall be writing to the Chief Constable about the high-handed way in which you have conducted yourselves.'

'Nobody's accusing either of you of doing anything,' said Detective Sergeant Porteus. 'But please try and understand how it might look from our point of view, Mrs Lockhart. Your husband comes in here to tell us that he's had a premonition that the MacRae boy is going to be murdered. Not just any boy, but a boy with a name. And now that same boy has disappeared.' He shrugged as eloquently as his bulk and his cheap suit allowed. 'You must admit it looks strange.'

'It's a pretty tenuous chain of causation you have there,' sniffed Helen. 'I'm amazed you're taking this so seriously. I thought the Scots were supposed to be a hard-headed, sensible race. More like wooden-headed.'

'There's no need for that, Mrs Lockhart,' said Porteus. 'I tend to agree with you. The boy's disappearance is probably no more than just a coincidence and I expect he'll turn up before the end of the afternoon. They usually do.'

'He's dead I tell you,' Andrew declared forcefully.

Porteus sat back on his chair and raised his hands as if his point had been proved.

'For God's sake Andrew,' said Helen. 'Don't you think this performance has gone far enough? Look, I'm going to give you something, something to calm you down.'

Andrew shook his head firmly. His eyes were staring and when Helen touched him his skin was as cold as ice. Instinctively she pulled her hand away. She had never seen him like this before, not even when he'd finished making that film in the jungle, and it worried her more than her continued irritation with the Edinburgh police could make plain. She reached for his wrist to take a pulse but he pulled his hand violently away and wrapped himself in his arms, as if wearing a restraining jacket. A paranoid frown settled on his face as if something had dawned on him. Something unpleasant. He stood up slowly and went over to the window, his eyes glazing over as if he could after all see beyond what could be conveyed by his ordinary senses, to what was not known at the time to any of them.

'Andrew,' she gasped, as suddenly she realised that she was afraid of him, and when he spoke she hardly recognised his voice, for he seemed to have recovered some of his old Scottish accent.

'The boy's dead. But I think that if we went there, to Trinity, I could show you where to find him.'

Detective Sergeant Porteus looked at Helen and raised an eyebrow. He recognised the truth of what she had said about Lockhart, that the man was having some sort of breakdown, but in his guts he thought it might still be worth humouring him. 'It couldn't do any harm, madam,' he said quietly. 'Could it?'

'No, I suppose not,' Helen said dully, scared that somehow the harm was already done.

Porteus looked at Muir. 'Bring a squad car round to the front,' he told him, and then lowering his voice, he added: 'And you'd better alert the scene-of-crime boys. Just on the off-chance that Lockhart might actually be right.'

It was a short drive up Fettes Avenue and along Ferry Road. Helen stared unhappily out of the car window at the many school sports fields, the claret-coloured single-decker buses and the sensible little houses with their regular air of northern sanity: the practical, level-headed Scottish sanity of Alexander Graham Bell, John Dunlop, James Watt, Alexander Fleming and John Logie Baird. Nothing of what was happening to the two of them seemed to belong in this sceptical, scientific country, she reflected.

They turned left up South Trinity Road and pulled up beside the police car that was already parked on Zetland Place. Concerned Edinburgh citizens peered out from behind neat lace curtains or stood in their solid stone doorways and waited for something to happen. Helen felt their eyes upon her and shivered.

Andrew went through the gates of the little park and walked around as if considering the suitability of the location as she had seen him do so many times before. Porteus, Muir and a couple of uniformed policemen waited at a short distance, saying nothing, but willing the oracle to speak again.

The place meant nothing to him until he looked through the Arri that hung around his neck like an albatross, but when he did it was as if he had looked down a long, long tunnel to what was past and lay beyond. 'This way,' he said and led them to a gap in the shrubbery that bordered the little park. He pointed to the ground and told them to dig.

It seemed obvious to Muir that they would be wasting their time but he did what he was told and fetched some men wearing overalls with spades and shovels. They looked at the ground without much enthusiasm and then began to dig as if they were sure it was going to be a waste of time. The state of the ground seemed to say as much. They had dug about eighteen inches when from the edge of the park there was a cry and a police constable came running towards the excavating party.

'They've found the boy,' puffed the constable. 'Kenny MacRae. And he's all right. Says he ran away 'cos his mum cut his hair.'

'Thank God for that,' breathed Helen.

Detective Sergeant Porteus nodded at her and smiled.

'All right lads,' he said to the men digging, 'You heard him. You can stop now.'

But they had stopped already and one of the men was bending over to retrieve something spherical from out of the earth. For a moment Porteus thought it was a large potato until he realised that it was a human skull.

The darkness lifted from inside Andrew Lockhart's head as he suddenly remembered what his unconscious mind had kept hidden from him, what his hysterically dissociated brain had steadfastly refused to remember for twenty-five years (he could still feel the lethal, clanging vibration of the park-keeper's shovel in his murderous young hands and hear the lie he had told about swimming in Newhaven Harbour): he remembered what had really happened to his boyhood adversary, Fergus Gilmore. At last he knew, even as he was known.

Laughable really, how he had confused things, he said to himself. Helen would love that. He could almost hear the paper she would write about him now.

As She Turned

Maureen-the-nanny was back home in Ellesmere Port for a week. Richard-the-husband had taken the car to inspect sites. Sandy-the-wife-and-mother had been out buying food, and now she was hauling the big American shopping basket back home to Belgravia.

As Sandy turned into the mews, dragging the children and the caged food behind her, a sky-blue Citroën shot out at full tilt, splashing mud on her and on the wall behind her. The dark, rain-laden air made the interior of the car stand out as if aglow with inner light.

She looked inside. Within the bright box, in an aquarium of light, two heads were bobbing.

It was the two of them.

Arm casually stretched across the front seat, offering her his famous talking smile, no doubt about it, the husband was in the driver's seat, he was the man of the hour. Next to him sat the site he had been inspecting. Gleaming lips stretched wide, she was the she, no doubt about it, nodding, yes, it was Candida, her marcelled hair waving back like the Rolls Royce nymph, yes she was lapping it up right in the middle of London.

So much the wife saw in the fluorescent postcard.

Then gone, that moment gone.

Her mind flew back: 'If it's too *stressful* for you to carry your own groceries home, bubbie, then why don't you pick up the phone like a big girl and tell the man at Harrods what you want, tell *him* your problems, that's what he's paid for, because I don't want to hear, get it, I don't want to know about your little day.'

'What is this shit you got here? You don't expect me to eat parsnips, do you? Garbage soup tonight, eh, well not for me it isn't. What do you have in there anyway, you feeding an army or something?'

'You think I'm made of money?'

'I need you to type this and fax it off right away to NY so can you pay attention?'

'I *told* you the car is for business!'

Heaving chunks of the green, the dead, the frozen into the fridge, dump, clump, the wife slumped about, her tongue hanging out. A tramline of mud traced her track from door to kitchen across the pale carpet. Her children settled themselves down in front of a flickering screen, where they nibbled at sawdust and drank sugar.

Her hair was filthy, it stood out from her head and hung in separate lanky tendrils on her shoulders. 'I like it like that – it's on purpose really – it's Art Hair. I'm Walt Disney's Snow White – the most beautiful girl in the world! And some – someday – my prince will come!'

But the lyrical image did not hold. As she looked over her shoulder into the living room, the house was slowly but unmistakably getting up to one of its little exercises, one of the speciality acts it put on when its mistress had seen something she didn't like.

An empty vessel and literally nailed down, the modern mews home nevertheless had something of its very own to contribute. Like anything even remotely connected with Americans, it felt it had a right to express itself. And it expressed itself by seeming *like*.

Like. This time like an editorial feature in *House Beautiful* on the new hard home. Like a drop-dead style stab in *Elle Maison* about the new look of the morning after the last days of Pompeii.

Warily she peered round. The kitchen cabinets appeared to have been gouged out of fine grey pumice, the vinyl floor was hardening up-market into marble squares. In the dining area, before her very eyes, she now had a fabulous travertine table with matching chairs. Drapes carved of sober granite framed a window of translucent pinky-grey quartz.

So this is what they mean by picture windows! How modern! Notice how the window itself is what makes up the view. No need to depend on fine weather! All round, alabaster walls. And the droopy flowers have stiffened up into chalcedony, jade, opal and ruby, luxuriantly cool.

As she trudged heavily upstairs, carrying the leaden loo paper and boxes of glittering tissues, she saw the same thing under way up there. A soapstone teddy bear on a floor of dusty gypsum. Dust in the air. Her breath rasped in and out.

Seated in the limestone bedroom, stirring the brown carpet with her toe, she felt irritable-curious, an unworded sense, as if her period was coming on, except it wasn't. A familiar sense, hardly worth looking into. And yet.

She leaned forward into the vanity mirror, whose specular lustre gave her back its gift: an image of her face with two ugly sisters, one on each side. Button earrings looked out at her from the sides of their blobby faces. The hair of the three women was weirdly beautiful: wet, as if wet loved it and it loved the wet. Out from her multiplied head it waved in ever thicker living coils. Closing the mirror, she tossed her head and golden ringlets flew out. She tossed her head again, imperiously, and rainbow-like droplets arced across the room.

Such pleasures of the human and nearly-human.

Slowly, taking her time, she smiled. Appreciating the novelty. She had all the time in the world. Her strong long teeth gleamed white in the sunlight. Slowly she teased out her hair, her crowning glory, till shining ringlets twirled by a firm hand flowed out to the edges of her shoulders. She was a big woman.

It was a big day for her. She opened her blouse to let her skin breathe, and round each breast she drew a black circle, with lashes, so they too could see.

They will seek out her prey. The earrings are for side-sight. She exhaled a loud exuberant breath as all her eyes looked out.

To see what they could see. This is where she was, this is her landscape, her perfect London setting. Till darkness falls.

Into the closet went the boots, the hat and the wet, wormy pop-socks. She whirled quickly round the room, knocking over the coal-black telephone and table. She was a big woman. They looked better on the floor.

As she descended the grey stone steps, the horizontal sun struck her face. The pupils of her enormous eyes narrowed to slits and then dilated to eat the light. She turned her head, listening.

Who's that knocking? Who's that knocking at my door?

Enter their territory at your peril.

Her hand gripped the banister, her bare feet planted themselves on the steps.

And in he came, as he was fated to, in he came, turning his key and bursting in the door as she knew he would. His head was turned away, his face was dark.

So much the worse for him when he sees her.

She stuck out her tongue all the way. 'So!' And she laughed a loud, barking laugh, tongue circling round her lips. 'So! So!'

'Oh fuck!' He was looking at her breasts, which were looking back at him. He clambered over the sofa and yanked down the smoky mirror.

'Take a look at yourself! You look grotesque!'

Closing in, he waved the mirror at her. 'Com'ere you! Look at yourself!' The tone was not entirely welcoming, though doubtless sincere.

Yet come she did, head down, in one huge stride, grabbing his tie with the right hand while with the left she wrenched loose the mirror from his grip, swung it back to where it crashed against the wall and then, broken, flew forward again. Their eyes met.

He stopped stone dead, and in that instant a shard of mirror scythed across his neck and cut off his head. At a stroke!

The red head flew across the room, bouncing over the table, then it dropped and rolled further across the carpet, making a horrible but ever-fainter honking noise. Until it knocked against the base of the CD player and stopped, neck upwards.

She threw the broken mirror after the head, heaving it with such force that it stuck into the far wall, a sword of glass and mercury.

Fortunately for the carpet, not a drop of blood was shed. His stony body had remained bolt upright, arms held forward, like a votive statue or cigar-store Indian. The arms were at just the right height for holding a drinks tray, and now suddenly everything fell into place. At last! A use for that humungous great abalone shell lampshade Dick had shipped over from the Philippines. Set on the pin-striped shoulders, what with the style clash and all, it could be a very post-modern illumination.

He's a very bright fellow! A turn-on! A regular live wire! I always wanted a real standard lamp! And one that I made myself, too!

Gently she picked up the severed head, gently cradled it, gently gazed into the crystal eyes before dropping the lot into a spare Safeways bag. It felt heavy, even to a goddess like her, and indeed, it had been a long, hard day for all.

But now the day was over. She had done what she had been created to do.

She stood, almost immortal, at a great distance above the world. Relativities and relationships squirmed far below. She stood there, silent, as the primary world of absolutes flopped over and reversed back. Her world.

Evil: good. Known: unknowable. Her: him. All: nothing. She saw now what she was; she was what she was seeing.

Her mind looked down upon itself, silent, as it watched the dance of absolutes.

How lovely they are.

Raisins scattered on a white porcelain plate. Marshmallows in tar. Soot sinking into cream. Cherry blossom on a black bough. Dust devils on the unwritable page.

Then: diamonds set in onyx. A spattered wall. Aldebaran and the Peliades. Dots on a disc of snow.

It is bad of me to do this. It is bad to do this. Only a bad person would want to do something so absolutely bad.

It is not to be done, not to be thought of. I don't want to be bad.

Don't even think about doing it, it makes you bad, monstrous, just thinking about it. He isn't the issue, you are. It *bads* you, do it in your head just once, and you're bad, you can never be fully humane again.

You have to do your best not even to think about it.

It's unhealthy to keep thinking about what he's doing, don't brood about it all the time, it does you no good at all. It can make you sick thinking like that, in fact it's a self-indulgence. Work harder and be a better person and these thoughts will go away by themselves. You will stop thinking like that. A good person would not think like this. Only a bad person would throw hard looks like this out into the world, and it serves you right if they come back like a voodoo boomerang and hit you smack in the face.

You are a young matron with responsibilities, think of your children.

You do not want them to have a bad mother, do you, a mother with bad thoughts eating away at her? Are you a bad mother inside? If your children could read your thoughts . . . You see? You should be grateful the kids aren't a lot worse when they have you as their role model.

Can you be bad in yourself, the way grass is green?

Definitely, definite. Sickeningly obvious. Millions. Wherever you look.

But. To stand out, to have the full evil sun shine on your green badness and make it grow, you have to be bad *towards* something. Your power must be directed to ill, otherwise it is only a seed, a foetal deed.

Now – to explode into what you are, to become yourself fully and finally, you arch upwards, you vixen, into something glittering, golden-locked, and big as a city block.

Though made of snaking shadows, half-alive, insubstantial as a virus.

You have no idea . . .

Smack right out of time, out of humanity goes without saying . . .

But it feels so good! And it is absolutely the highest good of our age to feel good about ourselves.

In the new pragmatics, there's no interest in anything that can't be sensed or sucked or spent. And it felt good to me, I really cared.

So say you have a go, say you add a little absolute to your angle. Say you do it in black and white. Do two for the price of one.

Well, *vive* the difference, let me tell you.

You do see something special, something the others can't see. You see what only a murderess can see, and a wide-angle lens on things it is, because you have gained your perspective from standing on the body of another person.

What you see is magic, absolute magic. You enter majestic through the leaden gates. A queen. Beyond that is silence.

But what if you're wrong?

What if you have got it completely wrong because you're bad and can't think straight and you're heading for hell in a handbag?

You wouldn't be the first, not by a long shot.

So do it right.

He's testing your love. Don't attack him when he needs you most.

Now, in the moment of his greatest foolishness, it is for you to understand with compassionate love. Remember. Men are so sensitive, they're really only boys underneath.

Understand. A woman always understands, that is her true strength.

Perhaps, in years to come, you will see that it was all for the best. In the long run. Relax. Concentrate. Support.

For your own good, and for his sake. Be his home for him. Let him work out whatever . . . Rise above . . . whatever . . .

It is all part of his courtship of you, a courtship which is cosmic, endless. A courtship which may be at its most poignant when he seems most far. You are his centre. You must understand these heart-mysteries. Let him come back to you in his own time. They all do come home in the end.

Pay no attention to it. If anything, tease him, but no more. Keep those nicefires burning. What a big bad boy! They like a little role-play, now more than ever, since we have so many roles available. Black suspender belts, non-stop caring, the attentive smile of the sympathetic listener, and don't let your mind wander, they can tell.

Direct your thoughts away from the welter of confused subjectivity.

Think of others, think of what they might think and say of you.

Think of your future, your good name.

Think of your children, your home and him.

Think him.

Think *him*.

The men who have been killed in the minds of women . . . Their ghosts walk the earth in the form of living men.

Sandy once had a friend who could sit in his Toyota and from across the street he could spot women who wanted to get married. They dress conservatively, in mixed rich colours: ruby or brown or beige, always in skirts, and if they wear a sweater or suit it always indicates the bosom and the waist.

'There's one, the one in the pleated skirt waiting for the light to change!'

They wear flesh-coloured tights, and they walk slowly, one foot placed directly in front of the other, which gives them a gentle, unprovocative swing.

'Over there, quick, the one playing with her hair!'

And my friend, he was right every time. Now, thought Sandy, I can spot them too, even when I don't want to.

And these men . . . these men who have been killed in the minds of women and who still walk the earth. They look like living men but now I have the second sight, across the room, whether I want to or not, against my will I see the mark on them.

Their insides have been squeezed against their exterior shell for so long that there is only a cavity inside. An empty place where the soul once lived. But the man is dead, now that the organs of soulful desire are gone. During the jovial greeting, the eye remains fixed and glazed. The mouth grins but the rolls of flesh and the expression lines stay too long on the cheek.

He springs to open the door or unlock his car, but the gesture breaks down into its component parts. Now I am smiling at her. Now I am cementing the flattery with a winning look. Now I am taking out my keys and tossing them neatly as I grip the correct one and insert it into the car lock, still talking. This is my car. My hand is firmly on the handle.

They talk to themselves to accompany their actions: 'Ah, there' (of a key into a lock). 'Unnh!' (of a cork out a bottle). 'Mm, mmm' (of a tongue into a mouth). Their generally rather formal clothes are often just a little too tight. In a crowded drinks party there will be four or five such thought-slaughtered men. They speak with great confidence when they talk of business or of sex, but they tend not to do deals with each other. Their eyes move rapidly from face to face.

Styles change, but every generation breeds new candidates. There, do you see him? The one in the white Sierra, the black BMW, the red Jag. They speed through the light as it changes to red, and they curse the car in front.

Most of these men who have been killed in the minds of women are over thirty, the peak age is between thirty-seven and forty-three. The mind-slain appear immortal, untouchable, forever youngish, and so they are, because they are already dead.

Meanwhile the curtain rises in a modern mews house of the unreal city. One of many such houses.

The theme is Be Yourself. The authentic, almost candid you, sincerely and tastefully presented, cannot fail to make an impression. But do not bore him with the same old beans, add a little spice to life!

She hummed at her chores, with love she burned, she swept the floor, and all was in place when hubby came home and slammed the door.

Then, *quel surprise*! It's French night in Belgravia.

Be yourself – for him!

It's all in play, of course, more and more people like to play like this.

She had prepared *un menu bien elaboré pour épater les amis*, and she was the French maid there to serve, all in play in the name of love.

'Well – who's this sexy person?'

Even at this late date, enthusiasm, like a rose, can still be grafted onto humble domestic stock. He reacted, he cared. Blushing like an *ingénue*, she edged sideways up to him.

Short black taffeta maid outfit with purfled edge and little black petticoat peeking out . . . stiff white lace of the apron . . . slight scraping sound of silk stocking.

'*Un cocktail, m'sieu?*' Sound of silk slipping to and fro as legs were rubbed. . . .

'Oh yeah, I get it, toot suite!' To and fro as slender hairless legs were rubbed. . . .

There is a reason for some traditions . . . bowing and bobbing sideways as she popped open the champagne. Its joyous fluid spurted upwards, *zut alors*, until she wrapped up the bottle in linen and poured the elixir into a glass whose very stem had bubbles in it.

'Fit for a king, *m'sieu*.' As she bent over, a moony curve of thigh rose above the period-effect black stocking.

'So you're a saucy French maid for a change, are you?' No matter what lengths you go to, no matter how exaggerated the gesture, so long as it is for their pleasure, they are never surprised. Quite remarkable. They feel that the whole production is after all only natural, only part of a great tradition. Even that vital sense of play can get lost.

But he is responding. Always open to positive reinforcement, the dynamic initiator develops accident into advantage and goes from strength to strength.

'Aah–hm, *maid oui, mais oui* I mean.' Her round eyes widened, as if appreciating how well he knows the script. Rouged cheeks glistened with teardrops of champagne.

The white curve of thigh above the stocking repeated itself in the curved *bustier* with leather straps that reached up to the collar, covering feminine curves, that hint of bondage so up to the minute. No doubt we'll be hearing from you soon in some exotic spot.

They say there's actually *more* of this about, a sizeable minority are into it, though all in play of course.

Smiling winsomely, she trotted away on her spiky black heels, and back she trotted like a new pony with a fresh tray of goodies.

Every man wants to have a mistress, it's your responsibility to make sure it's you!

'Well! Will wonders never cease!' And the words of approbation slid into her incredulous ears, 'pink shells' as they are called.

She took a deep breath. ''Ere we 'ave *ze colpiettes*! From Rome, actually, *wiz ze pignoles, très mignonnes!*'

The one soft, the other strong, the one so very feminine, the other masculine. Head cocked, she waited. Knees bent, back arched, fingertips covering blushing buttocks, this is the Bunny Dip of the Fabulous Sixties, alive and half-living in London. You bend the knees to keep those swelling curves modest. It works better than ever, now that it is only in play.

She waits, she has given herself to the performance, quivering furry white like a little bunny, suddenly it matters utterly to her, she waits obsessed to see if he likes it, this eroticising of the dominant, and *ah, oui*, the meaty aroma has aroused him, he has placed one hand, as if for balance, on her fetish-French thigh, while he leans forward towards the plate, the scent has pulled him all right, he rubs his finger across the shiny round cheeks of meat. He picks up and eats. Coarsely chopped, then shaped and rounded, warm red pieces from whence the soul has flown.

The Only Only

The first ferry for a week was fast to the quay, the thick rope springs holding it to, looped fore and aft over iron cleats the height of children. The weather had been so hard and high that there was seaweed all over the island, brought in by the wind, and the east wall of each house was drifted up to the roof. The children dug in to these drifts and made blue caves to sit in, smoothing till the cave's inner ice melted and set to a clear lucent veneer.

Seven children lived on the island and attended the school together. Sandy was the only only among them; the rest had brothers or sisters. She was a girl of eight born to the teacher Euphemia and her husband Davie, who set and lifted lobsterpots for his main living, though the ferry company kept him on a retainer to attend the arrival and departure of the ferry, three times a week when the sea would let it through. Davie'd to hook up and untie the boat, watch for the embarkation of livestock and the safe operation of the davits on the quay. He had an eye to the secure delivery of post and to the setting in place of the gangplank so that it would hold in a swell.

He liked his job. It involved him with everyone who lived on the island and he was careful to respect this. If he knew that the father of a child off just now inside its mother on the ferry to be born on the mainland was not the man with his arm around the woman as the ship parted from the land, he did not say. Davie was not an islander born, although Euphemia was; she could remember her grandmother skinning fulmars to salt them for the winter and she herself could feel if the egg of a gull might be taken for food or if it was fertilised and packed with affronted life. Davie had boiled up a clutch of eggs once and they had sat down to them with a salad and pink potatoes from outdoors; the tapping and the faint window of membrane had seemed right enough, but when he'd got through to the boiled halfmade chick with its eggtooth sticking out like a sail needle's hook, he'd got sick. He still looked away when a seal heaved up the rocks to die after a gashing; the thickness of the blubber inside gave him a lurch, like seeing the legs above an old woman's stocking tops. In death a seal keeps its enthusiastic expression; the human face falls to neutral peace, but the seal appears to trust even death.

Because there had been no boat for some time, everyone was on the pier today. It was a social occasion although it was so cold. Something seemed to have slowed the sea, its salt particles surrendering to the grip ice has on water. On the Atlantic coast of the island, rockpools were freezing over, the crabs moving in under sea lettuce to escape seizure by the ice. Among the blue-brown mussels that clustered around the stanchions of the pier hung icicles at low tide. The sea was unusually quiet, hushed by the cold from lapping or thrashing the shingle or the harbour walls. Only the hardiest boats were still down in the water, fishing boats and a clam skiff that had been neglected and had taken in water that was now a hard slope of grey ice halfway up to the gunwales.

On the slip where the smaller boats came alongside there was a tangle of nets and a pile of polythene fishboxes. Yellow, orange, mauve and electric blue, the nets were neatly trimmed with a white buzz of rime. The impression of a deserted, frozen harlequinade was emphasised by a pair of red heavy-duty gloves lying on the weed next to a single yellow seaboot.

Sandy stood with Euphemia in a group of women. People asked the teacher about their children; in such a community there was no chance of going unnoticed. Talk was the pastime, talk and work the currency. Euphemia was pleased to be among women, with her daughter. When, as now, she was irked at her man she did not tell, or it would have been round the place before tea.

She wanted him to give up the boat and come into teaching

at the school with her. She could not see the future in working
on the pier. It took up a good day three times a week, when
the following up had been done, the cargo counted, the letters
sorted and settled in the red Land Rover to be taken round the
only road by the post; and by the time drink had been taken,
with the purser maybe, or with whoever came off the boat or
was in the bar off a fishing boat.

He was a good man, but where did these boat days go?
Whereas, should he come in with her at the teaching, they
would see their work as it grew day by day. And he could still
do the lobsters, if there were any left in the sea. With the French
and the Russians and the warm-water breeders at it, the sea was
full of mostly red herrings, forget the silver darlings.

Sandy now, she would see more of her father if he came in
with the teaching, and then Euphemia maybe, when it was all
settled, would get down to having another baby.

The purple line at the horizon lay over the slow grey sea.
The air smelt of weed, cigarettes and diesel; the post office van
was idling and the men gathered around it in their oilskins,
smoking for the warmth. The children of the island were standing against the rail at the end of the pier, their feet kicking
against the robust wire barrier with a bright harsh chiming. Six
of them red-headed, in shades of red from orangeade to a
bracken mixed with rough briar brown, and one of them with
the crow-black hair that does not shine and goes with blue
eyes. The children were waiting to wave, even those who were
waving no one off; it was the boat, which was the presiding
event of their lives, that they wished to acknowledge.

Against the folding evening clouds, and frosted by their
departing rims of hard light, the shining ruby-juice red of
Sandy's straight hair and the drained white of her face seemed
to Euphemia to be stamped like a royal seal set to important
words. It was not easy to think of Sandy with a brother or a
sister. But Euphemia did not approve of only children;
especially not here, where circumstances were already isolated
in the world's eyes. It was not possible to imagine loving Sandy

any less or loving any child more than Sandy was loved; it was hard to imagine the love that Davie and she bore for their child stretching to accommodate more, but Euphemia was convinced that this would occur naturally, without pain, like passing through a door into a new room with open windows.

The ferry was loaded. The gangplank was lifted on its ropes and let down to the pier for rolling and storage in the metal waiting room at the end where the children hung and bobbed and cuffed one another's bright heads. A long plaintive blast warned that the boat must soon go and the children hollered back to it through cupped hands. Lights were coming on in the boat; soon the dark would land over them all, steaming across the water from the purple edge of the sea.

Davie was checking that goods had been properly exchanged, the gangmower sent to the mainland for fixing by June time, the cowcake fetched up out of the hold, the canned goods and frozen gear stowed ready for the shop, the box of specially requested medicaments boxed up for the doctor, the beer rolled into the pub's Bedford van; detail was what mattered in this job, and he took a pride in it.

In the restful numbed cold silence, people began to prepare themselves to make farewell and to depart for their homes. The moment the children loved was coming, when they could wave to the boat as it pulled out and away from the island, seagulls over the wake like bridesmaids. They stood and waited at the pier end, looking out to sea.

There was a creak, a sodden tugging groaning. The seagulls gathered. The eighty people on the pier experienced the shared illusion that it was they and not the boat who moved. The rudder of the ship was churning deep under the water which, astern, showed silvery green below its surface and white above. The air was still enough for a hundred separate lifted voices to reach the ears intended as the twenty souls on the boat looked down to the crowd on the pier. The children waited.

The stern spring of the boat cracked free of the cleat from which Davie had forgotten to lift it. After the first tearing report of the bust rope came the whipping weight of sixty yards of corded hemp and steel, swinging out through its hard blind arc at the height of a good-sized child.

'Lie down, get down, for God's sake,' yelled a man. The women fell to the ground. Unless they were mothers, when they ran for their little ones to the end of the pier as the thick murderous rope lashed out, rigid and determined as a scythe to cut down all that stood in its way.

Sandy lay under her mother's heart, hearing it in the coat that covered them both. The concrete of the pier seemed to tremble with the hard commotion of the rope's passing over them.

Snapped out of her dreams, Euphemia held her only child.

The boat continued to move away, its briefly lethal rope trailing behind it, a lone seaman at the winch above, coiling it in to usefulness. The black ferrous patina on the big cleat had burned off under the seething tension of the rope; its stem was polished by force through to a pale refined metal blue. The children from the end of the pier comforted their mothers, who stared out to the disappearing ship seeing, abob in the water, the heads of children cut off at the neck, their frozen sweetness of face under the streaming curtailed hair; red, red, red, red, red, red or black, and to grow no more.

The Comforting Arms of Marilyn Monroe

One day, some addict or tramp passing through Madrid will clear his throat and spit and sigh, and ask me who's that old guy alone on the bench there, the one wearing the thick glasses with one lens missing, fingers crossed, wrapped up in inexplicable torment, holding a busy conversation with himself, and sometimes interrupting to sing snatches of *Yesterday* by the Beatles. Is he as mad as he looks? the newcomer will wonder. Is he safe to talk to?

As mad as he looks? I'll reply. Luis? Hard to tell. We'll watch him for a while and I'll picture, sometime in the near future, an unmarked tombstone in the rain and a schoolboy standing by it, clutching a Hondo guitar which has seen better days. The picture will affect me. I'll offer the newcomer my carton of wine. That's Luis, I'll say. He won't want to meet you. Let me tell you about him.

He was a lazy bugger, most of the time. The only person I ever met who couldn't be bothered to sidestep an approaching dog-turd. But once or twice a month, when he was rightly tired of the arguing and bawling of the rest of us in the square, he'd shuffle off and catch the bus to the Necropolis. He'd turn and wag his finger at us as though we were children, earnestly remind us of the murder of Lola a year ago for a packet of sunflower seeds: getting *so* angry about the *smallest* things! He would sit on the low Necropolis wall, his boots turned in at the toes, oozing melancholy as he scratched at his grey stubble, contemplating the memory of his dead wife Pepita, upon whose stone he would each week leave a single rose, donated by the fat flower-shop woman.

Luis sometimes told us that he'd like to bring them all back from under the ground, from out of their little pots, so that he could *talk* to them. Not just Pepita: all the friends he'd ever had, and all the ones he'd only heard about. The air of the Necropolis might *seem* calm, he'd continue, ignoring our jocose abuse, but it was ahum with stories. No, really: all you had to do was listen. The funeral rites had been read, but for Luis, above the graves there always hung a huge question mark, a thousand mute voices wanting to respond. This was part of his innocence, his madness, and it was part of the reason why he'd become a *vagabundo*. He was a thinker – he still is – and as Luis said, who ever earned any money by simply thinking?

One day towards the end of last December, he was plodding through the Necropolis towards Pepita, and there in a wall he saw a tombstone, dirty, blank; except that in the middle of it, there was one word, one of the nine words which he was able to read, scrawled small in blue indelible pen. He went up close, felt the cold stone breathing on his face.

MAMA

This word always affected Luis. Silently he mouthed it, fishlike, stupid. Ma. Ma. The first sound in the world. He had never known his own mother: he had apparently been born twenty minutes after her death.

'*You*, Luis?' Mari-Tere had said once, and she'd spat her fabulous multicoloured spit. No one else can spit all those colours and laugh at the same time. 'You, immaculate? *Joder*, I seen more immaculate pavements.'

Mama. Luis was interested. This was a luxury: something from *now* to think about, something around which he could turn his mind which wouldn't just carry him back in time down a sluggish reversed river. He decided to spend more time in the

Necropolis, in the hope that he would meet the person who had written the word.

What else was he to do with his time, anyway? Construct a bronze city? With a river of liquid gold?

I'll tell you the sort of life Luis's was – and mine, and all of ours, for that matter. Ours was the sort of life where, if war broke out in the Middle East, you didn't hear about it for three days. And when you did hear about it, usually from Piotr the Pole, the only one of them who could read properly, it meant nothing because it was Piotr the Pole telling it.

But if a famous Madrid actor died, you knew it within hours. Just by sitting and listening. Shrivelled arseholes, big ears: that was us, that was Luis.

So the gay gravediggers, Carlos and Jesus, came down the path towards him, stopped for a cigarette and then took a hammer and chisel to the edges of the blank gravestone.

'What's going on?' Luis called over to them. 'You can't do that.'

'Suck on this,' Jesus replied, patting his *paquete*. He always did that.

'We have to move this,' explained Carlos. 'Arturo Cruz has died.'

'Arturo Cruz?'

Luis was aghast, more aghast than usual on hearing of a death. If you were aghast every time somebody died round here, you'd be permanently aghast.

But Arturo Cruz was unusual. He'd been famous. Luis had used to go and see his films with Pepita. Unwillingly, of course: they were a joke, they stank. But he had gone along anyway: overblown, romantic yarns which had made Pepita cry and which had made Luis squirm with jealousy in his seat. Whenever he recalled that jealousy now, he was thankful for it because it had been *human*, an emotion felt by someone not entirely alone. He believed that the last film he had seen, ten years before, had in fact starred Arturo Cruz.

No. Luis had never managed to move Pepita as much as

Arturo Cruz had, and Luis had shared the same bed as her for twenty-nine years: something Arturo Cruz had never done once, not to Luis's knowledge.

'Murdered,' Jesus added.

'*Callate*,' said Carlos. 'You're not supposed to tell anybody that.'

'Well, anyway. Suck on this.'

'You can't move that stone,' Luis insisted. 'Murdered who by?'

'*No sé*. Famous Actor Murdered in Cold Blood.'

The gang was divided as to why Arturo Cruz should have been murdered. Mari-Tere, bright-eyed, balding, said it was drugs, but then she would. José Maria reckoned it was ETA, and Piotr the Pole made up an incredible story involving the American athlete Carl Lewis, the Mafia and himself.

Me, I just didn't know: however long I may have been in Spain, there are still a lot of things I don't understand.

Luis attended Arturo Cruz's funeral from a safe distance. His third famous funeral in a month. About two hundred people huddled beneath the yews, all laundered handkerchiefs and fur coats, the scrunched-up heads of chihuahuas peeking out. Weeping for the cameras. Afterwards, the Necropolis reeked of scent.

Several days later, a group of schoolboys came past. Cigarettes and swearwords, humour about testicles. One of the boys told his friends to go on ahead and paused, appearing puzzled. He wandered back and forth in front of Luis.

Luis sensed that this must be him. That this boy must have the story.

He removed his spectacles, conscious of the unpleasant effect they made on people, and approached the boy in a straight line. He wasn't so bad at first impressions: he could control the drink and speak a reasonable Castilian when he had to. However, the words flew out of his mind when he saw that the boy was crying, and not for any camera. Luis wished he had a handkerchief to offer.

'Do you want a sweet?'

The boy glanced at him for a moment, a little defiant. Then he sniffed.

'I have an allergy. Yeah, I'll have a sweet.'

'I don't have any.'

'I have. Gum. Sugar free. Want one?' The boy fumbled in his shorts pocket.

'*Gracias.*'

'I'd better catch up with them, then.'

The boy flicked his cigarette away. The two of them watched it settle in the gutter, continue to smoulder.

'Just one question,' said Luis. 'Before you go. Was she *your* mama?'

The boy looked shocked at that, and you can't blame him. This ancient, stinking ghost, asking him.

'*No sé . . .*'

'What do you mean you don't know?' Luis was discomposed. 'What's your name?'

'Miguel.'

'Did you write that, Miguel?'

'Yeah. Why've they changed it?'

Luis explained how they'd moved the stone and how it was now Arturo Cruz's grave.

'I suppose famous people can choose the best graves,' Miguel said.

'And you don't *know* if she was your mother?'

'No.'

'You want to find out?'

'Are you one of those mad people?'

No point in telling a lie to a youngster, Luis cautioned himself. They can see right through you. He'd spent a fortnight in jail in 1966 for not knowing that.

'Yes,' he said.

'Do you know the answers to things?'

'Some things. I can try. You want to know if she was your mother?'

'Where do you live, then?' Miguel asked, as if knowing the answer to this would make Luis real for him.

'In the back of a burnt-out Seat Ibiza. In Embajadores. Do you want to know?'

'I want to know she *was* my mother,' Miguel said after a while. 'I don't want to know she *wasn't*.'

'All right, Miguel,' said Luis. 'All right. I'll find out that she was your mother.'

It had been a long while since he had expressed an intention, had considered the future. The words felt strange in his mouth. It had also been a long time since he had said 'trust me'.

They met after school the next day. They went to a bar and Miguel, after buying Luis a coffee with milk and a *magdalena*, explained what he had meant when he had said he didn't know if she was his mother.

He had never known her. At three he'd been sent to live in Majadahonda, with family on his father's side. He'd never found out much about her: he hadn't wanted to ask, and the family hadn't wanted to tell. A case of avoiding trouble in the shape of awkward questions. We all do it. He was twelve now and, Luis reflected, wise for his age.

Two years before, an old woman had approached Miguel when he was coming out of the Metro at Callao, on his way to VIPS to meet some friends for a burger. The woman had stopped him short by saying the word Miguel, three times. A hoarse voice, full of cracked air. *Miguel, Miguel, oh Miguel.*

'Miguel,' he reminded Luis. 'That's my name.'

The woman had looked horrible, he said. Quite like Luis, in fact, all dirty and smelly, with hair like it was always raining on her and one of those dark, blotchy faces which show that you spend all your time in the street. A scar, she'd had, running clean through her right eyebrow, and quite a few scabs.

'I'm your mother,' the woman had said, and gripped Miguel's arm. Believe me. *Soy tu mama.* I have waited for you always. Believe me, Miguel.

Miguel had gone back home and repeated her words to his family. No, they'd said. No, Miguel. She's dead. She died a long time ago. They could at least have invented something, Miguel said. Oh, a long time ago. Dead. That wasn't her. That was one of those mad people. They'd gone on about it so much that Miguel had thought they were inventing after all.

But then, ten days before meeting Luis, Miguel had come out of the metro at Callao and observed a commotion. He went over to have a look and saw that, lying there dead on the ground at the foot of the steps, there was this woman. The same woman. He hadn't forgotten her, Miguel said: never would, now. It had been his first dead body.

'There'll be more,' Luis assured him.

Just as Luis had done for the funeral of Arturo Cruz, Miguel had hung around the Necropolis and checked with Carlos and Jesus that this was the same woman who had fallen down the steps at Callao. There'd been no one else there. After they'd gone, Miguel had written the word 'Mama' on the stone in blue indelible pen: he couldn't explain why, but Luis told him he exactly understood.

'Are they really homosexual?' he asked Luis. 'Carlos and Jesus?'

'Course they are.'

The woman's name had been Rosita, Carlos and Jesus had told him. Rosita Lerma. And that was the first step.

The first thing Luis instructed Miguel to do was to insist with his father's family. But Miguel said that would be useless.

Luis was galvanised. I'd never seen anything like it. Making enquiries wasn't easy, but it was easier having Miguel there behind him, looking forlorn, as he made them. He got José to have a word with Angel down at the police station, but there was nothing there; he got Piotr the Pole to scour his collection of newspaper clippings, but nothing. For about two hours, we were all galvanised in his wake. We went round the churches in the centre of Madrid, asking nuns, and up to the soup-kitchen, but nothing. Nobody knew who the woman was, where she had come from, and nobody cared: although they would have cared, as Mari–Tere said, had Luis been wearing a nice suit.

A week later, Antonio returned to the gang.

Somebody should write Antonio's life down. It's not a bad life for a dwarf. Antonio has had sexual intercourse with more than four thousand actresses, including Greta Garbo, Marlene Dietrich, Concha Velasco and Kim Basinger. Sometimes, he would just leave us and go away for a few days, hunting for comfort in their arms.

'*Venga*,' Luis said once, observing Antonio sceptically over the top of his spectacles. 'Concha Velasco?'

'*I* believe it's her,' Antonio said. 'If *I* can believe it, and I'm actually fucking *there*, why can't you? For Christ's sake, Luis. Our imagination's all we got.'

There was no answer to that. You would have believed it, too, to look at Antonio's head. It was like a walnut. It had all the normal creases, plus a dwarf's creases.

Miguel described Rosita to Antonio just as he had seen her, lying there at the bottom of the steps at Callao.

Antonio sat there, wiggling his toes through the open end of his right boot and nodding.

'Marilyn Monroe,' he said after a while. 'The scar.'

'Well,' said Luis. '*Está muerta.*'

Antonio glanced at Miguel, and then back at Luis, and took a slug from his carton.

'I told her,' he said. 'She was too bloody small to stand the drink. Too ambitious for her size.'

'You know anything about her?'

'We lived together for three months last year. Under that bridge. The one with the cars going under it. You know.'

Suddenly Antonio awoke to his present surroundings. What with his imagination and his memories, he didn't spend much time there.

'Who's the fucking kid?'

'*Hombre*, don't *swear*. This is her kid. Rosita's. Marilyn Monroe's.'

'She did talk about a kid,' Antonio murmured. 'Yeah.'

'That was me,' Miguel said. 'I was the kid.'

'You remember anything about her?'

Antonio racked his brain.

'Valencia,' he said slowly. 'She said Valencia.'

'Is that true about Kim Basinger?' Miguel wondered.

'Yeah. Oh God, yes.'

'Like hell it is.'

Antonio looked sorrowful for a moment. Then he felt about in his pocket and opened out his hand. In the palm there lay a lock of dirty golden hair.

'Could you get me her autograph?' Miguel asked, reeling: but Antonio only shrugged his shoulders.

'*Hijo*, I would. I really would. Only it's like this. The bitch can't write.'

Valencia, Luis thought. Might as well plan three months in Tahiti.

He told Miguel this and Miguel pondered him reproachfully, in a way Luis hadn't been looked at since Pepita.

'You haven't got *any* money?' said Miguel.

'Not a bean. Not a sausage.'

'Well where do you get your money from?'

'I ask people for it. Sometimes I sell tissues. Sometimes I just kneel down in the gutter. With the sign Mari-Tere did for me. They know me in the bars.'

'Do they give you things?'

'Sometimes they do, sometimes they don't. Depends how they feel.'

'Can you play the guitar?'

'The guitar? I haven't touched one for twenty years.'

The next day, Miguel rolled up clutching a Hondo guitar which had seen better days. He and Luis descended the steps into the La Latina Metro station and waited for Greasy Maria, whose spot it was, to finish. When she'd gathered up her change and left, Miguel set the guitar against the wall.

Luis watched it as though expecting it to explode at any moment.

'Well then,' Miguel said. 'It's not going to play itself, is it?'

Luis played the guitar for thirty seconds. Passers-by seemed torn between amusement and compassion. One of them recognised Luis and wondered when his new record was coming out.

'For Christ's sake,' Miguel called, having moved to a slight distance in his embarrassment. 'I've heard farts more musical.'

'It's my joints. Cheeky bugger you are. My joints are stiff.'

'Forget the complicated stuff, then. Just strum it.'

Luis haphazardly strummed. The following forty-five minutes brought them twenty-seven pesetas: hardly sufficient, as Luis pointed out, to get them onto the platform, let alone all the way to Valencia. The ends of his fingers were hurting.

'I got an idea,' Miguel said. 'You heard of the Beatles?'

'What do you take me for? I'm old enough to be your grandfather.'

'I just wanted to see if you were the only person in the world who hasn't heard of the Beatles.'

That night, they stood on a corner of the Plaza Santa Ana and performed rudimentary versions of songs by the Beatles and Simon and Garfunkel. Miguel sang, Luis played. Will you believe me if I tell you it didn't sound too bad?

Well, you're right. But people coughed up anyway; it was novel.

'*De puta madre*,' Luis said. 'Just think. Me, playing this.'

Within ten days they were on the platform at Atocha Station, and many passengers were hoping that they wouldn't get the seat next to Luis, and Miguel was handing him a carrier bag with *bocadillos*, fruit and Coca-Cola inside. And he'd brought Luis an old green shirt and a pair of brown corduroy trousers which his stepmother had been on the point of throwing away. The shirt almost fitted. There was a small crocodile on it.

In Valencia, Luis stayed in a *fonda* and enjoyed a proper bed and bath for the first time in nine years. He had three baths, in fact, one after the other, lying there till the water got cold and his skin was crinkled and soft, and then pulling out the plug and starting again. Nothing like it for the soul, he said afterwards, though you could have stood a spoon up in the water.

The next morning he went round to the Town Hall. He knew what he was looking for: a woman called Lerma, Rosa, probably born in about 1935. Miguel had written it down for him in case he had to read it. Luis was relieved to find that there was a thin woman with glasses at the Town Hall who was paid to do this sort of thing.

He loitered on a bench in a yellow tiled corridor, desperate for a drink. But during the two weeks since he and Miguel had become friends, Luis had started to feel a powerful, uncanny guilt about the drink. Miguel had told him it was doing him no good, and he was right about that: and now that he was here in Valencia, he wasn't going to spend the money they'd made together on alcohol. So he sat in the corridor scratching at his grey stubble, sweating, attracting curiosity, gripping the backs of his knees until his fingers ached from fighting the desire to drink.

'Perez Lerma, Rosa,' the thin woman said. 'Born 1937, Sagunto, Valencia Province. Daughter of Alfredo, a steel-worker. Anything else?'

'No. *Gracias.*'

There was a lot else. For example, there was fifty-three years of what happened between Sagunto and the Metro at Callao.

Luis had spent two days in Valencia and repeated the name of Rosa Lerma more than a hundred times before he came across a waiter called Jordi in a bar off the Plaza Victoria. Jordi said he had once worked with a girl called Rosa Lerma in a paint shop. Just up the road there. It was a video store now. Rosa? Jordi said. She'd been a beauty queen. Rosita Lerma? A girl with ambition, who hadn't seen eye-to-eye with the boss and who had haughtily walked out through the paint-shop door with the promise that one day, they would all see her from a cinema seat. A beauty queen, she'd been: that was why he remembered her.

'Why do you want to know?' wondered Jordi.

'Something to do,' Luis said. 'Something to live for in this life.' He hadn't quite been able to stay off the drink.

Jordi agreed and offered Luis something.

'No, *gracias*. No. Just a coffee with milk.'

'She had such a . . . *proud* look,' Jordi said, setting the coffee down. 'Such dignity. Like she owned the world. You'll forgive me for saying this, *señor*, but I – I fell in love with her.'

'I understand.'

'Just a little.'

'It's a terrible thing,' Luis murmured, 'when you realise you can't live without someone.'

He blew on the coffee.

At the public library, Luis was faced with a large problem. Stacked before him were two hundred and six copies of Valencia's local newspaper, all bound in large leather cases.

He sighed and asked another thin woman with glasses for a magnifying glass.

'Can you read, though?'

'*Hombre*, of course I can. Would I be asking to see these if I couldn't read?'

The thin woman hovered, pretending to check something. Luis slid out a volume at random. ROSA LERMA was etched on his mind: the straight lines of the 'R's, the harsher ones of the 'L' and 'M'.

'Please,' he whispered.

The thin woman pointedly coughed.

Luis heaved open the volume, turned over several pages and sneezed.

And then he saw a photograph of a beautiful face. Beautiful in a natural, old-fashioned way, dark-haired, clear-eyed. The face was happy, the lips parted in joy, and it reminded Luis, as many faces did, a little of Pepita's: her face at the beginning, not later, after everything had gone wrong. He brought the magnifying glass to the photograph and scanned it.

Then he slowly moved the glass to down below the photograph and a sharp pain ran up his right side.

'Come here,' he instructed the thin woman. 'What does that say?'

'*Qué*?'

'What does it say?'

'ROSITA LERMA: A YOUNG GIRL WITH A BIG FUTURE.'

Luis suddenly grew embarrassed.

'Give that magnifying glass here,' the thin woman said. 'You've got water on it, look.'

She photocopied the page for him, and five hours later Luis was on the night train back to Madrid with the page in his pocket. He reclined in the hot, dirty darkness, aware of the smell of soap on his body and wondering how long it would be before it wore off. He should have removed some from the bathroom. There'd been quite a bit of soap there he could have taken. And a towel. Nobody would have noticed. It was no wonder he was so poor. He never stole anything.

He held out to a man with a beard a box of toffees he had bought, and told him about what he had been doing, but the man with a beard refused either to eat the toffees or listen to the story. He appeared to be more interested in his crossword puzzle, and then he went to sleep with the magazine balanced on his face. Luis listened to the wheels of the train, feeling elation.

Elation was what he called it the next day, when he explained it to us: he said you had to separate it from the feeling you had when you were drunk. Elation was a clean, bright feeling which kept you from sleeping, he observed poetically. He went on to explain about destiny, and how only destiny could have drawn him like that so quickly to the name of Rosita Lerma.

Mari-Tere asked Luis if he had been taking drugs. And in Piotr the Pole's experience, anybody who uttered the word 'destiny' must be in love.

I read the article out for him. It stated that Rosa Lerma's ambition had been to become an actress, and that her greatest ambition of all had been to play alongside Arturo Cruz.

'How are we going to find out about that?' asked Miguel.

'Destiny.'

Luis spent several days exploring the contents of rubbish-bins, under the impression that this was where destiny was to be found. All he came up with was an old pair of steel toe-capped boots: not as exciting as destiny, Mari-Tere pointed out, but a damn sight more useful. The gang's theory was that a combination of destiny and the bottle was tipping Luis over the edge. All this activity was doing him no good.

Shortly afterwards he began to intercept middle-aged women on the street, holding up a photocopy of Rosa Lerma's face for the purposes of comparison.

Miguel grew irritable.

'Did she become an actress, or didn't she?'

'Of course she did. You've seen how beautiful she was. You were blessed with a very beautiful mother, Miguel. Don't you worry your head.'

'You don't even know she *was* my mother. You don't even know that yet.'

'These things take time. There's a lot of history to go through. Be patient, please.'

'I don't like history.'

The face they had seen on the newspaper cutting occupied both their minds while they slept at night: Luis bunched up on his side in the back of the burnt-out Seat, fearing rain, Miguel cosy under a Fido Dido continental quilt, the box of toffees from Valencia sitting untouched on his bedside table. Neither

Luis nor Miguel thought particularly about the other, apart
from occasionally wondering how the other lived, what the
other was doing at a particular time of day. Miguel thought: I
will do everything I can not to end up like that. Luis thought:
Poor bugger, if he's not careful, he'll end up like me.

The problem with Destiny, Luis said, was not *if* she would
reveal her secrets, but *when*: if you were lucky, you were still
alive when Destiny played her hand.

He was resting on the kerb outside the Apollo Theatre in the
Plaza de Tirso de Molina when a motor car, hugging the kerb
so as to get past a parked lorry, ran over his right foot. Shocked,
he rolled back onto the pavement. He lay there and realised
with a shock that a motor car had just driven over his foot. He
clutched it, imagining all sorts of terrible goings-on inside his
boot. He was wondering why he felt no pain when a girl came
running out of a bar.

She squatted down and replaced Luis's spectacles on his nose
for him. Then she removed them again, took out a tissue and
polished them.

'You could do with a new pair,' she said. 'Hey. Didn't I see
you playing the guitar a few weeks back? With a kid?'

'No.'

'Yes, I did. In La Latina. You were pretty good. Crazy.'

'No, no. Not me.'

'So how come you were playing the guitar, then?'

'So how come my foot isn't crushed to pieces?'

'Your boots.'

'Craftsmanship,' Luis said. 'Destiny.'

The girl helped Luis to his feet.

'*Vale*,' he said. 'I'll tell you what. I'll tell you my story for a
cup of coffee.'

'*Vale*.'

'With milk. And a *magdalena*.'

They sat in the bar next to the Apollo. Luis told his story.
He was going *loco*, he said worriedly, with not being able to

find her. He was on the edge of a discovery which would alter his whole life and perhaps alter history as well.

'Rosita who?' the girl said.

'Lerma. Rosita Lerma.'

An old woman, supported by two sticks, shuffled in like a haystack, paused and looked slowly about before waving to the girl. Luis observed her as she made her effortful way over to their table and considered the disagreeable changes which time wreaked on the human body, not least his own.

'Are *you* Rosita Lerma?' he enquired vaguely when she had arrived and was settling into a seat.

The girl laughed, shook her head.

'This is my grandmother. *Abuelita*, this is Luis.'

'Rosita?' the grandmother said, still breathing heavily. Luis was surprised that her mind moved so fast. 'No. But I knew her. You young people,' she admonished the girl, 'you have no idea how things fit together.'

A drink was brought to the table and set before the grandmother.

'You want to know about Rosita?' she said.

The grandmother remembered Rosita Lerma. She did become an actress, yes, just as she'd forecast to Jordi: she'd been famous in a small way, in her time, although hers had not been the sort of fame which survives a generation. She had acted opposite Arturo Cruz, too, hearing which made Luis tremble slightly.

The grandmother remembered it well. She had been working as an attendant at the Apollo at the time. One first night Arturo Cruz had taken the grandmother's hand and kissed it: her hand had been black as night before she'd washed it again.

'Very sad about Rosita,' she said, and Luis's heart skipped a beat. This was a dangerous day for his health.

'It must have been about 1955 when she left the theatre. She was going to make a film.'

'A film?'

'Are you deaf, old man? A film. With Brigitte Bardot and Claudia Cardinale.'

'Brilliant memory for names you've got,' mused the girl affectionately. 'Can't catch her out on names of things, can we, *Abuelita*?'

'What was the name of the film?' Luis asked.

'*Los Petrolíferos.*'

'What did she do in the film?'

'Don't recall.'

'And what's so sad?'

'Because of what happened after. She came back to the theatre to tell us all she was getting married. She brought us all a cake. Banana cake.'

Luis was disappointed to hear that Rosita Lerma had been married, and again felt the pain down his right side. He was not sure he wished to hear more.

But he found that the grandmother was talking anyway, and that he was listening.

'She went to live off the Paseo de Extremadura. With a man called Enrique. She wanted to settle down. Then Enrique died and everything started to go wrong. You know what I mean.'

Luis took a bite of *magdalena* and went through in his mind what those two words, 'went wrong', meant for him personally. First, the death of Pepita from cancer of the bowel, and then the drink; then the eviction order, and the half-hearted attempts to defeat the might of the law, half-hearted because the drink stole your fight.

All this was destiny, too. Rolling through the night like a train.

'It's a big world,' he said.

'*Qué?*'

'Yes. I know what you mean.'

Then Luis remembered Miguel.

'Did they have any children?'

'*Hombre, claro.* Just one.'

'Do you recall his name?'

'Of course I don't,' said the grandmother. 'I can't remember things I've never known, can I?'

That was what Luis did over the following weeks, however. He went absent, and remembered things he had never known: he imagined a different part for himself. He remembered that he himself had been Enrique, welcoming Rosita back from a day at work, offering her fine wine. He remembered him and Rosita going out together to restaurants and being given the finest tables by waiters, and he remembered his feelings of pride on strolling down the Gran Via, with the elegant, famous Rosita Lerma on his arm, proud with achieved ambition. The heads she turned! The softness of her body and the fresh smell of her perfume Luis also remembered, and the joy of living in her eyes, and saying things to make her laugh just so that he could listen to the sound of it.

He told us he remembered these things. He played us the song he had written for her, which was *Yesterday* by the Beatles but with different words, and he painted such a pretty picture that we agreed it would be a shame to tell him that he had gone mad.

The photocopy from the newspaper had become grubby and hard to make out.

'What did I tell you?' Piotr the Pole said, and we nodded our heads in sombre agreement.

'Being in love,' Antonio said on his return, oddly we thought, from the comforting arms of Marilyn Monroe. 'That's fine. But being crazy with love? That's hell.'

They showed *Los Petrolíferos*, made in 1956, one month later at the Filmoteca during a season of Brigitte Bardot films.

Prior to their entering the cinema, Miguel stood by embarrassedly in the lavatory as Luis noisily retched with nerves. He was wearing the green shirt with the small crocodile and an old grey jacket, and the rose which he would normally have laid across Pepita's grave occupied the buttonhole.

'Will you recognise her?'

'*Hombre*, do I recognise myself?'

'I don't know.'

Luis sat forward in his seat, breathing noisily and making clicking noises with his tongue in a way that would have disturbed the audience, had there been any audience to disturb.

I asked him afterwards what the film had been about. He said he hadn't noticed.

Then a girl wearing a light cotton dress, sitting on a river bank with other women, turned to the hero and smiled.

'I'll be waiting for you when you return,' she said. 'I have waited for you always.'

Luis leapt from his seat, clutched his side and swore. His glasses fell off and he brought his left boot down on them.

'That's her!' he shouted, and did not stop shouting until Miguel had led him safely onto the street outside.

'That was your mama, Miguel. That was her from the newspaper.'

'I know. I know. The same words, too. You've smashed your specs, you silly old bugger.'

'Doesn't that make you feel anything? She was beautiful, Miguel.'

Miguel went red and turned away. He muttered at the pavement.

'I just wish she'd made a better job of her life. I mean, who did she think she was?'

For the first time, Luis grew angry with Miguel. He started shouting things which he would not afterwards properly remember, about respect, and love.

'She's *my* mother, not yours,' Miguel said. '*Hombre*, calm down.'

'Young people don't understand *anything*, do they? The *abuelita* was right.'

'You'll have a heart attack if you go on like this. Do you think you're my fucking Dad?'

'You should know better at your age.'

'You should know better at *your* age, Luis. You're mad.'

'Of course I'm mad. I told you I was mad. I never said I wasn't mad.'

Luis took his spectacles back from Miguel and analysed them. The left lens was smashed. He spat and shoved them into his trousers pocket.

'I'm no good for you,' he said. 'We know she's your mother now. Maybe you should go back to your normal life. Your studies.'

'Yeah. Maybe I should.'

'Maybe you should.'

'Yeah.'

'You go back to your future again, Miguel. I'll look after the rest.'

'*Qué?*'

'See you tomorrow then? Normal place?'

The following day, Luis waited until it was almost dark by the Necropolis gates, but Miguel didn't turn up. Luis had thought he mightn't.

A week later, Luis was telling his story to the grandmother on the steps outside the Apollo.

'It's keeping me alive,' he said.

'I know what you mean. It's keeping the teeth in your head.'

The grandmother pointed in the direction of the window and whispered into his ear.

'That's Maria Luna. Getting out of that taxi. Arturo Cruz's wife.'

By squinting, Luis was able to make out a small woman with tiny, sharp eyes and bright red hair.

'She's as old as I am,' the grandmother complained. 'Though you wouldn't know it. Look at the cut of that coat. What happened to Rosita'll never happen to her. Look at those bloody heels, man.'

Maria Luna brought a glass of wine to her lips and sipped, and then she laughed gaily at a comment made by her companion.

'Where are you going?' the grandmother asked.

Luis, a paper napkin attached to the heel of his boot, was carefully approaching Maria Luna.

He placed a hand on her shoulder.

Maria Luna turned, shocked; and an expression passed across her face which Luis tried to describe to us later that evening. Remembrance and shock: like you'd look if you met yourself from forty years ago, he said, adding that probably we wouldn't understand that. And indeed we didn't.

'Maria,' he said. 'I'm Enrique. Rosita Lerma's husband.'

Maria Luna turned to her companion and stepped back.

'Go on,' grunted Maria Luna's companion. 'On your way.' He jerked his head in no particular direction.

'I love her,' said Luis, giddy under the impact of Maria Luna's perfume.

The companion sighed, removed some small change from his pocket and held it out.

'Show more respect for the *señora*,' he whispered fiercely. 'Get yourself a drink. Go on.'

Luis nodded slowly and returned to the table.

'You,' said the grandmother, 'are *loco*. What did you say, man?'

'I've understood something,' Luis said.

That evening, the grandmother and Luis drank more than would have been good for them forty years before, let alone now. Luis explained what he had understood. He had seen it: it had been in his mind. Encouraged by the young barman, people gathered round.

Rosita Lerma left her bench in Callao one evening to carry her sorrow around the streets of old Madrid. She had an empty Galerias carrier bag stuffed into her pocket. She had drunk too much, and had no particular destination: maybe she'd go and visit Antonio, and maybe she wouldn't. She wished she was free to visit Miguel, but there was too much old shame.

When she came to the Apollo, she turned left into a side-street and stopped. She stood and watched as a taxi pulled up. She thought she saw Arturo Cruz climb from this taxi, and then his wife, and a companion or two.

Luis paused, scratched at his grey stubble, working it through his mind, living it.

Rosita Lerma stood, wobbly, and recalled with tenderness a time many years before, when she had realised her dream of acting in a film with this man. He had been so handsome and strong, and now he was ancient and slightly bent, and this they shared. She felt an odd, overwhelming blend of admiration and sadness which was powerful enough to propel her towards him, to compel her to place a hand on his shoulder.

Arturo Cruz turned: in his eyes there was no remembrance and no shock, no surprise: simply boredom at being recognised by a stranger.

Automatically his hand moved to his pocket.

'Arturo,' she said quietly. 'It's Rosita. Rosita, Arturo. You remember me.'

'On your way,' the companion said. 'Go on. Get yourself a drink.'

Arturo Cruz was already moving away, his arm through Maria Luna's. Together they made a perfect circle which Rosita Lerma could not hope to break. She felt anger and sadness, and felt them strongly. She felt injustice and hurt.

Later that evening, reckless now, maddened by drink, pride and worthlessness, Rosita murdered Arturo Cruz. Murdered him, for not having a memory, and not giving the past its due.

'You're *loco*, Luis,' repeated the grandmother.

'She was a proud woman of great dignity.'

'How did she murder him?' somebody said.

'She shot him. *Hombre*, I don't know. *No importa*. Then she returned home and threw herself down the steps of the metro at Callao. Or maybe she just fell. Poor Miguel. Poor Rosita.'

Then Luis recalled the theft of Rosita's gravestone by Arturo Cruz.

'*Qué bastardo!*' He gave a big shout and banged the table-top. Someone laughed and clapped.

'You should have been a bloody detective, Luis man. Putting it all together in your head.'

The grandmother cackled with satisfaction and, from sympathy with Luis, also banged the table-top.

'I wish I could tell you you were wrong,' she said, 'but I can't.'

Luis thought he'd be relieved at getting the story over and done with in his mind. It had been there since December, and it was April now. But tonight he found he couldn't sleep for worry. It took him more than two hours of fuddled thought to realise what he was worried about, but then it struck him and forced him upright, causing him to bang his head on the roof of the burnt-out Seat Ibiza and also to awaken Antonio and myself.

He was worried that one day the police would discover that Rosita Lerma murdered Arturo Cruz, and he was also worried about the pain that this would cause Miguel, seeing her badly reproduced face in the newspapers next to that of the man for whom she had always waited.

He was worried about this complicated new burden of truth.

Luis scuttled to the police station at five o'clock in the morning and asked to see Angel, urgently. Angel wandered out of a back room, dabbing fruitlessly at some coffee which he had just spilt over his shirt.

'I did it, Angel,' he said. 'It was me.'

Angel looked up and smiled.

'*Hombre*, what?'

'Killed him. It was me. I killed Arturo Cruz.'

Luis worked the inside of his right ear with his little finger.

'This ear has heard the screams of a murdered man, Angel.'

'Go back home, Luis. I don't like to see you like this. My wife is pregnant. Go on, now.'

'Angel. *Por favor*. These hands have held – '

'Does coffee stain, Luis?'

'I don't know.'

Luis hovered.

'We're full up, Luis. *Hombre*, I told you. Get back home.'

That's the police for you.

Last Days and Nights

Extract from a novel in progress, *A Gift of Going*

This Crazy Night
28 December

My mother fell out of bed again while Rebecca and I were out yesterday, visiting the Science Museum as I had promised and promised.

My father said it was the worst moment in his life. It wasn't like the first time. Then she was in their old bed. This time there was the metal bar side. She slipped under the lower bar up to her chin and stuck, feet dangling. (Her feet were dangling the way Dr Gustaffson said to dangle them when she was pregnant.) My father said, 'She could have broken her neck.'

It could have broken my father. He's so agitated, he doesn't want to be left alone for a minute.

I don't want to picture it: how she went under the bed naked; feet, legs, hips, flat belly and flat pods of breasts. Her neck cords like blue strings.

With other children, Rebecca was stroking an alligator.

I saw my mother like an alligator sliding through a fall of air. Only her head held her back. I saw her head locked in the stockhole of her bed – her grey hair pasted to the skull, the eyehole dead, the skin tight as a stocking mask. I didn't want to see this. I cut my father off. I retorted, 'But she's all right.'

He rescued her. His hands like a pair of forceps clasping her skull. He pulled her up by her head. Her body was like the tail of an alligator slithering after.

Then her rings were lost, diamond and gold braid. He is beside himself searching.

And I've been sick, so sick, on my knees retching into the toilet.

Time hasn't stopped. Now it's four o'clock in the morning.

Since evening, she's had a fever. She's been so hot, so dry, so full of mucus. Could it be pneumonia?

Laurel's phoned twice, before and after I phoned the hospice. Laurel said Mom had a night like this before. The hospice said to try Tylanol suppositories, infant-size. Judith drove all over Boston to find a late-night pharmacy that had infant-size; and then she drove here. She asked, 'Do you think you can get them in?' The nurse said, 'It should bring the fever down.' The nurse added, 'Tell your mother she's not going to choke. It's better for her not to worry about it. If she does choke, it will be worse for you than her.'

Four-fifteen. It's four-fifteen a.m. A small blessing: my headache's fading. And Judith took Rebecca home with her.

He said, 'She fell out of bed again.' (And we were at the Science Museum.) He said, 'Thank God you're back.' Rebecca threw her arms around my father. 'Poor Grandpa. Poor Grandma.' I looked at my mother. I felt her face. Mine was hotter than hers. 'But she's all right,' I said to him. I looked at her left hand and saw that the rings were missing. Later, when it was dark, the fever rose. 'I don't have a fever,' she said. 'Well I have a migraine,' I said. 'You can rest in my bed, Ellen,' she said.

I couldn't rest in her bed. And I couldn't deal with the Tylanol. I tore the packaging off a pair of surgical gloves, more disposables from the hospice. I pulled the gloves on, pushing the fingers down. I saw how unnaturally smooth and white my hands looked. Then I retched again.

Bubbles and froth. Mouthfuls of sour mucus. And she wanted to know if I thought her imaginings were just imaginings.

My Mother's Party
29 December

She wants to have a party for her special day. 'When is it?' She
shook her head carefully. 'We don't know. But we have to get
ready. We should have the family and the ancestors. Ellen, in
the morning first you will go for your jog. Then there will be
a picnic with no insects. Very special. My brother Arnold will
be there and all the young people. We will open our tent to the
wayfarer and help the stranger. My mother will make her cheese
blintzes. Imagine sour cream and my mother's cheese blintzes.
I've done my arithmetic. We'll need loads of paper plates, more
than fifty. I'm inviting all the cousins. And this is such wonderful news. You'll never guess what I found this morning. They're
coming to the party too, a troop of lost children hidden in a
cave in Spain. One of the men in the search party will be their
father. What a wonderful thing! And another wonderful thing!
He's getting married. A father and a mother for the children.
Such joy. You tell Ernest Mailor to take his weeping away.
Remember Korczak, the Polish doctor? He's bringing all his
orphans from the ghetto. They are carrying a green flag, green
for freedom. Hush.' She put a finger to her lips. 'Listen.' I
listened and heard from the floor above the doctor creeping
around. In a few minutes, he would be down the stairs, on his
way out for his jog around Fresh Pond and the river route.
'Listen,' she repeated. 'They are singing in the box-cars. It's so
wonderful I don't want to wait. Peace. Peace-*Shalom*. Imagine
I am here.'

'Mom,' I whispered, 'you are here.'

'Hush,' she said. 'Imagine. Imagine the children singing.
Imagine the door opening.'

I saw the door of the unmarked box-car slide back. 'It's
opened,' I told her.

'The children are running and leaping,' she said, 'and shouting
and laughing. And hillsides ring. Imagine.'

'Yes,' I said.

'Imagine Fresh Pond,' she said.

'Yes,' I said, and I saw us having our picnic on the hill, just us, Laurel and me and my mother before Judith was born. My mother's face was round because of Judith. My mother was all round. I remembered.

'And the seas,' she said, 'and the trees of Poland, a willow by the water. Imagine lonely hearts,' she paused and made a gesture of disbelief. 'Unimaginable. I am here.' I reached for her hand and held it gently. She continued, 'Imagine our children, hundreds of trees. Imagine the unimaginable, all the tears that don't quench our thirst. Imagine our thirst.'

It was hard not to imagine her thirst. How could she go on talking when she couldn't swallow, when she was living on droplets of ice?

'Imagine silence and joy. Imagine paradise found again. The ordinary everybody people are here – mamas and papas and popsicle-eaters.'

'And mumsicle-eaters,' I said softly.

'Don't give me a mumsicle or a popsicle. Not now,' she said. 'Now you and I make our way alone like one last grasshopper. Tomorrow green pastures. Imagine. And Merry England. And Poets of the World. And Young Words. Imagine this Happy New Year waiting for the children waiting to be born.'

**New Year's Morning
1 January**

'Mom,' I said when I opened the door at seven this morning, 'It's Ellen.' I let the blinds up and a grey daylight came through the curtains. She was lying as I had left her six hours earlier. She was flat on her back, her head well-pillowed, the covers to her chin. I saw no change at all, only her mouth was opened wide. I looked at her mouth and then realised that she was speaking from her throat. She was making throat sounds, ba-ahing. They stopped almost immediately. I wondered if it was because I was there. Perhaps she had been making them for hours, calling for me with a sound I hadn't heard. Perhaps she had been trying to say my name. 'Mom,' I repeated, 'It's Ellen.'

I felt she had quieted. I felt she knew I was there. Watching, listening, I heard the clicking of the radiator and thought of long fingernails tapping. So I decided to cut her fingernails. She was so quiet, she had become wholly mine to care for. I went to her dresser for her nail scissors. I saw the early cloud was already dissolving, the sky turning blue. 'It's going to be a fine New Year's Day,' I told her. I think she heard me. I know the hearing is the last to go. I had the small scissors in my hand. Then I noticed that her teeth and gums were brown. Something like molasses was stuck to the side of her face. It had dripped from the corner of her mouth, tracing a path over her cheek and jawbone and pasting her hair to her neck. I put the scissors on the side table beside her stopped clock and went to fetch a basin of warm water. It wasn't until later that I thought about where the molasses could have come from. At that hour, I just washed it off. I washed her carefully, her chin, around her mouth, her cheek, jaw, neck, and the sticky parts of her hair. I changed the water and washed the rest of her face. I patted her dry, put the basin away, found the skin lotion, and rubbed where I had dried. Then I decided to clean her teeth and gums. The hospice nurse had left me a bag of medicated toothettes. They were coloured sponge cubes skewered on toothpicks. They looked a little like lollypops. I wet one and rubbed it against my mother's gums. I worked tooth by brown tooth, gum space by gum space, undisturbed. This too I didn't think about at the time: that she didn't bite down or suck at the lollypop sponge. She made no sound and no movement. As if she were anaesthetised, her jaw stayed open. And when I moved her arm and lifted her hand and took hold so I could cut her nails, her fingers were limp. Perhaps I was too intent upon my tasks to pay attention. Or perhaps I was calmed by her calm which, in retrospect, I see was exceptional. Before leaving her, as the hospice nurse had showed me, I rolled up a towel and tucked it under her head. I straightened her body on the bed, checked that the sheets were dry, and readjusted her covers. Then, although Rebecca was calling because she wanted her breakfast, I stopped for a moment. I placed my hand on my mother's forehead as if in benediction and studied her face as if to relearn what might be lost. Small but shapely, I reminded myself, with high cheek bones and a modest but determined chin. The remaining eyebrow curved neatly above the remaining eye. The eye was closed and twinned with the brown crusted ulcer on the left side. Dry, the ulcer gave off no scent. As for the visible tumour, the swelling above the bridge of her nose, it disappeared in that early light. Or I kissed it away, and my lips touched a warm dryness. At that moment, I saw her skin as the ivory of good bone.

Rebecca, my father and I were having breakfast when a visitor knocked on the apartment door. I went to open it. She was a sturdy middle-aged woman dressed for winter walking, and she carried a small canvas pack on her back. She introduced herself as one of the Early Birds. She used to meet my parents having Early Bird breakfast at Friendly's. 'Oh yes,' I said, 'they often used to go there.' 'How is your mother?' she asked. 'She isn't very communicative,' I said, 'but you're welcome to see her. Hold on a minute. I'll let her know you're here.' 'Tell her it's Edith. She'll know Edith-the-Early-Bird. Newcome,' she added, 'Edith Newcome.'

I noticed that I'd left the nail scissors on the side table and picked them up to put away. Then I noticed my mother's teeth, the teeth I'd sponged only half an hour before. They were all rotted, brown as mud, and the gaps between them looked black. They made an ugly display. I remembered how many years had passed since she'd been to a dentist, since our old family dentist had died of cancer from the x-ray machine. 'When they're ready,' she had insisted, dismissing treatment, 'they fall out. Who cares about an old tooth?'

Just then, I cared. And I didn't understand why I was seeing her teeth exposed in this way. Then I noticed how wide her

mouth was opened, how stiff and stretched her jaw as if straining to make space for air; as if it couldn't open wide enough to
take the air she needed.

I had to be very careful. I put the scissors down. I didn't
want to make a mistake. Suddenly I sensed how silent she was,
as silent as her unplugged clock. My heart stopped beating. I
wasn't ready to touch her face yet.

Instead I pulled the sheet back, stared at the faded bloodstains
on her T-shirt and pressed my cheek to her shrunken stomach.
It was still warm from the live blood pooled there. Then my
heart started pounding all over my body like a bird gone wild
in a trap. I jerked myself up, covered her to the neck, and cried
out, 'Dad, Dad, Dad, she's dead.'

My father brought his hand to her mouth and held it, feeling
for feather-breath. As I watched, I saw the moles on the back
of his hand proliferate as if she could be breathing them into
him. Then his hand dropped away. He nodded one slow nod,
cupped her chin, and pressed her mouth closed. 'I'd better call
Judith,' he said.

Alone in the room and unseen, I took hold of my mother's
head. It was hard and cold and her hair felt rough against my
palms. I drew my cheek down to her cheek and let out a howl.
I howled with an animal's brute mastery, not caring who heard,
wanting to be heard, and hearing the power of the noise as if it
was my right above and over all. Later I thought of the sound
carrying through all the apartment walls, through the walls of
the brick building, and into the streets of Cambridge. My howl
was the crashing of old church bells, the bellow of warning
horns, the gallop of iron-clad feet, the town crier's call.

Rebecca answered it. She fell on me, hooking my neck with
a hot thin arm and pressing her hot head so hard against the
side of mine, my ear still burns.

Then it was done. I pulled away, disentangling us from my
dead mother, and took Rebecca with me into the bathroom. I
filled the sink with icy water and plunged my face in. The bell

ringers, playing a medley for the New Year, began 'Auld Lang Syne'.

Harvard Square
1 January

As soon as the body was gone, we wanted to be gone too. We thanked the nurse for all the hospice had done and said we would be sending a contribution soon. In a rush we gathered the laundry for the home aid worker and heaped it on the old double bed along with a box of soap powder and an envelope of coins for the machine.

Outside the air was so warm and the day so bright, we were dazzled. In a dumb parade, we trooped to Harvard Square. My father was in the lead, Rebecca and I next, Judith and Marty last. Overnight the university students had returned. We saw them everywhere smiling the smiles my mother thought were the most beautiful thing in the world, and entertaining one another with their youthful looks, wits and performance skills. On the brick pedestrian terrace at the start of Brattle Street, entertainers were at work. They were juggling, fire-eating, unicyling, story-telling and playing music. As we continued along the pavement, we came upon others. Buskers stood in doorways beside their instrument cases which were opened for contributions. A saxophonist swayed to the melancholy of a jazz solo and the gleam of the metal tubing swayed in the picture window behind him. At the corner, in front of the Harvard Cooperative Society, Conservatory students were playing a wind trio. My father stopped to listen to them and stopped us. I found the sweet leaps of their tones too painful to feel and looked across the road at the French bakery café. The corner was filled with sunlight and so crowded, people were standing around those who were seated and everyone was talking and eating regardless. The glassed-in self-service section also looked impossibly crowded. It seemed that everyone was out celebrating the first day of the New Year right there. Everyone had decided upon lunchtime cappuccino at Au Bon Pain.

Suddenly we didn't know which way to turn. The light, the brightness, the hubbub, the happy energy, and the crowding bewildered us. Rebecca turned to me and I turned to Judith and Marty; then we all looked to my father. He led us away from the crowds by leading us out of the sun and into a narrow side street. There we found a cold, empty ice cream parlour and sat at metal tables on metal chairs with ice cream and paper cups of strong coffee. When we had finished, none of us thought of going anywhere but home.

The closer we came to the apartment, the more agitated we felt and the faster we talked. It was as if we were hurrying home to my mother, as if she might still be lying in the bed, waiting. Crossing the courtyard, I felt the recurring anxiety of the past weeks that something had happened to her while I had been out and I wondered that I had left her. My father opened the apartment door with his key and then called out, 'Hello? Anybody home? I'm home.' Rebecca turned to me with a quizzical expression and mouthed, 'Who's he speaking to?' I said, 'It takes time to learn. He's forgotten.' Instinctively we went to the bedroom as if to check on my mother. The sides of the hospital bed were lowered; the electric cord coiled snake-like on top of the plastic-covered mattress, and the sheets the home aid had laundered were piled there sorted into sets and sizes. I picked up the single sheets to put them away. Judith said, 'Wait a minute.' 'What is it?' I asked, glancing at her. She was looking at the sheets in my arms. 'One's missing.' I looked down. It was as if I couldn't see it. 'The pink blush with the pencil-striped pattern. That was my favourite,' she said. 'We bought it together, Laurel and I, last month.' 'Nobody would have taken it,' I said. 'Well where is it?' Judith insisted. 'Maybe it's with the doubles,' I said, putting the singles back on the bed. Rebecca pressed against me. 'Mom,' she whispered, 'Grandpa said they could take it.'

Then I saw it. I saw it again. He lifted one side of the pencil-striped to cover her locked face and overlapped it with the other side. Again I heard myself say to him in an abrupt command, 'Wait.' He waited. They all waited, the two men from the funeral home, my father who was standing at the foot of the bed, and Rebecca. I pulled the sides of the sheet back and uncovered her face. I bent. I kissed her cheek again, her cold cheek. Then I pulled the pencil-striped rose-blush percale over her face myself.

'Judith,' I said. 'It was Mom. Mom took it.' Suddenly I was laughing a terrible laugh and Judith was crying and Judith and Rebecca and I were hugging each other clumsily and hard.

We put the sheets in the cupboard and then Judith said, 'Let's get rid of the old bed now.' Rebecca said, 'Grandma told me to throw it out the window.' Judith said, 'Marty, you're good at throwing.' Marty picked Rebecca up and counting 'one, two, three', he swung her towards a window as if he was going to swing her through. Again I heard my mother say, 'I want to be outside.' I imagined her as a Mary Poppins sailing through the window. Out she went, open-eyed and smiling, with the covers pulled up to her chin.

Marty stood Rebecca back on her feet and directed the dismantling of the bed. We inched the pieces around the hospital bed, up the corridor, out of the apartment and through the elevator door. Then Judith and Rebecca and I stood at the bedroom window where my mother had so often stood watching for the mailman, and we watched the dismembered bed making its way to the trash hut. They carried it together, my father and Marty, going back and forth until it was done. Then Judith fetched a broom and dustpan from the kitchen and started sweeping up tissues and other leavings. Rebecca crouched with the dustpan. 'The ring!' she shrieked suddenly. 'Grandma's wedding ring. Both rings!' she added, pulling the diamond from a crack between the floorboards. We ran out to my father who was on the way in and pressed the rings into his hand. He looked at them as if they couldn't be real and then handed them back 'for the granddaughters'. 'That's what your mother would want,' he said. He passed us and went back into the bedroom. He looked around the room and then turned to the window from where he could see that the trash hut door was closed.

Mount Auburn Cemetery
1 January

Judith and Marty left. Then Rebecca wanted to go out again. She didn't care where. 'Mom, let's just go.' 'What about Grandpa?' 'Laurel will be here soon.' My father said, 'Sure. You go.' 'Okay, we're going,' I said. There was one place I wanted to go and only one: the cemetery. 'You'd better hurry,' he added, 'I can feel the temperature dropping.'

The afternoon was fading and already winter was back. The wind, gusting from the north, layered clouds against the sun and pushed them on, turning cobalt to charcoal and charcoal back to fire. Fiery edging spread into streaks and patches as the sun was briefly freed. Colour speared the branches and a wild run of tints was unleashed. 'Purple,' said Rebecca, 'green, gold, silver, lemon, slate grey, London grey, orange, puce. Mom, are you looking?' I looked up and then at her. The look on her face was so like my mother's, it took my breath away. In rapt absorption, Rebecca stared until the clouds covered the sun entirely, turning the sky back to charcoal. Then she said, 'I wish I hadn't left my watercolours in London.' And I wished I could tell my mother that Rebecca wanted to paint her glowering cemetery sky.

I said, 'We can get some in the Square tomorrow.'

'I might not remember till tomorrow.'

'Yes you will,' I said. 'Make yourself remember.'

'I can't make myself.'

'Come on,' I said. 'We're looking for our spot.'

Was it happiness I felt wandering along the footpaths and up and down the hills with Rebecca? And was it because of the thought: this is where my mother would be forever? The men had carried her out strapped into a stretcher. She would be laid here in a box. I recalled my mother telling me about the burial of my cat; how comfortable she had made Kitty, couching her on moss.

We dipped into Consecration Dell and climbed to the Norman Tower lookout. 'There,' I said, pointing to the further side of Willow Pond. 'Grandma will be over there.' I noticed a bench beside one of the willows and imagined my father sitting on that bench in springtime. The branchlets above would turn from green to yellow and hang like a rain of gold soft as hair. I imagined my father's face rippling in the pond among the mirrored branches. The sun would pour through them like a blessing.

I heard the echo of my mother's blessings. Then I was suddenly anxious. Suppose Laurel was still *en route* from New York and my father was alone. Now I saw the emptiness of the hospital bed in the swept bedroom. I felt the cold of the encroaching night, the wind biting, the sky darkened to a brutal lid. How could it be that only this morning my mother was alive, singing her sheep's song, calling to me in a language I had failed to understand? She stopped singing and opened her mouth wide, wider than ever before. I scrubbed her black-and-brown gums with a pink sponge toothette and I watched my hand drop the toothette into the wastebasket near her stopped clock. The clock was still stopped. In the late light, I made out a statue of a lamb on a pedestal, a cold cast-iron lamb. I turned around, suddenly confused. My own lamb, Rebecca, where was Rebecca? The sun was setting. The land was freezing. Gravestones were falling away on all sides. It was as if they were being swallowed up by the night, carried off to join those dug under. 'Rebecca!' I cried out. 'Rebecca!'

She heard my fear. 'Mum?' she answered. Where was she? 'Here,' she called. Why was she laughing? There was a leak of sunlight, a shaft which burst over her and I saw her set in the landscape tucked under a wide evergreen branch. She was a bundle of pinks and reds caught in a burnished red light. 'Why are you hiding there?' I scolded. 'Imagine I'm a gravestone,' she said. What kind of gravestone was this? She leaped up and raced to another tree and again tucked herself close to the thick trunk with a branch like a roof over her head. 'We could bury Grandma here.' 'You're a gravestone,' I repeated. 'Imagine. Imagine.' I heard the echo of my mother's voice. And then the warning bell clanged across the hills from the office half a mile away. 'Come on.' I reached for Rebecca's mittened hand and pulled her up. 'We've got to run.' Hand-in-hand, we ran all the way and through the cemetery gates and across Mt Auburn Street. In a blur, I saw the red lights and headlights like a crowd of eyes.

My father and Laurel were in the dining room when we returned. He was seated at the table with a book opened in front of him. Laurel was painting his portrait. 'Rebecca,' Laurel cried, interrupting herself to rip a blank sheet from her pad, 'I've been waiting for my niece. Come and paint with me.' Rebecca sat down beside Laurel. I went into the kitchen to prepare some food.

To Be a Pilgrim

It's galling to have to ask for Purseglove at Reception. I get a beamer from the desk clerk, sunrays spread out from the counter: smiles are à la carte here, this is a Country House Hotel.

He checks to see if there is a note for me, an anything. He doesn't rummage – I am the only frenzied being – he enquires, meanderingly, like a lazy river on a sunny day. I am water from a viler spout, a gargoyle. Struggling to restrain the gush, to flow a little, I look round.

An open book, hardbacked, marbled, octavo, probably unreadable, Walter Scott? Some half-rimmed specs, a decanter of brown water. I feel like giving it a shake or two with the stopper off, I'm not the kind of idiot to go along with it: brown water equals Madeira? No.

Yes there is a note. Purseglove has gone for a wander among the tree ferns. I hope they drip. I am not hopping around on leaf mould seeking Purseglove here and there.

This is not the sort of floor you can flounce out on, the thickness of the carpet absorbs petulance, I cannot slam an open door. My car – I should have known – has been removed to a distant, landscaped, parking place. Spotting it among the Daimlers, the Mercedes, the nippy sports, I get inside and sulk.

Purseglove's ancestry is northern. A grandfather ran a bar closed down by the local morality monger in the Twenties when some guy was spotted on a Sunday morning leaving on all fours: I don't think it was the drink.

I like this car lot screening me from tweed, I like it better than the pillared lobby. I feel safe. I'm in no mood for ramblers, for Guccis strolling after lunch. I'll kill Purseglove when I see her, not a luger but a letter for the lady and the sensation, a 'qualm' the clerk might call it, a qualm coming out of nowhere,

that she is going to creep up on the car with me inside. I keep
an eye out back through the driving mirror, adjusting it I see
my face. Stubble when I don't wish to be caught shaving, this
time not being the best time to look keen. Stubble doesn't suit
me though . . . could I roll in the sharp, washed, gravel?
Writhe, try to rub it off?

Although it's cold some kitchen staff sit around an upturned
barrel. The word 'private' does not appear here, or perhaps
there is a euphemism for it that I haven't twigged. The cooks
look like male nurses, I can feel them objecting to me, strongly,
as I pass them on the way up to the tennis court. Purseglove
affects me though I haven't caught a sight of her, she has remote
control.

She won't feel patronised, far from it, she'll have them running round. Hiding things, working with her, not against. A
team. Her team. And if the tree ferns drip she'll relish it; all
part of the fun.

I understood that country walks were always circular, this is
not the case. I have to backtrack, catwalk, nonchalant among
the nurses, and it hurts. I hope I won't have to sit through
dinner, the waiters are doubtless even worse.

I have done it, many times; dinner with Purseglove in hotels.
The conversation, if you can call it that, dries before we take
our seats. She's bored of course, too bored to order, too bored
to eat. Cigarettes are her poison, you get your turbot smoked.
And there wasn't a time when it was ever any better, there was
no beginning with Purseglove, all middle, all the time.

I'm edgier than ever. If she hasn't seen the car then she'll be
told I got the message. She may be leaning from a window:
stubble features can't look up. Or showering: for her own
delectation and not mine. Purseglove's body – confidence is
everything – I've seen it, been there, no great shakes.

Wracking shakes, my hands begin to tremble as I think. I
have to sit down but not near the barrel, in this joint surely if
my knees begin to buckle they'll roll out a davenport? God,
now I've met the nurses. They put my head between my knees.

I am out here, idiot, sitting with them on the bench. I would pretend to be foreign – they are foreign – it is better not to speak. I've made an idiot of myself without even seeing Purse-glove, this is how it goes.

I get out and break – the operative word – into an apologetic, jerking jog. Like someone who was just resting, in training for something other than what I have in mind. Stubble-features in the late afternoon. On the run.

I head towards the tree ferns, downhill all the way, the car keys jangling next to the letter in the pocket of my suit. God oh God and in all this vegetation I somehow can't get off the path and do it. Hide. Like a butterfly I slow my pace behind a pair of bright yellow culottes.

This time it's better. The grounds here are extensive, discussion of the gardens lasts a drink.

'Why go out when you're expecting me?'

I always ask the obvious, it's what she expects. And of course she bats my question aside. Not bats, not Purseglove. She strokes it out of sight. My question hangs round me at odds with the ambience – I read the brochure – the temperate climate – cover to cover – of the place. Ambience for God's sake. The Madeira, the half glasses and the book? She has a lovely suite which I am not invited to. I have a lovely room.

'Let's eat,' I say.

She'll smoke. She really likes the toadying, the comfort, more like a country house than a hotel. She actually believes that shit.

I stop myself from saying, 'You're paying through the nose for it.' Expressions I would never use add to the ugliness of me round her. I make the flowers saggy, I am a warthog by the pond. I skin and lump the sauces, turn the cream.

We both drink. I eat and drink. My drinking makes me drunk. All the time I'm thinking of the ammunition in my pocket, what I've got for her in the trousers of my suit. If she was talking I'd let her run but she isn't talking. Only looking, with confidence, around her: enjoying everything but me. I leave my napkin on my chair as I get up to go outside and shake.

They ought to make a feature, trailing me, trailing Purse-glove; the narration can be brief. I'd like to have it mentioned that I was once, indubitably, an ordinary man. This condition is not congenital; I started okay as a baby, the toddling stage was orthodox, my mother loved me. Still does.

I am smoking a cigarette I don't want. By that I mean that I need to set fire to a pack of twenty to get the sort of satisfaction that I crave. I could take the Madeira now if I was in reach of it, at a swig.

By the time I go back in she has left of course. I stand on coloured marble looking down at her, swimming in the heated pool. A one-piece swimming suit that doesn't do a lot for her, but does enough.

I envisage a scene. Me insisting on lying all over her body, breaking in. Taken off her by some flunky dressed in authentic twill. I've forgotten all about the letter. My passion is absolute.

Alone but not alone; the staff are so discreet. I wander the downstairs of the hotel which to me is just another place. It is a nightmare but of course I'm not asleep. I have the choice of half a dozen three-seater chintzes, easy armchairs that can't do a thing for me, scatter cushions in shot silk. The invisible staff are right there to help me when I require it but I am far beyond. I think of asking them for drugs. Poison, do it the hard and nasty way, draw attention to myself?

'You poison weeds here?'

'Everything is organic here, sir.'

Vanquish hope.

'Everything will seem better in the morning sir.'

He wants me to go up now but I won't.

In other places I drink with the flunkies. I downmarket myself, act the chameleon, imply that I am nearer them than us. Sometimes they go for it, they are bored as Purseglove's bored; a new face to watch crack up. They tend me with nap-kins, the hard corners of starched cloths. A warm woman might rub up against me, more than that if I strike lucky, whilst Purseglove quietly sleeps.

To tell Purseglove what I need to tell her is both too short and too long. Living without her won't kill me, I only wish it would. I'd like her to know what it feels like to be hanging on like this, waiting on organic death. I'm technically dead without her, 'I'm just a torso, Purseglove,' she might . . . might . . . laugh at that. To make her laugh is the only way in and I know it but there isn't much that's funny now about my state. A state of suspension, horror, shakes. Withdrawal from something I can't get into, or, if I do get into, somehow never have. Purse-gloves are not had by anyone. If they like you then they decide to give. You don't go for the jugular with Pursegloves, you find the funny bone. They yield when their fancy is tickled. For them passion is fun.

This Cornwall seems like the end of the line to me tonight. At the end of England, Purseglove quietly sleeping, me.

The lamp swings from my hand leaving an afterglow. It's rained since dinner, down towards sea level, squelch and soggy damp. Down by the water, exhausted, further stubbled, I get some strange and tantalising glimpses around the time darkness gives way to the dawn.

Water, still colourless, slaps against the hotel's little boats. On tired ears the lapping sound is womb-like, lullabying. Solace laps the little hulls and whispers, 'You are not the first or only one.'

I sit on a wet rock when the shakes come, I turn the lamp out only when I realise that it has been unneeded for some time. I suppose a bottle should float by and I should put the letter in it, but life . . . it doesn't happen quite like that.

You keep the letter for a long time, a very long time. Particles of pocket fluff in the creases of the envelope, until the ink outside, 'By Hand', begins to fade. You keep it fifty years or so and someone finds it after the sweet releases of organic death. They are embarrassed by it. It has, at least, some delayed effect. Or one day, you wake knowing that you've grown out of it, that it's finished. You are embarrassed by it; it doesn't hurt to drop it in the trash now, let it go.

You marry someone else. She marries. She marries someone so idiotic that it might just as well have been you. You wonder what happens to her. You want to drop a note to a mutual friend on the lines of 'Let me know, won't you, if something happens', or more precisely, 'Put me on the list.' Too much to drink, you spill it out to someone who isn't listening, someone who is waiting for a space in your maudlin story to cap the lines with something worse. What are friends for? I don't know.

Am I going to drop this note now where she'll never find it or leave it at Reception on the desk? Birds have started singing, rain-forest noises turned down very low. Mist rises, tree ferns drip.

To leave it in the centre of the maze would be sensational, I just don't know whether I have the energy to spend the narrow time in hedges turning round. Keep it in the glove compartment until I sell the car? Or is this Purseglove running down the wet slope, calling out? How worried she was about me, how none of the staff – her friends – knew where I'd got to. I'm upset so I can mistake a jogger for the beloved. For the beloved, of course, won't come.

'Glorious morning,' he says as he passes me. I even got the sex wrong, and the whiff that isn't Purseglove for a Purseglove does not sweat.

Should I shove the letter out at him as if it were a baton? Let him wear it in his pocket? Carry what I've been carrying? Pass it on?

I feel spectacularly awful. The stubble is better now that there is more of it but I haven't slept and apart from a glimpse of salvation sucking round the varnished hulls of rowboats, I suffer just the same. Cold to the bone the passion flares in me. Where is death when I need it, where is the potion, lotion, the un-elixir that could make my heart go numb?

I crawl into the lobby, sunbeams steam my suit. I leave a message at the desk for Purseglove.

'Why drive me to stay out all night?'
That's what she expects.

Mouths of Nectar, Mouths of Knives

All my life they were building their tomb for me. It was to be a marvel, a triumph of their architectural skills. They brought masons from Thebes and marble from Paros. They cut deep into the rocky hillside, close to the palace walls, a long passage that opened into a circular chamber. In the centre of the chamber there was a bier. There I was to be placed, pickled in nitre, sceptre in hand, hair bound in braids of state, and caparisoned from head to toe with the gold that I had so detested in life. I was to lie in that manner forever, breathing in the close chill air. For my spirit could not move on; even the shades of the Styx would reject it.

But I was not afraid. Briomene had taught me that you cannot bury what is not dead, and you cannot kill what never lived. They may cast my bones wide beyond the palace gates to be eaten by dogs, as Calchas wanted it, arguing that I had forfeited all human status, and was a bitch to be devoured by bitches; or they can bury me in state, insisting, with Orestes, that my punishment was less important than the reinstatement of the law. But they cannot destroy me. I am a principle. I am invulnerable. They do not even know, those singing bands of masons, why their hands like to carve out the long passages to the deep chambers in the heart of the hillside.

I was born in the town of Sparta, fifty miles or so from Mycenae, on the slopes of the mountains of Lacedaemon. My father was Tyndareus, ruler of Sparta, my mother Leda, who slept with Zeus in the form of a swan, and bore Helen.

My childhood was a free one. I was allowed to wander wild on the rugged slopes of Lacedaemon. I knew the rivers and streams, the mountain ash and the wild antelope; I knew the snow-dusted peaks where orchids grew in spring and the slate screes where you could chute down the hill in seconds. Sometimes, when my father wasn't looking, I worked the chariots, lashing the panting teams in the traces, making my brothers cry out with the risks I took. Or I would spend hours entirely alone except for the river gods, my feet deep in the peaty water, drowsy with the scents of sage and mint. Above my head only an old eagle made hot circles, and glided off.

I knew the secret shrines in Dionysius. I would hide behind the sacrifice stone and see them burning their offerings, emptying flagons of wine, dancing wildly to drums and strings and bells. My own god was Artemis. She dwelt among the winds and the clouds, the surging pines, the fierce chatter of running water, the beat of hooves on the mountain. I spoke to her continually; we were co-warriors on the wind.

Perhaps that's why later I could not endure the terraces of Mycenae. The continual boiling of those stones. Nothing around but the rim of the burning mountains. Not a twig or a bush, a cloud or a leaf. Nowhere to hide from yourself. Brine-hazes off the sea burnt up as quick as the film of an eyeball. And then the blaze of all that gold, that parched empty glittering gold. Twice I was to go mad. Inspecting the dust, I had a delirium of fresh oaks fanning stiff spring leaves over pools with mossy boulders; I heard the beat of an antelope's hoof. I ran beyond the palace gates and had to be brought back. Afterwards they put it about that it was my longing that had shaped Agamemnon in a dust-cloud, returning from the wars.

My father was a squat, dark man, seething with avarice and ambition. All the time I was growing up he was counting what he could earn from Helen, who was so beautiful she could turn the minds of hermaphrodites and old women. He bought adornments for her as an investment, and pinned them to her with trembling hands, as she stood entranced, for hours at a time, before her own image in the long polished stones. And each day her beauty exceeded his estimates. Late in the night I would see the light at his window, his shadow humped over the table as he drove himself crazy with his revised calculations.

My mother was a vague and submissive woman. I had the feeling throughout my childhood that she was hardly there. She would go out to wander on the hillside, without so much as a spear or bow to protect herself, and there she was repeatedly raped by the gods in one form or another. Though on one occasion she hit the jackpot and bore Helen, on many others, which are not mentioned, she bore monstrous and disfigured creatures: creatures with slimy tails or webbed feet, ears like asses and toes in their nostrils. These all had to be taken away secretly at dead of night and left on the hillside. I think the grief of these repeated pregnancies may have cracked her wits. She would hum to herself and scatter flowers. Towards the end of her life she suffered from prolapsis of the womb; her womb fell out and hung between her legs, making it difficult for her to walk. She would spend all day in the house, never going out. She tied herself up with woollen cloths, partly to keep things as much as possible in their proper places, and partly, I think, to protect herself finally from the trauma of those earlier experiences. But it was too late. I remember her sitting in front of the loom just staring at it. She had forgotten how to weave, but spent hours examining the pattern of the threads as if they had something to tell her; she would rock her head back and forth, hum to herself, and pick the petals out of flowers.

When she was dying she recovered her wits briefly and called me up to her. The flesh had melted off her face, which had become as fine as a bone needle. She looked like a young girl again, rather like Helen in fact. She signalled to me that I was to bend down. 'Be a . . . woman,' she croaked. I could not hear her. I bent closer. 'Be a . . . woman,' she repeated. Her eyes pawed my face like frightened animals. 'Good woman?' I said, my heart knocking between my ribs. She swallowed, gave a tiny movement of her head that I interpreted as assent, and sighed. A blue mottle spread all over her body. I reached forward and pulled shut her eyes, whose wide staring terror had frightened me.

I do not blame my mother. She taught me what she could. It is from her, after all, that I learnt how to thread a needle and skim a shuttle in several colours. And though I would rather have driven chariots, I am not entirely sorry. In the early months on the hot terraces when they gibbered at me violently in their strange tongue, her songs were my only comfort. In them I recovered my home, the hills and streams, the wooded shrines and flowers of Sparta.

Yes, my mother taught me many things. And I am not ungrateful. But one thing she didn't teach me. She did not teach me how to fight. She didn't teach me how to block and parry, fist and shove. She didn't teach me how to resist and butt, assault and batter. She did not teach me how to kill. She taught me how to step aside, how to cower and how to shrink. Because any man, however brutal or ill-seeming, however wretched and paltry a creature he might be, was greater than I. And she taught me how to shield my head and beg, when he should choose to prove it.

So how could I resist the visions when they came? I had gone beyond you, mother, by many years. For they invited me to dream of power. I ran a kingdom after all, for ten years, a woman, alone. And when I began to dream there was no stopping; there were no roots to hold me fast. You hardly thought of this, did you, when you tossed on that bed, reached down to cut the cord and said with an exhausted grunt: 'Too bad, a girl.' But that girl became a legend. Her name was remembered through all history. She would not lie down. Oh yes, their frantic pens damned her beyond all circles of hell, beyond all the rivers of Styx, all fields of the dead, but they could not leave her alone. Her name excited them more than the others, it burnt in their veins like a poison. Cly – tem – nestra!

After my mother's death, my father decided it was time to

start realising his capital. So he married me to Tantalus, son of Thyestes. 'Daughter,' he said, calling me down into the hall where a large man with a great deal of beard was standing. 'Here is your husband. He has great flocks and acres of land. He is famous, nephew to Atreus, ancient king of the Greeks. Be a good woman. Obey him.' I did not look at the man, but walked straight up to my father. I threw my chariot whip to the floor. 'I will not marry him,' I said. 'I will remain single, a virgin to Artemis.' On the night of my wedding, I was still black and blue from the thrashing he gave me.

For a year I was two people. When he climbed on top of me, I vanished. I was no one, a creature without time or space or history. Small as dust, wide as the air. Only on the mountains, at my shrines, I was myself again. I began to learn hatred, the type that deposits itself slowly, drop by poisoned drop, like the lignification of a tree.

Then I came back from the hillside one evening and found my husband dead. He was slaughtered by the altar of the house. So too was my child. A man with even more beard than Tantalus stood astride the bodies, holding a thick sword steaming with entrails, staring at it with large eyes high in his head like a sheep. My father was kissing the bloodied greaves of this man and whimpering. 'Please! Have any gold you want! Have the goats! The oil! The wine!' He caught sight of me. 'Have her!' he said. 'She's hardly used. I'll give a big dowry.'

When I arrived in Mycenae they gave me shining garments. They gave me chemises made of silver thread and capes made of gold. They gave me tunics woven of wool and dyed purple – a royal Tyrian – in the crushed veins of the shellfish murex. They gave me jewels: diadems of opal and garlands of sapphires from the mines of Ethiope; crowns and harnesses made from the gold leaf which their own craftsmen fashioned, half-blind and cross-legged, beating it out all day long in the dusty alleys with their fine hammers. The gold that was so plentiful they shovelled it into the graves of their dead kings. They gave me goblets and sandals, pigments to paint myself with and amphorae decorated with wonderful medusas or the tales of their battles, that stored oil and wine, and kept the water cool.

And for a whole year he did not bother me. He wanted me to want him of my own accord. The pride of that man knew no bounds.

He assumed that after the fits of grief, the storming and the weeping, after the vicious rages, the gold cast shattering across the floors, the water jars broken, after all the songs for Lacedaemon and the nights of insomnia, tossing wild on a too-soft bed and swearing my hatred, I would exhaust myself. Then I would fall into a calm. I would commit the treachery of sleeping beneath a foreign sky. When I woke, sweet morning would assert itself. The blood of youth would steal along my veins. And when desire had unfurled itself inside me, my eye would fall upon him, the greatest of the Greeks, a man made like a god and a hero; and I would say: 'Ah well, after all it is a king.'

But he had not counted on Briomene.

Sometimes, when I came back from playing on the hillside, my mother would emerge from her dreamy state, and say: 'Clytemnestra, what is that strange plait you have made in your hair? It is not at all attractive dear. The hair must be worn flowing, in the manner of the gods. You should take a note from Helen.' Or: 'Clytemnestra, what is that way you have of standing. Your legs apart and hips jutting. It is not at all ladylike. You should examine the statues, dear.' And once, when she found a sickle-shaped cut on my cheek, decorated with small red spots, she became truly angry. I was beaten by my father and locked in my room for three days. But I would not confess.

For it was a love-mark, the mark of Briomene's people.

Briomene came from the land of the Nile, and her people built the mountains of yellow brick that grazed the sky. She was picked up by ships from Greece when she was a child and sold into slavery. My father took a fancy to her at the market and brought her home for his amusement. The rest of the time she worked the fields, digging ditches, grafting and splinting the olives like a man.

She had eyes like ebony, deep and softly gleaming. And when she moved, it was like watching water or flame: there was no seam.

We met in the granaries at dusk. It took me a whole month to make her look up at me. We whispered fierce and quiet amongst the drifts of golden chaff, while outside, in the trees, the nightingale sang.

She told me the stories of her people, their gods and magic. She told me of women with the heads of eagles who brandished serpents and sceptres; she told me of men with the heads of rams. She told me of snakes that did not hide themselves in bushes but moved openly, whipping sideways on the sand. And she told me that this life is a series of stations that must be passed through, one by one, like houses left vacant, until you reach the real home of the soul, which is the sun.

It was from Briomene that I learnt the secret of myself. It was she who kissed me to life on the nape of my neck, in the hollow of my elbow, my rounded belly, the soles of my feet, the place between my thighs. All these areas I learnt to love because of her. Her tongue made bright blossoms fall out of the darkness in front of me; and through her I learnt my own existence. I learnt my strength and nature, my authority, how to glide like an eagle on the wings of my own power. And the last thing she taught me was how to defend myself. If they came gently, she said, I was to be a flower of nectar, and afterwards I was to love them. But if they came brutally, like a thief in the night – and here she shook her head and frowned and I knew she was thinking of my father – I was to turn myself immediately to a mouth of knives.

Much later, when I realised what it meant to be queen, I sent messengers secretly all over the empire. But my father had got tired of her and sold her to a merchant from Smyrna. There was no trace.

After a year the hatred of Agamemnon's courtiers exhausted me and I conceded. But I had learnt from Briomene, and he found no satisfaction. Each time, he toppled from me with the same expression that was on his face the day he killed Tantalus: a smirk, modified at the edges by a shadow of self-doubt. Of course he preferred the dancing girl, Chryseis.

And then Orestes was born. He was the loveliest thing I had ever dreamt, and for a while I was almost reconciled. He was a slip of sunlight, running water, a joyful thought made flesh. He chattered all day, and brought me the wild flowers that grew between the crevices of the palace walls. He pulled the silver threads from my loom, wondering at their shine, and splashed in the waterjars, to make the handmaids laugh. He asked for songs, and more songs, always the songs of Leda, which I had almost forgotten. I fed him from my own milk, perhaps too long.

And the priests watched us. They watched with jealous eyes, covetous and hot. There is nothing more dangerous than an old priest. There is the grave in front and a life of murdered desire behind. Whatever you hide from them, they will spy out, and what they cannot spy, they will invent. Their thoughts split and multiply themselves, like a pit of angry vipers.

Calchas, chief of the oracle, was the worst.

He said Orestes had been too long at the breast of his mother, so he was taken from me and given to a tutor. They turned my lovely laughing boy, the youth who delighted the handmaids, into a replica of his father. A boor, short in wits and ripe in swagger, who boasted of ripping the head off a horse and rooting in its entrails. He learnt to sneer at women. 'Mother,' he said thickly in exact mimicry of his father, when I tried to take the flagons from him for he was still only a child. 'Go to your woman's work, can't you?' and banged the table. How they roared with pride, and Agamemnon the loudest.

But it was not so simple. For Orestes had taken in my language, my songs, my thoughts, with my milk. He was always torn. I pitied him: for what person is more pitiable than the one who must kill the person he loves to prove his love for the person he hates? When Orestes saw his father dead he could not rest till he had cleared himself. But he loved me above all others. That only a fool would deny.

When the news came that Helen had run off with Paris I was not surprised. Helen had grown up in a kind of trance of self-love. Her beauty had taken her beyond herself, and made her forget her function as property for investment. It was hardly surprising that the lovely Paris, wooing her with poetry and wit, youth and opportunities for travel, should win her heart. I wished her luck, until I heard that the whole Greek army was going to Troy to recover her.

And that was when Calchas struck his second blow. Not content with taking one child, he demanded the life of another, my darling daughter Iphigeneia.

I have observed that the men of this country combine extreme boastfulness with great metaphysical cowardice. I have not found one that is prepared to think for himself. Even Aegisthus, when he first slept with me, had to burn a score of thigh bones to appease the gods. We exhausted our passion with torches flaming all around the bed, and the reeking smell of fat. It did not occur to him that by our act we had placed ourselves beyond all law, beyond any possibility of appeasing those gods. And later, when we plotted to take the king's life, he was the same; he scarcely had time to remember the speeches I taught him, so intent was he on his sacrifices, working the altars with trembling hands.

For me it was different.

On the day when Agamemnon killed my daughter, when I saw him lift her onto the altar at Aulis, with the same expression on his face that he had when he killed Tantalus, and when he rolled his great body off mine each night, in the very moment that he lifted his knife against her young flesh, I knew there were no gods.

I looked up at the sky, blank blue and pitiless, and knew it for what it was. Empty of everything except my own invention. I swore a mighty curse against all priests, against Calchas and the oracles, and above all, against the king, my husband, this 'father' who for the price of a wind to send him to Troy, had murdered his own daughter.

I folded the hatred into my heart. Pleat by pleat and square by careful square. I folded it the way you fold a deed of property to a kingdom, or the broad beautiful cloths I spent my days weaving, length after vivid length, waiting for the day when he would return from Troy and I would spread them in the red banners of revelation beneath his feet.

I took Aegisthus for my lover. I chose him because he was an exile, a man without a patrimony. He knew the pangs of famished revenge, disinherited, as he was, by Agamemnon. I took him for his shame. He was the offspring of his father's union with his own daughter. It made him walk always a little stooped.

Oh yes, Aegisthus was a dark, shambling, shame-faced, restless man. Product of a house that had turned on itself, to devour its own flesh. And he suited me.

We met in the long afternoons, in the colonnades by the baths. I taught Aegisthus the secrets that Briomene had taught me and he learnt willingly. Perhaps his self-doubt had given him more capacity for kindness than other men. For ten years we were happy, with that desperate reckless kind of happiness of people who have taken themselves beyond the law.

But all that time I knew I was waiting. And when, with a sudden premonition, I saw the whirling speck of dust below me on the Argolid plain, it was as if ten years had fallen away to a day. It was yesterday that Agamemnon had heaved his body onto mine, yesterday that he had turned my son against me, yesterday that he murdered my daughter like a goat on the altar at Aulis.

My hands shook, not with fear, but exhilaration.

Aegisthus lost his nerve completely. The desire for revenge, too long unsatisfied, had rotted inside him, weakening him. 'We have done something terrible,' he said, 'Terrible!' and he began to torch the altars in contrition.

'Are you mad?' I said. 'We have much worse to do. Now listen!'

All night, while the beacons flamed the news of Agamemnon's triumph at Troy, I rehearsed him in his speeches of welcome. Then in the morning I sent him to the coast. I knew that Agamemnon's pride was our greatest ally. Such pride would never examine a speech for flattery, unctuousness for deceit, hospitality for malice. The total abasement of the rest of humanity was always his due. So he would accept Aegisthus's offer, and come to the halls to feast.

I was waiting in the colonnades. In the torchlight. With my axe.

It is said that the floor ran with blood. That the mixing bowl was overturned and the cries rang for miles. It is said that Agamemnon died like an ox in a stall, and all his followers with him. It is said that I turned away while Agamemnon beat the ground with his hands and would not look, and that I would not even close his eyes for him when he was on the point of going down into Hades.

It is all true.

But what is not spoken of is my joy.

I was filled from the bottom-most particle of me to the top with astonishing joy. In the blows that I brought down on his head, I was alive for the first time in my life. It was a miracle, as if that killing of another taught me my own existence. It was better even than the time with Briomene.

Afterwards, I did not care what happened. I ruled two years, three years, perhaps even ten. I cannot really remember. And of course, they came for me in time.

My poor Orestes. Smuggled out of the land to become his sister's killing machine. But his hand shook on the axe he lifted above me; his eyes were wretched. Only Electra, her back pressed to the door, screaming at him 'Strike! Strike! Strike her down as she struck my father!' made him do it.

And Electra, that poor desperate child, living in a fantasy of her father. A father who would have sacrificed her like any goat for any priest with a poisoned heart. I was her protectress, though she would never admit it. And in her nature she was more like me than she knew.

But I did not care. I did not care about any of it.

For that one act had taught me a truth that made me proof against it all. I learnt to be as tall as the blank and pitiless sky. As remorseless. I learnt that my nature is no different from it, blank and free and wild. I learnt my limits and my power. I had lived more in those seconds than in all the rest of my life. I had broken through from their laws and invented others.

They placed me in the long tombs and sealed up the entrances. They covered me with gold, and spoke the language I abhorred over my corpse when it could not defend itself. They thought they had fixed me.

But they could not quiet me. I am a problem that would not lie down. There were strange knockings in the mountainside, dreadful cries and labourings of the earth. All night, in the golden palace, the shape of their fears would pursue them in their dreams: knives and daggers, adzes and axes, the soft curves of a woman's arm raised in vengeance. And though they would rather have forgotten me, I had a tendency to stalk the pages of the greatest of their writers.

And for many years Orestes was hunted, house to house, land to land, by the vengeful Furies.

The Turfcutter's Medicine

Jimmy Kavanagh often feared he was cutting into flesh when he sank the slane in the wet earth. He heard tell of many bodies disappearing in bogs, drifting with their screams and coming to rest among the rotting trees. Plenty of times he'd dreamt of coming across a swollen finger pointing out, or a bloated foot, and he'd pictured faces in the blackness with O on their mouths and hollows in their eyes. Some evenings he saw as many as twenty with arms outstretched, pleading.

Jimmy worked faster to blot them out. On a good day he could turn 900 sods. There was an art in it. He'd been cutting turf nearly ten years by the time Pat Madden bought land next to his. Pat was dead four years and his daughter who upped and married the Greek was easily thirty by now so he was slaning the best part of forty-five years.

He left down the slane and surveyed a day's work. He was slowing a bit but then he was no young chicken either. He spat into his hands and looked up. Moist earthy smells always raised his spirits and made him a cheerful giddy. He blinked away the sweat seeing lots of colours in the sky, greens and blues and patches of pink.

The sun had gone a while. The ground was still warm but the long evening's waltz with summer was nearly over. Jimmy walked back to the lines of turf he'd footed the previous day. There was good drying, a lot of the sods were turning to a lighter brown at the edges. He filled the wooden barrow and led it to where he had the stacks. Rows of waist-high bee-hived stacks of turf lined a stone track that ran to his house. It was just possible to see part of the black slate roof from here. The rest was guarded by a big gnarldey hawthorn which was flat-headed from the prevailing wind.

He topped off some of the stacks with care and precision, making sure they were nicely rounded. When the barrow was empty he set off for home.

Smooth stones pressed and tucked into the soles of his feet through worn boots. He knew the feel of every ridge and at times he'd give a half hop out of his stride to see if he'd come across one he hadn't met before. The first thing when he got into the house was dispense with the boots and into the slippers. The fire was going grand. He poked it and threw on a few more pieces of turf. Jimmy kept a fire year in year out. He couldn't remember a fire not being on the go. Every night he banked it by burying a fresh sod among the embers. A pot of beef and barley was simmering on the stove. He'd tell P.J. the next time he came that there was one of the best cuts of meat he'd given him ever. P.J. came on the Tuesday with the travelling shop, rain or shine. Even the time when he burst his ankle jumping down off the van P.J. was there on the day. Tuesday was the day of plenty. P.J. had everything from eggs to alcohol on his shelves.

Jimmy always ate supper looking at the fire. Two tinkers came to the door one day trying to sell him a television. He told them to go away as he had his own station. Small bright tongues of orange and yellow stuck out and he saw the same people from the bog dancing in the flames. They seemed happier, livelier at least. Little pieces of his own past mingled with the different molten figures. He saw his mother's hands rubbing together and the shape of his father's shoulders. It was comforting. Jimmy had heard of men who could tell the future by gazing into fires. He looked hard at the burning shapes and tried to concentrate. Nothing more came. He smoked a cigarette, had a cup of tea with a drop of whiskey in it and went to his bed. He imagined the sky lighting up with an explosion and became afraid. Then he slept.

He woke with the wind pushing against his bedroom window and remembered part of a dream with him in Ryan's dance hall as a young man. He looked sharp in a fresh white shirt that glowed under his chin. There was a woman looking over at him. He was startled by the dark gaze of her. Then she was gone just as he'd built enough courage to ask her up.

Raking squawks of crows surrounded the house. Jimmy put porridge on the stove and a couple of eggs in the pan to tempt his appetite. He brought out the boots for a polish. Greet every day with a pair of shining shoes – his grandfather's advice. The morning was cold for August. Through the window the scutch grass and furze were glistening a heavy dew. The sky was a motley of toffee brown, grey and white. Jimmy was an early bird, always was. Catching each sunrise was like learning the quietest new secret. The sun began to stretch long angular beams over a grumpy hill in the distance and its slopes became a velvet baize.

Jimmy heard a scratching at the door. He opened it and in strolled Hughie the cat, bold as you like. 'Good morning Master Hugh, nice of you to drop in.' Hughie ignored him and padded into the room, rubbing against the legs of the chair and table. He climbed up to a commanding perch on top of the dresser and peered down at Jimmy. He was a wild tom that sometimes took to sleeping indoors. He had lime-green marbled eyes that spoke in a stare. His coat was jet black except for the dab of white on his chin, the nape of his neck and the spotless gentleman's gloves on his paws. Jimmy reckoned there was something noble about the cut of Hughie and on occasion took to calling him 'your lordship'.

With the slane over his shoulder Jimmy walked the path to the stacks. From thirty feet away he saw something askew. Some of the stacks had been disturbed as if the tops had been blown off but there'd been no storm last night and there was no missing turf lying around. The thought hit him like a blow to the head. Somebody had stolen his turf. Someone had lifted a few bags for themselves. Never in all the years this, never before, never, bastards, dirty bastards, dirty filthy dirty dirty stinking dirty bastards. He saw where feet had trampled grass near the stacks and found some discarded sods on the ground.

The choosy cur had taken his time for sure. Jimmy hadn't felt as furious since he knocked John Keogh to the ground in a row over slating the roof at the back of the house. John Keogh had asked him for more than the price agreed and then called him a name. Jimmy put him down on the flat of his back with his right fist. Again he felt the sickening anger in his stomach. And the roof still leaked in places.

He followed the path to the road. He picked up two fallen sods. Oh yes he'd taken the lazy man's load as well. There were tyre marks in the grass margin of the small road. He would have heard the car coming and going. Not if the crafty bugger came the back road with the engine switched off. It was down-hill from Pat Madden's to well past his house. He could coast down with the incline to get back on the main road at Bowden's pub. Like cowardly vermin coming in the dark, snapping at your heels. The anger was close to tears. I'll have you, bastard.

He went back to the stacks and counted the damage. About five bags worth at the most. That would have taken at least two runs up the path at it. He'd make that up in a couple of hours but that wasn't the point. The poison. The sheer poison, like a snake had slithered off leaving some of it in him. He set to work like a demon and nearly wore himself out after half an hour. He propped himself against the handle of the slane. He felt dizzy and his legs were going from under him. Pull yourself up straight man. Keep the chin up. Don't let it take anything out of you. Then he cursed the slow-moving clouds and the scattered trees and the stone walls and the mountains and the birds and God for watching an old man cry.

He started cutting again, going at his own steam remembering 'the hastier you are the behinder you get'; and other words his mother said flowed over him like a soft balm.

There was a full moon that night. Jimmy sat by the window and looked hard at it. He'd heard of men going mad for less. Slowly a face became clearer looking down at him. There could be hundreds looking up at that face at the same time, or no one at all. He felt like a silver statue. The moon throbbed and grew bigger. Jimmy opened his eyes wider. So what would you do mister if someone stole your turf. A dull cloud in the shape of a horse and chariot slipped past the moon and rode on. The moon had a disinterested smile. Thank you. The chant of a lone hawk stabbed the silence.

Jimmy looked at his reflection in the window. He saw himself again as a young man with a proud face, not vain. The determined look in the glass gave him courage. The sky was full of cloud, blackberry seas and oceans tossed before him. The moon stood back in a blue- and brown-ringed frame. A tiny star flickered in black. Outside hawthorn and furze and bush were frozen in a silent vigil. Jimmy felt a light, tingling energy surge through him. Then he apologised formally in his thoughts to each and every thing he had cursed that afternoon. P.J. was due the next day. Better to say nothing or the whole county would be laughing at him. Jimmy slept in the chair by the window with Hughie in his lap.

'Nothing strange Jimmy?' 'Nothing much P.J.' 'I see you're building the great wall of China with the turf, you'll be doing sentry duty on it soon.' 'That was some cut of meat you gave me last Tuesday P. J.' 'Stop it, I'm too good to you – all right for the tea and sugar?' 'I'm sweet enough, how much can you do me for?' 'Ah, I'm too soft call it eighteen pounds even, and that includes the spuds.' 'Go on you larrier P.J. the softest part of you is your teeth.'

The travelling shop bumped up and down the track to the road and disappeared.

Jimmy had thought of asking P.J. in for a cup of tea or a stronger drop but he left it, thinking P.J. might find out there was something amiss, might catch a look in his eyes. If a man couldn't protect his property he wasn't worth a hen egg. And what if that thieving cur came back. Would he stop now? Like hell he would – an old man and a cat wouldn't stop him. Jimmy felt darts of pain in his chest. He had pain like it before. The doctor said it was to do with his heart and had a long name for it in Latin. Jimmy had kept the bottle that he'd got on the prescription behind a picture on the mantelpiece. The picture was of two Highlander bulls in the wild that somebody had brought back as a souvenir from Scotland. Jimmy didn't know who had brought it back. It was there since he was a little child but for the first time the bulls didn't look wild any more. They looked sad and tired from standing on the same mantelpiece for too long.

The label on the brown glass bottle read: 'Mr James Kavanagh . . . glycerol trinitrate tablets . . . two to be taken twice daily . . . keep out of the reach of children.' The doctor had made efforts to explain the chest pains to him at the time, mentioning ventricles in the heart and valves opening and closing. Jimmy hadn't had much cause for doctors. He wouldn't even have taken the pills if it hadn't been for Mrs Clarke at the chemist's insisting that they'd work if he'd follow the instructions. There were two tablets left in the bottle. He'd never been able to believe that the pills were the cause of the pain going away but he'd no better explanation. He put the two pills on his tongue, swallowed and washed down the bitter dry taste with a mouthful of lukewarm tea from the pot. The small empty bottle felt snug in his hand and he squeezed it tightly, daring it to break and cut into his palm, gashing and hurting. He tried to imagine the face of the man who had stolen his turf in pain. The bottle stayed hard and warm in his hand. Jimmy sat in his chair for a while, his thumb and fingers rubbing the smooth contours of glass.

The afternoon was grey with thin drizzle coming from the north-west – a bad day for working outdoors. At the side of the house Jimmy lifted off some plastic fertiliser bags he used for covering his bike. He hadn't used it since Easter. There was a bit of rust on the rims of the wheels, everything else was sound. Jimmy looked up at the sky. Those clouds were down for the day but at least there was no wind and with a bit of luck he'd make it to Lonergan's petrol station and back an hour before dark. He closed the front door looking around for Hughie. There was no sign. Worse you're getting Jimmy, thinking the cat would look after the house. He set off at a steady pace with the squeak in a pedal keeping time.

Lichen-smattered stone walls and rain-laced hawthorns drifted by. Jimmy pedalled faster and felt rewarded with tiny warm streams trickling down his cheeks. Water welled in his eyes and brown slashes of open banks of bog quivered and merged with grassy patches and slender wisps of bog cotton. He passed Matt Mahon's cottage. There was no one in it now, Matt's widow was living with their daughter's family a few miles back. The cottage was badly in need of a lick of paint and there were black bags tied over the chimneys to keep rain and crows out. The curtains in the windows were faded and torn. Weeds sprouted from the bulging thatch roof.

He ploughed on past Bowden's pub, past Willie Byrne's, not pausing for breath until he reached the outskirts of town. There was a young girl no more than twelve holding the fort at Lonergan's petrol station. 'Can I help you?' 'And who are you girleen and have you no school to go to?' 'My name is Annie Lonergan – Peter Lonergan is my Grandad, we've no school today because there's a teachers' meeting and I'm looking after the shop here while my brother goes and collects his good shoes that had to be mended because he was playing football in them and they were almost brand new.' 'Is that a fact? Well girleen you can do me a service. Do you see this little bottle here, see if you can fill it with petrol for me without spilling any.' 'Do you want super or regular or what?' 'Doesn't matter a whit girleen as long as it's petrol.' The girl held the nozzle of the pump carefully as the petrol dribbled into the small bottle in Jimmy's hand. 'I spilt a little bit.' 'I don't think it'll break the bank. How much do I owe?' 'Thirty-eight pence.' Jimmy handed her a pound note. 'Get a few toffees for yourself.' 'Thank you very much.' 'Thanks yourself.' Jimmy made sure the cap on the bottle was secure before slipping it into his coat pocket. Then he started the cycle home. It always seemed longer on the way back. The rain had stopped and there was a wind coming up with a cold bite in it. Overhead a flock of birds flew by in a lazy wavering V, off to warmer places if they had any sense. He was in a strange sort of mood, not happy, not sad, and nothing in between. He whistled and sang the verses of any songs he could remember for most of the journey back. Before he reached the house he collected a large damp sod of turf from a stack and carried it back with him.

After tea, Jimmy rooted through the drawer of the dresser and found an old pen-knife. It was stiff to open. He ran his finger carefully along the blade – sharp enough. He sat beside the fire and started to carve a small rectangular hole in the damp sod of turf. He saved what he cut from the sod on a sheet of newspaper. He pared the edges slowly, stopped to inspect it, then continued on. When he was satisfied he went to his coat and took the bottle from the pocket. He turned the bottle upside-down and shook it to make sure there was no leakage from the cap. He pressed the bottle into the sod – nearly there. He scooped a bit more and widened the edges. This time the bottle slotted neatly in – perfect fit. Using a cup of water he moistened the small pieces of turf he had cut from the sod and worked them back in on top of the bottle. When he had filled the hole he looked at the sod closely and away at arm's length, then he propped it a safe distance from the fire to dry.

Jimmy saw some more figures from the bog in the fire that night. They were waving and enticing him to join them. There was a black door at the back of the fire and Jimmy saw himself opening it. There was another black door behind it surrounded in flames and another behind that. When Jimmy tried to shut his eyes tightly all he saw were tiny orderly flames like stars dancing around his head.

The thief was back a fortnight to the day. What surprised Jimmy was the lack of anger he felt about it. Again the stacks nearest the path to the road were the ones interfered with and there were sods strewn along the trail. He took a bit more this time, stocking up for the winter. Well good luck and sorrow mend you. He collected the fallen sods and brought them back to the stacks. The sod with the bottle was gone.

A week went by.

'That was a heavy fall of frost last night Jimmy. Did you hear about those two brothers back at Lough na Fuaidh the other night?' 'What about them P.J.?' 'Some kind of explosion in the house. The story is they are no strangers to the drop of poitín.' 'What happened to them P.J.?' 'One still in shock with minor burns and the other is in the Regional. He lost an eye. Joe Mac told me, his daughter's a nurse. The fellah who lost the eye was babbling about seeing faces in the fire and then it blew up in his face. Oh they'll be all right I suppose. Imagine a fire exploding like that. Scare the life out of you. I'll see you on Tuesday Jimmy.' 'Good luck P.J.'

Jimmy waited until the travelling shop was out of sight then walked back to the open door of the house. The shock of the news was beginning to wear off. The wind was cooling his forehead and the sweat along the side of his neck. P.J. hadn't suspected anything. Nobody was any the wiser. The relief from the trouble and the constant worry was starting to make him feel light-headed. They won't be back. All his senses were growing stronger and more aware. He took a few deep breaths quickly and felt slightly drunk with a ringing in his ears. He could hear every living sound clearly and the deep regular thud that was a great drum beating in his body.

The medicine had done the job. His heart felt fine.

Promised Lands

Extract from a novel in progress

Sydney Cove, New South Wales, 28 January 1788

William couldn't sleep. The ground was hard as iron, and lumpy, after his hammock. And still: each time he managed to drop off, the unyielding stillness of the ground permeated his body and woke him in a sweat. He felt his own heart would stop beating. Its motion was too alien. Stillness would overwhelm it. He could not remember feeling like this after other long voyages. Now the lack of the waves' motion was an absence. As if a mother who gently rocked his cradle while he slept had withdrawn herself, leaving him alone as the dead in darkness. There was a chill in the night air too, draughting in through the tent flap, and a tinge of smoke, and the smell of land – distance – instead of the warm soothing fug of quarters aboard ship.

After the third waking he lay with his eyes open, listening to night sounds, telling himself there was nothing to be afraid of. Tench's breathing was soft and regular, he was sound asleep. From outside the tent, that same fitful breeze that brought the drifts of smoke brought snatches of distant voices – or maybe that murmuring talk was the wind in the leaves, not human at all. He told himself that outside there would be stars; a skyful, now, at quarter moon. Why not take the glass and charts and measure the positions of the brightest? But his body did not move, it had become as still and unresponsive as the ground it lay on. He was afraid.

He lay so rigidly still that pins and needles began to spread through his left arm and shoulder. He made himself sit up, bowing his head to his pulled-up knees, clasping his arms

around them. What was there to fear? The size, the stillness of
the land? Land cannot hurt you. Attack from the natives? A
watch was posted. But they would not attack. Besides, he was
not afraid of a skirmish, he was not afraid of danger: a fight
was a quick and obvious thing. No, he was afraid – perhaps . . .
of what would happen. Not in its minutiae – not in hard work
digging and sawing and measuring and drawing; not in tangles
with Phillip or the discomforts of insect bites or working in the
heat; not even in hunger, or mutiny, or sickness, not in physical
danger . . .

He was afraid in spirit. Afraid of this place. Afraid of presuming to act, presuming to have meaning – afraid, ludicrously, of
being inappropriate. Of being made nothing.

He *was* afraid, he checked his breathing and forced himself to
inhale more slowly, deeply – and to exhale in the same slow
rhythm. His heart was racing. It was foolishness. The future
was plain; having arrived safely, for which they must continue
to thank God, they would build a settlement and carve a home
in this wilderness. The convicts would be set to work and
would be reclaimed as worthful human beings, able to cultivate
and enjoy the fruits of their own honest toil. He would build an
observatory and chart these new skies, and watch the progress of
Maskeylene's comet – and other unknown heavenly bodies –
night by night. In so doing he would add to the sum of human
knowledge, and to the safety of all who sailed the southern seas.
He would do his duty as a marine, guarding the settlement
from attack by natives without and from rebellious convicts
within. And he would observe and learn from this new land,
cataloguing its strange array of flora and fauna, making friendly
contact with the innocent savages who roamed the woods, and
discovering the secret of their language and religion. This would
enable him and others to spread the word of Christ among
them. He would explore, build, observe, record, enlighten. He
would be instrumental in the establishment of this new world,
and he would try, from the bottom of his heart, to make it such
a New World as God might approve.

Well then. How, afraid? How, presumptuous? How, inappropriate? What bogeys of negative value, what black shadows was
he conjuring? How could such an enterprise be worthless? If
that was worthless, then what was there of value in the world?
Wouldn't other men – men in England – give their eye-teeth
for an adventure with such challenge and purpose?

But the challenge and purpose, though he could articulate
and itemise it, was, tonight, ethereal. While the land, the stony
hard ground, was all too real beneath him, his purposes seemed
wafer thin: painted scenery to this hard rock; a frippery thing
that might be blown away in the next gust of wind. He might
be, simply, nothing. A leaf on a tree. A speck in the dark.
Nothing. And in the end it might be as if he had never existed.
This land might obliterate him: obliterate them all.

It was an illogical fear and all the resources of his intellect
strained to argue it down. Because it was not even the fear of
failure – was it? Even if they failed, they would have failed in a
noble attempt. No; it was the fear of being completely, insanely
irrelevant. Of performing actions which could have no value.
Of displaying courage which was worthless.

His tensed buttocks ached where they pressed on the stony
ground; he could feel the bony imprint of his knees on his
forehead, through the thin layer of blanket. And in this uneasy
position he slumped into sleep at last, waking again with a jerk
as the first rays of the rising sun penetrated the tent flap.

His heart lifted at the light. Tench was still snoring peacefully.
Dawn meant it was nearing 5.30; soon they would beat reveille.
He shuffled stiffly from his blankets and crawled out, taking his
rolled-up trousers with him. The camp was completely still,
strangely lit by the horizontal rays of a sun just emerging from
the rim of the Pacific. He pulled on his trousers and boots, and
turned away from the sun and the dazzling sea. The tents he
passed were silent – a pathos of empty boots stationed near each
flap. He was surprised not to see the look-outs pacing, but then
noticed them down away to his left, crouched over a kettle on

a small smoky fire. He saluted them silently and they jumped up belatedly and returned the salute.

His shadow was a stripe of darkness preceding him into the wood. Nothing moved – nothing – only he. In the sharp early light colours were very bright against the dark backgrounds of their shadows. The grey Australian plants were almost an English green, in this light; there was a rich luminous edge to everything – a kind of perfection. He noted with surprise the lack of dew. Two brilliant blue butterflies, their wings like the eyes on a peacock's tail, danced before him, plaiting the air with colour. The silence was broken by a sudden racket of bird noise; a fast, repetitive, single-note call which he traced to a gum tree ahead. In silhouette against the pale sky the bird was the shape of a kingfisher, only too big; the same sharp dart of a beak. It did not fly off as he drew nearer; the call, which had been alarming at first, now began to seem more like laughter. It was answered by a faint, distant, copycat call. The trackless space became territory, the territory of a pair of laughing birds.

Suddenly he felt less like a trespasser; not minding so much the crunches and crackles of his own footfalls, now the silence was broken. Almost imperceptibly the land had been rising, and he now found himself on the crest of a gentle slope, able to look out over a great expanse of scrub ahead, which melted away into a lavender-blue distance.

As he stopped to take in the view he had the curious impression that the bushes in the middle distance were shifting – were moving. Staring more intently, then, he made out that they were not bushes at all, but animals – quite large animals, with the bulk of their bodies upright like a man's – tall animals, who moved hesitantly then froze. He took a step forward. And suddenly, they were off – moving in great leaping bounds, through the bushes they so exactly resembled – bouncing like rubber balls over the ground, large ones, small ones. All suddenly in motion – and as suddenly, gone. It must be the creature Banks had drawn; that strange marsupial kangaroo. The sudden exhilaration of their movement had made him catch his breath.

He let it go now, slowly, eyes straining across the still grey landscape for any further motion.

The sun was already hot on his neck; hot in earnest, like a banked-up fire. He turned to look back the way he had come; the same still trees and bushes, the pale smooth trunks of the gums, with their long irregular branches, and glitter of leaves; the sudden dart of a red and green parrot from one bush into another. He noticed that the bush itself was red and green, with small red flowers whose thin petals stood up like hairs.

Quite suddenly, he had a sense that it would resolve. This dreadful huge stillness would resolve. Into moving creatures; moments of beauty; sudden brilliant flashes of sound and colour; unknown shapes of beasts and flowers. Suddenly he was in Eden, and he was a child – innocent – wide-eyed before its wonders. There were squawks and shrieks overhead and he looked up to see a great flock of birds passing over. Their plumage was grey – or maybe pinkish – the size of pigeons, he judged; but as they flapped their wings they concealed and revealed a patch of dark glowing pink on the inside of each wing – in their armpits, as it were – a hot, pulsing pink against the clear blue sky. He stared until distance swallowed them, and the huge blue arc of the heavens, and all the golden heat that was in it, made his head swim and float. The black night, with its pitiful tatters of fear, dropped away. He breathed in deeply and the strange smell of eucalyptus was a pleasure, and the flies that were settling on his chest and upper arms were a wonderful detail – enough to set him laughing aloud – for they seemed to want no more than to be carried upon his clothes, like sailors on a ship, and offered him no harm whatsoever.

He heard the drummers beat reveille while he was still making his way back. It sounded right. The drums belonged in this landscape: heralding civilisation, order, the gifts they could bring to a wild but peaceful land; a land which lay spread open wide before them like an offering.

Port Jackson, New South Wales, 29 January 1788

When the charting expedition's boats left Camp Cove, they were heading north for the point that divides south and middle harbours. The native women who had remained at the northerly end of the cove, in their canoes, jumped out and ran into the woods. Their men followed the boats, running along the shore up to the point where the women were hiding. It seemed that they feared their women being carried off.

William was overcome by waves of tiredness; he kept his eyes fixed on the distantly approaching shore, but it seemed to drift and dance in the sunlit water. How would it be if one day this series of bays and coves, with its pretty wooded shores and islands, its blue and green wilderness colours, became one of the world's great harbours? If it was busy with tall ships and barges and brigs; if storehouses and quays lined its shores, and roads, houses, shops, factories, were ranged on the hillsides? If narrower points were spanned by great bridges, like those over the Thames in London: if carts and carriages and pedestrians and livestock streamed across them, from one part of the city to another? He wondered if such a transformation was possible. He wondered what the natives would make of it. That was a little hard to imagine.

But once the natives understood the superiority of the white man's civilisation – might they not throw themselves whole-heartedly into the work of establishing a city? No, that wasn't right, there was a better reason for them to be glad of the English coming. . . . He was nearly asleep, and could not make his brain think. It was nonsense anyway, there were a thousand reasons for them to be glad. There were the English medical skills which would alleviate pains and illness; luxuries of food and drink of which their poor palates were insensible; the pleasures of culture – music, poetry, painting, books – reading. They would learn to read. And there was something else too. Ah yes, God, that was it, religion. His eyes closed. The sun was warm on the left side of his body.

If they thought we were spirits, as Bradley says, they would not expect us to stay. Only visit. They would imagine we lived elsewhere. The sky, or perhaps the sea. Mind you, Cook only visited. We are the first whites to stay. They may imagine we have other purposes. If strange beings arrived in England, how would we interpret them? He tried to imagine creatures whose purposes and appearance were entirely alien, and failed; in fact he could not imagine what it was he was trying to imagine or why, only a knotted kind of thread was lowering him down and getting darker, but with an anxiety which he couldn't quite make out. . . .

He woke with a start, and found his face buried in Bradley's shoulder.

'I'm terribly sorry, you should have woken me –'

Bradley smiled. He looked happy. 'It's all right. You can stay here. I'll do the measurements with Waterhouse.'

Belatedly William realised that they were anchored close in to the rocky shoreline, and that Bradley and two others were exchanging places with seamen in the small boat. This part of the coast seemed deserted. There were no natives, and no vessels in sight; only the moving sea, the wooded shores and the rocky outcrops above. It could be an unpeopled world.

He watched Bradley and Waterhouse scramble over the rocks in a business-like fashion and set their quadrants on a flat stone. He was pleased by their practicality. An unpeopled land was a terrible thought: the pointlessness, the waste of it. The sheer vegetable stupidity of the seasons circling over an uninhabited landmass; of seeds germinating, growing, flowering, withering – all unseen and unharvested by man; of trees providing shade; of streams flowing; of pasturelands growing, of fruits rotting. 'Where man is not, nature is barren.' With satisfying exactness, Pope's line capped his thoughts. The land was made to serve man, to be worked by him and to render back to him the fruits of his labour. The land was man's backdrop, his setting. Land without man would be as futile as a stage with no actors.

[Stephen broke off here.]

A stage with no actors. Beckett? . . . or Ionesco? Both, maybe. No you're thinking of Beckett's Breath *— curtain up on an empty stage, a breath indrawn for half a minute, exhaled for half a minute, curtain down. The inhalation and exhalation is the human element, the human breath is the actor. So that doesn't count. And Ionesco? — a stage full of furniture, I think. More and more furniture, proliferating. That of course presupposes a human presence, makes a comment on human behaviour, greed, love of material possessions, capitalism, etc. OK then, so far as I know no one has presented a stage with no actors. Prose writers have done human absence. Rooms without people; Virginia Woolf and her billowing curtains. But again, it's the absence that's the point. Painters have — yes. Painters are the ones who do nature without man.*

Really? Well . . . romantic views of gothic ruins. Craggy mountains with windswept forests. They're all humanised, aren't they? Pictures of moods. Sweet Samuel Palmer's hare on a hill; landscape aglow with human vision. Yes, but surely the point was at least man wasn't the central item in the pictures any more. Isn't that Romantic? They were interested in nature without man. Big views, big skies, little people almost afterthoughts, near the edges of the canvas. Not central. Didn't Wordsworth spend his days stalking nature on the lakeland hills — hunting its moral force, finding it where man was not? The mountain that reared its head when he stole a boat. The scene imbued with sense and moral value not by the human component (which was little and craven and naughty) but by the majestic hills. Where man is not, nature is splendid. Yes.

Oh the strong curving pleasure of an idea that runs! Now. Today. Greenies desperate to save the world's wildernesses. Lying down in front of bulldozers. Making a religion of rainforests. All industrial and architectural achievement seen as so much vandalism. Pollution. Extinction of species. Etc. Where man is, nature is raped and pillaged. Dug up, burnt down, blown to smithereens and covered with crap. (No, that would be recycling. Covered with nuclear waste.)

Where man is, nature is stuffed. And isn't it oh isn't it the glory of man? His ambition his greed his wanton excesses. Doesn't he have the innocent charm of a rampaging toddler, all ego all growth? He can destroy the planet that supports him — boldly bravely wilfully. Isn't it the most glorious thing of all that he can say FUCK IT! Eat drink slash and burn. For tomorrow we die. And if we lived like pennypinching wraiths on recycled corncobs and hairy handspun vests, what would it buy us? An extra century? An insult! For Christ's sake, blow it! Enjoy it! Spend spend spend!

He wonders if he could be more convincing. Don't you Stephen my boy. Wonders if there is maybe a touch of protesting too much. Wonders if he will be sussed entirely if he starts chanting 'Kill the whales! Kill the whales! Kill the whales!' He wonders what he thinks. Thank heavens for an innocent hero, living in simple times.

And where does that leave William Dawes, faced with a sealed, self-sufficient, harmonious continent, a viable ecosystem, untouched by white men?

Well, at a loss. What a fucking stupid question. The damn thing doesn't even exist for him. If a continent is in balance, if its predators and preyed-upon all flourish, if its animal and vegetable occupants have evolved to survive its ferocious climatic extremes; if black humans live in it without disturbing these natural balances, without so much as scarring the face of the earth by building or farming; intervening only to burn off an area from time to time, which stimulates regeneration: then so what? as far as William is concerned. So what. Because that is in the absence of Europeans. White men are not there to witness it. And therefore IT DOESN'T EXIST. It can't be acknowledged, or preserved, any more than a perfect ecosystem on Uranus could be. It is OUTSIDE the known. William cannot value it or lament the fact that it is under threat because it is not a thing he can know. All he can see is empty (going to waste) land. With a scattering of poor savages who don't even have the wit to build proper shelters. He does not have the words — the ideological equipment — to deal with the notion that it might, in any way, be better to not build than to build. It would be nonsense; literally, unthinkable. Thank you Stephen. Therefore William would not think it.

It's tedious anyway, straight up its own bum. Consumption = bad. Earth's resources = finite. The only thing to do, in all fairness, is to die in very great numbers, in order to give the earth a chance to

*regenerate and heal the damage inflicted by human presence. And if
we all died, well; there'd be a most satisfactory wilderness. And no
one to enjoy it. Where man is not, nature is barren.*

*But those paintings. There's something else to fish after, in that.
Start with Romantic landscapes; then you've got Constable, with his
terribly English domestic landscapes, oozing human presence. But then
what about Turner? What about Turner and sea and sky and no
humans? What about painting light, and having no interest whatsoever
in humans? Where man is not, sunsets are glorious. Right away, at
the edges of sea and sky, as far away from small pathetic land-creeping
man as possible. What about glorying in a world free of people?*

*It's not, though, is it. Because by some sleight of hand Turner has
become a transcendental expression of the soaring heights of the human
spirit. It's not actually extra-human (as in, extra-terrestrial); it's the
highest form of human. Like the last movement of Beethoven's Ninth.
Right then, a blind alley. A dried-up stream-bed. Return to William
Dawes. Who has, who will have a proper sense of man's insignificance
in the universe, despite being an eighteenth-century man and able to
quote Pope; because he is a stargazer. In gazing at the stars he can't
help but know there are movements, and destinies, beyond the human
scale, and that there are galaxies where man is not, and where he
cannot get close enough to know if they are barren, but that it might
be presumptuous to assume that so much and so many and so far are
all entirely barren: it might be reasonable to give them the benefit of
the doubt, as one would try also to give those poor noble savages the
benefit, and assume – if necessary in the face of evidence – that their
lives were not entirely brutish and barren. Yes. William is innocent
but not pompous; enlightened but not lacking in humility. He is on
his way to being romantic. He believes in freedom and equality, and
is opposed to the slave trade. He believes in noble savages. And in the
perfectibility of man. Here endeth the interruption.*

With Bradley and the others back in the boats, they headed
across the mouth of middle harbour to Grotto Point. The wind
had dropped, it was a glorious calm sunny evening, and a school
of dolphins was moving parallel to the boats, diving out of and
into the water with effortless energy.

The westerly side of Grotto Point was well sheltered, with no more than a slight swell to the water. Hunter decided they would sleep afloat, on the longboat. But they landed first and the men spread out across the beach, some to find a private spot to relieve themselves, others throwing out lines into the lapping shallows in the hope of catching some supper.

The fishermen were surprisingly successful, the fish had come right in on the tide and they pulled out one after another, twelve inches long and bigger. A fire was lit, and the seamen gathered around it cooking their fish and chatting quietly as darkness fell. William sat at a distance, enjoying the smells of smoke and cooking fish, keeping an eye out for the first stars. As the sea darkened it became velvety. The air was still warm, and the rocks he sat on, hot from the sun. He pulled off his boots and stockings, rolled up his trousers, and crossed the fine crunching sand to the water. It was shuddery cool, suddenly he felt wide awake and full of energy. There was Sirius, already more brilliant than he'd ever seen in England. And that – upside-down! – he worked out the belt, the arm, yes that was Orion.

'Mind the sharks, sir.' Nagle's voice called mockingly in the darkness.

'Lubbock's just caught a crab as big as yer 'ead, sir,' came another, warning voice. William searched for a witty reply but none came and the silence lengthened, so he simply said, 'I'm keeping a good lookout for crabs, Bryce,' and was rewarded with a couple of soft chuckles. That bright star to the South East – with the three fainter – Crux Australis? It must be. He had expected it to be overhead, though, no wonder he had not found it before. He stood staring, the blue of the sky was deepening, minute by minute, and the stars lit up against it like sparks on a chimney back. The only one to rival Sirius for brightness was directly overhead, he was not sure what . . . Perhaps it was Canopus, leader of Argo? He remembered the name from Maskeylene's charts. Suddenly he heard Bradley's voice, from the shore close by.

'Come and look at this, William.' He waded back, curling

his toes into the warmth of the soft sand at the bottom. Bradley was crouching over something on the sand. William squatted beside him.

'What is it?'

Bradley snorted, and whispered, 'It's stopped now, of course. Just hold still a minute and keep your eyes on this patch of sand.' William did as he was told, staring at the dark patch of sand just as he had earlier stared at the dark sky, waiting for a star to appear. Suddenly there was a spot of light in the sand. He leaned closer, but could make out nothing beyond the yellow speck.

'What is it?'

'I don't know. Something like a glow-worm, I imagine. It goes out – Ah!' As he spoke the thing went dark, and they both peered to make out the shape. But it was too dark – and it really did seem as if there was nothing there but flat sand – until the tiny light appeared again.

'It's surprisingly bright, for such a small creature.'

'Yes.' They stared at it in silence for a while, then William tilted his head to look up at the stars again. There were hundreds, now, the sky was brilliant with them. He smiled to himself at the perversity of staring at a minute faltering speck of light on the ground, while countless galaxies radiated a steady brilliance overhead. But the little light was near, the stars far far away. The little light was close enough to touch. He looked down for it and, with half the star-spangled night sky sweeping past his eyes, overbalanced. The sky seemed to reel around him in points of light; Bradley was holding him by the shoulder, heaving him into a kneeling position.

'Are you all right?'

'Yes – stupid – I looked up and lost my balance. Did I squash it?' his eyes searched the dark sand.

'I don't know. It's gone out, anyway.'

He was conscious of Bradley's warm hand still clasping his shoulder: suddenly conscious that they were both conscious of it, for a long moment in which he held himself utterly still, immobile. He felt his stillness communicate itself to Bradley, and Bradley got up quickly and stumbled away across the soft dark sand.

William remained on his knees, staring for the spot where the glow-worm had been, his mind as stopped as his body. When he permitted a thought, it was that he hoped the creature would light up again. But after five minutes' waiting he was getting cold. He got up stiffly and went over to the seamen's fire to warm himself. On the longboat he took a blanket aft, and quickly lodged himself in the first space he could find, securely hedged in by Waterhouse and Hunter.

[Stephen broke off here.]

This is an unnecessary complication, lad, and one that descendants of Bradley at the nth generation may not thank you for. (They may rejoice, of course; 'Great-great-great-great-grandpa's come out, and let us all be gay!') But did he have children? Easy enough to check.

You labouring cretin.

I am afraid for them.

For all of us. For that moment of need. For the touch, the look, the second in which the question is asked and the rejection given.

It never comes back, it is never undone. Like a drop of the most concentrated dye, it tinges ever after with its colour. Oh how I am sorry for those who need love. Oh how I pity them.

Brave Stephen. Stephen mon brave. The world's most perfectly contained man. Needing no one. And suddenly weak with grief at my lack.

Bradley, I honour you.

Lisa Appignanesi was a university lecturer in European Literature before becoming first, Director of Seminars, then Deputy Director of London's Institute of Contemporary Arts. An occasional critic, broadcaster and television producer, she now devotes most of her time to writing. Her recent books include the novels *Dreams of Innocence* and *Memory and Desire* (Harper Collins) and a study of *Freud's Women* (with John Forrester, published by Weidenfeld).

Richard Barlow was born in 1953 in Birmingham, where he was educated. He moved to Leicestershire in 1979, and gained a PhD from Loughborough University in 1987. He now lives and works in Leicester. He started writing short stories in 1992; *The Phone Would Ring* is his first to be accepted for publication. In October 1993 he began an MA in Creative Writing at Lancaster University.

John Berger was born in 1926. He studied at the Central School of Art and the Chelsea School of Art. The city of Troy features in his trilogy about peasants, *Into Their Labours*. He is a novelist and short story writer and won the Booker Prize in 1972 for his novel *G*. Other awards have included the Guardian Fiction Prize, the James Tait Black Prize, the George Orwell Memorial Prize, the New York Critics Prize for screenplay, the Barcelona Film Festival Europa Award and the Austrian State Prize. He now lives in France.

Alison Brackenbury was born in 1953. Her most recent book is *Selected Poems* (Carcanet, 1991).

Alan Brownjohn was a teacher and lecturer until 1978 when he became a full-time writer. His novel *The Way You Tell Them* was published in 1990. His *Collected Poems*, bringing together the work of seven earlier volumes, came out in 1988, and a new book of poems, *In the Cruel Arcade*, will be published in 1994.

Lynne Bryan was born in Leicester in 1961. She moved to Glasgow after completing the MA in Creative Writing at the University of East Anglia. She is an Information Worker for a Women's Support Project, and was a founding director of the Scottish feminist magazine *Harpies and Quines*. Her writing has been published in anthologies by Faber and Polygon. She is currently working on a collection of short stories and a novella.

John Burnside was born in Scotland in 1955 and now lives and works in Surrey. He has published three books of poetry, *The Hoop* (Carcanet, 1988), *Common Knowledge* (Secker and Warburg, 1991), and *Feast Days* (Secker and Warburg, 1992). His next book, *The Myth of the Twin*, is to be published by Secker and Warburg in April 1994. He works as a computer systems designer.

Simon Burt was born in Wiltshire in 1947, and educated at Downside and Trinity College, Dublin. He now lives in North Kensington, London. He has written a collection of short stories, *Floral Street*, and two novels, *The Summer of the White Peacock* and *Just Like Eddie*.

A. S. Byatt studied at Cambridge and taught at the Central School of Art and Design before moving to University College London to teach English and American literature. She is now a full-time writer. Her first novel, *Shadow of a Sun*, appeared in 1964, and was followed by *The Game* (1967), *The Virgin in the Garden* (1978), *Still Life* (1985) and *Possession* (1990) which won the Booker Prize for Fiction. Her collection of short stories, *Sugar and Other Stories*, appeared in 1987, and a volume of critical essays, *Passions of the Mind*, in 1991. In 1990 she was Chairman of Judges of the European Literary Prize. Her most recent book was *Angels and Insects* (1992).

Suzanne Cleminshaw was born in Boston, Massachusetts in 1964 and raised in Ohio. She moved to England in 1990. She is currently writing her first novel.

Andrew Conway lives in Birmingham. He was a runner-up in the 1991 *Stand* international short story competition and was published in the first issue of *Cascando*. In 1992 he was featured in the Stagecoach festival of new writing at the Birmingham Repertory Theatre, and has recently returned from a prolonged stay in Hungary where he worked as a co-deviser on *Mrs Bricklayers*, a play about Hungarian women which has toured both Hungary and Britain.

Jim Crace was born in 1946 and read English at London University as an external student before working in educational television in Khartoum. He has travelled extensively on journalistic assignments and has published three novels: *Continent* (1986), which won the David Higham Prize for Fiction, the Whitbread First Novel Prize and the Guardian Fiction Prize, *The Gift of Stones* (1988) and *Arcadia* (1992). He is married, with two children, and lives in Birmingham, where he initiated and directed the first Birmingham Festival of Readers and Writers.

Patricia Debney was born in Texas in 1964, grew up in Virginia, and has been living in Britain since 1988. She took an MA in Creative Writing at the University of East Anglia, and now teaches literature and creative writing in Norfolk. She is currently revising her first novel, *The Best Place in the World*, and beginning work on her second.

K. M. Dersley took Latin Honours at Swansea University in 1973, and has since worked as Post Office clerk, petrol pump attendant, lorry driver's mate, cleaner, hospital orderly and busker; he is now a clerical assistant with Suffolk County Council. His poems, stories and articles have been appearing in magazines since 1974. Collections include *The Gentle Art of Camouflage* (Fetish Books, 1980) and *Pediments Above* (Appliance Books, 1993).

Maura Dooley grew up in Bristol and now lives in London. Her published work includes *Turbulence* (Giant Steps Press, 1988) and *Explaining Magnetism* (Bloodaxe Books, 1991). She has also co-edited *Northern Stories II* (Littlewood Press, 1990) and *New Poetry International* (Harwood Academic Press, first issue due 1994). She won a major Eric Gregory Award in 1987.

John Fuller was born in 1937. His latest collection of poems is *The Mechanical Body* (1991) and his most recent work of prose fiction is *The Worm and the Star* (1993), both published by Chatto and Windus.

Janice Galloway was born in Ayrshire, Scotland, where she taught for ten years. Her first book, *The Trick is to Keep Breathing*, won a Scottish Arts Council Book Award and was shortlisted for the Whitbread First Novel Award and the Scottish First Book of the Year in 1990. *Blood* was published in 1991 and the title story won the 1991 *Cosmopolitan*/Perrier Short Story Award. She lives in Glasgow, and her new novel will be published in the spring of 1994.

Lesley Glaister was born in Northamptonshire in 1956 and took a first class degree in English literature with the Open University in 1986, followed by a Master's degree in Socio-Legal Studies at Sheffield University. Her novel, *Honour Thy Father*, was published by Secker and Warburg in 1990 and won a Betty Trask Award and a Somerset Maugham Award in 1991. Her second novel, *Trick or Treat*, was published in 1991.

Sarah Gracie was born in 1961 in Bahrain and grew up in England and Scotland. After taking a first in English at Oxford, she taught English in prisons and psychiatric hospitals. She has an MA in Creative Writing from the University of East Anglia and is working on a doctoral thesis on post-war British fiction at Oxford. She has won prizes for her poetry and short stories and is now working on her first novel.

Romesh Gunesekera was born in Sri Lanka and now lives in London. His first book, *Monkfish Moon*, a collection of stories, was published in 1992. His next, a novel, will be published by Granta Books in 1994.

Georgina Hammick has published two collections of short stories, *People for Lunch* and *Spoilt*, and is the editor of *The Virago Book of Love and Loss*. She has contributed to various magazines and anthologies and several of her stories have been broadcast on BBC Radio 3 and 4. She is on the Executive Committee of English PEN and lives in Wiltshire.

Jane Harris was born in 1961. She has published many short stories in magazines and anthologies and in 1991 was a runner-up in the *Stand Magazine* short story competition. She has done an MA in Creative Writing at the University of East Anglia and is Writer in Residence at Durham Prison.

Jonathan Holland was born in 1961 in Macclesfield and was educated at the universities of London and East Anglia. Between 1985 and 1989 he lived in the south of Italy. He now lives in Madrid, teaching and writing occasional book reviews for *The European*. His short stories have been published in Faber's *First Fictions 11* (1992), in *Best Short Stories 1993* and in *Stand Magazine*. His first novel, *Stranger*, is to be published by Faber in 1994.

Grace Ingoldby has published four novels, *Across the Water* and *Head of the Corner*, both set in Ireland where she lived until 1976, *Last Dance with You* and *Candles and Dark Night*. She has written a social history of the island of Sark, *Out of Call or Cry*, and has just completed her fifth novel. She is currently working at Broadmoor Special Hospital.

Philip Kerr was born in Edinburgh in 1956 and studied law at the

University of Birmingham. He has published four crime novels, *March Violets*, *The Pale Criminal*, *A German Requiem* and *A Philosophical Investigation*. His latest novel, *Dead Meat*, was published in 1993 and televised by the BBC. He is editor of *The Penguin Book of Lies* and *The Penguin Book of Fights, Feuds and Heartfelt Hatreds*. He lives in London.

Hilary Mantel was born in Derbyshire in 1952. She lived for some years in Africa and the Middle East, and was the first winner (1987) of the Shiva Naipaul Memorial Prize for travel writing. She has published five novels, the latest of which, *A Place of Greater Safety*, won the Sunday Express Book of the Year Award for 1992. She is married and lives in Berkshire.

Philip MacCann was born in England and moved to Ireland at an early age. His stories have appeared in *New Writing 1* and Faber's *First Fictions*.

Helen McNeil is an American who has been living and writing in England for over twenty years. She lectures in American literature and film at the University of East Anglia. 'As She Turned' is a section of a novel about expatriation, murder and the ruin of dreams. Its provisional title is *The Special Relations*.

Candia McWilliam was born in 1955 in Edinburgh, where she was educated until, at the age of 13, she went to school in England. She has a son and daughter by her first marriage and a son by her husband with whom she lives in Oxford. Her first novel, *A Case of Knives*, appeared in 1988 and was followed by *A Little Stranger* (1989).

Ameena Meer grew up amidst a chaos of cultures and countries. Now she is an Indian of the diaspora, living either in Brixton or Mexico City, with her daughter, Sasha Iman Douglas. Her first novel, *An Evening in Paris*, will be published by Serpent's Tail. Her writing also appears regularly in *Bomb* and *Interview* magazines, among others. She is currently working on a fictional history of her complicated extended family.

Joan Michelson, Associate Senior Lecturer, University of Wolverhampton, has published poetry, fiction and essays in American and British periodicals including *Spare Rib*, *Stand*, *Ambit* and *Panurge*. Further excerpts from *A Gift of Going* have appeared in *Writing Women* and *The Tel Aviv Review*.

Padraic O Beirn was born in Dublin, where he now lives, having lived and worked in Canada, Spain, England and the west of Ireland. His work has appeared in magazines and newspapers. He is currently working on his first collection of short stories.

Julia O'Faolain is the author of the Booker short-listed *No Country for Young Men*, *The Irish Signorina* and, most recently, *The Judas Cloth*. She is currently working on a collection of short stories. Married to the historian Lauro Martines, she divides her time between London and Los Angeles.

Kaite O'Reilly was a winner in the Royal Court Young Writers' Festival and Second Wave's Young Women's Playwriting Festival, both in 1988. She worked as a performer before writing for the theatre and was Theatre Writer in Residence at Essex University in 1990. She has recently written 'The Storyteller' for BBC Radio 4 and is included in the Women's Press anthology *Tomorrow I'm Going to Rewrite the English Language*. She is currently writing a novel and lecturing in Performance and Theatre Writing at the University of Glamorgan.

Ursula Owen was born in Oxford in 1937 and spent the first eighteen months of her life in Berlin. After studying physiology at Oxford, she spent five years working on psychiatric problems in the community and then lived in the Middle East and America. In the early 70s she worked for various publishing companies before becoming, in 1974, a co-founder of Virago Press, where she was Editorial Director and later Joint Managing Director. In 1991 she was appointed Cultural Policy Adviser to the Larbour Party. In 1993 she was appointed Editor and Chief Executive of *Index on Censorship*. She is the editor of *Fathers: Reflections by Daughters* (Virago 1983) and co-editor of *Whose Cities?* (1991).

Peter Porter was born in Australia in 1929 and has lived in London since 1951. He has published thirteen collections of poetry, and collaborated with the painter Arthur Boyd on four books of poems and pictures. He is also a reviewer of literature and music in journals and on the BBC. After his *Collected Poems* (OUP, 1983), his recent publications include *The Automatic Oracle* (1987), *Possible Worlds* (1989) and *The Chair of Babel* (1992).

Caroline Price was born in 1956. She studied music at the University of York and violin at the Guildhall School of Music and Drama, London. She has worked as a violinist and teacher in Glasgow, London and now Kent. Her first collection of poetry, *Thinking of the Bull Dancers*, was published by the Littlewood Press in 1987; her second collection will be published by the Rockingham Press in April 1994.

Simon Rae is a freelance writer and broadcaster, presenting *Poetry Please!* for Radio 4 and contributing a weekly topical poem to the *Weekend Guardian*. He is editor of *The Faber Book of Drink, Drinkers and Drinking* and his collection of *Guardian* poems, *Soft Targets* (with cartoons by Willie Rushton) was published by Bloodaxe Books. He has just finished his first novel, *Pomroy's Last Tour*.

Peter Redgrove was born in 1932 and read Natural Sciences at Cambridge. From 1962 to 1965 he was Gregory Fellow in Poetry at Leeds University and in 1966 became Resident Author at Falmouth School of Art, a position he held until 1983. From 1985 to 1987 he was Leverhulme Emeritus Fellow. He was made a Fellow of the Royal Society of Literature in 1982. He has won many prizes for his volumes of poetry, which include *The Man Named East, The Mudlark Poems and Grand Buveur* and *In The Hall of the Saurians*. His first novel, *In the Country of the Skin*, won the 1973 Guardian Fiction Prize. His plays have been broadcast on radio and television and include *Martyr of the Hives*, winner of the 1981 Giles Cooper Award.

Daniel Richardson is a mathematician who lives in Bristol. He edits the *Avon Literary Intelligencer*.

Michèle Roberts was born in 1949 and is half-French. She divides her time between England and France. She has published six novels, the most recent of which, *Daughters of the House* (Virago), was short-listed for the Booker Prize and won the W. H. Smith Literary Award. Her most recent collection of poetry is *Psyche and the Hurricane* (Methuen, 1991) and her most recent short story collection is *During Mother's Absence* (Virago, 1993). She has also written for the stage, film, television and radio.

Jane Rogers has written four novels including *Her Living Image, The Ice is Singing* and *Mr Wroe's Virgins*, which she adapted as a four-part drama for BBC television. She has two children and lives in Lancashire.

Alan Rusbridger is Deputy Editor of the *Guardian*. He was born in 1953 and read English at Cambridge. He joined the *Guardian* in 1979, working as a reporter and columnist. In 1986 he joined the *Observer* as TV critic, moving to the *London Daily News* as Washington correspondent the following year. He returned to the *Guardian* in 1987, working successively as editor of the Weekend section, Features Editor and Deputy Editor. He is married with two children and lives in London.

Robert Saxton was born in 1952 in Nottingham and started writing in 1985. He has had poems published in the *Times Literary Supplement, Poetry Review,* the *Spectator, PN Review,* the *Observer* and other periodicals, as well as Faber's *Poetry Introduction 7.* In 1988 he was joint first prizewinner of the *TLS*/Cheltenham Festival Poetry Competition. He was featured in the New British Poets issue of *Poetry Review* (Autumn 1990), and was one of the readers in the Poetry Society's 'Catchwords' Festival, also in autumn 1990.

Kate Sekules was born in London. 'Jack Sprat's Wife' is her first published short story. She is now living in New York and working on more short stories and a novel.

Jo Shapcott won first prize in the National Poetry Competition in 1986, and again in 1991 with 'Phrase Book'. Her first collection, *Electroplating the Baby,* published in 1988, was awarded a Commonwealth Prize. She has won several other awards and prizes for her poetry. In 1991 she was the Judith E. Wilson Senior Visiting Fellow at Cambridge University. Her second volume of poems, *Phrase Book,* was published in 1992.

Penelope Shuttle was born in 1947 and lives in Cornwall with her husband Peter Redgrove and their daughter Zoe. Her fifth book of poems, *Taxing the Rain,* was published in 1992 (OUP). She is currently working on a new volume of poems and a collection of short stories.

Matthew Singh-Toor, the son of an Indian father and an English mother, was born near Leicester in 1967. Since his first degree he has travelled and worked in India, co-founded a national group for lesbians and gay men of mixed racial heritage and taken an MA in Creative Writing at the University of East Anglia. He is currently working on a novel and a screenplay.

Elizabeth Smither is a New Zealand poet who has published widely in Britain and Australia. Her first collection of stories, *Nights at the Embassy,* was published by Auckland University Press in 1990. She is presently working on a second collection. A small collection of her poetry, *A Cortège of Daughters,* was published in 1993 (Cloud Press).

R. S. Thomas was born in 1913 and read Classics at the University of Wales, Cardiff. He took orders in 1937 and held livings in various Welsh parishes between 1942 and 1978. He has published over 30 collections of poetry, including *Selected Poems 1946–1968* (1973, republished 1986) and *Collected Poems 1945–1990* (1993). His most recent collections are *Mass for Hard Times* and *Frieze*. He has edited *The Batsford Book of Country Verse*, *The Penguin Book of Religious Verse*, *A Choice of George Herbert's Verse* and *Selected Poems* by Edward Thomas. He is the subject of numerous critical studies, and was awarded the Queen's Gold Medal for Poetry in 1964.

Adam Thorpe was born in Paris in 1956 and brought up in India, Cameroon and England. He has had two collections of poetry published by Secker and Warburg: *Mornings in the Baltic* (1988) and *Meeting Montaigne* (1990). His first novel, *Ulverton* (1992) is a sequence spanning three centuries of a fictional English village. He lives in France with his wife and three children.

Charles Tomlinson was born in 1927. His paperback *Collected Poems* appeared in 1987 and *The Door in the Wall* in 1992. There are volumes of his work in Italian, Spanish and Portuguese, a large number of critical articles on it and four full-scale studies. In 1989 he received the Cittadella Premio Europeo for the *face-à-face* Italian edition of his poems. In 1993 he was given *The Hudson Review*'s Joseph Bennett Award in New York. He is also a painter (*Eden: the Graphics of Charles Tomlinson*) and a literary critic (*Poetry and Metamorphosis*). He has translated widely from Spanish and Italian and edited the Penguin *Octavio Paz*. His *Selected Poems of Attilio Bertolucci* was published by Bloodaxe in 1993.

Rose Tremain was born in 1943 and graduated from the University of East Anglia. She has published six novels and two collections of short stories as well as having had numerous radio and television plays performed. She won the Dylan Thomas Prize for Short Stories for *The Colonel's Daughter*, the Angel Literary Award for *The Swimming Pool Season* and the *Sunday Express* Award for *Restoration*, which was also short-listed for the 1989 Booker Prize. Her most recent novel, *Sacred Country*, won the James Tait Black Memorial Prize. In 1983 she was chosen as one of the Best of Young British Novelists. She lives in Norfolk and London with the biographer Richard Holmes.

Barry Unsworth was born in 1930 in a mining village in Durham and attended Stockton-on-Tees Grammar School and Manchester University. He has spent a number of years in the eastern Mediterranean area and has taught English in Athens and Istanbul. He now lives in Italy. He is the author of ten novels, of which *Mooncranker's Gift* received the Heinemann Award for 1973 and *Pascali's Island* was short-listed for the Booker Prize in 1980 and later filmed. His most recent novel, *Sacred Hunger*, was joint winner of the 1992 Booker Prize. He is a Fellow of the Royal Society of Literature.

Jane Westaway was born in Watford in 1948, and has lived in Welling-ton, New Zealand, on and off since 1964. Her journalism and book reviews have appeared in many New Zealand publications, and her short stories have been anthologised. She is currently completing a novel.

Susan Wicks grew up in Kent and has since lived in France, Ireland and the United States. Her first collection of poems, *Singing Underwater*, published in 1992, won the Aldeburgh Poetry Festival Prize and was a Poetry Book Society recommendation. Her second, *Open Diagnosis*, will be published in 1994. She has a D.Phil degree in the modern French novel and works as a part-time tutor for the University of Kent. She lives in Kent with her husband and two daughters.

Kit Wright was born in Kent in 1944 and studied at New College, Oxford. His publications include *The Bear Looked over the Mountain* (1977), *Bump-Starting the Hearse* (1983), *From the Day Room* (1983), *Real Rags and Red* (1988) and *Poems 1974–1983* (1988). He has also published five volumes of poetry for children, as well as editing *Soundings: A Selection of Poems for Speaking Aloud*, *Poems for 9-Year-Olds and Under* and *Poems for Over 10-Year-Olds*. He won the Geoffrey Faber Memorial Prize in 1978.

BOOKER

KEY LINKS IN THE FOOD CHAIN

WE BELIEVE
IN FOOD
FOR THOUGHT

SPONSORS OF THE BOOKER PRIZE FOR FICTION

Malcolm Bradbury & Judy Cooke

NEW WRITING

New Writing is a platform for the best, by writers of note and writers to look out for – a stunning collection gathered together in this, the first of a series of annual anthologies published by Minerva in association with the British Council. Comprising specially commissioned stories, essays, poems, drawings, articles, interviews and extracts from work in progress, it bursts with the literary talent of today.

Fiction – comic or tender, realistic or more experimental – displays its diverse pleasures alongside a variety of non-fiction, work which includes the polemical and the reflective, personal and broad-ranging by turns, in a volume to engage passions and stimulate debate.

Gilbert Adair • Martin Amis • A S Byatt • Angela Carter • Geoff Dyer • Lucy Ellmann • Penelope Fitzgerald • Alasdair Gray • Michael Ignatieff • James Lasdun • Doris Lessing • David Lodge • Hilary Mantel • Ben Okri • Craig Raine • Graham Swift • Rose Tremain • Marina Warner • Dannie Abse • Paul Bailey • Christopher Bigsby • Mel Calman • Wendy Cope • Paul Cox • Valentine Cunningham • Fred D'Aguiar • Carol Ann Duffy • Suzannah Dunn • Lesley Glaister • Georgina Hammick • Peter Kemp • Philip MacCann • Glyn Maxwell • Clare Morgan • Peter Reading • Lorna Sage • Adam Thorpe • Anthony Thwaite • Hugo Williams • Adam Zameenzad

A Selected List of Fiction Available from Minerva

While every effort is made to keep prices low, it is sometimes necessary to increase prices at short notice. Mandarin Paperbacks reserves the right to show new retail prices on covers which may differ from those previously advertised in the text or elsewhere.

The prices shown below were correct at the time of going to press.

☐ 7493 9145 6	**Love and Death on Long Island**	Gilbert Adair	£4.99
☐ 7493 9130 8	**The War of Don Emmanuel's Nether Parts**	Louis de Bernieres	£5.99
☐ 7493 9903 1	**Dirty Faxes**	Andrew Davies	£4.99
☐ 7493 9056 5	**Nothing Natural**	Jenny Diski	£4.99
☐ 7493 9173 1	**The Trick is to Keep Breathing**	Janice Galloway	£4.99
☐ 7493 9124 3	**Honour Thy Father**	Lesley Glaister	£4.99
☐ 7493 9918 X	**Richard's Feet**	Carey Harrison	£6.99
☐ 7493 9028 X	**Not Not While the Giro**	James Kelman	£4.99
☐ 7493 9112 X	**Hopeful Monsters**	Nicholas Mosley	£6.99
☐ 7493 9029 8	**Head to Toe**	Joe Orton	£4.99
☐ 7493 9117 0	**The Good Republic**	William Palmer	£5.99
☐ 7493 9162 6	**Four Bare Legs in a Bed**	Helen Simpson	£4.99
☐ 7493 9134 0	**Rebuilding Coventry**	Sue Townsend	£4.99
☐ 7493 9151 0	**Boating for Beginners**	Jeanette Winterson	£4.99
☐ 7493 9915 5	**Cyrus Cyrus**	Adam Zameenzad	£7.99

All these books are available at your bookshop or newsagent, or can be ordered direct from the publisher. Just tick the titles you want and fill in the form below.

Mandarin Paperbacks, Cash Sales Department, PO Box 11, Falmouth, Cornwall TR10 9EN.

Please send cheque or postal order, no currency, for purchase price quoted and allow the following for postage and packing:

UK including BFPO	£1.00 for the first book, 50p for the second and 30p for each additional book ordered to a maximum charge of £3.00.
Overseas including Eire	£2 for the first book, £1.00 for the second and 50p for each additional book thereafter.

NAME (Block letters) ....

ADDRESS ....

....

☐ I enclose my remittance for ....

☐ I wish to pay by Access/Visa Card Number

Expiry Date